FIFTY YEARS IN FAMILY LAW

ESSAYS FOR STEPHEN CRETNEY

Edited by
Rebecca PROBERT
Chris BARTON

intersentia

Cambridge – Antwerp – Portland

Intersentia Publishing Ltd.
Trinity House | Cambridge Business Park | Cowley Road
Cambridge | CB4 0WZ | United Kingdom
Tel.: +44 1223 393 753 | Email: mail@intersentia.co.uk

Distribution for the UK:
Hart Publishing Ltd.
16C Worcester Place
Oxford OX1 2JW
UK
Tel.: +44 1865 517 530
Email: mail@hartpub.co.uk

Distribution for the USA and Canada:
International Specialized Book Services
920 NE 58th Ave. Suite 300
Portland, OR 97213
USA
Tel.: +1 800 944 6190 (toll free)
Email: info@isbs.com

Distribution for Austria:
Neuer Wissenschaftlicher Verlag
Argentinierstraße 42/6
1040 Wien
Austria
Tel.: +43 1 535 61 03 24
Email: office@nwv.at

Distribution for other countries:
Intersentia Publishing nv
Groenstraat 31
2640 Mortsel
Belgium
Tel.: +32 3 680 15 50
Email: mail@intersentia.be

Fifty Years in Family Law. Essays for Stephen Cretney
Rebecca Probert and Chris Barton (eds.)

© 2012 Intersentia
Cambridge – Antwerp – Portland
www.intersentia.com | www.intersentia.co.uk

Cover pictures: left: The Divinity School, Postcard of "The Divinity School" Ref.
UK/CP2067 © The Bodleian Libraries, The University of Oxford
middle: The Convocation House, Postcard of "The Convocation
House" Ref. C274 © The Bodleian Libraries, The University of
Oxford
right: Magdalen College, Oxford ©Oxford Picture Library/Chris
Andrews

ISBN 978-1-78068-052-1
NUR 822

British Library Cataloguing in Publication Data. A catalogue record for this book is available from the British Library.

FOREWORD

I have had the privilege to be the first to read this book of essays, in proof, from soup to nuts. It is a great collection. For a great man.

Stephen Cretney's modesty, so widely acknowledged in these pages, would lead him to downplay the significance of his contribution to the beneficial development of family law during the last 50 years. In fact, however, its significance is hard to overstate. It goes much wider than the quality of his contribution as a Law Commissioner, important though that was. Prior to 1970, as Stephen has demonstrated in his towering *History*, family law was deeply impoverished. One important reason was the lack of academic interest in it. The two rival manuals for use by practitioners – *Rayden* and *Latey* – expounded it but were (as one would expect) largely uncritical of it. Writers like A.P. Herbert had lampooned its most egregious absurdities. But there was little intellectual analysis of it, in particular of its archaic and futile hunt for matrimonial 'guilt' and 'innocence' as the determinants of legal rights.

But things changed with the advent in the 1960s of family law as a subject of undergraduate study. The fascinating complications inherent in the application of law to family relationships led many students to exercise the option to study it. Generations of them began to read and write about it. Then they moved on. Many became lawyers; some later became judges. A few became politicians. But, whatever they were doing, these graduates helped to widen the debate. Family law became a matter of national discussion. The result was that over the years beneficial changes in it were wrought both by legislation and also, massively if imperceptibly, by judicial decision. Legal academic study had discharged one of its most important functions: it had fertilised the law. Today family remains the area of law which attracts about the highest level of public interest – up there with criminal sentencing and the reach of Article 8 of the European Convention.

Credit for the achievement of putting family law on the map as an important subject for academic study must go to quite a few people, including – very definitely – some of the writers of these essays. Here, however, Stephen's insistence on fairness, hovering over me, guides my pen to identify the seminal contribution of the late Peter Bromley. You must read the essay on the great case of *Cretney v. Bromley* in 1974: it's riveting. Yet no one would object to my identification of Stephen himself as perhaps the most influential single contributor to this achievement. His contribution was by his inspirational book *Principles*; by his lectures; by the breadth of his other legal activities and the energy with which he pursued them; by the respect for family law which his intellectual stature engendered among lawyers in other fields; and by his profound and stimulating expositions of issues in family law, never too hard to understand, which, like a magnet, drew those who read and heard them into a real and lasting interest in them.

This collection of essays is worthy of Stephen. They fall across a wide spectrum of subjects relating to family law and are written with astonishing clarity, originality and intellectual sophistication. Above all, however, they exude the warmth of one of those glorious English summer days of which we have about six each year. This, says each page, is for Stephen. The affection for the man is palpable.

Nicholas Wilson
Candlemas, 2 February 2012   The Supreme Court

ACKNOWLEDGEMENTS

We are grateful to Baroness Ruth Deech for arranging the planning meeting at the House of Lords and to Warwick Law School for providing funding for participants' travel. Similar thanks are due to Dr Susan Jenkinson of Staffordshire University Law School and to All Souls College for the launches at Stoke-on-Trent and Oxford respectively. Finally, much is owed to Ms Cheryl Morris for taking time off work and to Mrs Joan Morris for coming out of retirement to proof-read this book and to Ms Ann-Christin Maak of Intersentia for not allowing her honeymoon to interfere with the vital assistance she provided. We thank them all.

We are pleased to say that, at Stephen Cretney's request, all profits from the sale of this book will go to the National Association for the Care and Resettlement of Offenders (NACRO), and we are deeply indebted to Intersentia for their generosity in taking no profit from the publication themselves.

Rebecca Probert
Chris Barton
March, 2012

CONTENTS

Contents

LIST OF AUTHORS

Andrew Bainham is a barrister of the Middle Temple and a tenant at 14 Gray's Inn Square, representing local authorities, parents, children and other family members in public law and private law children cases. He has been at the University of Cambridge since 1993 where he is Reader in Family Law and Policy and a former fellow of Christ's College. For over a decade he was editor of the *International Survey of Family Law* published on behalf of the International Society of Family Law. He is author of many publications in family law, especially the law relating to children, including *Children: The Modern Law* (3rd edition, 2005) to which Stephen Cretney contributed when in its first edition in 1993.

Chris Barton is Emeritus Professor of Family Law (Staffordshire University), Academic Door Tenant at Regent Chambers, an Emeritus Member of The Society of Legal Scholars and a Vice-President of the Family Mediators Association. He has taught family law since before the Divorce Reform Act 1969 and is author, co-author and part-author of a number of books. He has also published in learned and professional journals and in broadsheet newspapers. Stephen Cretney, who gave him the honour of being the England and Wales Law Commission's first researcher (1982/83), has since been his major source of professional inspiration and advice.

Elizabeth Cooke is a Solicitor; she qualified in 1988. In 1992 she became a lecturer in law at the University of Reading, and was awarded a personal chair in 2003. She has published on many topics within family law and land law, and particularly on land registration and on family property. In 2008 she was appointed a Law Commissioner for England and Wales, for a five-year term until 2013, which has now been extended to 2016; as a Commissioner she has particular responsibility for family and property law projects.

Ruth Deech, now Baroness Deech of Cumnor DBE, started her career as an assistant to the family law team at the Law Commission; then she taught law at Oxford University, where she was for a while a colleague of Stephen Cretney's. They are fellow honorary benchers of the Inner Temple. Baroness Deech was Principal of St Anne's College Oxford from 1991–2004, a pro-Vice-Chancellor, and is now an Honorary Fellow of the College. She was chair of the Human Fertilisation & Embryology Authority from 1994–2002, a Governor of the BBC from 2002–2006, a trustee of the Rhodes Scholarships from 1996–2006.

After retiring from Oxford she became the first Independent Adjudicator for Higher Education, resolving student complaints from all the universities in England and Wales. She is Gresham Professor of Law 2008–2012 and chair of the Bar Standards Board from 2009. In 2005 she was created a Life Peer and sits as a crossbencher in the Lords.

Gillian Douglas obtained her LLB at the University of Manchester and her LLM at the University of London (LSE). She became a Lecturer in Law at the University of Bristol in 1978, and spent a year as a Visiting Teaching Fellow at the National University of Singapore in 1983/84, before moving to Cardiff University in 1989 where she has remained, becoming Professor of Law in 1998 and serving as Head of the Law School between 2005 and 2010. She had the great good fortune to work with Stephen Cretney during her time at Bristol University, sharing the teaching of Family Law with Stephen and Nigel Lowe, and becoming, with the two of them, a Case Reports Editor for the journal, *Family Law*, an association which Stephen initiated in 1986 and which Gillian continues. She is co-author (with Nigel Lowe) of the 9th and 10th editions of *Bromley's Family Law* (1998, 2007) and (with Chris Barton) of *Law and Parenthood* (1995) and has written numerous other works, including *An Introduction to Family Law* (2001, 2004). She was awarded an LLD by Cardiff University in 2011 for her contribution to scholarship in the field of Family Law.

John Eekelaar was Fellow and Tutor in Law at Pembroke College, Oxford from 1965 to 2005, sharing some family law teaching with Stephen Cretney when Stephen was Tutorial Fellow of Exeter College between 1969 and 1978. He was a founder member of the International Society of Family Law, and founding co-editor of the *International Journal of Law, Policy and the Family*. He has written and researched widely in family law. He was elected a Fellow of the British Academy in 2001 and Distinguished Visiting Fellow by the New Zealand Law Foundation in 2005. His books include *Family Security and Family Breakdown* (1971), *Family Law and Social Policy* (1978, 1984), *Regulating Divorce* (1991) and *Family Law and Personal Life* (2006, 2007).

Stephen Gilmore, of Lincoln's Inn, barrister, is Senior Lecturer in Family Law at King's College London. His research focuses on the law of parental responsibility, children's rights and the courts' resolution of parental disputes. He co-edited (with Rebecca Probert and Jonathan Herring) *Responsible Parents and Parental Responsibility* (2009) and *Landmark Cases in Family Law* (2011). His journal articles include: 'Disputing Contact: Challenging Some Assumptions' (2008) 20 *Child and Family Law Quarterly* 285; and (with J Herring) '"No" is the hardest word: consent and children's autonomy' (2011) 23 *Child and Family Law Quarterly* 3.

Brenda Hale is the first, and so far the only, woman Justice of the Supreme Court of the United Kingdom. She joined the top court in the country in 2004 when it was still a committee of the House of Lords, after a varied career as an academic, law reformer and judge. In all three capacities, her primary interest has been in Family and Social Welfare Law. In 1978, she was due to collaborate with Stephen Cretney in writing a book which he inspired (later published as *The Family, Law and Society – Cases and Materials*), when he had to withdraw because of his appointment as a Law Commissioner. When he left the Law Commission in 1984 to become a Professor at the University of Bristol, she replaced him as the Commissioner in charge of Family Law. And in 2007, as Chancellor of the University of Bristol, she was delighted to be able to honour his achievements in Family Law by conferring upon him the degree of Doctor of Laws, *honoris causa*.

Sonia Harris-Short is a graduate of Christ Church, Oxford (and was a family law student of Stephen Cretney's whilst an undergraduate) and has an LLM (by research) from the University of British Columbia, Canada. She currently holds the position of Professor in Family Law and Policy at Birmingham Law School, University of Birmingham where she is also the Director (Research) of the Centre for Professional Legal Education and Research. She is the author of a recent monograph examining aboriginal child welfare and self-government in Canada and Australia and the co-author (with J. Miles, University of Cambridge) of *Family Law: Text, Cases and Materials*, a major family law text for OUP. She has published extensively in leading journals on a range of family law issues including adoption, the interaction between family law and human rights, shared parenting and gender and the law. She also serves as a Deputy District Judge (Civil) on the Northern Circuit.

Joanna Harwood graduated from the University of Warwick in July 2010. It was at Warwick that she developed her interest in family law and when she first became aware of Stephen Cretney's immense contribution to this area of law. In the year following her graduation, Joanna worked as a volunteer for her local women's refuge and Citizens Advice Bureau. She also worked as a researcher for Rebecca Probert and as a seminar tutor at the University of Warwick, an experience which enabled her to study family law from the other side of the seminar desk. Joanna has delivered two papers at Soroptmist International study days held at the University of Warwick, both papers focusing on family law and domestic violence; these papers have recently been published in *Optimistic Objectives* and *Tackling Domestic Violence*. She is currently working as a research assistant at the Law Commission and hopes to return to Warwick in the future to do a PhD.

Jonathan Herring is Professor of Law and a Fellow of Law at Exeter College, University of Oxford, where Stephen Cretney was once a Fellow. Jonathan is the author of several textbooks including *Criminal Law: Text Cases and*

Materials (4ᵗʰ ed. 2010); *Criminal Law* (6ᵗʰ ed. 2009); *Family Law* (5ᵗʰ ed. 2011) and *Medical Law and Ethics* (3ʳᵈ ed. 2010). He has also written monographs on the law and older people (*Older People in Law and Society* (2009)) and family law and human rights (*European Human Rights and Family Law* (with Shazia Choudhry) (2010)). He has written widely on criminal law, family law, medical law and ethics, and elder law. He was lectured by Stephen Cretney as an undergraduate and has learned an enormous amount from his writing.

Sue Jenkinson, formerly a businesswoman in property development, returned to education in 1995, and obtained her LLB, LLM and PhD from Staffordshire University where she is now a senior lecturer and Director of the Staffordshire University Centre for Family Law and Policy. Her teaching and research interests focus on divorce and its legal history, very much inspired by Stephen Cretney's work.

Sanford N. Katz holds a Doctor of Laws degree from the University of Chicago Law School and was U.S. Public Fellow at Yale Law School. He is the Darald and Juliette Libby Millennium Professor of Law at Boston College Law School where he teaches Family Law and Contracts. He served as Editor-in-Chief of the *Family Law Quarterly* from 1970 to 1983 and now serves as an Overseas Editorial Adviser for the *International Journal of Law, Policy and the Family*. He is the author of *Family Law in America* (2011) and co-editor (with John Eekelaar and Mavis Maclean) of *Cross Currents* (2000). He was a Visiting Fellow at All Souls College, Oxford in 1997 while Stephen Cretney was a Research Fellow. He also was a Visiting Fellow at Pembroke College, Oxford in 2000 and 2006. A founding member of the International Society of Family Law, he was President from 1982 to 1985 and now serves on its Executive Council.

Penny Lewis graduated from the University of Warwick in July 2010, having spent part of her final year working as a research assistant in both company law and family law. Since joining the Law Commission as a research assistant in September 2010 she has primarily been working in the area of socio-legal history and now in her second year she is assisting in the preparations for the Statute Law (Repeals) Bill for introduction into Parliament in 2012. Penny has written for the *Child and Family Law Quarterly* and has delivered a paper at the Waseda-Warwick Joint Seminar in Tokyo which examined human rights and criminal and family law in an international comparative context. She hopes to do a PhD in the future in the area of family law and literature and continues to take inspiration from the books and articles written by Stephen Cretney which have added colour and texture to the otherwise black letters of law.

Nigel Lowe LLB, LLD, Barrister of the Inner Temple is a Professor of Law and head of Cardiff Law School, Cardiff University, Wales. He specialises in Family

Law, particularly Child Law. He is co-author of White, Carr and Lowe, *Children Act in Practice* (4th ed. 2008); Lowe and Douglas, *Bromley's Family Law* (10th ed. 2007); Lowe, Everall and Nicholls, *International Movement of Children – Law, Practice and Procedure* (2004); and Lowe and White, *Wards of Court* (2nd ed. 1986). He was a colleague of Stephen Cretney at the University of Bristol, 1983 – 1991, a joint case note editor with him for *Family Law*, 1986–1991 and they were both members of the Judicial Studies Board team on the training of the judiciary on the Children Act 1989.

Mavis Maclean, CBE, is a Senior Research Associate in the Department of Social Policy and Intervention in the University of Oxford, and Senior Research Fellow of St Hilda's College. She set up the Oxford Centre for Family Law and Policy with John Eekelaar in 2001. Together they have carried out empirical research in family law for over thirty years. Books include *The Parental Obligation* (1997), with John Eekelaar, *Family Lawyers, The Divorce Work of Solicitors* (2000) with Sarah Beinart and John Eekelaar, *Family Law Advocacy* (2009) with John Eekelaar and most recently *Making Family Law* (2010) with Kurczewski. She is currently observing the work of family judges in the lower courts. She has acted as an academic adviser to the Ministry of Justice for many years. She is a Fellow of the International Institute for the Sociology of Law in Onate, Spain, and a past president of the ISA Research Committee on the Sociology of Law.

Judith Masson is Professor of Socio-Legal Studies at Bristol University, specialising in child law and socio-legal research. Whilst she was working on a commentary on the Children Act 1989, she was invited to join Stephen Cretney as co-author of *Principles of Family Law*, and has written the chapters on child law from the fifth edition onwards. Judith Masson has undertaken numerous studies on the application of child law including step parent adoption – *Yours, Mine or Ours* (1983); representation of children in care proceedings – *Out of Hearing* (1999); partnership with parents of children looked after long term – *Lost and Found* (1999); and emergency intervention in child protection – *Protecting Powers* (2007). Her most recent research examines care proceedings quantitatively – *Care Profiling Study* (2008), qualitatively *Just following instructions?* (2011) and the pre-proceedings process *Families on the edge of care proceedings* with grants from the ESRC. Judith was a specialist adviser to the Constitutional Affairs Committee Inquiry into Cafcass (2002–3) and the Justice Committee Inquiry into the Family Courts (2010–11). She has been a member of the Judicial Studies Board and Academic Member of the Family Justice Council.

Joanna Miles is a Fellow of Trinity College and Senior University Lecturer in Law at the University of Cambridge, and an Academic Door Tenant at 1 Hare Court, Temple, London. She is the co-author, with Sonia Harris-Short (see above), of *Family Law: Text, Cases, and Materials* (2nd ed. 2011). In preparing to write each of her chapters for the first edition of that book, she made a point of first reading the relevant chapters of Stephen Cretney's *Family Law in the Twentieth Century* in order to ensure that her account of the contemporary material was connected to the broader historical narrative. She has written extensively on financial and property issues in family law, including marital agreements, and was seconded to the Law Commission for England and Wales to work on its Cohabitation project.

Walter Pintens is Professor of Law at the University of Leuven, Belgium; Honorary Professor at Saarland University, Germany; Secretary General of the International Commission on Civil Status (Strasbourg); and Member of the Organising Committee of the Commission on European Family Law (CEFL). On his publication list are several books and more than three hundred articles in the fields of family law, succession law, comparative law and private international law. He is the editor of the volume *Family and Succession Law* in the *International Encyclopaedia of Laws*, member of the editorial board of the *Rechtskundig Weekblad*, corresponding editor of the *Zeitschrift für Europäisches Privatrecht*, co-editor and chairman of the International Advisory Council of the *Zeitschrift für das gesamte Famillenrecht* and co-editor of the *European Family Law Series*. He had visiting positions in Berlin, Cambridge, Freiburg and Pretoria.

Christine Piper is a Professor at Brunel Law School. After graduating from Bristol University with a history degree she taught in schools before she undertook further study and doctoral research. Her research and teaching interests are focused on family and child law and policy, sentencing and youth justice. Her books include: *Investing in Children, Policy, Law and Practice in Context* (2008), *Sentencing and Punishment, The Quest for Justice* (2005, 2008, 2012) (with S. Easton), *How the Law Thinks About Children* (1990, 1995) (with M. King), and *The Responsible Parent* (1993). She is a member of the Editorial Board of the *Child and Family Law Quarterly*, an associate Director of the Brunel Law School's Criminal Justice Research and Family Law Research Centres, and a member of the Parent Abuse Research Network. She met Stephen Cretney at many seminars and is grateful for his historical research which she has used for postgraduate teaching and her own research.

Rebecca Probert studied law at Oxford, where her interest in the history of family law was first engaged by Stephen Cretney's lectures. She worked as a research assistant at the Law Commission and then taught family law at the University of Wales, Aberystwyth and at Sussex before moving to Warwick, where she is now professor of law. She took over responsibility for *Cretney's Family Law* in 2003 and contributed to the eighth edition of *Cretney: Principles of Family Law* in 2008. Her other major publications include *Marriage Law and Practice in the Long Eighteenth Century: A Reassessment* (2009), *The Rights and*

Wrongs of Royal Marriage (2011) and *The Legal Regulation of Cohabitation, 1600–2010: From Fornicators to Family* (2012).

Neil Robinson is Director of The Mediation Centre. In a former life, as child care lawyer, he was Legal Aid Family Lawyer of the Year 2007. He is currently Vice-Chair of the Family Mediators Association, and a member of the Resolution and Family Justice Council ADR Committees. He chairs the Stoke on Trent LFJC ADR Committee. He has recently been Consulting Editor to the second edition of Lisa Parkinson's *Family Mediation* textbook, and has been a contributor to the Resolution ADR Handbook, Family Law Protocol, and *Family Law*. A much longer time ago as an Oxford undergraduate, he benefited from Stephen Cretney's wisdom, even if not much of it rubbed off. He is a trainer for the Family Mediators Association and Resolution, an experienced family lawyer, family and civil mediator and Professional Practice Consultant, and a Mental Health Tribunal Judge. Neil has a particular enthusiasm for developing creative mediation practice that will meet the needs of entrenched, complex and mixed civil/ family conflicts.

Simon Rowbotham was called to the bar on 28 July 2011 by the Honourable Society of the Middle Temple. He is undertaking his family law pupillage at Deans Court Chambers under the supervision of Bansa Singh Hayer and Francesca Fothergill. He studied Law at Hughes Hall, Cambridge, under the encouraging eye of his Director of Studies, John Hopkins, in the course of which he studied Family Law under the enthusiastic eye of Dr. Jens M. Scherpe and with the invaluable assistance of *Cretney's Principles of Family Law* (8th ed.). This chapter is his first work to be published.

Jens M. Scherpe is a University Senior Lecturer in Law at the University of Cambridge, a Fellow and Tutor of Gonville and Caius College in Cambridge, an Honorary Fellow of St. John's College in Hong Kong and an Academic Door Tenant at Queen Elizabeth Building (QEB) in London. Previously he was Research Fellow and Head of the Department for the Law of the Nordic Countries at the Max Planck Institute for Comparative and International Private Law in Hamburg, a member of the Legal Advisory Group of the Law Commission of England and Wales' Cohabitation Project and has held visiting positions in Belgium, Germany, Australia, Spain, New Zealand and Hong Kong. Jens also is a member of the International Advisory Board of the *Zeitschrift für das gesamte Familienrecht* (FamRZ) and member of the Wissenschaftliche Vereinigung für Familienrecht e.V. His recent publications include comparative studies on the legal status of cohabitants, legal issues of transsexuality, financial relief upon divorce and marital agreements.

INTRODUCTION

Rebecca Probert and Chris Barton

Although Stephen Cretney took pride in his North Country origins and liked to think of himself as a Mancunian,[1] he was in fact born on 25 February 1936 at Witney, Oxfordshire, where his father was for a short time manager of the Witney Blanket Company. Throughout his childhood the family home was in the Cheshire suburb of Cheadle Hulme where Stephen attended the local grammar school – not perhaps an intellectual forcing house but staffed by some inspiring and encouraging teachers.

Schooldays involved (as one might expect) voracious reading and (perhaps more unexpectedly) a cycle trip to London in 1951 for the Festival of Britain, as well as attendance at Hallé concerts, meetings of the Manchester branch of the Esperanto Association and (during the school holidays) a number of defended divorce trials, sowing the seeds of an interest that was to grow during the subsequent years.

Having been elected to a Demyship – a Major Open Scholarship – in Modern History at Magdalen, Stephen completed two years of then-compulsory National Service before going up to Oxford in 1956. By the time of his arrival, however, he had decided to read Law rather than History, a decision that was subsequently vindicated by the award of a Distinction in his first-year examinations and a First-Class Honours degree at the end of the three years. During that time he also wrote occasional articles for the student magazine *The Isis*, his first publications tackling such weighty issues as the need for reform of the abortion laws and the injustices of the system of courts martial.

After graduation he spent a period as an articled clerk at Neish Howell and Haldane (later known as Macfarlanes), being admitted as a solicitor in 1962 and accepting a 'salaried partnership' in 1963. The prospect of a full partnership, however, posed a dilemma: as he put it, 'in those days accepting a partnership… meant effectively accepting a moral obligation to stay with the firm until death

---

[1] Although the surname 'Cretney' is Manx – a matter of great pride to him.

or old age… Though I had become technically well-equipped to deal with the tax and inheritance problems of rich private clients my heart was not really in this.'

Instead, in a dramatic change of course, he accepted a two-year contract to lecture at the Kenya School of Law. Upon arriving in Nairobi, 'I was told I would have to teach Family Law (as well as Succession, Land Law, Trusts and Accounts) beginning my courses within forty-eight hours.' Since at the time his knowledge of English family law derived from attending five lectures on the subject at the law 'crammers', Gibson & Weldon, 'I learned along with my students. That is how Family Law became a subject I professed.' Careers are built on such chances of fate; later generations of family-law students certainly owe a debt of gratitude to the person in Nairobi responsible for the teaching allocation that year.

Returning to England in 1968 he took up a post as lecturer at the University of Southampton, and then in 1969 as a fellow at Exeter College Oxford. Despite his teaching experience in Kenya – and his publication of a number of law review articles dealing with family law issues[2] – he still regarded himself as mainly a property or tax lawyer,[3] and it was to a University Lectureship with special responsibility for the course in personal taxation that he was appointed in 1972.

But family law was becoming his real focus of research. This emerging interest was reflected in the writing of *Principles of Family Law* in 1973 with the aim 'not only to explain the law as it is, but to give an account of its historical background, to analyse the factors underlying its development and to stimulate discussion of its effectiveness as an instrument of social policy…'[4]

The policy dimension of family law was to assume still more importance in the following years. Having been invited to act as the Rapporteur at the Council of Europe's Conference on the Harmonisation of Family Law in Vienna, Stephen was invited to take up an appointment at the Law Commission. Here he was to serve for five years, from 1978 to 1983: a busy period for law reform in the field of family law.[5]

---

[2]   S. CRETNEY, 'Jurisdiction in Matrimonial Causes in Kenya' 2 *East African Law Journal* 72; 'Some Problems in the Marriage Laws of Kenya' 3 *East African Law Journal* 1.

[3]   See e.g. S. CRETNEY and G. DWORKIN, *Theobald on Wills*, 13th ed., Stevens & Sons, London 1971; S. CRETNEY and G. DWORKIN, 'Rectification and Indemnity: Illusion and Reality' (1968) 84 *Law Quarterly Review* 528.

[4]   It also had an impact on Stephen's own family life. At the time the English graduate Antonia Vanrenan was college secretary at Exeter College, and she and Stephen were married in July 1973. Their two sons, Matthew and Edward, were born in Oxford in 1975 and 1979 respectively.

[5]   See also LAW COMMISSION, *Nineteenth Annual Report, 1983–4* Law Com. No. 140, HMSO, London 1985, para. 1.23.

Upon stepping down from his role as a Commissioner in 1983, he took up a Chair at the University of Bristol, where he also served as Dean of the Faculty for a number of years. During the next eight years he also took on responsibility for the monthly case analyses in the Bristol-based *Family Law* journal, as well as persuading the publisher, Jordans, to go into the business of continuing professional education conferences for practitioners (a long-standing area of interest). He also became a member of the Civil and Family Committee of the Judicial Studies Board, served on the Departmental Committee on the Prison Disciplinary System and on the Lord Chancellor's Advisory Committee on Legal Education, acted as a trustee of the Bristol Courts Family Conciliation Service, chaired the Committee of Heads of University Law Schools and the Working Party established by the National Association for the Care and Re-Settlement of Offenders to examine the operation of s. 53 of the Children and Young Persons Act 1933, and sat for eight years as a part-time Chairman of the Tribunals established to deal with appeals against decisions about entitlements under the Social Security system. As he put it, with characteristic understatement, 'it was a busy life.'

Another change took place in 1993, when Stephen was elected to a Senior Research Fellowship at All Souls College Oxford. There he completed his major work, *Family Law in the Twentieth Century: A History*, which was published by Oxford University Press in 2003. This was universally well reviewed, and in 2004 was one of six titles shortlisted for the British Academy Book Prize, awarded for books in the humanities and social sciences judged to be not only 'academically outstanding' but also 'appealing to the general reader'.

This research did not, however, lead him to neglect other aspects of public service. He was a member of the Judicial Studies Board Working Party and Steering Group on Training the Judiciary for the Children Act 1989. He chaired Medical Appeal Tribunals, Disability Appeal Tribunals and the new Child Support Appeal Tribunals. He chaired the Jurisprudence section of the British Academy from 1991–95 and was a member of its Council from 1994–96. He also acted as President of the National Council for the Divorced and Separated, and served as a member on the Lord Chancellor's Ancillary Relief Advisory Group. Having been appointed as honorary Queen's Counsel in 1992, he became an honorary Master of the Bench of the Inner Temple in 2006.

His sense of public duty, scrupulous regard for accuracy and detail, and ability to communicate ideas to a general audience, were all subsequently reflected in his appearance on *Panorama* in February 2005 to explain the legal problems associated with the apparently straightforward announcement that the Prince of

Wales was to marry Camilla Parker-Bowles in a civil ceremony.[6] It was saddening that some less well-informed commentators seemed to regard those highlighting the legal obstacles as inconsiderate troublemakers.[7] Given that the basic obstacle to marrying in Windsor Castle – the fact that it had not been approved as a venue for civil marriages, and that such approval would allow any person to marry there – would have been discovered sooner or later, at the very least it can be said that Stephen's intervention saved Clarence House from the embarrassment of writing to a list of illustrious guests to inform them that the venue had changed. On the more fundamental issue – the fact that the legislation seemed to exclude members of the Royal Family from an English civil marriage – the authorities did not accept his view, and it remains the case that the law governing the formalities for civil marriage is less clear than it should be in this area.

Even in retirement – since 2001 he has been an Emeritus Fellow of All Souls College – he continued to research and lecture, giving the prestigious Clarendon Lectures in 2005 on the topic of same-sex relationships and – fittingly – one in a series of lectures entitled 'All Souls and the Tradition of Public Service in the Twentieth Century.'[8]

Given the enormous breadth of Stephen's interests, the task of the editors in deciding which topics to cover, even within the (admittedly flexible) confines of family law, was a difficult one, but this in turn eased the demands placed on the individual contributors: whatever topic they chose, there was invariably an erudite article or chapter by Stephen for inspiration. The extent to which *Family Law in the Twentieth Century: A History* constitutes a resource for scholars is reflected by the sheer number of references to it in these pages.

It is a tribute to the esteem and affection in which Stephen is held by the family law community that the response to invitations to contribute to a volume in his honour should have been so overwhelmingly positive. This collection brings together some of the most eminent figures in the field of family law with some who are just embarking on their academic careers – the latter being especially important, given the efforts that Stephen has made to encourage more junior scholars over the years. Indeed, readers may think that seniority counts for nothing here.

---

6   See further S. CRETNEY, 'Royal Marriages: the Law in a Nutshell' [2005] *Family Law* 317.
7   S. BATES, 'Blunders cast a shadow over big day for Charles and Camilla' *The Guardian*, 23.02.2005.
8   See now S. CRETNEY, 'Simon: A Lawyer in Politics' in S.J.D. GREEN and P. HORDEN (eds.), *All Souls and the Wider World: Statesmen, Scholars and Adventurers, c. 1850–1950*, Oxford University Press, Oxford 2011.

Having rejected both the simple solution of arranging the contributions alphabetically, and the potentially explosive one of placing them in order of seniority, we have chosen to structure the book by first focusing on Stephen's contributions in particular areas (at the Law Commission, in the teaching of law and in the historical depth of his research) before moving on to examine the family law issues in the order in which they might be experienced (though not, one would hope, by any one family).

We start, therefore, with Brenda Hale's evaluation of Stephen's contribution to the reform of family law during his time at the Law Commission. During this time he played a part in widening the pool from which the Law Commission recruited, as set out in the chapter by Joanna Harwood and Penny Lewis, leading to the introduction of Research Assistants to the Commission. Stephen's contribution to the range and scope of family law textbooks then comes under the spotlight, with Simon Rowbotham imagining the student of 1974 faced with the choice between Cretney's *Principles* and Bromley's *Family Law*. Next, Stephen Gilmore focuses on the extent to which Stephen Cretney's work has been judicially cited and his contribution to the development of the common law and statutory interpretation in the fields of family and child law. Christine Piper's chapter looks at Stephen the historian while also providing powerful examples of legislation being marketed 'for the sake of the children' and an excellent demonstration of the lessons that can be (but often are not) learnt from history.

We then move from the position of children born outside marriage in Andrew Bainham's chapter to planning for marriage in Joanna Miles' contribution on pre-nuptial agreements and thence to the ceremonies/registration, together with the informal options, in the contributions from Chris Barton and Rebecca Probert. The impact – or not – of marriage on property rights forms the subject of Jens Scherpe's chapter on community of property regimes. Turning to the children of the union, the use of adoption and of wardship (as very different ways of protecting children) are considered by Sonia Harris-Short and Nigel Lowe respectively. The consideration of rights on death is usually postponed to the end of any family law text – if it is considered at all – but Lizzie Cooke's chapter on succession is placed next, in order to emphasise the often-overlooked fact that most marriages do still end in death rather than divorce.

Divorce is, of course, a crucial part of modern family law, and in his chapter Jonathan Herring considers the scope for greater private ordering. This option – now being energetically promoted by the government – stands in stark contrast to the earlier history of divorce reform, which Sue Jenkinson describes in her chapter on the history of the co-respondent. The consequences of divorce then fall to be considered, with Gillian Douglas' chapter on the division of assets illustrating one of the problems with the current emphasis on autonomy and agreement.

How such disputes could – or should – be resolved is the topic of the next set of chapters, with Neil Robinson examining the contribution of mediation and John Eekelaar exploring the difficult issue of arbitration provided by Muslim Sharia Councils (and the still broader issue of how the state should approach the family laws of minority communities). Ruth Deech discusses the contribution that barristers may make to the resolution of family disputes, along with the issue of how the Bar should be regulated. Judith Masson's chapter on judicial case management then analyses the attempts that have been made to streamline the working of the family law system (with, as yet, limited success), while Mavis Maclean focuses on recent attempts to ensure greater openness and transparency in the family courts.

We close with two comparative perspectives: Sanford Katz provides a panoramic overview of American family law over the past fifty years – as well as an explanation of how the policy context in the States is very different – and the collection closes with Walter Pintens' striking tale of another royal wedding.

Editing this book has been a privilege and a pleasure – not least because of the very different ways in which the contributors have approached their task. Given that the focus of this book is a person, rather than a topic, we have not attempted to impose uniformity on the individual chapters: each stands alone as a contribution on the discrete topic and as that person's own distinctive contribution.

COLLECTIVE RESPONSIBILITY
Law Reform at the Law Commission

Brenda HALE

Contents

1.   INTRODUCTION

In 1979, shortly after Stephen Cretney became a Law Commissioner, Michael Zander described the creation of the Law Commission as 'the single most important event in this century's history in the field of reform of the law'.[1] That could not be said with such confidence today. The heady days are long gone when its statutory task – to 'take and keep under review all the law... with a view to its systematic development and reform, including in particular the codification of such law...'[2] – was thought remotely feasible. But the Commission has achieved more towards that aim in family law than in any other field and Cretney's astute tenure as a Commissioner played a large part in that.

The Commission is required to put forward programmes for the examination of different branches of the law to the Lord Chancellor and can only proceed with his approval.[3] In the early days, however, the approved subject matter was so broadly stated that it was allowed to do pretty well what it liked. The first

---

[1]   M. ZANDER, 'Promoting Change in the Legal System' (1979) 42 *Modern Law Review (MLR)* 489, 502.

[2]   Law Commissions Act 1965, s. 1(1).

[3]   Ibid., s. 3(1)(b).

programme[4] contained some discrete topics,[5] such as reform of the grounds for divorce, but also some large codification projects, happily approved by its progenitor, Lord Gardiner. In 1968, the first programme was supplemented by an even more ambitious second programme. This included not only the comprehensive examination of the whole of family law with a view to its systematic reform and eventual codification, but also an examination of the jurisdiction of the courts dealing with family matters.[6]

2. BEFORE THE CRETNEY ERA

Wisely, the Commission got on with the law reform first. Its study of the family courts was suspended when the Finer Committee on One-Parent Families took up the topic in the early 1970s and never resumed. Between 1965 and 1971, a remarkable programme of family law reform was completed: remarkable because family law had only been recognised as a proper subject in the 1950s – specifically in 1957, when Graveson and Crane published *A Century of Family Law 1857 – 1957*, marking the hundred years since the introduction of judicial divorce, and Peter Bromley published the first edition of his textbook, *Family Law*. Bromley brought together the law of matrimonial causes, inherited from the ecclesiastical courts, and the common and equitable law of husband and wife, parent and child, and presented them as a coherent whole. Marriage was a status which imposed a series of legally enforceable rights and obligations looking very like contractual rights and obligations. No sooner had Bromley produced this analysis, however, than the Law Commission set about pulling it apart.

The first wave of reforms covered the grounds of divorce,[7] nullity of marriage,[8] the powers of the courts to make financial and property orders following nullity and divorce,[9] and the abolition of remedies to enforce the obligations of marriage and contracts of engagement.[10] Together these revolutionised the law. A contract to marry was no longer enforceable; a husband could not enforce his wife's marital obligations against outsiders; neither husband nor wife could obtain a

---

4   *First Programme of Law Reform* Law Com. No. 1, HMSO, London 1965.
5   Largely taken from the list in G. GARDINER and A. MARTIN (eds.), *Law Reform Now*, Victor Gollancz, London 1963.
6   *Second Programme of Law Reform* Law Com. No. 14, HMSO, London 1968, items X and XIX.
7   *Reform of the Grounds of Divorce: The Field of Choice* Law Com. No. 6, HMSO, London 1966, implemented by Divorce Reform Act 1969, consolidated in Matrimonial Causes Act 1973.
8   *Report on Nullity of Marriage* Law Com. No. 33, HMSO, London 1970.
9   *Report on Financial Provision in Matrimonial Proceedings* Law Com. No. 25, HMSO, London 1969.
10 *Proposal for the Abolition of the Matrimonial Remedy of Breach of Conjugal Rights* Law Com. No. 23, HMSO, London 1969; *Breach of Promise of Marriage* Law Com. No. 26, HMSO, London 1969.

decree of restitution of conjugal rights ordering a deserting spouse to return. Irretrievable breakdown of the marriage became the sole ground for divorce, provable in defined ways which made no serious attempt fairly to allocate the blame for that breakdown. On divorce, all the couple's actual and foreseeable resources, both income and capital, could be put into a notional pot and shared between them as the court thought fit. Following the precedent set by the Matrimonial Homes Act 1967, the remedies were all gender-neutral, available on the same terms both for and against both husband and wife.[11] Discretionary remedies governed by a flexible series of factors based largely upon need had supplanted the contractual model.

In the 1970s, the Commission turned to the law of marriage itself, but with much less success. By 1978, as Cretney has commented, some of the early glamour had worn off and the problems inherent in bridging the gap between a non-political advisory body and a politicised legislature had become apparent.[12] The 1973 report on the formalities of getting married[13] has never been implemented. A comprehensive review of matrimonial property law produced two principal recommendations. One, for automatic joint ownership of the matrimonial home, has also never been implemented.[14] The other, for improved discretionary powers to re-allocate resources after the death of a family member, has.[15] Flexible discretionary remedies proved politically more acceptable than automatic property and succession rights, whether during the marriage or on death or divorce.

By contrast, the Commission's only early contribution in the field of child law was on the proof of paternity in civil proceedings.[16] The Family Law Reform Act 1969, which lowered the age of majority from 21 to 18 and revolutionised the succession rights of children born to unmarried parents, was the work of others.[17] So too were the Guardianship Act 1973, which gave married mothers

---

[11] See also *Report on Matrimonial Proceedings in Magistrates' Courts* Law Com. No. 77, HMSO, London 1976.

[12] 'The Law Commission: True Dawns and False Dawns', in S.M. CRETNEY, *Law, Law Reform and the Family*, Clarendon Press, Oxford 1998.

[13] *Report on Solemnisation of Marriage in England and Wales* Law Com. No. 53, HMSO, London 1973.

[14] *First Report on Family Property. A New Approach* Law Com. No. 52, HMSO, London 1973; *Third Report on Family Property. The Matrimonial Home (Co-ownership and Occupation Rights) and Household Goods* Law Com. No. 86, HMSO, London 1978.

[15] *Second Report on Family Property. Family Provision on Death* Law Com. No. 61, HMSO, London 1974.

[16] *Blood Tests and the Proof of Paternity in Civil Proceedings* Law Com. No. 16, HMSO, London 1968.

[17] *Latey Committee on the Age of Majority* Cmnd 3342, HMSO, London 1967; *Russell Committee on the Law of Succession in relation to Illegitimate Persons* Cmnd 3051, HMSO, London 1966.

equal parental rights and authority with their husbands, and the Children Act 1975, which brought about the comprehensive reform of the adoption law.[18]

The Commission's role was to propose 'changes and improvements in any part of the law which can appropriately be put forward by a body of lawyers on the basis of legal principle and pragmatic common sense, after public consultation'.[19] In other words, a project is suitable for the Law Commission if it is a suitable one for lawyers. So it was odd that the private law of the family was thought suitable, and was for a long time so profitable an area for reform, steeped as it is in moral and social issues and gender politics. Cretney's explanation was that private family law fell within the departmental responsibility of the Lord Chancellor's own department, with its close relationship with the Commission and professional lawyers in policy making roles.[20]

3. THE CRETNEY YEARS

Before joining the Commission, Cretney had been critical of the 'Bromley' approach to family law. His own textbook, *Principles of Family Law*, emphasised the social and political context within which it operated.[21] So he was uniquely well-qualified for the policy-making task, but he modestly wonders whether it was his role as Rapporteur at the Council of Europe's Conference on the harmonisation of Family Law in Vienna in 1977 which brought him to the attention of the Lord Chancellor's officials.[22] When he arrived in October 1978, to take charge of the Commission's work in family law and land registration, he inherited (or revived) some projects and initiated others.

His principal inheritance was replete with social context and gender politics. In 1976, impelled by the law's anomalies and the need to ratify the 1975 Council of Europe Convention on the Legal Status of Children born out of Wedlock, the Commission had set up a working party, consisting mainly of officials from interested government departments, to help to prepare a working paper on illegitimacy. This was completed in March 1979, less than six months after Cretney's arrival and three months before the landmark decision of the European Court of Human Rights in *Marckz v. Belgium*.[23]

---

[18]   *Report of the Departmental Committee on the Adoption of Children* Cmnd 5107, HMSO, London 1972.
[19]   Sir M. Kerr, 'Law Reform in Changing Times' (1980) 96 *Law Quarterly Review* 515, 516.
[20]   S. Cretney, 'The Politics of Law Reform' (1985) 48 *MLR* 493, 510.
[21]   See further Rowbotham, this volume.
[22]   Personal communication from Stephen Cretney.
[23]   (1979–80) 2 EHRR 330.

The principal question raised[24] was whether reform should simply seek to remove the legal disadvantages of illegitimacy as far as they affected the child or to abolish the concepts of legitimacy and illegitimacy altogether. In the Commission's analysis (which Cretney could well have stimulated), this inevitably meant giving unmarried fathers the same rights and authority as married fathers. But the notion that the best way of improving the status of a child was also to improve the father's status proved controversial, not least because it was seen as potentially making the lives of unmarried mothers bringing up their children alone even more of a struggle through unwanted paternal interference. Hence, while the working paper had favoured the more radical proposal, the eventual report[25] favoured the less radical solution.[26] The attached Bill also continued the traditional legislative practice of referring to the status of the child – now to be described as 'marital' or 'non-marital' rather than 'legitimate' or 'illegitimate'.

As Cretney predicted, the Government found space for such a necessary and comparatively uncontroversial reform in its legislative programme for the session 1986 to 1987, in the run-up to the general election of June 1987. However, although the Government liked the policy, they did not like the Bill. The Scottish Law Commission had reached the same conclusion on the substance of the reforms, but also argued that it was unnecessary and undesirable to attach any kind of label to the child.[27] Where distinctions were necessary, they should be made between fathers rather than between children. If it was necessary to distinguish between people on the basis of whether or not their parents were married to one another, it should be done in just those terms. The Law Reform (Parent and Child) (Scotland) Act 1986 adopted that approach.

So it came about that the Law Commission, now with a different membership,[28] was urgently and secretly approached by officials from the Lord Chancellor's Department, concerned that if the Lord Chancellor were asked to introduce the Bill annexed to the Law Commission's Report, he would decline to do so. A busy summer's work between Commissioners and Parliamentary counsel resulted in a new Bill along similar lines to the Scots', published with the Commission's second report on illegitimacy in October 1986.[29] Its principal feature was a new rule of construction, applicable to legislation and other legal instruments unless a contrary intention appears, that references to any familial relationship are to be

---

24   *Illegitimacy* WP No. 74, HMSO, London 1979.
25   *Illegitimacy* Law Com. No. 118, HMSO, London 1982.
26   See further BAINHAM, this volume.
27   SCOTTISH LAW COMMISSION, *Illegitimacy*, Scot. Law Com. No. 82, HMSO, Edinburgh 1984.
28   The new Commissioners were Sir Roy Beldam, Trevor Aldridge, Julian Farrand and Brenda Hoggett. Only Brian Davenport QC remained of the signatories to the earlier Report.
29   *Illegitimacy (Second Report)* Law Com. No. 157, HMSO, London 1986.

construed without regard to whether or not any person's mother and father were married to one another at the material time. So a father's sister is the child's aunt, and the child her niece, irrespective of whether or not the child's mother and father, or the father's and sister's parents, were married to one another. There would no longer be any need expressly to include 'illegitimate' or 'non-marital' children or relationships in legislation or other legal instruments.

It was sad that this work had to be done without consulting the Commissioner who had been responsible for working with Parliamentary counsel on the first Bill, but Cretney accepted it with his usual good grace.[30] It was a comparatively mild and benign departure from previous Commissioners' policy, unlike the Commission's project on offences against religion and public worship.

This was undertaken in the wake of the conviction of the editor of *Gay News* for the common law offence of blasphemous libel in publishing a poem about a Roman soldier's feelings for Christ on the cross.[31] Common law offences were inconsistent with the Commission's programme to codify the criminal law. A working paper was published in April 1981, when Sir Michael Kerr was Chairman,[32] proposing that the common law offences be abolished without replacing them with any offence protecting religious feelings. This prompted a huge response, those against abolition without replacement (generally organised religion) heavily outnumbering those in favour (generally lawyers, professional groups and academics).

Shortly after the working paper was published, Sir Ralph Gibson became Chairman and Brian Davenport QC the new barrister member. The new Commission decided still to recommend abolition of the common law offence, but, perhaps in the hope of sugaring the pill, also to recommend a new offence of injuring religious feelings. These proposals joined the queue for Parliamentary counsel to draft a Bill, but kept on being postponed – until the composition of the Commission changed once more.[33] Sir Ralph Gibson and Brian Davenport QC still thought that there should be a replacement offence: 'We would therefore wish adherence to a religion, with the reverence for the sacred which goes with it, to be recognised by the State as deserving of such protection as the State can give without impairment of the rights of others.'[34] The three new Commissioners,

---

[30] Apart perhaps from the decision to apply the new rule of construction to the word 'heir'.

[31] See *Whitehouse v. Lemon* [1979] AC 617.

[32] *Offences against Religion and Public Worship* Law Com. WP No. 79, HMSO, London 1981; the other Commissioners were Stephen Cretney, Stephen Edell, W.A.B. Forbes QC, and Peter North.

[33] Cretney, Edell and North were replaced during 1984 by Trevor Aldridge, Julian Farrand and Brenda Hoggett.

[34] *Offences against Religion and Public Worship* Law Com. No. 145, HMSO, London 1985, Note of Dissent, para. 3.2.

on the other hand, did not agree that religious feelings were so different from any others that their protection was, without more, a sufficient justification for interfering with freedom of speech. Unsurprisingly, the majority Report languished without implementation for more than 20 years, until blasphemy was abolished by section 79 of the Criminal Justice and Immigration Act 2008. At a National Secular Society 'Bye-bye blasphemy' party, Sir Ian McKellan made the offending poem sound much better than it reads on the page. The moral for the Commission is 'never let them say never'. Parliament as well as the Commissioners can change its mind.

The change in personnel may explain another change between the first and second Reports on Illegitimacy. In the first, the Commissioners reluctantly agreed that the court should be able to make declarations of parentage,[35] as well as declarations of legitimacy and legitimation. But they were so worried about the potential for abuse if there were no 'proper contradictor' of a collusive assertion that X was the father of the child that they had recommended several restrictions.[36] Then early in 1984 came the report recommending a new and more consistent scheme for declarations of marital and legitimacy status.[37] The second report on illegitimacy in 1986 recommended that children of unmarried parents who wanted a declaration of parentage should not be subject to a more limited and onerous regime than people who could apply for a declaration of legitimacy or legitimation when the issue was essentially the same.[38] The feared abuses do not seem to have materialised.

Illegitimacy is one field where Cretney made a major impact. The other is financial provision on divorce. Here again, gender politics loomed large. These emerged as the full implications of the first wave of family law reforms began to sink in during the 1970s. If all the assets and income are notionally pooled, the parties' respective contributions to the welfare of the family equally valued, their marriage dissolved because it has broken down, but the court is instructed to assume that it has not in deciding how their assets will be divided, the richer spouse will have to provide for the poorer one irrespective of fault. Had the marriage not broken down, they would have continued to enjoy a roughly equal standard of living. But they would also have continued to do so for life or until re-marriage – hence the so-called 'meal ticket for life'.

The Commission handled this hot potato with a care and caution typical of the 'gradualist approach' which Cretney favoured: the issue raised difficult questions

---

[35]   Above n. 24, paras. 9.2–9.35.
[36]   Above n. 25, paras 10.6–10.27.
[37]   *Declarations in Family Matters* Law Com. No. 132, HMSO, London 1984, following WP No. 48, HMSO, London 1973.
[38]   Above n. 29, para. 3.14; see Family Law Act 1986, ss. 55 and 56.

about the nature of marriage itself and the respective functions of husband and wife. It would not be appropriate for the Commission to advance even tentative proposals for reform. Instead it produced a discussion paper, ostensibly in response to a request from the Lord Chancellor, 'to provide advice and information to government departments' under section 3(1)(e) of the 1965 Act.[39] It was not easy to answer the question 'whether the law, which no longer seeks to enforce many of the traditional obligations of marriage, should still continue to enforce an obligation of financial support'; but various 'models for a law' were discussed. When reporting on the response,[40] it declined to adopt any particular model, recommending only that the statutory objective be repealed, that priority be given to providing adequate support for the children, and that each party should do everything possible to become self-sufficient. It was left to the courts painfully to work out a rationale both for redistributing the existing assets and awarding any continuing provision for the future.[41]

The approach of the Scottish Law Commission, undertaking the more comprehensive task of reviewing what powers of financial provision and property adjustment should be available on divorce, was very different. It linked those powers to a set of quite precisely defined principles, placing more emphasis upon the principle of equal sharing of marital assets than upon provision for marriage-related needs or compensation for marriage-related sacrifices.[42] This produces harsher results for home-making spouses when capital is limited than does the more flexible and pragmatic English approach.[43]

The same pragmatic caution appears in the project on financial relief after foreign divorce, of which Cretney can be justly proud. Greater mobility made it easier for people to establish a sufficient connection to give the foreign country jurisdiction to grant a divorce (or to validate a non-judicial divorce such as a *talak*) which English law would recognise. The parties might have a much closer connection with this country or have considerable marital property here but none of the remedies to enforce the obligation to maintain were available if they were divorced abroad. The resulting hardship and injustice had to be set against the risks of forum shopping and the problems of the courts in deciding whether it was appropriate to make an order. Forum shopping was to be deterred by

---

[39]   *The Financial Consequences of Divorce. A Discussion Paper* Law Com. No. 103, HMSO, London 1980.

[40]   *The Financial Consequences of Divorce. The response to the Law Commission's Discussion Paper, and recommendations on the policy of the law* Law Com. No. 112, HMSO, London 1981.

[41]   *White v. White* [2000] UKHL 54; *Miller v. Miller* [2006] UKHL 24.

[42]   *Report on Aliment and Financial Provision* Scot. Law Com. No. 67, HMSO, Edinburgh 1981.

[43]   *Miller*, above n. 41, per Lord Hope, [110]-[121].

requiring an ex parte application for leave to a High Court judge.[44] Guidance was given as to the factors to be taken into account in deciding whether England and Wales was an appropriate venue for making the application. However, hardly anything was added to the existing guidance as to the factors to be taken into account in deciding what order, if any, to make. In particular, the legislation did not make it clear, as had been suggested in the working paper, that the jurisdiction was designed for 'the occasional hard case'.[45]

Once again, the Scots' approach to the same problem was very different. While the English chose a broad basis for assuming jurisdiction and a leave filter to weed out the undeserving cases before the respondent was troubled, the Scots chose a narrower basis for assuming jurisdiction, with no leave filter, and then treated the case in all respects as if it were a Scottish application.[46] The English, on the other hand, could take the foreign connections into account in deciding what order, if any, to make and might well award less than an English court would have done.

Cretney was also responsible for the reports clarifying the courts' power to order a sale of property when redistributing the parties' assets on divorce[47] and reducing the time which married couples had to wait after the wedding before they could be divorced.[48] Making them wait three years unless they could show 'exceptional hardship' or 'exceptional depravity' was hard to reconcile with the policy of burying dead marriages with as little 'bitterness, distress and humiliation' as possible.[49] Some Commissioners favoured a one- or two-year absolute bar while others favoured making it procedurally more difficult to obtain a divorce within two years of the marriage. The absolute bar won.

The reports on financial relief after foreign divorce and time restrictions in nullity and divorce were produced with such speed and efficiency that they could be implemented alongside the changes to the law of financial provision in the Matrimonial and Family Proceedings Act 1984.

---

44   *Financial Relief after Foreign Divorce* Law Com. No. 117, HMSO, London 1982.
45   *Financial Relief after Foreign Divorce* Law Com. WP No. 77, HMSO, London 1980, para. 51; see *Agbaje v. Agbaje* [2010] UKSC 13.
46   *Report on Financial Provision after Foreign Divorce* Scot. Law Com. No. 72, HMSO, Edinburgh 1982.
47   *Orders for Sale of Property under the Matrimonial Causes Act 1973* Law Com. No. 99, HMSO, London 1980.
48   *Time Restrictions on Presentation of Divorce and Nullity Petitions* Law Com. No. 116, HMSO, London 1982.
49   See also *Law Reform? An invitation for views – divorce in the early years of* marriage, HMSO, London 1980; *Time Restrictions on the Presentation of Divorce and Nullity Petitions* Law Com. WP No. 76, HMSO, London 1980.

Cretney also played an important part in the projects on recognition of foreign nullity decrees[50] and on conflicts of jurisdiction between different parts of the United Kingdom in cases concerning children,[51] both of which reported after he had left the Commission at the end of 1983. He was party to the report which recommended that the solution to the problems caused by the overriding interest of a party (usually a spouse) in actual occupation of land registered in the name of another lay in registration of co-ownership interests, including implementation of the Commission's scheme for co-ownership of the matrimonial home.[52] He was also productive as Commissioner in charge of the Law Commission's long running project to modernise the law of land registration.[53]

But apart from these specific projects, his great achievement was to re-establish the Commission as a valuable producer of family law reform, upon which his successors were able to build.

4. AFTER THE CRETNEY ERA

Work continued on the family law programme after he left at the end of 1983, on both legacy and new projects. The legacy project was another review of the ground for divorce.[54] Cretney ensured that this was not forgotten, not least by hosting a seminar at Bristol University in December 1985 'to seek further information and canvass views' to enable the Commission to formulate a consultation paper.[55] Eventually the Commission produced a simple proposal for a year-long breathing space during which it was hoped that the parties would be able to agree the practical consequences of their divorce.[56] This was complicated by the government after further consultation and even more complicated during its passage through Parliament. Many thought the results completely unworkable, so it was no surprise when a later government announced that it would not be brought into force. Whatever his views of the original proposals, Cretney was scathing about the excuse – that pilot studies had shown that fewer couples than expected chose to resolve their affairs through mediators rather than through

---

50   *Recognition of Foreign Nullity Decrees and Related Matters* Law Com. No. 137, HMSO, London 1984.
51   *Custody of Children – Jurisdiction and Enforcement within the United Kingdom* Law Com. No. 138, HMSO, London 1985, Scot. Law Com. No. 91, HMSO, Edinburgh 1985.
52   *The Implications of Williams & Glyn's Bank Ltd v. Boland* Law Com. No. 115, HMSO, London 1982; and see the case-note by S. FREEMAN (widely believed to be Cretney himself), 'Wives, Conveyancers and Justice' (1980) 43 *MLR* 692.
53   Earlier working papers were exhumed and a Report, *Land Registration* Law Com. No. 125, HMSO, London 1983, published during his tenure.
54   *Fourteenth Annual Report 1978–79* Law Com. No. 97, HMSO, London 1980, para. 2.24.
55   *Twentieth Annual Report 1984–85* Law Com. No. 155, HMSO, London 1986, para. 2.22.
56   *The Ground for Divorce* Law Com. No. 192, HMSO, London 1990.

lawyers – noting that there was 'nothing in them which would come as any surprise to those who have taken even the most superficial interest in this subject over the years'.[57]

Rather more success was achieved with three new projects. The Commission's proposals to simplify and modernise the law on rights of occupation of the family home and protection from domestic abuse[58] also had an eventful time in Parliament. They made most of their way through Parliament in the 1994–1995 session before a few MPs raised last-minute objections which meant that the Bill had to be withdrawn. Greatly to the Government's credit, it was re-presented as part of the Family Law Bill in the following session, and reached the statute book comparatively unscathed.

The Commission's project on the private law of guardianship and custody[59] was a companion piece to its work with the government on the Review of Child Care Law. This was a new style of working, suitable to a reform project which fell within the core responsibilities of a government department: the Commissioner sat on an inter-departmental working group chaired by an official from the lead department and the family law team supplied the legal expertise alongside the policy expertise of departmental officials. Delay in implementing the Review's proposals meant that both the public and the private law could be presented to Parliament in a single Bill; the Law Commission's privilege of direct access to Parliamentary counsel had shown how it could be done. The Children Act 1989 was the result. A similar model of working was adopted with the 1992 Adoption Law Review, which eventually resulted in the Adoption and Children Act 2002.

These were the last substantial pieces of legislation to emerge from the Commission's traditional family law programme. For a while the Commission decided to concentrate on other matters, not surprisingly, given how much energy had been devoted to family law over its first 30 years. But there was still a great deal to do. The Commission made a welcome return to family law with its Consultation Paper and Report on Cohabitation: the Financial Consequences of Family Breakdown.[60] This complex work was completed in double-quick time partly because it was not accompanied by the usual draft Bill. It is disappointing that a government which was apparently enthusiastic that a project be undertaken became markedly less enthusiastic about implementing its recommendations. Recently the Commission has published a Report on Intestacy and Family

---

57   See [1999] *Family Law* 517.
58   *Domestic Violence and Occupation of the Family Home* Law Com. No. 207, HMSO, London 1992.
59   *Review of Child Law: Guardianship and Custody* Law Com. No. 172, HMSO, London 1988.
60   CP No. 179, TSO, London 2006; Law Com. No. 307, TSO, London 2007.

Provision Claims on Death[61] and a Consultation Paper on Marital Property Agreements.[62]

But the way in which the Commission decides upon projects has now changed.[63] The approved programmes of law reform are regularly updated after negotiations with Government. The Commission will not pursue even a good idea if there is no governmental enthusiasm for it. This may enable the Commission to take on topics which it might not have done in earlier years. It is also hoped to improve the chances of implementation.

5. CONCLUSIONS

What are the messages? Most of what is currently on the statute book in family law is the result of the work of the Law Commission in its first 30 years. Three factors combine to explain this. The Commission was given a relatively free hand by Government to reform the private law and allowed to take a leading part in the reform of the public law of child care and adoption. It had a specialist family law team led by Commissioners who were either specialists or had a special interest. And the private law of the family was then the responsibility of the Lord Chancellor's Department, which also had responsibility for the Law Commission and a peculiarly lawyer-based policy team.

That combination no longer exists. With a current Commissioner who is expert in (among other things) family law, serious work has been resumed. But the Commission has less of a free hand in choosing projects than in earlier days. The Lord Chancellor's Department has metamorphosed into the Ministry of Justice. Departmental responsibility even for private family law is diffused and policy-makers are no longer lawyers. The days when it was enough to demonstrate a clear need for a remedy have also gone by. The greater the need, the less likely it is to be provided, because that will cost money either in the courts or in legal aid or both.

Discretionary remedies were once seen as easier to devise and provide for than fixed rules of entitlement or even fixed principles of adjustment. Now, there is more enthusiasm for fixed rules or at least for fixed principles. The Commission has so far declined to undertake another review of the financial remedies on divorce but any such review would undoubtedly aim to clarify the principles of

---

61   Law Com. No. 331, TSO, London 2011.
62   CP No. 198, TSO, London 2010.
63   See *Eleventh Programme of Law Reform* Law Com. No. 330, TSO, London 2011, Part 1 and Law Commission Act 2009.

the exercise and narrow the scope of the courts' discretion. The current exercise on marital agreements can only result, if the present law is to be changed, in giving further weight to the agreements made by individual couples, whether at the beginning, or during, or at the end of their relationship. This is the antithesis of the open-ended discretion, for example, to award financial relief after foreign divorce.

But why were some of the most innovative steps in family law the work of others? Why was the Commission not responsible for the Guardianship Act of 1973? Why did the Commission not spot the gaps which led to the Domestic Violence and Matrimonial Proceedings Act of 1976? Why was the Commission not behind the civil partnership legislation in 2004? If it had taken up the subject of unmarried relationships (as opposed to home-sharing), as it surely should have done in the later 1990s, would it have ended in the same place? These were real break-through moments – equality for married mothers, family law remedies for unmarried victims of domestic abuse, and a whole new legal status for same-sex couples. Is it because the Commission is good at improving what is there already but less good at spotting the need for wholly new law?

Another message is about the differences between being an academic lawyer and a Law Commissioner and between being a Law Commissioner and a judge, even in a collegiate appellate court. An academic lawyer does not have to make a decision. Whether, like an advocate, he can decide what he wants the answer to be and then find arguments to support it is debatable. But he can certainly argue any case which appears to him to be intellectually and empirically sustainable. In the end it does not matter because the decision does not lie with him but with Parliament and the judges.

A Law Commissioner, on the other hand, does have to make a decision. He has to formulate a policy precise and coherent enough to satisfy Parliamentary counsel that it can be expressed in Parliamentary language. But it is a collective decision. Any credibility the Commission has must stem from its collective wisdom. If five distinguished lawyers of different professional backgrounds can agree that something is wrong with the law, that it needs a solution and that the solution proposed is the best available, their conclusions should carry greater weight than the view of any individual Commissioner, however brilliant.

The tradition is to strive for internal consensus – there are very few dissents and most publications represent the considered views of all five Commissioners. Inevitably, compromises have to be made – particularly over the way in which certain recommendations are explained. But it is unlikely that the recommendation would be one with which the Commissioner in charge of the project did not agree. Not only this, the Commission tries hard to be loyal to its predecessors even when modifying or departing from their views. There is, of course, no doctrine of precedent. But there is a sense of continuity over time, promoted by the practice of referring to 'we' and 'our' even when the publication in question was the work of a completely differently constituted Commission.

The Commission also looks for external consensus. As most reforms are achieved by legislation, it wants Government and Parliament to agree with its recommendations. So it first consults the interested parties in the hope of discovering the balance of opinion before rather than after it decides what to recommend. It then tries to find solutions that will command the widest possible respect. So it is entirely possible that a Commissioner will recommend the less radical solution to a problem while privately supporting a more radical approach.

Decision-making and continuity-respecting are also features of the judicial life. An appellate court gains much of its credibility from its collective wisdom. But the difference between an appellate court and the Commission is that the court is deciding what the law is and the Commission is deciding what it ought to be. The Commission can take a much wider range of sources into account in doing this – precedent, principle, and even common sense, but also empirical research about the operation of the law and the experience of people affected by it and the views of a wide range of organisations and individuals.

Even then, as Cretney recognised, there is often room for at least two views about where the best answer lies to what are essentially value judgments:[64]

> '... throughout my period of office as a Law Commissioner I constantly found myself asking the question – to which there rarely seemed to be an answer: *whose* interest should the Commission seek to advance?'

The answer may be easier when advancing the interests of children at the expense of adults, but what about mothers at the expense of fathers, breadwinners at the expense of homemakers, victims at the expense of persons accused of violence, or any of the other multitude of interests with which the law is concerned every day? Cretney was a pioneer in promoting the understanding of law in its social, economic and political context. Perhaps that is why he was so cautious in the many reforms which he did recommend and why he was so successful in getting them onto the statute book.

---

[64]   CRETNEY, above n. 20, 506.

A PAEAN FOR THE LAW COMMISSION
A View from the Inside*

Joanna HARWOOD and Penny LEWIS

Contents

1. INTRODUCTION

Stephen Cretney has been eminent in the field of law reform throughout his legal career: in legal practice, in academia and in his work at the Law Commission, where he was a Law Commissioner from 1978 to 1983.[1] During this period,

---

*   We are grateful for the help we have received from the Law Commission in writing this essay. Any errors or opinions expressed are the sole responsibility of the authors.

[1]   The Law Commission is a non-departmental advisory public body sponsored by the Ministry of Justice. It functions to keep the law under review and to make recommendations for reform.

Cretney worked on a number of influential family law projects, ranging from the law on illegitimacy to the financial consequences of divorce, with his work leading to major legislative developments in family law, including the Matrimonial and Family Proceedings Act 1984.[2] Cretney's commitment to making the law simpler, clearer and more accessible to those governed by it continues to underpin and inform every aspect of the Law Commission's work.

In 1985 Cretney published 'The Politics of Law Reform – A View from the Inside'.[3] This article – from which we take inspiration for the title of our essay – was based on his Inaugural Lecture given at the University of Bristol in 1984 and focused on his experience of working at the Law Commission. It considered the extent to which the Law Commission could accurately be described as having heralded a 'new dawn' for law reform, which meant examining the fundamental meaning of 'law reform' itself. What we aim to provide here is some insight into the current workings of the Law Commission and to demonstrate its continuing importance.

Our essay is written from the perspective of two of the Law Commission's current research assistants – one working for the Property, Family and Trust Law team and the other for the Statute Law Repeals team. As such, we are greatly indebted to the subject of this book as he played a significant part in introducing research assistants to the Law Commission, a role which was formally created between 1983 and 1984.

2. THE GENESIS OF THE LAW COMMISSION

Before the establishment of the Law Commission, the task of law reform fell to a number of Ministerial Committees rather than to any permanent and cohesive body charged with this responsibility. The need for a unified body devoted to law reform was first voiced in 1963 in *Law Reform Now*,[4] a need later restated in a 1965 White Paper:

> 'One of the hallmarks of an advanced society is that its laws should not only be just but also that they should be kept up-to-date and be readily accessible to all who are affected by them. The state of the law today cannot be said to satisfy these requirements... There is at present no body charged with the duty of keeping the law as a whole under review and making recommendations for its systematic reform... it

---

[2]   For discussion of Cretney's work at the Law Commission see HALE, this volume.

[3]   S. CRETNEY, 'The Politics of Law Reform – A View from the Inside' (1985) 48 *MLR (Modern Law Review)* 493.

[4]   G. GARDINER and A. MARTIN (eds.), *Law Reform Now*, Victor Gollancz, London 1963.

is evident that comprehensive reform can be achieved only by a body whose sole task it is and which is equipped with a professional staff on the scale required.'[5]

And so, in 1965, a Law Commission for England and Wales was created with the purpose of keeping the law under review and making recommendations for reform.[6] Section 3 of the Law Commissions Act 1965 details the scope of the Law Commission's intended role:

'To take and keep under review all the law with which they are respectively concerned with a view to its systematic development and reform, including in particular the codification of such law, the elimination of anomalies, the repeal of obsolete and unnecessary enactments, the reduction of the number of separate enactments and generally the simplification and modernisation of the law...'[7]

The creation of the Law Commission was seen as a move to replace the 'desultory and unsystematic approach to law reform'[8] with a cohesive, professional approach and it is therefore difficult to overstate its importance. Its formation has been described as 'the single most important event of this century in the field of law reform', a view shared by a number of commentators, including those divided on other legal issues.[9] The Law Commission has also helped to shape the current statutory framework; it is responsible, as our current Chairman has stated, for a number of statutes now taken for granted, including the Children Act 1989 and the Mental Capacity Act 2005.[10]

3. STEPHEN CRETNEY: FIFTY YEARS IN FAMILY LAW – FIVE INFLUENTIAL YEARS AS LAW COMMISSIONER

'Stephen Cretney, during his time as a Law Commissioner, made a great and distinguished contribution to the reform and codification of family law... in all of the work of the Law Commission his acuity and ability to draft were used to help his colleagues and to improve the work produced.'[11]

---

5   White Paper, *Proposals for English and Scottish Law Commissions* Cmnd. 2573, HMSO, London 1965.

6   Scotland and Northern Ireland each have a separate Law Commission; information about these Law Commissions can be accessed from <www.scotlawcom.gov.uk/> and <www.nilawcommission.gov.uk/index.htm> accessed 30.12.2011.

7   Law Commissions Act 1965 (c. 22) s.3.

8   CRETNEY, above n. 3, 493.

9   Ibid., 494.

10   J. MUNBY, 'Comment: Law Commission Consultation' [2010] 40 *Fam Law (Family Law)* 685.

11   LAW COMMISSION, *Nineteenth Annual Report 1983–1984* Law Com. No. 140, HMSO, London 1985, pp. 9–10.

His achievements at the Law Commission are comprehensively addressed in Baroness Hale's essay in this collection. What we provide here is a brief discussion of his views on the scope of the Law Commission's role, as outlined in his 1985 article, 'The Politics of Law Reform – A View from the Inside'.[12] He described the terms of the Law Commissions Act 1965 as 'breathtakingly wide'; it is responsible for reviewing *all* the law'.[13] However, he argued that the question of what should constitute the 'proper sphere' for the Law Commission's work may ultimately be answered pragmatically: the remit of the Law Commission could be shaped by 'analysing the experience of where it has in fact been effective'.[14] He suggested that the corollary of this pragmatic approach could be that the Law Commission should focus less on 'the original ambitious plans for codification' and more on 'the numerous small scale problems which reduce the efficiency of the legal system'.[15]

The precise scope of the Law Commission's role continues to attract debate today. In contrast to Cretney's 1985 view on codification, there have recently been calls for the Law Commission to refocus its attention on this area, in part in response to the mass of new statutes entering the statute book.[16] This difference in emphasis may be indicative of the flexibility inherent in the Law Commission's role, and also of the changing legislative environment in which it operates. However, whichever view is taken, this does not detract from the Law Commission's continuing value, particularly since – as Cretney has emphasised – it goes some way towards 'bridging the gap between government and the governed'[17] and contributes to upholding the rule of law.

4.   LAW REFORM, THE LAW COMMISSION AND THE RULE OF LAW

The relationship between the rule of law and the role played by the Law Commission in its promotion is complex, and one to which we cannot do justice in this short section. However, two aspects of the Law Commission's work are of particular relevance to the rule of law and deserve mention: first, its role in ensuring that those subject to the law can understand why, and by what, they are bound; and secondly, its careful and considered approach to law reform.

---

12   CRETNEY, above n. 3.
13   Ibid., 493 and 496.
14   Ibid., 514.
15   Ibid., 514.
16   D. NEUBERGER, 'General, Equal and Certain: Law Reform Today and Tomorrow', Annual Lord Renton Lecture 2011, London, 28.11.2011 <www.statutelawsociety.org/__data/assets/ pdf_file/0014/101381/RentonLectureNov2011Final.pdf> accessed 30.12.2011.
17   CRETNEY, above n. 3, 515.

Lord Bingham has described one of the 'sub-rules' of the rule of law as being that the law must be 'accessible and so far as possible intelligible, clear and predictable'.[18] The Law Commission's role is predicated on the pursuit of this objective. It informs all aspects of its work: reviewing outdated or incomprehensible areas of law; giving a voice to those subject to the law; and ensuring that the Law Commission's work is capable of being understood by lawyers and non-lawyers alike. As Sir Terence Etherton has stated:

> 'The establishment of the Law Commission was indeed a truly inspired vision, promoting in a radically new way the right of citizens to laws which are intelligible, accessible and which meet their needs. The Commission has achieved a quite remarkable impact on large areas of our national life in pursuit of that principle.'[19]

A further valuable aspect of the Law Commission's work in relation to the rule of law is its careful and measured approach to law-making. Lord Neuberger has called for resistance to the '"something must be done – and done now" school of thought'.[20] He has cautioned that rushed legislation may result not only in 'bad' law, but that it may also risk the rule of law acquiring a 'bad name'; in his view, there is often a trend to 'legislate in haste and repent in litigation'.[21] Lord Neuberger therefore advocated a more 'deliberate approach to law-making';[22] the Law Commission's philosophy on law reform may be seen to encompass this approach. Law Commission recommendations are the product of a widespread review of the problems associated with a particular area of law, consultation with members of the public, legal specialists and interested parties, and a meticulous approach to Bill-drafting.

5.   THE LAW COMMISSION TODAY

The remainder of this essay takes as its focus the current operation of the Law Commission, providing an overview of its structure and the process of law reform, in addition to personal accounts of aspects of our work as research assistants.

---

18   T. BINGHAM, 'The Rule of Law', The Sixth Sir David Williams Lecture, Cambridge, 16.11.2006 <www.cpl.law.cam.ac.uk/Media/THE%20RULE%20OF%20LAW%202006.pdf> accessed 30.12.2011.

19   T. ETHERTON, 'Law Reform in England and Wales: A Shattered Dream or Triumph of Political Vision?', Bar Law Reform Committee Lecture, London, 14.11.2007 <www.justice.gov.uk/lawcommission/docs/Etherton_lecture_Bar_Law_Reform_Cttee_20071114.pdf> accessed 30.12.2011.

20   NEUBERGER, above n. 16.

21   Ibid.

22   Ibid.

5.1. STRUCTURE

Five Law Commissioners, appointed by the Lord Chancellor and Secretary of State for Justice for terms of up to five years, are responsible for overseeing the work of the five teams of the Law Commission: Commercial and Common Law; Criminal Law; Property, Family and Trust Law; Public Law; and Statute Law Repeals. One of the Commissioners is appointed as Chairman for up to three years and, since 2007, he or she must be a judge of the High Court or Court of Appeal.[23] This change has been described as a 'powerful symbolic reflection' of the Law Commission's independence.[24]

The five teams are each headed by a team manager and have the expertise of a number of team lawyers. Research assistants are recruited to each team on fixed-term posts. The Law Commission also benefits from having its own economic advisers and Parliamentary Counsel. Despite its apparently hierarchical structure, all members of the Law Commission adopt a collaborative style of working and take an interest in the work of all teams, in addition to their own.

5.2. THE LAW REFORM PROCESS

> 'Law reform has been likened to making love to an elephant: it is extremely difficult to achieve and it takes 2 years to produce anything.'[25]

Sir Peter Gibson, in drawing the above analogy, was recognising the importance of the 'careful procedures' adopted by the Law Commission in its pursuit of meaningful law reform, rather than criticising its methods of working.[26] Once a particular area of law in need of review is identified – a process influenced by factors such as the availability of resources, the responses received following consultation and the suitability of the project for the Law Commission – the teams will work to create a scoping or discussion paper. This stage is crucial to ensuring that a realistic timeframe is established and that the key issues for consideration are identified.

A consultation paper is then published, providing a summary of the current law, its defects and proposals for improvement. Consultation papers are publicly available and anyone who wishes to respond is encouraged to do so. The

---

[23]   Tribunals, Courts and Enforcement Act 2007, s. 60.
[24]   ETHERTON, above n. 19.
[25]   P. GIBSON, 'Law Reform Now: The Law Commission 25 Years On', 1991 Denning Lecture, London, 1991 <www.bacfi.org/files/Denning%20Lecture%201991.PDF> accessed 30.12.2011.
[26]   Ibid.

challenges associated with consultation have, however, been emphasised, by Cretney as well as others. Writing in 1985, he saw one particular problem as being the extent to which consultation can claim to be representative.[27] It may now be argued that, at least to some extent, the increased availability of the internet has helped address this problem, with Law Commission publications being more readily accessible to a wider audience. What is not disputed is that the consultation process provides a valuable opportunity for anyone to share their views or expertise on the area of law under discussion.

If it is decided, following the consultation process, that reform is needed, a report is produced. In order to ensure that recommendations will work in practice and to ease the process of implementation, Law Commission recommendations that require primary legislation for their implementation are usually contained in a Bill, drafted by Parliamentary Counsel assisted by the relevant team. Once the report and the Bill have been published, it is for the government to decide whether to implement the recommendations.[28]

Research assistants play a significant role in all stages of the law reform process and contribute in a direct and meaningful way to the formulation of policy. At the early stages of the reform process, the work can include looking at the current law and its defects, a research task which often involves examining the law of other jurisdictions. At the consultation stage, research assistants are commonly given responsibility for evaluating consultation responses. If a project is taken forward following consultation, they can become closely involved in the creation of the policy paper, which is presented to the Law Commissioners to seek their approval for the proposed reform suggestions. Research assistants can also help instruct Parliamentary Counsel and, if the government decides to implement the recommendations, they may assist with the introduction of legislation to Parliament.

The research assistant role is therefore both varied and challenging. It provides recent graduates with experience of the law in its social context and enables them to make a direct contribution to the process of law reform. It is to a discussion of the research assistant role and our experiences that we now turn.

---

[27]   CRETNEY, above n. 3, 504–507.
[28]   In some cases, it is also possible for Law Commission recommendations to be taken forward in a Private Member's Bill.

5.3. THE RESEARCH ASSISTANT ROLE

'Each generation has its duty to keep the law in conformity with the needs of the time.'[29]

During his time as Law Commissioner, Cretney not only made 'a great and distinguished contribution to the reform and codification of family law',[30] but also played a significant role in establishing the research assistant system within the Law Commission: a legacy which has since benefited over 200 law graduates. In 1981, discussions had been underway to invite academic lawyers to spend periods of sabbatical or other leave working on a project with the Law Commission. It would be left to the Law Commissioners to consider which specific topics would benefit from this outside assistance. Such an opportunity was announced in the Society of Public Teachers of Law (SPTL, now the Society of Legal Scholars) Newsletter at the beginning of 1982.[31]

In 1982, Chris Barton – then lecturer at what was then North Staffordshire Polytechnic – had invited Cretney to give a lecture at the university on the Law Commission and family law. The university had started to show an interest in research, and Barton approached him to see whether the Law Commission might need a researcher. It did, or rather he did, and Barton took up the research post by starting his six-month secondment in September of that year.

Barton's recollections of his time as the 'first researcher' in Conquest House – where the Law Commission was then situated, and where perhaps many members of staff still wish they were[32] – offer an insight into the early days of the assistant at work:

'Life at Conkers House was great fun. I was given a nominal quarter desk in the room occupied by two or three young Law Com lawyers but, for everyone's sake, I spent my time in the Library, which was half-sunk below street level.

I was to look into cohabitation contracts, and after a month or so, I had amassed a fair amount of material. I kept on amassing because I didn't know what to do with it once finally amassed...'[33]

---

[29]   Lord Denning cited by J. MUNBY, 'Shaping the Law – the Law Commission at the Crossroads', 2011 Denning Lecture, London, 29.11.2011 <www.justice.gov.uk/lawcommission/docs/20111129_Denning_lecture_Lord_Justice_Munby.pdf> accessed 30.12.2011.

[30]   LAW COMMISSION, above n. 11.

[31]   Law Commission Minutes of Commissioners' Meetings 1981, 02.12.1981 (File No. 1/6/14).

[32]   Gone are the days of individual offices and complimentary biscuits.

[33]   We are very grateful for Chris Barton's help and insight into the research role at this time.

But eventually, and finally amassed, his work was published in *Cohabitation Contracts: Extra-Marital Partnerships and Law Reform*,[34] and Sir Ralph Gibson, the then Chairman of the Law Commission, wrote a Foreword for the book acknowledging the association that Cretney had initiated:

> 'This book is an example of co-operation between an academic lawyer and the Law Commission which we hope will be repeated.'

Co-operation with the SPTL continued to develop: Cretney drafted further notices and announcements in the Newsletter expanding on the opportunities for effective collaboration between the Law Commission and academic lawyers in law reform work.[35] He thought it was desirable that the Commission should continue to invite outside staff to work on the Law Commission projects in the future.

5.3.1. A sea change

Though the scope of Barton's work was somewhat different to that which is expected of current research assistants, the Law Commission had seen value in using outside researchers to aid them in their reform work. So, when the time came for the Commission to address its financial situation by way of staff restructuring,[36] students were the obvious pool in which to cast the recruitment line – they were young, intelligent, enthusiastic, and perhaps most significantly, they were cheap. The formal arrangements of these new research assistant posts, or RAs as they are often referred to, were recorded in the 1983–1984 Nineteenth Annual Report. They were to become permanent fixtures in the Law Commission framework:

> 'Young and exceptionally able law graduates with or without professional qualifications can be taken as research assistants for terms of up to three years. They work as members of our law reform teams and their contribution is substantial. These posts afford an opportunity to participate in the process of law reform and to gain experience of important aspects of the law before going on to practice, academic work or the public service.'[37]

---

34   C. BARTON, *Cohabitation Contracts: Extra-Marital Partnerships and Law Reform*, Gower, Aldershot 1985.
35   Above n. 31 and Law Commission Minutes of Commissioners' Meetings 1981, 28.10.1981 (File No. 1/6/14).
36   Under the Civil Service employment structure, the Grade 5 post that was held by the Assistant Solicitors was deleted in nearly every case, which, as a result, meant that the lawyers had to seek employment elsewhere. The money made available as a result of this was then used to fund the research assistant posts.
37   LAW COMMISSION, above n. 11, p. 40.

Five law graduates were employed as a result of the first recruitment campaign, all working as research assistants in the legal teams. One of these RAs, Jonathan Whybrow – who worked as an RA for three years in Baroness Hale's newly formed Family Team – writes about his time at the Law Commission:

'It was a life changing experience because, after getting my law degree, I did not want to be a lawyer. I had been well and truly put off. I worked with children in care and homeless people in Birmingham for several years before training to be a school teacher. It was through meeting children solicitors and barristers that I saw the light and decided to qualify as a legal aid lawyer specialising in children cases. I only met these lawyers when the Law Commission consulted the professions about children law reform.

I think the post of RA provides a great opportunity for the lost to be found and gives an injection of the outside world to the civil service. I have made lifelong friends from some of the people I knew at Conquest House. I will never forget sitting on Gray's Inn Fields with one of the team mulling over ideas for reform of the threshold for care/supervision orders. What a privileged position for an outsider to be in!

As a solicitor I was later able to practise in and train others in the very areas I had been working on. The RA job was probably the luckiest break I've ever had!'[38]

Following the success of that first year, and the years that were to follow, the research assistant structure gradually began to increase; in the 2011 cohort, 16 RAs were recruited. The importance of this set-up should not be overlooked. For the first time, legal graduates with no professional qualifications were given the opportunity to engage in reform work that could change the very legal landscape where they would later be working. Young graduates were given the opportunity to examine the law in context. Cretney highlighted the importance of this when he stated that it was now accepted that:

'The student should not only be a master of what is (sometimes pejoratively) referred to as "black letter law" but that he or she should be alive to the implications for policy of the law and particularly of its application in practice.'[39]

Allowing young graduates at the start of their careers to understand the importance of policy issues, to involve them directly in the reform process, and to encourage them to ask *how can the law be better?* no doubt provides a valuable lesson.

---

[38] We would like to thank Jonathan Whybrow for kindly providing this contribution to our essay.

[39] CRETNEY, above n. 3, 514.

5.3.2. The recruitment campaign

And so began the yearly intake of wide-eyed and bushy-tailed research assistants, all eager to participate in the process of reforming the law. The Law Commission asked that applicants were able to demonstrate five key skills that were to be essentials in the research assistant's toolkit: research, policy awareness, communication, team working, and legal knowledge.

The current recruitment campaign details the expectations of the research assistant:

> 'Research assistants carry a considerable responsibility for analysing the law on given topics with a view to identifying problems and their implications, and developing a range of solutions. They work closely with the Commissioners and qualified lawyers, and take part in meetings and discussions with Government officials, the judiciary, expert practitioners, industry bodies and other interested parties.'[40]

Though only *assisting* in the reform process, research assistants account for over 40 per cent of the Law Commission's total legal staff. Each year then, the Commission invites a large proportion of new employees to carve their own impression into a particular reform project, all from different universities, backgrounds and cultures, and all with different skills, ideas and experiences. With the constant stream of fresh recruits flowing through the Commission, it ensures that the reform process will not go stale or become out of touch with reality.

Further, contrary to some perceptions, research assistants are not recruited only from Oxbridge, but are taken from a diverse range of institutions from around the world, some at the beginning of their legal careers, others, even, coming towards the end of their careers. The Law Commission values this yearly injection of creative and enthusiastic thinking, and as the Law Commissioners too are only engaged on fixed term contracts, the process of law reform continues to evolve with each new intake.

5.3.3. The Property, Family and Trust Law team: a research assistant's perspective

I started at the Law Commission in September 2011 and therefore write this account from the perspective of a relatively new recruit. What attracted me to studying law at university is in many respects what also motivated me to apply

---

40 LAW COMMISSION, 'Research Assistant Posts 2012: Guide for Applicants' (2011), p. 4 <www. justice.gov.uk/lawcommission/docs/RA_Guide_2012.pdf> accessed 30.12.2011.

for the research assistant role at the Law Commission: an appreciation that the law does not exist in a vacuum. The law is shaped by – and itself plays a role in shaping – the social, historical, political, economic and cultural environment in which it operates. As a University of Warwick law graduate, a university well-known for its 'law in context approach', I can identify with Cretney's view that:

> 'One of the most welcome developments in legal education in recent years is that most (if not all) law teachers now accept that the law is best studied in context…'[41]

Working at the Law Commission requires that at the forefront of every research task, every policy discussion and every recommendation, is a focus on the likely consequences of the operation of the law in practice. My legal education at Warwick provided a firm foundation for the approach to law reform required by the Law Commission. Having graduated, I was keen to gain some practical experience of the law before applying for the research assistant role. I therefore spent a year working for Colchester and Tendring Women's Refuge and also for my local Citizens Advice Bureau, which enabled me to observe first-hand the reality of the law as experienced by a diverse range of groups, the importance of the law generally, and the need for it to be both clear and accessible.

For me, the research assistant role provides a unique opportunity to combine academic knowledge acquired at university with practical experience gained after my graduation. What I find appealing about the role is that it is, by its very nature, highly academic but it is also inherently practical. This is of course challenging, but it continues to inspire me to think about the law holistically with a creative and critical eye.

It was at Warwick that I was able to develop my interest in family law, and I feel very fortunate to have been given the opportunity to take this interest further at the Law Commission. Family law permeates most aspects of personal life; we will all be touched by it at some point. It is a fast-moving area of law, and one that needs to be responsive to changing family forms, structures and expectations. In the light of the wide-ranging impact of family law and its continued evolution, the Law Commission's commitment to making it clearer, more accessible and more relevant to the people it serves, is ever more crucial.

An aspect of the work at the Law Commission – and indeed of family law more generally – which I find particularly engaging is its connection with the seemingly most basic questions: *what* constitutes 'a family'; *to whom* do we owe a 'duty'; and *to what extent* should the law regulate the private affairs of individuals? An appreciation that the answer to these questions may change

---

[41]   CRETNEY, above n. 3, 514.

depending on the social, historical, political, economic or cultural lens through which they are viewed is an important aspect of the Law Commission's work and is part of what makes the research assistant role so exceptional.

The work of a research assistant in the Property, Family and Trust Law team is therefore both exciting and challenging.[42] Many of my research tasks have parallels with the type of work I carried out at university. However, the tasks also require a more flexible and creative way of thinking, and an approach that looks not only at the problems associated with a particular area of law but also possible solutions.

The research assistant recruitment campaign emphasises the opportunity for research assistants to influence directly changes in the law.[43] I was aware of this when I started working at the Law Commission but I have been surprised by the extent to which my team was interested to hear my views on the topics under discussion and keen to take them into account. The Law Commission embodies a genuine enthusiasm for dynamic ways of thinking about legal problems. This is reflected in its recruitment of research assistants from a range of different experiences and educational backgrounds.

Our Law Commissioner, team manager, team lawyers and my fellow research assistants make working for the Property, Family and Trust Law team a truly enjoyable experience. What is obvious from observing the work of the Law Commission from the inside is that there is a total commitment and interest from all members of staff in the law and how it may be improved. There is an enthusiasm for discussion of ideas and academic concepts, an enthusiasm firmly rooted in an evaluation of how to translate these ideas into workable solutions in practice. I have only been at the Law Commission for a relatively short period but the experience has met – and I am in no doubt that it will continue to meet – my expectations of the research assistant role... and more.

5.3.4. The Statute Law Repeals team: a research assistant's perspective

I imagine that to many readers, especially those interested largely in the area of law *reform,* the work of the Statute Law Repeals (SLR) team conjures up a rather colourless picture of law at its least appealing;[44] there is no reform, little policy,

---

42   Information on the Property, Family and Trust Law team can be found at <www.justice.gov. uk/lawcommission/areas/property-family-trust-team.htm> accessed 30.12.2011.

43   LAW COMMISSION, above n. 40.

44   See, for example, J. ROZENBERG, 'Clean Up Your Acts' 2008 *LSG (Law Society Gazette)* <www. lawgazette.co.uk/features/clean-your-acts> accessed 30.12.2011 where it was said that 'running the statute law repeals team at the Law Commission doesn't sound like a lot of fun.

and, as the name suggests, there are plenty of statutes. The purpose of the Statute Law Repeals team is to:

'Modernise and simplify the statute book, reduce its size and save the time of lawyers and others who use it. This in turn helps to avoid unnecessary costs. It also stops people being misled by obsolete laws that masquerade as live law. If an Act still features in the statute book and is referred to in text books, people reasonably enough assume that it must mean something.'[45]

During the four-year cycle, the SLR team will work their way through the statute book, identifying suitable candidates for repeal selected on the basis that the Acts are no longer of practical utility – that they are spent, unnecessary or have been superseded by later legislation. The team relies on a catalogue of Acts which lists every Act of Parliament ever enacted, known as the Chronological Tables of Statutes, to identify which Acts have been repealed, shown in italics, and which Acts are still live, shown in bold – this then provides a good indication of which areas of law need repealing. Different Chronological Tables are used depending on whether the Acts are local, private, or public general legislation. The statutes proposed for repeal are selected on a topic-by-topic basis rather than chronologically, and then within these topics each Act is thoroughly researched, the findings written up and sent out for consultation.

Much like the street sweeper in autumn who spends all day sweeping up the fallen leaves to keep the streets clean, the SLR team works hard to tidy up the statute book. Since 1965 the team has promoted the repeal of over 5,000 statutes, in whole or in part, and with over 30,000 Acts of Parliament still live on the statute book, the work of the team is important in keeping the path clear. And although the leaves continue to fall and pile high around us, with our 2012 Bill seeing the likely repeal of over 800 Acts of Parliament dating from 1267 to 2010, the work of the SLR team certainly has its value.

My first research task, on joining the Law Commission in 2010, was on the London Project which looked into a bequest of a Mr George Palyn, who had left £100 to St Mary-le-Bow's Church in London with the intention of setting up a weekly lecture or sermon to be given to the poor people in the parish of St Mary-le-Bow. It appeared that the *St Mary-le-Bow Lecturer's Trust Act of 1799*[46] was a suitable candidate for repeal as there was no evidence that the lectures were still being given and it was likely that the money had been used up some decades ago.

All your colleagues spend their time thinking up new laws. Your job is to get rid of the old ones'.

[45] Information on the Statute Law Repeals team can be found at <www.justice.gov.uk/lawcommission/areas/statute-law-repeals-team.htm> accessed 30.12.2011.

[46] 39 Geo.3 c.lxxxi (1799).

I was 'simply' to find out when these lectures had ended. After exhausting every internet source imaginable, and being informed that St Mary-le-Bow's Church had no record of any such bequest being left or indeed any lectures being given, I realised that perhaps this was a job for the Archives. So off I went to the London Metropolitan Archives with my research note under my arms, confident that I would find this out in a couple of hours. Two days later I was still head deep in dusty manuscripts, carefully turning the pages of 19th century Vestry Meeting minutes with cotton gloves on my apparently corrosive fingers, and a pencil in my hand recording any mention of this elusive Mr Palyn.

What I learnt from that first task was not only information on the lectures themselves, but more importantly, I was able to see the story – the narrative – behind an Act of Parliament. For the period that I was researching the 1799 Act, the law was positively alive. I knew *who* Palyn was, *why* he wanted to set up the lectures, *who* would benefit from them, *how* much it cost to send the Bill through Parliament and eventually, *why* the lectures had ceased to be given. I followed the trail like it was a chase and eventually caught my hare.

Whilst the *repeal* element of the SLR work must not contain any contentious issues of policy, the research behind the repeal candidates allows one to understand the reasons *why* an Act was created and *why* it was no longer necessary. Each Act is looked at in its social, economical and historical context. As Cretney has written:

> 'Law reform properly comprehends all the great social issues of the time, from the repeal of the corn laws, the ending of the slave trade, the prohibition of the use of children as chimney sweeps, through such matters as the rights and legal status of women (in public as well as in private law), down to the decriminalisation of homosexuality, the legalisation of abortion and the abolition of capital punishment.'[47]

The repeal of these expired statutes is not 'putting history at risk' and these Acts are not 'under attack from British reformers'.[48] On the contrary, the thorough research and interesting repeal notes of the SLR team go some way to *revive* and *restore* the little pockets of history that have been lost along the way. George

---

[47] CRETNEY, above n. 3, 495.
[48] The repeal of obsolete statutes from the 17th to 19th centuries relating to turnpikes in Essex, Sussex and Norfolk had caught the attention of toll-road enthusiasts in the United States, who not only declared that 'Britain's great turnpike heritage [was] at risk' but also that 'a panel of legal fussies called the Law Commission are trying to purge hundreds of harmless old turnpike laws from the British statutes... toffs like this, if they still had their way over here would "modernize" America by legislating out of existence the great turnpikes' of various states <www.tollroadsnews.com/node/1599> accessed 30.12.2011.

Palyn, for example, had been completely forgotten: a man who sought to educate the poor and left a vast amount of money in order to do so.

The role of the research assistant in the SLR team has been hugely varied, interesting, challenging and creative. I have walked the streets of London in the 17th century, watched it burn in the Great Fire and seen it rebuilt again. Streets have moved, monarchs have changed and society has developed – things that we now take for granted, such as cleaning or lighting the streets, had once been a difficult and expensive project to establish in a rather dreary and impoverished Dickensian setting. Though we may now live in a world of the NHS, the Human Rights Act 1998[49] and the Children Act 1989, some concerns remain the same, as they did all those centuries ago: how to support the sick, how to educate the poor and how to care for our children. Perhaps it is understanding our past that will allow us to change our future.

6. CONCLUSION: THE FUTURE OF THE LAW COMMISSION

'One should not go out to fight for freedom and justice wearing one's best trousers. So, law reformers should not expect to engage in the business of political decision taking without expecting that sometimes those decisions will be questioned.'[50]

The Law Commission is as much needed today as it was at its inception in 1965: a link is still required between those charged with making law and those subject to the law; laws still should be intelligible, clear, accessible, predictable and relevant to the context in which they operate; and the rule of law must still be upheld. Three recent developments demonstrate the recognition given to the importance of the Law Commission. Firstly, the Law Commission Act 2009 now places a duty on the Lord Chancellor to report to Parliament on the extent to which Law Commission proposals have been implemented by Government. Secondly, a statutory protocol has been introduced, setting out the way in which the Government and the Law Commission should work together on law reform projects. And thirdly, it is worthy of note that Law Commission law reform Bills are now subject to a House of Lords procedure which is intended to ease the implementation of Law Commission recommendations.[51]

---

49   Though I have had several genuine requests from the public to repeal this Act on the grounds that it 'is pointless' – so too, apparently, is the entire Criminal Justice Act 2003 and PACE 1984.

50   CRETNEY, above n. 3, 515.

51   For further information, see MINISTRY OF JUSTICE, 'Report on the Implementation of Law Commission Proposals', 24.01.2011 <www.justice.gov.uk/publications/docs/report-implementation-law-commission-proposals.pdf> accessed 30.12.2011 and MUNBY, above n. 29.

However, the Law Commission has not been immune from the tensions associated with the current economic turbulence; its ability to function, its independence, and even its continued existence, have all been shaken. It has faced significant reductions in funding; it also fell within the Government's review of arms'-length bodies, sailing close to abolition as a result of Schedule 7 to the Public Bodies Bill. Had this Schedule been taken forward – thankfully it was not – this would have resulted in both the composition of the Law Commission and its functions being capable of amendment by the government through statutory instrument.[52]

Despite facing new and complex challenges, the continuing recognition of the importance of the Law Commission amongst its supporters has, for now, enabled it to maintain its position. As students we observed the value of the Law Commission from the outside; now working as research assistants, we have been fortunate to view its significance from the inside. The Law Commission engages in comprehensive examination of areas of law in need of reform, but it also provides a forum for discussion, bringing academics, practitioners, students, members of the public and other interested parties together for one common purpose: to reform the law and to use each other's knowledge and experience in order to do so. As the pages in our statute book continue to increase, it is more crucial than ever that we should have an independent body whose purpose it is to ensure that the law is as modern, simple and as accessible as possible. It is therefore to be hoped that the words of Sir Peter Gibson will not be forgotten: 'whatever the state of business generally, the business of law reform is not in recession'.[53]

---

[52] Munby, above n. 29.
[53] Gibson, above n. 25.

IN THE MATTER OF *CRETNEY*
V. BROMLEY (1974):

Stephen Cretney's *Principles of Family Law*

Simon ROWBOTHAM*

Contents

1. INTRODUCTION

For the student of Family Law today, faced with an array of textbooks on the Blackwell's shelf, the eighth edition of *Principles of Family Law*[1] might appear a somewhat traditional option next to those modern textbooks containing suggested reading lists and diagrammatical representations of the law.[2] This traditional book, however, was once itself the 'modern' option. As with other areas of academic law, the names of S.M. Cretney and P.M. Bromley are remembered by students as *Cretney* and *Bromley*; more book titles than the actual authors. It is time to remind ourselves of the pioneering contribution

---

*   Inevitably, my acknowledgements are many but I reserve this footnote for one Ethel Rowbotham, to whom I owe my wig and gown.

1   J. MASSON, R. BAILEY-HARRIS and R. PROBERT, *Cretney's Principles of Family Law*, 8th ed., Sweet & Maxwell, London 2008.

2   See e.g. S. HARRIS-SHORT and J. MILES, *Family Law: Text, Cases, and Materials*, 2nd ed., Oxford University Press, Oxford 2011.

Cretney made, not only to Family Law as a subject but to its study at undergraduate level.

This author applied somewhat questionable criteria in selecting his textbook for the academic year 2009–2010, probably including economy. Suffice it to say he alighted on *Principles*. The decision was a difficult one, perhaps in part because the differences between the books available today are not as vast as they once were; for the undergraduate undertaking that same exercise in 1974, the year *Principles* was first published, the choice was very different.[3] By then, Bromley's *Family Law*[4] was in its fourth edition and 'Bromley-land' had, since 1957, been 'the only undergraduate country on Planet Family Law'.[5] Cretney's was a 'new breed of family law textbook'[6] that looked beyond the law to the social policy behind it, a shift from Bromley's focus on the 'hard black letter law'.[7] For those embarking on the then relatively novel 'Family Law' courses, *Bromley* was tried and tested; *Cretney* was not. From reviews in the contemporary legal publications, and in examining the fourth and first editions of *Bromley* and *Cretney* respectively, we will attempt a historical reconstruction of the choice faced by the student of 1974.

2.   1974 AND ALL THAT

Our student of 1974, standing in a bookshop humming a David Bowie song, can probably be forgiven their ignorance of the historiographical context of their decision. 'Family Law' remained a relative novelty to the academic syllabus; compared to its legal siblings, it was late to develop as a distinct subject in England and Wolfram Müller-Freienfels has documented its slow development out of disparate and discrete areas into a unified whole under the umbrella of 'Family Law'.[8] Despite first appearing as a coherent course in the academic year 1951–1952 as the 'Law of Domestic Relations' at the London School of Economics, led by Professor Otto Kahn-Freund, Family Law was not offered as an

---

3   S.M. Cretney, *Principles of Family Law*, 1st ed., Sweet & Maxwell, London 1974; hereon referred to as 'Cretney'.

4   P.M. Bromley, *Family Law*, 4th ed., Butterworths, London 1971; hereon referred to as 'Bromley'.

5   C. Barton, 'Family Law in the Classroom' (2004) 34 *Fam Law (Family Law)* 264, 264.

6   Baroness Hale, 'A Minority Opinion?', The Maccabaean Lecture in Jurisprudence on 13.11.2007, rep. in (2008) 154 *Proceedings of the British Academy* 319, 324.

7   Preface to N. Lowe and G. Douglas, *Bromley's Family Law*, 10th ed., Oxford University Press, Oxford 2007.

8   W. Müller-Freienfels, 'The Emergence of *Droit de Famille* and *Familienrecht* in Continental Europe and the Introduction of Family Law in England' (2003) 28 *Jo Fam Hist (Journal of Family History)* 31, 39–43.

undergraduate paper at Oxford, Cretney's own institution, until 1970.[9] What the student of 1974 may not have known, examining *Bromley* on the bookshelf, was the important role that book had played in this process: a 'pioneering work'[10] that had not only cemented the words 'family law' as a book title[11] but also, as Baroness Hale describes it, 'managed to bring together the common law of husband and wife, parent and child, and the ecclesiastical-turned-statute law of divorce and matrimonial causes, into a single coherent whole'.[12] Such was the regard in which Bromley's textbook was held, having batted off its potential challengers,[13] that by 1972 one reviewer thought it 'a book which will undoubtedly remain pre-eminent in its field'.[14]

Of course, *Bromley* and *Cretney* were not the only options. Even by 1967, J.C. Hall had declared that '[t]en years ago there was not a single book on English family law. Today the position is quite different'.[15] The problem was not a shortage of books in the field but the paucity of work in the 'textbook' format. In 1965, E.L. Johnson had published the second edition of his textbook, though with the enormous statutory developments since its publication and with no third edition in sight that book was not an option by 1974.[16] Reviewing *Bromley* in 1967, Hall wrote:

> '... many of those teaching the subject have been conscious recently of the need for an up-to-date textbook of an intermediate size, falling somewhere between Professor Bromley's distinguished work... on the one hand and Mrs. Puxon's *The Family and the Law* on the other.'[17]

Perhaps this 'need' was a symptom of a deeper requirement for what Baroness Hale hails a 'new breed of family law textbook'. Now that *Bromley* had begun to make sense of the law, to 'discover the concepts and principles which make it a coherent whole', it was time for a textbook examining 'the law as it is experienced

---

9   MÜLLER-FREIENFELS, above n. 8, p. 44; see also R. PROBERT, '"Family Law" – A Modern Concept?' (2004) 34 *Fam Law* 901, 903, who notes that other universities 'were slow to establish comparable courses' to the LSE's.

10   See A. BAINHAM, book review of P.M. BROMLEY and N.V. LOWE, *Family Law*, 8th ed., Butterworths, London 1992, published in 'Book Reviews' [1993] 52 *CLJ (Cambridge Law Journal)* 336, 336.

11   MÜLLER-FREIENFELS, above n. 8, 44–45.

12   BARONESS HALE, above n. 6, 323; cf. PROBERT, above n. 9, 902–903, noting the earlier attempt by W.P. Eversley to unite the disparate topics under the title of 'Domestic Relations' in 1885.

13   E.g. E.L. JOHNSON, *Family Law*, 2nd ed., Sweet & Maxwell, London 1965.

14   ANONYMOUS, review of *Bromley*, 4th ed., above n. 4, published in [1972] 2 *Fam Law* 21, 21.

15   J.C. HALL, review of Johnson, above n. 13, published in 'Book Reviews' [1967] 25 *CLJ* 123, 123.

16   JOHNSON, above n. 13; see also MÜLLER-FREIENFELS, above n. 8, 44–45.

17   HALL, above n. 15, 123.

by the people or organisations it affects'.[18] Reviewing *Cretney* in 1974, Hall remarked:

> '...whereas students of Family Law are already well served by a standard textbook which has stood the test of time, they have hitherto lacked a book which both sets out the law and debates in some detail the policy problems with which this subject abounds.'[19]

No doubt the 'standard textbook' was *Bromley* and a retrospective glance at its fourth edition reveals a book that was increasingly old-fashioned in its 'black letter' approach.[20] Indeed, the continued prominence of 'consortium' and Bromley's use of a comma in 'STIRLING, J.' were archaic even by 1974.[21] With the enactment of the Divorce Reform Act 1969 and the Guardianship Act 1973, the bookshelves had a gap for a new, up-to-date textbook.

3. THE FIELD OF CHOICE: *BROMLEY* OR *CRETNEY*?

3.1. DEMOGRAPHIC AND PRICE

For the student faced with this choice in 1974, *Bromley* or *Cretney*, target market would have been crucial and Cretney, unhesitatingly, put the student at the centre of his work. While his publisher's synopsis declared *Principles* 'a major new students' textbook', Cretney stated in his Preface:

> 'This book is intended primarily for the use of degree and other students of Family Law...The book is not intended as a practitioners' manual, in the sense of providing a comprehensive coverage of all the topics within its title; on the contrary I have been deliberately selective, concentrating on extended discussion of what I believe to be the issues central to a student's understanding of the law.'[22]

Cretney referred to 'students' four times in his Preface; *Bromley* did not mention them once except to acknowledge their assistance.[23] Perhaps *Bromley* was already showing signs of what Andrew Bainham would later describe as attempting 'to

---

18   BARONESS HALE, above n. 6, 323–324.
19   J.C. HALL, review of *Cretney*, 1st ed., above n. 3, published in 'Book Reviews' [1974] 33 *CLJ* 340, 340.
20   LOWE and DOUGLAS, above n. 7.
21   See *Bromley*, 4th ed., above n. 4, p. 9 and ch. 4.
22   Publisher's Synopsis (back cover) and Preface to *Cretney*, 1st ed., above n. 3, p. vii. Note that Sweet & Maxwell's synopsis also talks of 'practitioners', evidently concerned not to narrow the audience unduly.
23   Preface to *Bromley*, 4th ed., above n. 4, pp. v-vi.

straddle the student and practitioner markets'.[24] Indeed, up to his third edition in 1966, Bromley had reprinted the 'Preface to the First Edition' in which he stated that he had 'written this book having in mind the present needs of [his] own students at Manchester', though even then adding 'I also hope that some practitioners will find the book of value to them'.[25] If originally aimed at students, *Bromley* was never solely a students' textbook in the way that *Cretney* was; Cretney was 'to be congratulated', said one reviewer, for 'sticking to the objective' of writing for students.[26] This fact would not have escaped the attention of our book-buying youth.

Cretney further nailed his colours to the student mast in omitting several chapters on the 'courts and the family, the enforcement of financial orders, and tax matters' for the purpose of economy: '[s]ince this is a student's text it has been produced at a price which it is hoped will be within their means'.[27] This attracted the attention of many reviewers, not all favourable,[28] though on the whole the 'comparatively modest price of £3.75' received favourable comment.[29] In the cost arena, *Cretney* won – if only just – compared to *Bromley* at £4 in paperback, both books being available in hardback (or 'cloth') at £6.[30] Whether an empathetic display for student poverty or an entrepreneurial manoeuvre, for the prudent student of 1974 a potential saving of 25 pence was at stake (or, perhaps, two pints). Of course, the difference between the textbooks went deeper than mere marketing; let us turn, then, to the concerns of the more scholarly student.

3.2. A NEW BREED OF TEXTBOOK

In 1974, *Bromley* and *Cretney* represented fundamentally different approaches to legal scholarship. Baroness Hale, delivering the British Academy's Maccabaean

---

24 BAINHAM, above n. 10, 336.
25 P.M. BROMLEY, *Family Law*, 3rd ed., Butterworths, London 1966, pp. vii-viii.
26 N. MICHAELS, review of *Cretney*, 1st ed., above n. 3, published in 'Reviews and Notices' [1974] 90 *LQR (Law Quarterly Review)* 565, 565.
27 Preface to *Cretney*, 1st ed., above n. 3, p. vii.
28 See e.g. B. HADFIELD, review of *Cretney*, 1st ed., above n. 3, published in 'Book Reviews' [1975] 26 *NILQ (Northern Ireland Law Quarterly)* 250, 250: 'The author himself gives the ubiquitous and eminently practical reason of economy, but one wonders whether such exclusions can be fully justified in a book which sets itself the aim of stimulating discussion of the law's "effectiveness as an instrument of social policy"'.
29 See e.g. MICHAELS, above n. 26, 565; and HALL, above n. 19, 341.
30 See e.g. E. GRIEW, review of *Cretney*, 1st ed., above n. 3, published in 'Reviews' [1975] 38 *MLR (Modern Law Review)* 360, 360. It might be of amusement to note G.S. WILKINSON in 'Book Reviews' [1967] 25 *CLJ* 122, 122: 'the difference in price between books bound in hard covers and those with paper covers recently led a writer in a legal journal to point out that the binder seems to make as much out of the book as the author, printer and publisher combined'.

Lecture in 2007, discussed these two jurisprudential forms and cited Bromley as the 'prime exponent' of an approach that aimed to distil the statutes and judgments that comprise our law to 'discover the concepts and principles which make it a coherent whole'.[31] This manifested itself in *Bromley*, a work Michael Freeman describes as being 'rooted within a positivistic and legalistic framework'.[32] Had the student in the bookshop opened *Bromley* at its preface, he would have been faced with a list of statutes (the Rent Act 1968, the Guardianship of Minors Act 1971, the Family Provision Act 1966 etc.).[33] While Bromley referred to these Acts being the 'inevitable consequences of the social revolution that we have been experiencing in this country for many years', he went no further: the law 'was a discrete entity, not part of a social continuum'.[34] Where in 1957 Bromley's approach had been pioneering, by 1974 it was traditional if not old-fashioned.

Baroness Hale went on to discuss the 'change in the direction in which family law went, after the reforms which took effect in 1971 destroyed so much of the conceptual coherence which Peter Bromley had discovered'. This change, driven by a very different approach to legal scholasticism, asked 'not about the law in the law reports, but about the law as it is experienced by the people or the organisations it affects'.[35] This shift gave birth to a 'new breed of family law textbook' to be 'exemplified by Stephen Cretney' in *Principles*.[36] Where previous authors had almost unanimously employed the title *Family Law*, in a symbolic break indicating his jurisprudential leanings Cretney entitled his textbook *Principles of Family Law*. 'Principles' meant going beyond the law itself:

> 'I have tried not only to explain the law as it is, but also to analyse the reasons for its development and to stimulate discussion of its effectiveness as an instrument of social policy.'[37]

This was undoubtedly the angle marketed by Sweet & Maxwell, the back cover proclaiming that Cretney 'writes believing that the law can be fully understood only in the light of the policy considerations behind it'. For the student diligent enough to read reviews, this was the feature that attracted most attention. Writing for the *Modern Law Review*, Edward Griew commented:

---

[31]   BARONESS HALE, above n. 6, 323.

[32]   M. FREEMAN, 'Family Values and Family Justice' (1997) 50 *CLP (Current Legal Problems)* 315, 318.

[33]   Preface to *Bromley*, 4th ed., above n. 4, p. v.

[34]   FREEMAN, above n. 32, 318; see also MÜLLER-FREIENFELS, above n. 8, 44.

[35]   BARONESS HALE, above n. 6, 324.

[36]   Ibid., 324 (esp. fn. 21).

[37]   Preface to *Cretney*, 1st ed., n. 3 above, at p. vii. This change in title might be seen in light of MÜLLER-FREIENFELS' distinction between 'Family Law' as a mere collective term and as referring to a codified area of law with an internal, coherent conceptual basis; see above n. 8, 38–39.

'It is right that the student's principal companion in the subject, while providing a solid basis of legal principle and paying due regard to the authorities, should at the same time be forward looking and policy-based, and should draw its critical and expository strength from non-legal as well as from legal sources. All this can be said of Mr Cretney's book.'[38]

Cretney plugged that gap, noted by Hall, for a textbook examining 'the policy problems' of Family Law. Contemporaneous reviews, while not unanimously sure that Cretney had succeeded,[39] generally reveal a palpable sense of achievement: that Cretney had 'gone a long way towards producing the family law textbook to meet the needs of the modern student'.[40] With its neat green cover (plate 1), novel title and new jurisprudential approach, *Cretney* must have looked modern to the student of 1974 next to *Bromley*; the Apple to *Bromley*'s Microsoft. The true test, of course, was to be found between the covers.

A fair comparator would be to examine how *Bromley* and *Cretney* dealt with the same discrete point: care orders under section 20(1) of the Children and Young Persons Act 1969. Clearly, the two legal approaches bore very different fruit. Bromley wrote:

'(c) A *care order* committing the child to the care of a local authority. Unless the order is varied, it remains in force until the age of 18 or, if he has already reached the age of 16, when it is made, the age of 19. There are powers to extend orders to the age of 19 if this is in the child's interest or the public interest in view of his mental condition or behaviour, and if he is over the age of 15, the local authority may apply to a juvenile court to have him sent to a borstal institution...'[41]

His description of a care order continued in that fashion, fixed on the letter of the law. In contrast, while Cretney dealt with the same points of law, he went on to examine their underlying policies and possible effects on society, that is, the law considered 'as an instrument of social policy'.[42] Commenting on local authorities' discretion under section 27(2) to act contrary to their duties towards children in order to protect the public, he stated:

'...the unfortunate result is that the statute confers on authorities extensive powers only really justifiable in the context of major anti-social behaviour. It is therefore even more likely that the result of the Act...may be [citing O.M. Stone (1970) 33 *MLR* 649 at 658] "to nudge those children who have been neglected or ill-treated but show no anti-social tendencies into what largely amounts to a juvenile delinquents' court and sphere of treatment."'[43]

---

38   GRIEW, above n. 30, 360.
39   See e.g. HADFIELD, above n. 28, 250–251.
40   GRIEW, above n. 30, 360.
41   *Bromley*, 4th ed., above n. 4, p. 294.
42   *Cretney*, 1st ed., above n. 3, p. vii.
43   *Cretney*, 1st ed., above n. 3, pp. 304–305.

It is interesting to note how the two scholastic approaches manifested themselves in writing style: Bromley's material was, inevitably, of somewhat drier stuff than Cretney's, allowing Cretney to show more opinion, perhaps even personality, through indicating his own thoughts as well as reproducing the dramatic words of Stone.

3.3. A CASE STUDY: DIVORCE

If *Cretney* exemplified the 'new breed' of textbook, his chapter on 'Divorce' exemplified his jurisprudential approach in action. Under the subheading 'The Social Policy of Divorce Legislation', Cretney traced the history of divorce law in its social context, beginning with a myth-busting discussion of divorce rates in England (pages 79–82), looking at the law's policy of protecting 'the sanctity of marriage' (pages 82–83) before finally tracing the rise and fall of the 'Doctrine of Matrimonial Offence' (pages 83–91). This was well received: 'an unusual but well-conceived textbook introduction to the subject'.[44] It was certainly a world away from the traditional introduction of *Bromley*, which opened with a reminder of the archaic 'divorce *a vinculo matrimonii*' and 'divorce *a mensa et thoro*' before offering a brief overview of the path to the Divorce Reform Act 1969 from a principally statute-led perspective.[45] For the student of 1974, the content of *Cretney*, drawing upon varied and numerous sources, made its exposition of family law 'unusually readable... for a student' in areas often considered 'dull'.[46]

Content aside, merely glancing into *Bromley* at page 203 (see plate 2) and *Cretney* at page 79 (see plate 3) reveals how the two academic approaches were instantly appreciable through their different manifestations on the page. On page 203 dense blocks of text are seen, with long sentences producing weighty paragraphs. Where Bromley's prose was heavy, with often complex sentence structures, Cretney erred on the side of brevity; his sentence construction, often staccato, kept colons and semi-colons to a minimum. As Hall observed, Cretney's writing had a 'refreshing crispness'[47] and his inclusion of numbers and statistics in the text, far from presenting a visual distraction, was considered 'never unduly obtrusive and... most helpful in assisting the student'.[48] This produced a very different and more student-friendly look when printed, as seen on page 79: note the almost bullet-point appearance and the use of lists to format the body of the text.

---

44   Griew, above n. 30, 360.
45   *Bromley*, 4th ed., above n. 4, ch.8 (esp. pp. 203–206).
46   Michaels, above n. 26, 566.
47   Hall, above n. 19, 340.
48   Michaels, above n. 26, 568.

Where page 203 shows a relatively thin strip of regimented footnotes, Bromley's superscript numbers appearing strictly after punctuation marks, page 79 includes a block of footnotes twice as long, the text littered with numbers at the ends of headings, subheadings and the words '1858', 'adopted' and 'trend'. This difference might be explained by jurisprudential approach. Though they include the occasional academic article, the bulk of Bromley's footnotes cite statutes, law reports and further points of law to substantiate his legalistic textbook; from page 203 onwards, they consist predominantly of references to the Matrimonial Causes Acts of 1923, 1937, 1963 and 1967, reminders of Latin terminology or Parliamentary anecdotes.[49] In contrast, Cretney's policy-focused approach led to a set of footnotes drawing on all manner of additional material from statistical reports to sociological essays to Law Commission papers. Page 79 exemplifies what would be known by the third edition as Cretney's 'unique amalgam of detailed analysis of the law, highly critical comment, historical development, social context and policy issues for the future'.[50] This was an engaging, student-centric approach that our student of 1974 would have seen from the pages without needing to stand and read them.

3.4. A RESERVED RECOMMENDATION

The untested nature of *Cretney* might have led our cautious student to scour the reviews. Though most thought that Cretney had 'gone a long way towards producing the family law textbook to meet the needs of the modern student', the tenor of the critical reception was that he had not quite gone *all* the way.[51] As Griew stated:

> 'There is… in this first edition the makings of a very good, attractive and appropriate textbook. If from this point I concentrate upon some of its defects, I do so in order to suggest that Mr. Cretney has a good deal of work to do to make the second edition, to which we shall all look forward, a substantial improvement upon the first. Enthusiasm makes one wish to recommend this book unreservedly. There are many reasons why one cannot yet do so.'[52]

Frankly, some of the criticisms were of little consequence.[53] Others – like Brigid Hadfield's doubts that Cretney had achieved the balance between 'a textbook on

---

49 *Bromley*, 4th ed., above n. 4, pp. 203–206 (esp. fns. 11–18). Note that Bromley's Table of Statutes at pp. xi-xxi extended to 11 pages compared to Cretney's 7 at pp. xxix-xxxv.

50 S. MAIDMENT, review of S.M. CRETNEY, 3rd ed., published in 'Reviews and Notices' [1982] 98 LQR 159, 159.

51 GRIEW, above n. 30, 360.

52 Ibid., 361.

53 It appears to have been the unfortunate approach of reviewers in the 1970s to produce page-by-page lists of typing, grammatical and referencing errors; e.g. GRIEW, above n. 30, 361–362.

general principles' and a 'recitation, with critical comment, of the relevant cases and statutes' – were unsupported by fellow critics and easily dismissed.[54] Some criticisms, however, were of more concern to the student of 1974.

Family Law's youth meant an absence of consensus on what its textbooks should contain, though Cretney's selection and organisation was considered 'essentially traditional, at least as far as the chapter headings go'.[55] Even then, some remained 'unhappy, for student purposes, with some of Mr Cretney's decisions',[56] particularly in Part III on 'Matrimonial Litigation'. Where Bromley dealt with marriage, divorce, children and then matrimonial property, Cretney moved children to the end to deal with divorce and matrimonial property together.[57] Naomi Michaels was concerned that, by discussing matrimonial property immediately after divorce but before the court's discretionary powers of relief, 'the significance of these sections may appear distorted',[58] while Griew decried that:

> '...the material on matrimonial orders and the grounds on which they are made is all over the place: for instance...wilful neglect to maintain is cut off from other grounds in such a way that the student may not pick up the fact that it founds the same order as adultery or persistent cruelty...'[59]

The student reader 'needs to perceive structure and direction' but, for Griew, *Cretney* did not facilitate this, his chapters containing 'too few' signposts while the overall course of the book was 'very difficult to follow', not helped by a Contents table 'limited to chapter titles'.[60]

Much criticism stemmed from the book's perceived rushed nature[61] and relative brevity, in light of which the sections on marriage were thought 'unduly lengthy' and 'self indulgent', leaving other areas 'deficient in detail'.[62] Some wanted more ink spilled on matrimonial property[63] while others wished for more focus on 'children's rights' and 'conflict of laws'.[64] One flaw however, on which the reviewers were unanimous, could have been the deciding factor for our student. As Hall put it, the 'price that has to be paid in order to confine the book to a size

---

54   HADFIELD, above n. 28, 250–251.
55   Ibid., 250.
56   GRIEW, above n. 30, 361.
57   Contents page(s) in *Cretney*, 1st ed., above n. 3, p. ix; and *Bromley*, 4th ed., above n. 4, pp. vii-x.
58   MICHAELS, above n. 26, 567.
59   GRIEW, above n. 30, 361.
60   Ibid., 361.
61   E.g. GRIEW, above n. 30, 361.
62   MICHAELS, above n. 26, 566 and 569.
63   Ibid., 567.
64   HADFIELD, above n. 28, 250.

of something under 400 pages is the exclusion in general of exposition of cases'.[65] The effect, from a student's perspective, was clearly negative:

> 'Comparatively few cases are actually described in the text, as opposed to being attached as footnote names to statements of principle or to judicial observations. The most notable sufferers from the shortage of clear case law illustration are the long chapter on matrimonial property and financial obligations (the student surely needs to know what actually happened in such cases as *Wachtel, Trippas* and *Harnett...*)'[66]

In an extreme example on page 144 (see plate 4), disembodied case names are found footnoted to legal principles but without supporting facts. Hadfield and Michaels were also critical, Michaels alleging that Cretney's claim – to have 'dealt fully with the Court of Appeal's decision in *Wachtel* v. *Wachtel*'[67] – was 'unsubstantiated'.[68] Even the second edition would be described as 'a companion to the law reports without itself becoming entangled in the intricacies of the decided cases'.[69] Perhaps this represented Cretney's non-legalistic approach giving too little focus to cases for undergraduate purposes. Evidently, there is no substitute for reading law reports and that is perhaps the ethos with which Cretney approached his writing; as one critic wryly commented, 'the student who expects to be "spoon-fed"...can perhaps take consolation in the knowledge that...the cases on this subject tend, on average, to be noticeably shorter than those encountered in other areas of the syllabus'.[70] Nevertheless, to a student looking for a Swiss-Army textbook, *Cretney* might not have appealed when contrasted with *Bromley* and its generous attention to cases.

The usefulness of a textbook, however, inevitably depends 'to a large extent on what teachers of courses on family law demand from their students'.[71] In 1974, Cretney might not have benefitted from this. Writing in 1993, Bainham commented:

> 'There is no doubt that the book [*Bromley* 8th ed.] is at the "black letter" end of the spectrum and as such will suit the more traditional courses. Those teachers who take a more contextual or inter-disciplinary approach are likely to opt for *Cretney...*'[72]

---

65 HALL, above n. 19, 340.
66 GRIEW, above n. 30, 361.
67 *Cretney*, 1st ed., above n. 3, p. vii.
68 HADFIELD, above n. 28, 251; MICHAELS, above n. 26, 567.
69 J. PRIEST, review of S.M. CRETNEY, 2nd ed., published in 'Reviews and Notices' [1977] 93 *LQR* 616, 617.
70 Ibid., 617.
71 MICHAELS, above n. 26, 569. I am informed by Professor Masson and Neil Robinson that Professor Cretney would have declined – out of modesty – to recommend his textbook to his own supervisees.
72 BAINHAM, above n. 10, 337.

In this observation, as true for 1974 as for 1993, a problem lay in the fact that Family Law was still struggling to gain recognition as a subject of weight, a problem not aided by the negative views of the judiciary.[73] Contemporary opinion indicates that Cretney was thought by some to be walking a dangerous line: 'that too much plugging of "law and its environs" will lead to Family Law degenerating into a hotch-potch of general inconclusive principles', damaging its attempts to gain credibility.[74] It is questionable how many supervisors would have dared part with the tried and tested textbook and, as such, the student of 1974 may well have visited the bookshop with a clear recommendation of *Bromley*.

4. THE FUTURE OF *PRINCIPLES*

For the student who did leave the bookshop with *Cretney* in hand, intending to follow its subsequent editions, they were to be well rewarded. In the second edition, published in 1976 and still 'intended primarily for students rather than practitioners',[75] Cretney had heeded the comments of his peers. His 'greatly improved table of contents, expanded from one page…to nearly four' offered 'a detailed breakdown of each chapter.'[76] He undertook 'a substantial rearrangement of the contents' to give a 'far more logical and coherent treatment of the matters discussed' and the book itself was extended by some 85 pages.[77] Although the price too would increase (to £7.50 in paperback; £11.00 in hardback) so too would the areas covered, the most notable addition being chapter 11 entitled 'The Courts and the Family', omitted from the first edition[78] but that would go on to be praised as 'one of the best general introductions to the subject'.[79] This chapter, especially the section entitled 'Reform – The Case for a Family Court', remains of particular interest in light of the 'Norgrove Report'.[80] Such were these improvements that one critic suggested *Cretney* 'must surely now be guaranteed a place as a long-term survivor in the competitive market for student texts'.[81]

---

[73]   I am grateful for the recollections of Baroness Deech on this point.
[74]   HADFIELD, above n. 28, 251.
[75]   Preface to S.M. CRETNEY, *Principles of Family Law*, 2nd ed., Sweet & Maxwell, London 1976, p. vii.
[76]   PRIEST, above n. 69, 617; Contents page of *Cretney*, 2nd ed., above n. 75, pp. xi-xiv.
[77]   Ibid., 616. Note however that in his Preface to *Cretney*, 2nd ed., above n. 75, p. vii, Cretney made it clear that he would not rearrange his chapters on divorce: 'I am not convinced that any other treatment of the subject would be better'.
[78]   Preface to *Cretney*, 2nd ed., above n. 75, p. vii; see MICHAELS, above n. 26, 565.
[79]   MAIDMENT, above n. 50, 160; see also PRIEST, above n. 69, 616.
[80]   See the *Family Justice Review, Final Report* (Ministry of Justice, November 2011).
[81]   PRIEST, above n. 69, 618.

The third edition, published in 1979 and now £14.00 in paperback (£19.00 in hardback), was again 'intended primarily for the use of degree and other students'.[82] Although it would gain another 145 pages, with a new section on 'Protection' and domestic violence, as Susan Maidment put it the book had 'not only grown in length but also grown in stature'. In just five years, *Cretney* was heralded 'a classic' and Cretney's subsequent appointment as a Law Commissioner made his 'critical views, expressed throughout the book, of the utmost relevance'.[83] The fourth edition in 1984 would swell to 982 pages to be cut to 713 for the fifth edition in 1990.[84] The enactment of the Children Act 1989 necessitated the recruitment of Judith Masson, who re-wrote the sections on children for the fifth edition and whose continued contribution would secure the survival of *Cretney* into its subsequent editions.[85] Along the way the book would collect two more distinguished contributors, Rebecca Bailey-Harris joining for the seventh edition and Rebecca Probert for the eighth. In 1996, the book survived the Canary Wharf bombing in which the Sweet & Maxwell offices were hit[86] to produce a sixth edition in 1997 and, in 2008, *Cretney* survived the retirement of Cretney himself to enter into its eighth edition.

Even after retirement, Cretney continued 'with his important work of identifying a picture for the cover that would capture an aspect of family life in art', a practice started with the selection for the fifth edition of *Waiting for the Verdict* by Abraham Solomon (1857).[87] Cretney suggested that 'the cover picture may give some indication of [his] personal feelings about the appropriateness of unnecessary involvement of the legal system and the traditional court structure in family life and personal relations'.[88] In *Waiting for the Verdict*, an anxious family in muted reds and yellows stands out against the shadows of a Dickensian court corridor, symbolising the focus of *Cretney* on the family, not the law. Perhaps in line with the growing emphasis on child law, Cretney's next selections – *La Famille Bellelli* by Edgar Degas (1858–1867) on the sixth edition, *The Daughters of Edward Darley Boit* by John Singer Sargent (1882) on the seventh edition and *Ernesta (Child with Nurse)* by Cecilia Beaux (1894) on the eighth edition – all depict monochrome little girls in white dresses, each held under the watchful eyes and controlling hands of adults, present or invisible. Cretney believed 'that many great works of art tell a story, or at least convey messages and

---

[82] Preface to S.M. CRETNEY, *Principles of Family Law*, 3rd ed., Sweet & Maxwell, London 1979, p. vii.

[83] MAIDMENT, above n. 50, 159–160.

[84] Note that the fourth edition was reprinted twice, in 1986 and 1988.

[85] See the Preface to S.M. CRETNEY and J.M. MASSON, *Principles of Family Law*, 5th ed., Sweet & Maxwell, London 1990, p. v; and the 'Valedictory Note by Stephen Cretney' in *Cretney*, 8th ed., above n. 1, p. ix.

[86] The bombing occurred on 9th February 1996; I am indebted to Judith Masson for this story.

[87] MASSON, Preface to *Cretney*, 8th ed., above n. 1, p. vii.

[88] Preface to *Cretney*, 5th ed., above n. 85, p. vi.

different views';[89] these illustrations would allow his covers to become as much a part of his discussion of social policy as the text they contained.

5. CONCLUSION

Perhaps it is a reality of any textbook, once established, that the student emphasis begins to dwindle. By the fourth edition, the reference to 'students' in the Preface had gone, to be replaced by a hope that 'those who have to advise' on legislative change would find assistance in the work.[90] That was the allegation made against *Bromley* and is perhaps a reflection of the academic weight both books attained.[91] Such a transition can in no way, however, diminish the epic achievement of Cretney in redefining what a Family Law textbook for students should be. Indeed, *Bromley* (now in its tenth edition and edited by Nigel Lowe and Gillian Douglas) owes much to the 'new breed', while a *newer* breed under Jonathan Herring appears to be its logical descendent.[92] Whether or not one textbook can truly meet the needs of a student,[93] the statutes annotated approach is extinct; thanks to Cretney, family law is no longer viewed in isolation of its social context. By the 1990s, *Cretney* was referred to as *the* 'principal rival' to *Bromley*, a laudable achievement for a book then half the age of the other.[94] Our student in the bookshop of 1974 could have done far worse than heed the words of Hall in his review of that year: 'there is no doubt at all that the book as it now stands makes an important contribution to the literature on this subject and should certainly be read by everyone who studies Family Law at a university'. In 1982, it was said that a new edition was not just a 'necessity' but a 'certainty'; let us all keep our pocket money ready in the hope of a ninth edition.[95]

---

89   CRETNEY, 'Valedictory Note', above n. 85, p. ix.
90   Preface to S.M. CRETNEY, *Principles of Family Law*, 4th ed., Sweet & Maxwell, London 1984, p. vii.
91   BAINHAM, above n. 10, 336.
92   See J. HERRING, *Family Law*, 5th ed., Longman, 2011. I defer to Chris Barton on this point.
93   BAINHAM, above n. 10, 337; and HADFIELD, above n. 28, 251.
94   Ibid., 336.
95   MAIDMENT, above n. 50, 160.

*Plate 1**

*   S.M. Cretney, *Principles of Family Law*, 1st ed., Sweet & Maxwell, London 1974.

Simon Rowbotham

Plate 2*

during that time from which the petitioner, as a reasonable person, would conclude that the other spouse was still alive.[3]

It should be noticed that the petitioner is not bound to rely on this period of absence. The court may accept any satisfactory evidence from which it may be presumed that the spouse is dead:[4] the inference to be drawn from the seven years' absence is of particular importance when there is no evidence at all of what has happened since.

If the proceedings are brought by the husband, he must be domiciled in England; if they are brought by the wife, she must either be domiciled in this country or have been ordinarily resident here for a continuous period of at least three years immediately preceding the commencement of the proceedings.[5] But in order to determine the wife's domicile, the husband is deemed to have died immediately after the last occasion on which she had reason to believe him to be living, so that *for the purpose of these proceedings* the wife may acquire a separate domicile in England if her husband was not domiciled here.[6]

B. DIVORCE

I. HISTORICAL INTRODUCTION

We have already seen that the doctrine of the indissolubility of marriage was accepted by the English ecclesiastical courts after the Reformation, so that these courts had no power to pronounce a decree of divorce *a vinculo matrimonii* which would permit the parties to remarry.[7] In addition to decrees of nullity and jactitation of marriage, they could pronounce decrees of restitution of conjugal rights and divorce *a mensa et thoro*. The former called on a deserting spouse to resume cohabitation with the petitioner, and the latter (which was granted on the grounds of adultery, cruelty or the commission of an unnatural offence) relieved the petitioner from the duty of cohabiting with the respondent without severing the marriage tie.[8] The only way in which an aggrieved party could obtain a divorce *a vinculo matrimonii* was by Act of Parliament, the expense of which was sufficient to put relief beyond the hope of most.[9] In addition, by the end of the eighteenth century, the practice of the House of Lords was to give a reading to a bill introduced on behalf of the husband only on the grounds of adultery and then only after he had obtained a divorce

[3]*Thompson* v. *Thompson*, (*ante*). A mere speculation will not be enough to rebut the presumption. *Quaere* whether the petitioner is bound to make all reasonable enquiries: *ibid.*, at pp. 605 and 421, respectively. *Cf. ante*, pp. 53-55.
[4]*E.g.*, the otherwise inexplicable disappearance of an explorer.
[5]Matrimonial Causes Act 1965, s. 14 (2).
[6] *Ibid.*, s. 14 (5).
[7]*Ante*, p. 59. See generally, Jackson, *Formation and Annulment of Marriage*, 2nd Ed., c. 2.
[8]Readers unfamiliar with ecclesiastical reports before 1858 are warned of the confusing terminology. The word " divorce " *simpliciter* always means divorce *a mensa et thoro;* occasionally " divorce *a vinculo matrimonii* " is used, in which case it always means nullity.
[9]There were on the average less than two divorces by statute a year.

*   P.M. Bromley, *Family Law*, Butterworths, London 1971, reproduced by permission of Reed Elsevier (UK) Limited, trading as LexisNexis.

Plate 3*

CHAPTER 5

DIVORCE

THIS Chapter is divided as follows:
  (i) The Social Policy of Divorce Legislation.
  (ii) The Matrimonial Offence and Bars.
  (iii) The Modern Law of Divorce.
  (iv) Other Kindred Matrimonial Litigation.

THE SOCIAL POLICY OF DIVORCE LEGISLATION [3]

DIVORCE RATES AND THEIR SIGNIFICANCE [4]

In 1858 [5] there were 244 divorce petitions. In 1914 for the first time the number exceeded 1,000; in 1942 it rose above 10,000.[6] In the first year of the operation of the Divorce Reform Act 1969 there were 110,017 petitions, and in 1972, 111,077.[7] This is only a crude indication of divorce rates, but whatever statistical test is adopted [8] there is an upward trend [9] over the years.

It should not be assumed that this necessarily represents an increase in the number of marital breakdowns:

  (i) All divorces evidence breakdown of a marriage, but not all breakdowns are evidenced by divorce. A man who leaves his wife and establishes a " stable illicit union " [10] with another partner has done much the same as a man who divorces one wife and remarries, but it is only in the latter case that the breakdown is reflected in the Divorce Statistics.

  (ii) The rise in the rate may simply " reflect the fact that a growing

[3] See Max Rheinstein, *Marriage, Stability, Divorce and the Law* (1972).
[4] See generally: " Field of Choice " paras. 5–12; McGregor, *Divorce in England* (1957); *Eekelaar*, pp. 32–47; W. J. Goode, *World Revolution and Family Patterns* (1963).
[5] The first year in which divorce by judicial process was available.
[6] See Royal Commission Report, App. II, Table 1.
[7] Civil Judicial Statistics, 1971, Cmnd. 4982, and 1972, Cmnd. 5333, Table 10.
[8] The number of decrees absolute of divorce per 1,000 of the married population is the most meaningful of the readily available figures: this was 0·4 in 1931, 2·6 in 1951, 3·1 in 1966, 3·6 in 1968, 4·1 in 1969, and 4·6 in 1970: see Table 14 and the graph at p. 57, Social Trends (No. 1, 1970), and Table 7, Social Trends (No. 3, 1972) (H.M.S.O.), " Field of Choice " para. 10 and App. C. Other tests sometimes used are (i) the divorce rate per 1,000 marriages; (ii) the rate per 1,000 population; (iii) the rate per 1,000 married women (at specified ages). All statistical information is given in the Registrar-General's Annual Statistical Reviews—most recently for 1971, Part II. Commentaries on the statistical tables are published periodically.
[9] With, however, considerable short-term fluctuations, influenced by (*e.g.*) the availability of legal aid: this is graphically illustrated in *Eekelaar*, p. 34, and see " Field of Choice " para. 5 and App. B; the *Bedford College Survey*, p. 147.
[10] " Field of Choice " paras. 33 *et seq.* This may appear to outsiders to be a valid marriage: there is nothing to stop a woman adopting the surname of the man with whom she is living; " Mrs." is a courtesy title without legal significance.

79

*   S.M. CRETNEY, *Principles of Family Law*, 1st ed., Sweet & Maxwell, London 1974.

*Plate 4**

CHAPTER 6

MATRIMONIAL PROPERTY AND FINANCIAL OBLIGATIONS

"DIVORCE," it has been said by an eminent lawyer [1] "has become less about divorce and more about money." The parties to an unhappy marriage now have to accept that, sooner or later, it can be dissolved. The main scope for dispute is therefore about the financial arrangements which should be made.

Until 1970 although the courts had wide power to order income payments on divorce they had very limited powers over the parties' capital assets.[2] In order to achieve fairness in this respect the courts developed the law of property rights, so as to give both spouses some interest in "family assets." [3] This undoubtedly led to some distortion of orthodox concepts of property law.

The Matrimonial Proceedings and Property Act [4] gave the courts wide discretionary powers over the whole family finances, but for some time there was doubt as to how liberally these powers would be exercised.[5] These doubts have now been resolved,[6] so that the ascertainment of the parties' strict property rights will often be unnecessary [7] in disputes consequent on divorce. But the problem may still be relevant in some such cases,[8] and will be relevant if the dispute is between one spouse and strangers—*e.g.* a creditor, seeking to enforce his debt against one spouse's property,[9] or as to rights of inheritance.[10]

We therefore consider in turn:

    (i) Matrimonial Property;
    (ii) Financial Obligations on Breakdown;
    (iii) The Case for Reform.

[1] Jackson, p. v.
[2] See Law Commission 25, and P.W.P. No. 9, Part I; *Wachtel* v. *Wachtel* [1973] Fam. 72, 90.
[3] See *Pettit* v. *Pettit* [1970] A.C. 777 *per* Lord Diplock at p. 819.
[4] The greater part of which is now consolidated in M.C.A. 1973.
[5] *Infra*, p. 206.
[6] *Wachtel* v. *Wachtel* (*supra*).
[7] *Kowalczuk* v. *Kowalczuk* [1973] 2 All E.R. 1042, *per* Lord Denning M.R. at p. 1045; *Gordon* v. *Gordon* (1973) The Times, October 13.
[8] *Glenn* v. *Glenn* [1973] 1 W.L.R. 1016; p. 207 *infra.*
[9] *Ex p. Solomon* [1967] Ch. 573; *Re Cole* [1964] Ch. 175.
[10] *Re Cummins* [1972] Ch. 62.

144

*   S.M. CRETNEY, *Principles of Family Law*, 1ˢᵗ ed., Sweet & Maxwell, London 1974.

'WHY SHOULD THEY CITE US?'

Lessons From an 'Uncommon' Family Lawyer's Influence on the Common Law

Stephen GILMORE[*]

Contents

1. INTRODUCTION

Faced with choosing an appropriate topic for this chapter, I thought back to the first time I met Stephen Cretney, at the Society of Legal Scholars (SLS) conference in Oxford in 2003. I confess that we did not really chat informally at the conference, not from any lack of friendliness or approachability on his part, but through my own shyness and reticence to begin a 'family law conversation' with such an eminent family law scholar. I had read and admired much of his work, and his name was, for me, indelibly associated with the major family law textbook which bore his sole name at the time it was recommended for my

---

*   I am grateful to the participants at the seminar that preceded this book for providing me with helpful information and sources. I should also like to thank Professor Keith Stanton and Dr Alexandra Braun for sending me copies of their work.

undergraduate family law studies.[1] (To my shame, I did not purchase the book, but borrowed it frequently from the short loan room of the university library – the fact that copies of the book were stored in the short loan room says something about its popularity with, and usefulness for, students!)

Thinking back to that SLS meeting, however, I recalled a reply made to me during one of the conference sessions of the Family Law Section, which has stuck firmly in my mind since. The context is hazy, but I was making a point about the sparseness of academic commentary cited by judges in family law cases, to which Cretney retorted: 'Why should they cite us?' It is, of course, a very good question, raising profound issues about the respective roles of jurists and judges and their relationship. As to the questioner himself, the question perhaps demonstrates a certain modesty since Cretney's academic work has been cited by the English courts on many occasions. The English judiciary have thus seen some very good reasons for citing his work.

So it is that I am led to the subject matter of this chapter. I wish to examine the occasions on which Cretney's work has been cited in English case law and the use that has been made of it. I shall seek to demonstrate that an examination of the citation of his work can illustrate the value of citation of academic work in judgments more generally. Of course, it has not escaped me that Cretney was not so much questioning the usefulness of academic commentary, as whether academics could claim some legitimate role in the process of judicial decision-making. With that point in mind, the chapter begins with some general reflections on the roles of judges and jurists and their connections, before turning to examine Cretney's specific contributions. The chapter ends by offering some further general observations on the judge-jurist relationship, this time more specifically within the discipline of family law.

2. JUDGES, JURISTS AND THE COMMON LAW MOSAIC: AN ANSWER IN PRINCIPLE

In earlier centuries the role of stating legal principle was almost exclusively the preserve of the judges, the work of Sir William Blackstone in his *Commentaries on the Laws of England* being a rare exception. Since the second half of the 20th century, the increasingly important relationship between judges and jurists, and the role that jurists play in the development of the common law, has been recognised by senior members of the judiciary and in academic thinking. Lord Gardiner, addressing the Society of Public Teachers of Law in Lincoln's Inn Hall

---

[1]   S. CRETNEY, *Principles of Family Law*, 4th ed., Sweet & Maxwell, London 1984. For discussion of Cretney's textbook, see ROWBOTHAM, this volume.

in 1966,[2] suggested that the age-old warfare between dons and judges could be ended by the judges submitting at last to the proper guidance of the professors, since 'the ultimate source of judicial truth is to be found in the *Law Quarterly Review*; all that is needed is to incorporate this obvious fact into our jurisprudence'.[3]

Similarly, Sir Robert Goff (later Lord Goff of Chieveley[4]) in his Maccabaen lecture in Jurisprudence[5] at the British Academy in 1983 saw 'the whole corpus of the law as consisting not only of the statutes and cases, but also of the work of jurists who have expounded, interpreted, and often illumined the law'[6] and recognised that 'today it is the fusion of their work which begets the tough, adaptable system which is called the common law'.[7]

Over thirty years after Lord Gardiner had uttered his speech at Lincoln's Inn, Professor Peter Birks, the late Regius Professor of Civil Law in the University of Oxford, delivered a similar message from the Old Hall of the Inn,[8] commenting that 'the self-image of the common law as judge-made is incomplete':

> 'It is judge-and jurist-made. The common law is to be found in its library, and the law library is nowadays not written only by its judges but also by its jurists. The juristic function is to analyse, criticise, sift, and synthesise, and thus to play back to the judges the meaning and direction of their own daily work, now conducted under ever increasing pressure. Everyone who writes even so much as a case-note in a journal joins in that law-making function.'[9]

In his reference to a fusion of the work of jurist and judge, Sir Robert Goff recognised, however, that 'their roles are not the same'[10] and that each is conditioned by the work which he or she is called upon to perform:[11] for the judge, 'the overwhelming influence is the facts of a particular case'; for the jurist, 'it is the idea – often received, but sometimes an original brainchild'.[12] Furthermore, the vision of the judge, focusing as it does on the particular facts and issues of one case, is fragmented, whereas the jurist's concern is much more

---

2   Rt Hon Lord Gardiner, 'Law Reform and the Teachers of Law' (1966–1967) 9 *Journal of the Society of Public Teachers of Law* 190.

3   Ibid., p. 190.

4   A Lord of Appeal in Ordinary.

5   Read 05.05.1983, see R. Goff, 'The Search for Principle' (1983) 69 *Proceedings of the British Academy* 169–187.

6   Ibid., 186.

7   Ibid., 171.

8   Delivering the Twenty-first FA Mann Lecture on 26 November 1997. The text of the lecture is reproduced in P. Birks, 'The Academic and the Practitioner' (1998) 18 *LS (Legal Studies)* 397.

9   Birks, above n. 8, 399.

10   Goff, above n. 5, 170.

11   Ibid., 182.

12   Ibid., 171.

with 'the place of each decision in the law as a whole'.[13] Goff concluded that 'the roles of judge and jurist, though distinct, are complementary: they should be co-operative, not competitive'.[14] In a helpful analogy, Goff preferred to think of the common law, not as a seamless web, but as a mosaic. He explained:

> 'The legislature apart, it is the judges who manufacture the tiny pieces of which the mosaic is formed, influenced very largely by their informed and experienced reactions to the facts of cases. The jurists assess the quality of each piece so produced; they consider its place in the whole, and its likely effect in stimulating the production of new pieces, and the readjustment of others. In this their approach is certainly broader, perhaps more fundamental, and also more philosophical than that of the judges.'[15]

Therein, I think, lies the answer to the question of principle posed by Cretney's question 'Why should they cite us?'. The work of jurists should be drawn on by judges when, in the context of their task, its use will improve the mosaic; and basic politeness requires that if the work is used, it should be properly cited.

3. PRACTICAL CONSIDERATIONS BEARING ON CITATION OF MATERIAL

Of course the answer in principle must also contend with practical considerations.[16] The reasons why, in practice, commentators may or may not be cited are complex. As Stanton points out, the practical barriers to citation make a simple count of citations as an indication of judicial use of academic work of limited value; the context is important.[17] Citation depends not only on merit, but on the accidents of litigation which make academic work of some (general) relevance to the practising lawyer. The use of the work in a particular case is also then dependent on counsel becoming aware of the work concerned and his or her decision as to the relevance of the work to the particular arguments being advanced. The basic methodology of case law reasoning and resources should also not be overlooked: the principal sources upon which counsel will likely wish to rely are those which are most effective in persuading of his or her case, namely binding (or persuasive) case law precedents or statutory provisions. Where, as in most cases, such authorities are available to work with, academic thoughts on a relevant issue may become a somewhat secondary consideration. Also to be

---

13 Ibid., 184.
14 Ibid., 187.
15 Ibid., 186.
16 See generally, P. Darbyshire, *Sitting in Judgment The Working Lives of Judges*, Hart Publishing, Oxford 2011.
17 K. Stanton, 'Use of Scholarship by the House of Lords in Tort Cases' in J. Lee (ed.), *From House of Lords to Supreme Court: Judges, Jurists and the Process of Judging*, Hart Publishing, Oxford 2011, p. 204.

factored in are the cost of doing research, and the availability of time and resources, although in some cases, for example where an academic has engaged in a detailed analysis of relevant case law, reliance on academic research may save time in the long run. Even if academic work is drawn to the court's attention, there may be other reasons why there is a failure to cite, for example, the need for economical exposition, or the particular style of the judge.[18]

No doubt there are other more personal factors bearing on whether work is cited, such as the individual academic reputation of an author and the quality of his or her arguments. No family lawyer would doubt that these are significant factors in the frequent citation of Cretney's work in the law reports. Presumably the various professional encounters or partnerships which the academic concerned may have with members of the judiciary, and the academic's consequent visibility to the judiciary, is also a subtle factor. It seems clear that Cretney's work as a Law Commissioner and for the Judicial Studies Board, his annual lectures to the family law judiciary, his period spent as a case-note editor for the leading family law practitioner journal *Family Law*, and membership of the Thorpe Committee, quite rightly would have brought him to the attention of the judiciary as a commentator of some standing.

4. PRACTITIONERS AND JURISTS: A PARTNERSHIP

As noted above, it is possible that the partnerships which exist between judges and jurists may be important channels in the process of citation of jurists' work. Alexandra Braun has recently examined the nature and characteristics of the partnership between judges and academics in this jurisdiction, comparing it with those existing in France, Italy and Germany. Pointing to a multitude of ways in which the practice of law and academia interact in this jurisdiction, Braun concludes that 'in England academics and judges do not seem to belong to two distant, disconnected worlds.'[19] An increasing number of judges have had an academic career or at least have taught within the universities;[20] some retain visiting or honorary professorships.[21] Some judges publish not infrequently in academic journals. Judges are invited to speak at academic conferences. Some are on the editorial boards of academic journals. Thus, as Birks recognised, 'the universities hold no monopoly of the juristic function.'[22]

---

[18]   STANTON, above n. 17, pp. 207–208.
[19]   A. BRAUN, 'Judges and Academics: Features of a Partnership' in LEE, above n. 17, p. 227.
[20]   Braun identifies the following judges: Beatson J and Cranston J, Buxton LJ and Elias LJ, Kay LJ, Hooper LJ, Sir Mark Potter, Lord Collins, Lord Goff, Baroness Hale, Lord Hoffmann, Sir Robert Megarry, Lord Rodger and Lord Wright.
[21]   E.g., Baroness Hale of Richmond, Visiting Professor, King's College London.
[22]   BIRKS, above n. 8, 400.

Reaching out from the other direction, of course the understanding of law of the majority of practitioners who do a law degree is coloured at an early stage by exposure to an academic thinking. A number of academics are members of the legal profession, some practising or with an academic role in practice, such as an academic door tenancy. Some are invited to provide lectures to judges and other practitioners. Academics clearly sometimes write with the practitioner/judge audience in mind, particularly in the case of case commentaries, and I have myself, in my role as case law editor of *Child and Family Law Quarterly*, on occasion sent a case commentary on a Court of Appeal decision to counsel soon to appear in the same case before the Supreme Court. The Law Commission is also an obvious point of interaction of academics and practising lawyers, as well as providing a means for academic views to feed in to law reform.

Perhaps another pointer to a growing interaction of jurist and practitioner can be seen in the fact that the Honourable Society of the Inner Temple has recently begun to appoint a number of academic fellows with the specific aim of stimulating connections between the work of academics and legal practitioners. A further example of such interactions within the field of family law is the recently-established Centre for Family Law and Practice, of which Baroness Hale of Richmond is the patron. The aim of the Centre and its journal is to explore the interfaces between family law and practice.[23]

Braun's analysis identifies at least two significant ways in which the partnership between academics and judges in England differs from that in the continental jurisdictions she examines. The first highlights a fact which the English lawyer may rather take for granted: in England the relationship between jurist and judge 'evolves between individuals',[24] with the citation of a particular academic's work within a particular judge's judgment, rather than the engagement being between the members of *a court* (delivering a single judgment) and the doctrine of a particular academic group/school of thought. As already noted, this means that in the English approach the citation of an author's work is 'based principally upon his own reputation and the strength of his arguments'.[25] The delivering of individual judgments, possibly engaging with various individual academic perspectives, can be seen as a positive feature of the English system, and as something for a court to bear in mind when considering the option of delivering instead a composite judgment in which the detail of academic commentary may be suppressed. As Sir Roger Goff commented in 1983, perhaps it is more conducive to the law's healthy development if judges 'express their separate views

---

[23]   Several academics (including the author) and Mr Justice Jonathan Baker are on the editorial committee.

[24]   BRAUN, above n. 19, p. 228.

[25]   Ibid., p. 229.

in their different ways' rather than having one judgment 'insulated not merely from dissent but from differences in analysis and on points of detail which may later prove to be important'.[26]

The second difference is that in continental jurisdictions such as Italy and France, the dominant partner is the academic community whereas in England it is the judge. But that ought to be the case in a common law system in which pragmatism is the watchword, and the facts of individual cases are used to create or develop the law, for, as we have seen, deciding cases in this way is the principal focus of the judge not the jurist.

Despite the dominant role of the judiciary, the academic community has in recent times become more conscious of its role in the process of law-making.[27] Academic analyses already indicate 'a clear trend towards a greater transparency' in the interactions between judges and jurists in case law, the dialogue being initiated and sustained on both sides.[28] The reasons for this are no doubt complex. But it may reflect an increasing recognition that, as our society itself becomes more complex, more plural and secular, fragmentation and an unsystematic approach increasingly present a danger for practising lawyers.[29] The complexity requires greater sophistication in ensuring that the law is acceptable and can withstand criticism. As Birks points out, in this sense the rationalisation that jurists perform, 'goes hand in hand with legitimation'.[30]

In the next section, I examine more specific benefits of the citation of academic work, illustrated through examples of the citation of Cretney's work.

5. THE USEFULNESS OF ACADEMIC WORK IN JUDGMENTS[31]

5.1. NOVEL POINTS

One type of case in which academic commentary may prove particularly useful is a case in which a novel point of law arises, on which there is little if any direct authority. In fact, the first citation of Cretney's work in the law reports that I could locate is in just such a case: *Santos v. Santos*[32] a well-known decision on the

---

26   GOFF, above n. 5, 175.
27   F. COWNIE and R. COCKS, *A Great and Noble Occupation!*, Hart Publishing Oxford 2009.
28   BRAUN, above n. 19, p. 239. See e.g., the analysis of tort cases in STANTON, above n. 17.
29   GOFF, above n. 5, 185.
30   BIRKS, above n. 8, 401.
31   I have drawn on STANTON, above n. 17 p. 209 et seq. for some of the categories that follow.
32   [1972] Fam 247.

meaning of 'living apart' for the purposes of divorce law.[33] The case decided that the notion of 'living apart' incorporated a mental as well as a physical element of separation, although the mental element could be fulfilled by a unilateral decision which need not necessarily be communicated to the other spouse. In the recorded submissions of Mr Ewbank (later Ewbank J), representing the Queen's Proctor, appears the following:

> 'The problem here is completely new to English law. There are two interesting articles on this. Joseph Jackson Q.C. in the *Law Society Gazette*, July 1971, p. 341 in an article entitled "The new legislation in practice", supports the Queen's Proctor's submissions. The contrary view is taken by Mr. Stephen Cretney in the *Solicitors' Journal* in the issue of April 23, 1971, p. 295 in an article entitled "When does living apart start?"'

The submissions in *Santos* illustrate another useful purpose which academic work can serve when there is no domestic authority, namely analysis of similar laws in other jurisdictions: the court was also 'referred to the comprehensive and helpful review by Professor Wadlington in the *Virginia Law Review*, vol. 52 (1966), p. 32, of the effect of comparable provisions in the legislation of a large number of individual states of the U.S.A'.[34]

Although Cretney's article is not cited in Sachs LJ's judgment in *Santos*, it can be seen that by the early 1970s he was writing an article predictive of a difficult issue which new legislation might pose, and which was coming to the notice of counsel.

5.2. ACADEMIC DISCUSSION AS INSPIRATION FOR JUDICIAL REASONING

Whether or not a novel point arises, juristic work can present relevant arguments for counsel and consequently provide inspiration for judicial reasoning. The use of Cretney's work in this way can be illustrated by his commentary on the Court of Appeal decision in *Whiston v. Whiston*[35] in the *Law Quarterly Review*.[36] In *Whiston* the Court of Appeal refused on public policy grounds to exercise its discretion to make financial provision or property adjustment ancillary to a decree of nullity where the applicant was a bigamist, holding that there should be no profit from this crime. Cretney considered that the decision was 'certainly defensible; and the argument that a person who commits bigamy should not be

---

[33] Then in the Divorce Reform Act 1969, now consolidated in the Matrimonial Causes Act 1973, s. 1(2) (d) and (e).

[34] [1972] Fam 247, 257.

[35] [1995] Fam 198.

[36] S. CRETNEY, 'Right and Wrong in the Court of Appeal' (1996) 112 *LQR* 33.

in a better position than one who refrains from going through a marriage ceremony is undoubtedly a powerful one' yet he was also:

'...left with feelings of unease about what may be thought to be the simplistic approach taken by the Court of Appeal. First, the supposed principle that a claimant is not to be allowed to benefit from his crime is arguably today more flexible than the Court of Appeal seem to allow; and it is surely regrettable that the court gave no consideration to the decision of Peter Gibson J in *Re H (Deceased)* [1990] 1 FLR 441.'[37]

Cretney's commentary had direct impact in *Rampal v. Rampal (No 2)*[38] in which there is an obvious connection between the commentary and Thorpe LJ's reasoning.[39] The Court of Appeal distinguished *Whiston* to hold that the public policy bar should not apply in the case of a bigamous marriage to which the wife was a knowing and willing party. Having earlier referred to the fact that in the case of *Re H (Deceased)* Peter Gibson J held that public policy did not require the application of the forfeiture rule in every case of manslaughter,[40] Thorpe LJ concluded:

'The crime of bigamy can surely not be said to be so serious as to suspend the general rule that whether or not the principle of public policy can be invoked to bar a claim depends upon an appraisal of the seriousness of the crime in all the circumstances. As Dr Cretney pointed out in his commentary on the decision in *Whiston v. Whiston*, see 112 LQR 33, Professor Kenny followed his colourful description of the crime by saying that it, like manslaughter, is peculiarly elastic in its range.... Even the present case, not so exceptional on its facts, challenges the application of the rule in *Whiston* to all culpable bigamists.'

Ward LJ had also cited Cretney's commentary in his dissenting judgment in the earlier case of *S-T (Formerly J) v. J*[41] though his Lordship concluded that *Whiston* was binding. The fact that even when it did not support his conclusions Ward LJ should have cited Cretney's work to show that some commentators were surprised at the decision in *Whiston*, is a testament to the esteem in which Cretney's commentaries are held.[42] Another example can be seen in *Sorrell v. Sorrell*[43] in

---

37   Ibid., 34.
38   [2001] EWCA Civ 989.
39   With which Robert Walker LJ and Dame Elizabeth Butler-Sloss P agreed.
40   [2001] EWCA Civ 989, [16].
41   [1998] Fam 103, at 135[(meretricious marriage between woman and female-to-male transsexual person). The majority (Sir Brian Neill and Potter LJ) distinguished *Whiston* on the basis that the crime itself founded the marriage. 'Cretney and Masson, *Principles of Family Law* (Sweet & Maxwell, 5th ed. 1990), pp. 46–48' was also cited at p. 124.
42   See also *Woolwich Plc v. Gomm* [1999] All ER (D) 877, in which Cretney's commentary at [1998] Fam Law 666 on *Royal Bank of Scotland v. Etridge (No2)* [1998] 4 All ER 705 stimulated Ward LJ's anxiety 'to see whether there is any way in which that home can be preserved for this unfortunate family'.
43   [2005] EWHC 1717 (Fam).

which Cretney's views that *Lambert v. Lambert*[44] had created 'a community of property system imposed by judicial decision'[45] were put to counsel by Thorpe LJ despite his Lordship's clear disagreement with that viewpoint.[46]

Sometimes the academic criticism may provide validation for a judicial view, for example about the need for law reform. In *Cowan v. Cowan*,[47] in a section of his judgment headed 'The academic appraisal' Thorpe LJ referred to academic work, including two works by Cretney,[48] for the view that the case for statutory reform of ancillary relief has been much strengthened by the decision in *White v. White*.[49] The fact that a section of a judgment is so headed is perhaps an indication of the increasing judge/jurist connection discussed earlier in this chapter.

5.3. PLACING LAW IN HISTORICAL CONTEXT, OR PROVIDING BACKGROUND

A pitfall of the use of earlier case law in judgments is the danger of an unhistorical approach; interpretation of earlier decisions ought to take account of the historical context.[50] This is a task with which academic historical accounts can assist the judiciary and, unsurprisingly, given the fact that Cretney is regarded as the foremost historian of 20th century English family law and policy, there are several examples of Cretney's work providing the historical context for a judgment. The esteem in which Cretney is held by the judiciary in this context is neatly illustrated by the observation of Wall LJ in *Re S (a child) (adoption order or special guardianship order)*[51] at the beginning of a section of his judgment entitled 'The Historical Background':

> 'As is to be expected, there is a scholarly and informative chapter (chapter 17) on the legal adoption of children between 1900 and 1973 in Professor Stephen Cretney's magisterial history: *Family Law in the Twentieth Century*'.[52]

---

44   [2002] EWCA Civ 1685. [2003] 1 FLR 139.
45   S. CRETNEY, 'Community of Property Imposed by Judicial Decision' (2003) 119 *LQR* 349.
46   [2005] EWHC 1717 (Fam). See also *Gloucestershire County Council v. P* [1999] 2 FLR 61, in which Thorpe LJ, holding to his dissenting view, noted that Dr Cretney, in commenting in 1994 on the decision of Wall J in *Re MD & TD (Minors) (No 2)* [1994] Fam Law 489, expressed his reservations.
47   [2001] EWCA Civ 679, [114] and [115].
48   The 'erudite picture presented' in 'Trusting the Judges: Money after Divorce' (1999) 52 *CLP (Current Legal Problems)* 289, and his comment on *White v. White* in [2001] Fam Law 3.
49   [2001] 1 AC 596. See also *Wicks v. Wicks* [1999] Fam 65, endorsing Cretney's call for legislative reform in his comment at [1993] Fam Law 120.
50   GOFF, above n. 5, 175.
51   [2007] EWCA Civ 54.
52   Ibid., [5].

Wall LJ then dedicates five paragraphs of his judgment to Cretney's work, quoting three times[53] from Cretney's book, not only from chapter 17, but also chapter 20, by way of an account of the introduction of custodianship in the Children Act 1975 and the recommendations of the Houghton Report[54] which preceded that change. In *Clibbery v. Allan and anor*[55] a case on whether proceedings in private in chambers were confidential, Thorpe LJ, in three paragraphs of a section of his judgment similarly headed 'The historical background'[56] confessed that his review of the law's developing approach to confidentiality in divorce cases had 'drawn exclusively on chapter 4 of Dr Stephen Cretney's *Law, Law Reform and The Family* (1998) where the whole saga is traced with a judicious balance of scholarship and wit'.[57] Similarly, in *Re K; A Local Authority v. N and Others*[58] Munby J precedes a seven-paragraph discussion of parental consent to marriage and reasons for the decline in applications under section 3(1)(b) of the Marriage Act 1949 with the comment: 'I take the historical background, with gratitude, from Professor Stephen Cretney's magnum opus, *Family Law in the Twentieth Century: A History* (Oxford University Press, 2004), pp. 57–68'.[59]

An historical analysis can provide not only important background for a judgment, but on occasion may even assist in pointing the way forward. In *R (Kehoe) v. Secretary of State for Work and Pensions*[60] the Court of Appeal had to consider whether the payment of child support could be enforced in the courts, by the mother of a child, or whether enforcement measures had been exclusively placed in the hands of the Secretary of State by the Child Support Act 1991. Ward LJ referred to the then 'very recently published magisterial magnum opus, *Family Law in the Twentieth Century*'; quoting a passage[61] which suggested that over time the view had emerged that 'the attempt to deal with maintenance obligations by judicial process was outdated and that court procedures should be replaced by a system of administrative assessment and recovery', he asked: 'Does therein lie a clue to the resolution of this case?'[62]

---

53   Quite extensively from pp. 624, 626–627, and 705–706.
54   (Cmnd 5107) (1972).
55   [2002] Fam 261.
56   Ibid., [87]-[89].
57   Ibid., [89]. The chapter, entitled '"Disgusted, Buckingham Palace…": Divorce, Indecency and the Press, 1926', deals with the circumstances leading to statutory restrictions being placed on press reporting in divorce cases.
58   [2005] EWHC 2956 (Fam).
59   Ibid., [73]. For another example, see Munby J in *Pawandeep Singh v. Entry Clearance Officer, New Delhi* [2004] EWCA Civ 1075.
60   [2004] EWCA Civ 225.
61   S. CRETNEY, *Family Law in the Twentieth Century: A History*, Oxford University Press, Oxford 2003, p. 455.
62   [2004] EWCA Civ 225, [16]. Cretney's 'masterly history' was also cited by Baroness Hale in the House of Lords decision: see *Regina (Kehoe) v. Secretary of State for Work and Pensions* [2005] UKHL 48, [62].

5.4. A CONVENIENT METHOD OF SUMMARISING A BODY OF LAW

As well as providing historical background, academic work can also save judges time in affording a convenient reference point for summarising a body of law as a starting off point for discussion or as confirmation of a viewpoint. For example, in *Sheffield City Council v. E and another*, Munby J, presumably bolstering his conclusion that the legal test for capacity to marry should not be set so high as to require detailed knowledge of the legal incidents of marriage, commented:

> 'as Dr Stephen Cretney has pointed out (*Cretney, Masson & Bailey-Harris, Principles of Family Law*, 7th ed. (2002), para. 3–001)…"it is virtually impossible to give an account of the legal consequences of marriage which is coherent, much less comprehensive."'[63]

Another example is provided in Ralph Gibson LJ's judgment in *F v. Metropolitan Borough of Wirral DC and Another*,[64] using 'Cretney, *Principles of Family Law* (4th ed. 1984), ch. 10, pp. 287 et seq.' as a reference point for the whole body of law relating to parent and child and its development in the 20th century.

I hope that the foregoing account of Cretney's citations in the law reports has managed to convey the esteem in which members of the family law judiciary hold his work, and the range of his work upon which they have drawn. It illustrates that the family law judiciary is not unreceptive to the judge/jurist collaboration. In the final section of this chapter, however, I wish to argue that nevertheless there is no room for complacency.

6. ROOM FOR IMPROVEMENT?

This is not the occasion for a detailed assessment of the overall use of academic commentary by English family law judges, and space precludes anything more than a brief outline of two examples which illustrate, in my opinion, a failure on the part of judges in family law cases to engage adequately with areas of relevant academic work. Both examples concern the courts' decisions in children cases.

The first relates to the use of social science research evidence when the courts are providing guideline judgments for applying the paramountcy principle in section 1(1) of the Children Act 1989. The courts' track record in this area is poor. At worst, there has been a complete failure to engage with research evidence in some

---

63   [2004] EWHC 2808 (Fam).
64   [1991] 2 FLR 114.

areas. An example is the courts' approach to shared residence. To my knowledge, in none of the Court of Appeal's guideline judgments in this area is there any reference to research findings. This is so even though summaries of the principal findings of research are available,[65] together with legal academics' reflections on their implications for legal decision-making.[66] Of course the role of such research cannot, and should not, be to tell the courts the appropriate outcome, but the research can provide important insights into factors bearing on a child's welfare in this context, which can be considered on a case-by-case basis.

In the case law on contact with a non-resident parent, the picture is a little, but not much, better: at least the role of research evidence is recognised in the case law. Unfortunately, however, as argued elsewhere,[67] the Court of Appeal's use of research evidence to conclude that there should be an assumption that contact is beneficial relies on limited sources, is arguably a misreading of the expert opinion put before the court in the Sturge/Glaser report,[68] and is not supported by the research evidence as a whole. Yet, despite the fact that the research has been reviewed, and these criticisms made, in mainstream family law journals, the judges have, as yet, not seen any need to engage further. These failures have led me to wonder whether we should not put in place a more systematic approach to ensuring that counsel and judges are guided by findings from relevant research in applying section 1, findings that are subjected to rigorous examination, and transparent to all. After all, the judges are not unused to such guidelines, for example in matters of sentencing.

The second example also relates to the paramountcy principle, this time to its interpretation as a matter of law in the light of implementation of the Human Rights Act 1998. There has been a distinct failure to engage with academic commentary pointing to the differences between the requirements of the paramountcy principle (focusing solely on the child's welfare) and of Article 8 of the European Convention on Human Rights (weighing of the various interests engaged), differences which impact on the process by which decisions are taken, and in some cases potentially on the outcome.[69] Perhaps the worst example of

---

65   For reviews, see L. TRINDER, 'Shared Residence: A Review of Recent Research Evidence' [2010] 22 *CFLQ (Child and Family Law Quarterly)* 475 and references cited therein.

66   S. GILMORE, 'Contact/Shared Residence and Child Well-being: Research Evidence and its Implications for Legal Decision-Making' (2006) 20 *IJLFP (International Journal of Law, Policy and the Family)* 344; S. GILMORE, 'Court Decision-Making in Shared Residence Order Cases: A Critical Examination' [2006] 18 *CFLQ* 478.

67   S. GILMORE, 'Disputing contact: challenging some assumptions' [2008] 20 *CFLQ* 285; S. GILMORE, 'The Assumption that Contact is Beneficial: Challenging the "Secure Foundation"' (2008) 38 *Family Law* 1126.

68   'Contact and domestic violence – the experts' court report' [2000] *Family Law* 615.

69   See e.g. S. CHOUDHRY and H. FENWICK, 'Taking the Rights of Parents and Children Seriously: Confronting the Welfare Principle under the Human Rights Act' (2005) 25 *OJLS (Oxford*

this failure is the decision of the House of Lords in *In re G (Children)*[70] in which, without any reference to Convention rights at all, the House declared that it should not entertain any weakening of the statutory position, which it said was 'plain: the welfare of the child is the paramount consideration',[71] by which it meant 'the sole consideration'.

7.   AN OPTIMISTIC CONCLUSION

In a contribution celebrating the great work of a leading academic, it would be wrong to end on a downbeat note. So I would like to bring this chapter to a close with more positive, optimistic comments. Going back to the question of partnership discussed earlier, we are blessed in family law with a close and warm academic community and close connections with some of the judges working in the area which, I believe, we value greatly. We have been fortunate to be able to mix with senior members of the judiciary in the informal setting of the family law section of the Society of Legal Scholars conference in recent years and at other events. The Current Chairman of the Law Commission, Lord Justice Munby, is a prominent family law judge. The connections are illustrated by the fact that two of the family law specialists in the Supreme Court are contributors to this book and were present at the meeting in the House of Lords to discuss the contributions. It was most promising to hear Lord Wilson of Culworth state at that meeting that there is far too little interrelationship between judges and jurists. By way of responding to those words and ending on an upbeat note, I can perhaps do no better than to repeat the words of Sir Robert Goff in his Maccabaen lecture:

> 'We should welcome each other's assistance in our work; and, while doubtless conscious of each other's shortcomings, recognize and appreciate each other's strength and the nature of our respective contributions in the unceasing restoration and embellishment of the mosaic which is the common law.'[72]

Journal of Legal Studies) 453 and references cited therein.
[70]   [2006] UKHL 43.
[71]   At [30].
[72]   GOFF, above n. 5, 187.

CHILD FOCUSED LEGISLATION:
FOR THE SAKE OF THE CHILDREN?

Christine Piper

Contents

1. INTRODUCTION

The passage of legislative provisions which are intended to improve the lives of (some) children and young people has never been conflict free. What is considered to be in the best interests of children is a contested area, subject to changing values, knowledge, fears and aspirations. It is also an issue which cuts across what adults, notably mothers, fathers, governments and commercial enterprises, consider to be in their best interests. Stephen Cretney's research on key pieces of legislation affecting children has shown how 'immense scholarship'[1], an historian's persistent 'digging',[2] and meticulous attention to detail can uncover complexities of motivation which undermine naïve assumptions about causation and open up new avenues to explore in relation to all legislative reform.

An example of such an assumption can be found in Cretney's introduction to an article on the genesis of the Children Act 1948 in which he notes that

---

[1] The phrase used by N. LOWE in his review of S. CRETNEY, *Law, Law Reform and the Family*, Clarendon Press, Oxford 1998, in (2004) 18 *International Journal of Law, Policy and the Family* 256, 256.

[2] I love the following quote about historians from Dr Johnson but this definitely does not apply to Stephen Cretney: 'Great abilities are not requisite for an Historian... he has the facts ready to hand so there is no exercise of invention. Imagination is not required in any high degree; only about as much as is used in the lower forms of poetry' (R.W. CHAPMAN (ed.), *Boswell's Life of Johnson*, Oxford University Press, Oxford 1953, p. 304).

commentators still often presume that the death of a child – Dennis O'Neill – in foster care in 1945 led to the government's decision to set up the Curtis Committee. In fact it had been established that the decision had preceded the death.[3] This and other 'puzzling features' prompted Cretney to comment that 'The truth is that the background to the legislation is more complex than is often assumed'.[4] His analysis of the factors and pressures leading to that Act also led him to suggest that 'the way in which the response to the various pressures for change is reflected in the legislation may be of interest to lawyers and indeed others who have an interest in law reform'[5] but in that comment he characteristically underestimates the value of this sort of research. What Reece sees as a weakness in the way the research is presented – 'that it is at times difficult to decipher what Cretney wants us to take from the historical material'[6] is also, as she acknowledges, its strength: it is a repository to be mined many times for otherwise unknown historical documents and new insights. Above all, perhaps, it tells us that the devil is often in the detail.

However, it was the article discussing the genesis of the Guardianship of Infants Act 1925 which first stimulated me – and several cohorts of postgraduate students – to think more carefully about the way women, in one way or another, influenced the passage or the detail of legislation relating to children. Section 1 of that Act is seen as a milestone in child law and is a provision which in practice has operated for the sake of the children. It introduced the principle by which the welfare of the child is the paramount consideration of the court when it makes decisions about the child's upbringing. Reece comments in her review of Cretney's 1998 book[7] and the discussion of the 1925 Act in Chapter 7, 'It would be impossible to overemphasize the significance of this development'.[8] As Cretney points out in relation to the interpretation of 'paramount' since 1970, 'It is doubtful whether this interpretation … adequately reflects the intentions of those responsible for the terms in which the Guardianship of Infants Act finally reached the statute book'.[9]

Yet it becomes very clear from Cretney's research that section 1 was a very carefully crafted compromise, the outcome of campaigns and negotiations that did not focus on the children *per se* but, rather, on parental rights. Cretney used the

---

[3] By R. A. PARKER in 'The Gestation of Reform: the Children Act 1948' in P. BEAN and S. MACPHERSON (eds.), *Approaches to Welfare*, Routledge and Kegan Paul, London 1983.

[4] S. CRETNEY, 'The state as a parent: the Children Act 1948 in retrospect' (1998) 114 *LQR (Law Quarterly Review)* 419–59, 419.

[5] CRETNEY, above n. 4, p. 419. Chapter 9 of S. CRETNEY, *Law, Law Reform and the Family*, Clarendon Press, Oxford 1998 also discusses the factors that led to this Act.

[6] H. REECE, 'The Development of Family Law in the Twentieth Century: Informed Reform or Campaigns and Compromises?' (2000) 63 *MLR (Modern Law Review)* 608, 609.

[7] CRETNEY, above n. 5.

[8] REECE, above n. 6, 614.

[9] S. CRETNEY, '"What Will the Women Want Next?" The Struggle for Power within the Family, 1925–1975' (1996) 112 *LQR* 110, 129–130.

rhetorical question 'What Will the Women Want Next?' in the title of his 1996 article,[10] a question which had been posed by an official on a Home Office file recording a later meeting in 1929. The fact that the attendees at that meeting were the Prime Minister, the Chancellor of the Exchequer,[11] and a Deputation of Representatives of Women's Organisations reveals the great political importance of the 'woman question' which underpins a measure apparently focused on infants.

The research into these two pieces of legislation points up the importance of grappling with a complexity of motives for reform where children are affected by the outcome; it also alerts us to the fact that legislation which is (ultimately) of benefit or detriment to children (and perhaps their mothers as well) may be a by-product of legislation passed for quite different reasons.[12] It is with these points in mind that this chapter will focus not only on the 1925 Act but also on other pieces of legislation which are not quite what they seem and which may or may not have been passed for the sake of the children.

2.   THE FACTORIES ACT 1844

The Factories Act of 1844[13] has often been seen as part of a long and distinguished history of legislation which has benefited children in England and Wales. Perhaps the best known 19th century Acts are those which concern children climbing chimneys, going down mines or working in factories: many school children have been taught about the efforts of people like Lord Shaftesbury, Mary Carpenter and Dr Barnardo to give children homes, improve their conditions of work or remove them from employment or imprisonment. In the 20th century the Children Acts passed in 1908, 1948 and 1989 established, *inter alia*, juvenile courts, Local Authority duties to children in need, legal criteria for care orders, and a system of inspection of foster homes and nurseries. As well as child protection legislation, free compulsory education was introduced: at the 'elementary' level by legislation between 1870 and 1891 and at the secondary level by the 1944 Education Act.[14] There is no question that (some of) those pressing for such changes were motivated, at least in part, by concern for

---

10   Ibid.
11   Stanley Baldwin and Winston Churchill, respectively: see ibid., at fn. 1.
12   Conversely Acts named as for children may only tangentially be so. For example, the Act for the Relief of the Orphans and other Creditors of the City of London. 5 & 6 Will & Mary cap 10, often referred to as the Orphans, London Act 1694, was one by which duties could be levied on coal by the City of London in the same way as the duty set up after the Great Fire of London to pay for rebuilding, notably of St Paul's: see I. Doolittle, 'The City of London's debt to its orphans 1694–1767' (1983) 56 *Bulletin of the Institute of Historical Research* 46.
13   7 & 8 Vict c. 15.
14   For further discussion of the development of child-focussed legislation see C. Piper, *Investing in Children, Policy, Law and Practice in Context*, Willan/Routledge, Abingdon 2008, chs. 1 and 2.

the deprivations endured by children: their campaigns for reform were presented as 'for the sake of the children'.

An example of evident sympathy for the children in question and a desire for reform can be found in the poem which Caroline Norton[15] sent anonymously to Lord Ashley (later Lord Shaftesbury) in October 1836 in which the ninth verse reads as follows:

> 'Ever a toiling *child* doth make us sad:
> 'Tis an unnatural and mournful sight,
> Because we feel their smiles should be so glad,
> Because we know their eyes should be so bright.
> What is it, then, when, tasked beyond their might,
> They labour all day long for others' gain,–
> Nay, trespass on the still and pleasant night,
> While uncompleted hours of toil remain?
> Poor little FACTORY SLAVES–for You these lines complain!'[16]

In her covering letter to Lord Ashley, Norton wrote of the 'Factory Question' that 'I cannot but think it is incumbent on all who feel, as I do, that there *is* an evil which it behoves Christian lawgivers to remove – to endeavour to obtain such a portion of public attention as may be granted to the expression of their conviction' but she went on to acknowledge that 'There will be delay – there will be opposition: such has ever been the case with all questions involving interests, and more especially where the preponderating interest has been on the side of the existing abuse'. The opposition the promoters of the Bill had to overcome was not just from industrialists and other commercial interests but also from church leaders and other parties whose strongly held ideas about the family were threatened by the sort of regulation being discussed. Visions of 'pathetic' children such as those in Norton's poem – conjured up in parliamentary debates well into the 20th century – proved to be very powerful, indeed essential, aids to the reformers, and the speeches of Lord Shaftesbury in Parliament have been seen as examples of the 'politics of pathos'.[17] Norton's poem, entitled 'A Voice from the Factories', evoked what was a very common aspect of the image of the child used – to be found also in Elizabeth Barrett Browning's 'The Cry of the Children' (1843),[18] Andrew Mearn's 'The Bitter Cry of Outcast London' (1883) and John

---

[15] Norton is perhaps best known in relation to the scandal and ensuing court case over her alleged relationship with Lord Melbourne but she became a campaigner for issues relating to women and their lack of rights to custody of their children. Consequently she was influential in the passage of the Custody of Infants Act 1839 and the Matrimonial Causes Act 1857.

[16] Available at <http://digital.library.upenn.edu/women/norton/avftf/avftf.html> (accessed 24.11.2011), capitals in the original.

[17] G. BEHLMER, *Child Abuse and Moral Reform in England 1870–1908*, Stanford University Press, Stanford California 1982, p. 3.

[18] For the full text see <http://classiclit.about.com/library/bl-etexts/ebbrowning/bl-ebbrown-cry.htm> (accessed 5.11.2011).

Spargo's 'The Bitter Cry of the Children' (1906)[19] – that of children without a voice who silently 'cry'.[20] Barrett Browning's poem, for example, voices the child's woes in 13 verses, the 6th verse of which includes the following:

'For oh,' say the children, 'we are weary,
And we cannot run or leap
If we cared for any meadows, it were merely
To drop down in them and sleep.
...
For, all day, we drag our burden tiring,
Through the coal-dark, underground –
Or, all day, we drive the wheels of iron
In the factories, round and round.'

And that image of the silent, worn-down child can also be found in the earlier speech of Sadler when he was pressing for the passage of the Ten Hours Bill in 1832,[21] 'I wish I could bring a group of these little ones to [the] bar [of the House of Commons] – I am sure their silent appearance would plead more forcibly in their behalf than the loudest eloquence'.[22] We may denigrate such Victorian sentimentality but, as King noted at the beginning of his book entitled *A Better World for Children*, 'Little in life arouses moral indignation and demands moral judgements and action more than the suffering of children'.[23] The amount of indignation and pity was often what determined the success or failure of a Bill which entailed increased local or national taxation, had economic costs for employers or parents, or threatened a dominant ideology.

It is the fear of the undermining of an established order which is very clear even in the speech of Lord Ashley in 1844 in the debate in committee on the Factories Bill. I have quoted this long extract before[24] but I do so again because it indicates what was to be increasingly important in policy negotiation and campaigns, and no more so than in the Guardianship of Infants Act 1925, and that is the role of women.

---

19   Originally published in the USA and reprinted in 1969.

20   For further discussion see C. PIPER, 'Moral Campaigns for Children's Welfare in the 19th Century', in M. KING (ed.), *Moral Agendas for Children's Welfare*, Routledge, London 1999.

21   This Bill – and the pressure for a 'ten hours clause' in a later Bill – failed although an Act of 1802 had already limited – with little effect – the hours of work for children, and the Labour of Children etc in Factories Act 1833 (3 & 4 Will. IV) c. 103 confirmed the maximum hours of work of children aged 9–13 as 8 hours a day plus an hour lunch break and young people aged 14–18 as 12 hours.

22   *Memoirs of the Life and Writings of Michael Thomas Sadler, M.P.; F.R.S.; &c.*, 337/379 1842, excerpted in J. WARD, *The Factory System*, Vol 2, David and Charles, Newton Abbot 1970, p. 102.

23   M. KING, *A Better World for Children: Explorations in morality and authority*, Taylor and Francis, London 1997, p. 1.

24   PIPER, above n. 20, p. 41.

'But listen to another fact and one deserving of serious attention; that the females not only perform the labour but occupy the places of men; they are forming various clubs and associations, and gradually acquiring all those privileges which are held to be the proper portion of the male sex... Here is a dialogue which occurred in one of these clubs, from an eyewitness:- "A man came into one of these clubrooms, with a child in his arms; 'Come lass,' said he addressing one of the single women, 'come home for I cannot keep this bairn quiet, and the other one I have left crying at home: 'I won't go home, idle devil', she replied, 'I have thee to keep and the bairns too, and if I can't get a pint of ale quietly, it is tiresome... I won't go home yet'". Whence is it that this singular and unnatural change is taking place? Because that on women are imposed the duty and burden of supporting their husbands and family, a perversion as it were of nature, which has the inevitable effect of introducing into families disorder, insubordination and conflict... No, Sir, these sources of mischief must be dried up; every public consideration demands such an issue; the health of the females; the care of their families; their conjugal and parental duties; the comfort of their homes; the decency of their lives; the rights of their husbands; the peace of society; and the laws of God.'[25]

Children and their welfare are not mentioned directly – the focus is on the female's care for the family: paternal authority and particular ideas about the wife and mother are at stake.[26] Indeed the 1844 Act did not significantly improve the hours of labour for children although it did limit the hours of women in textile factories to those of the 14–18 year old.

These ideas about the family and women's role were shared – and used – by working class leaders urging for factory reform at that time: they wanted a 10 hour day for all workers but, knowing this would be opposed by a powerful factory owners' lobby, focused first on a reduction of hours for women and children in the hope this would later lead to a reduction in the hours for men.[27] Much later the Charity Organisation Society argued against what was eventually

---

[25]   Quoted in J. Cairns (ed.), *The Nineteenth Century 1815–1914*, The Free Press, New York 1965, pp. 68–9.

[26]   Feminist historians have, therefore, examined the role of male trade unions in seeking reform of working conditions for women and children which would, as a side product, increase the male wage and improve the terms of employment for men. However I am grateful to Stephen Cretney for suggesting that restrictions on the parental rights of the economically dependent clearly did not 'count' and so class, as well as gender, is an issue (Cretney at the *CFLQ* Seminar, All Souls Oxford, 01.07.1997). See also the comment of Lord Thring, when arguing in support of the Custody of Children Act 1891, that 'It gives the poorer child the same protection given by the Court of Chancery to wealthier children.' (quoted in I. Pinchbeck and M. Hewitt, *Children in English Society: From the 18th century to the Children Act 1948*, vol. 2, Routledge and Keegan Paul Ltd., London 1973, p. 385).

[27]   Frederick Engels wrote two articles on this issue – 'The Ten Hours Question' – for *The Democratic Review*, a Chartist publication, and then 'The English Ten Hours Bill' for a German journal in 1850. For a translation of the latter article see: <www.marxists.org/archive/marx/works/1850/03/10hours.htm>.

passed as the Education (Provision of Meals) Act 1906[28] on the grounds that it would undermine familial authority: 'It is better, in the interests of the community, to allow… the sins of the parents to be visited on the children, than to impair the principle of the solidarity of the family … by the offer of free meals'.[29] Familial or paternal authority was more important than a child's hunger.

It is not just Cretney's research which has made clear that a version of history in the liberal historical tradition, assuming clear cause and consequence and benevolent motivation, and documenting what historians assumed would be further progress towards a better society, no longer holds. The influence, on the one hand, of Marxist and sociological approaches to historical research with their emphasis on economic conditions and the class and gender based interests through which change occurs and, on the other hand, of post-modernism with its undermining of optimism has made sceptics of us all. So we now expect that reform publicly 'sold' as being for the sake of the children had other desired outcomes and, at one level, that is to be expected: 'All laws [affecting children] are made by adults in order to create the kind of society that adults wish to have'.[30] A new law may well benefit children but it will also – or predominantly – benefit their parents or society more generally.

That the child's welfare is not always the main issue is clear from those instances where legislation manifestly aimed at the child's welfare could not succeed because of interests deemed stronger. So if, as occurred in the 1870s, child cruelty was still seen as less important than upholding paternal authority and the privacy of the family, then legislation protecting children from parental cruelty could not be passed. Such priorities were explicit. As Lord Shaftesbury replied in 1871 to a letter asking him to support such legislation, '[t]he evils you state are enormous and indisputable, but they are of so private, internal and domestic a character as to be beyond the reach of legislation, and the subject, indeed, would not, I think, be entertained by either House of Parliament'.[31] Further, the School Meals Act 1906 directed at the welfare of children living in poverty and mentioned above as having been opposed on such ideological grounds, was also supported by those wishing to improve the health of children for a purpose other than the welfare of the child at dinner-time.[32] Recruitment to the Second Boer

---

[28] See C. MOWAT, *The Charity Organisation Society, 1869 to 1913*, Methuen, London 1961, pp. 74–5 and pp. 154–5.

[29] Quoted by PINCHBECK and HEWITT, above n. 26, p. 358.

[30] M. GUGGENHEIM, *What's Wrong with Children's Rights?* Harvard University Press, Cambridge, Mass. 2005, p. 47.

[31] On March 15th 1844, quoted by PINCHBECK and HEWITT, above n. 26, p. 622.

[32] Coming originally from a Derbyshire working class family I have no problem with referring to the mid-day meal as 'dinner'!

War of 1899–1902[33] had made clear the poor physical condition of recruits and the militarisation of Germany suggested a potential future need for fit soldiers and sailors. A London County Council Report of 1907 which assessed 50–60 per cent of children as coming under the category of 'indifferent nutrition'[34] confirmed the need for pressure for implementation of the Act at local level, it being resisted.[35]

3.   THE FAMILY LAW ACT 1996

A much more recent example of legislation being 'marketed' as for the sake of the children with a particular image of the child evoked in debate and policy documents – but involving a very wide mix of imperatives and motivations – is Part 2 of the Family Law Act 1996. There had been criticism of the Bill for not focusing sufficiently on the welfare of children. James and Lyon had argued that there had been an 'almost complete absence of discussion concerning children'[36] in the preceding White Paper[37] which 'contains in total little more than two pages referring to the needs of children in divorce.'[38] A joint statement drawing attention to what they saw as a lack of attention to the needs of children in the Bill was also signed by nineteen child care agencies and professional bodies.[39] Yet the policy documents very effectively purveyed assumptions that the current divorce process was 'bad' for children and that the break-up of their parents' marriage could itself be a cause of harm to children.[40] The assumptions were not discussed in detail and there was little analysis of research to support the assumptions – hence the lack of 'quantity' in regard to the child's welfare – but they were used effectively. The White Paper had stated that 'Separation and divorce constitute a painful process for all the family members concerned but

---

33   In 1899, 32.9% of the recruits who were medically inspected were rejected as unfit: see M. HENDLEY, '"Help us to secure a strong, healthy, prosperous and peaceful Britain": The social arguments for compulsory military service in Britain, 1899–1914' (1995) 30 *Canadian Journal of History* 261, 263.

34   See M. ALDEN, *Child Life and Labour*. Headley Bros, London 1908. Significantly, in a time of peace after two major wars, and as part of a drive to reduce the cost of school meals, the 1980 Education Act removed the requirement that all school meals should have certain minimal nutritional standards.

35   J. BRANNEN and P. STOREY, 'School meals and the start of secondary school' (1998) 13 *Health Education Research* 73, 74; M. CROSS and B. MACDONALD, *Nutrition in Institutions*. Wiley-Blackwell, Oxford 2009, p. 7.

36   A. JAMES and C. LYONS, 'Editorial' (1995) 17 *JSWFL (Journal of Social Welfare and Family Law)* iii, v.

37   LORD CHANCELLOR'S DEPARTMENT, *Looking to the Future: Mediation and the Ground for Divorce* Cm 2799, HMSO London 1995.

38   JAMES and LYONS, above n. 36, iv.

39   See G. NEWMAN, (1996) *Childright* No. 124, 2.

40   See C. PIPER, 'Divorce Reform and the Image of the Child' (1996) 23 *Journal of Law and Society* 364.

particularly for the children'[41] and the preceding Consultation Paper had spelt this out more clearly:

> 'Almost inevitably the breakdown of a marriage is hard for one or both of the parties *and especially for the children*. I believe that a good divorce law... should seek to eliminate unnecessary distress for the parties *and particularly for their children* in those cases where a marriage has broken down irretrievably.'

> 'It is clear that, when a marriage breaks down and there are children of the marriage, *they are very vulnerable to consequent damage.*'[42]

These and many other assertions in the policy documents painted a picture of the child as a vulnerable person who did not want his or her parents to divorce and was damaged by both the process of divorce and its consequences. It is, therefore, arguable that not only did this justify key divorce reform proposals but also that policy debates at that time led to the powerful image of the child as 'the victim' of divorce which has persisted and for whose sake there should be particular desired aims. The reforms the image justified in 1995–6 related to processes to encourage the use of mediation and delay divorce on the grounds that this would reduce parental conflict and possibly reduce the number of divorces at the end of the 'period of reflection' – both seen as in the best interests of children. As the White Paper noted 'it is conflict between the parents which has been linked to greater social and behavioural problems among children... A reduction in bitterness and hostility was seen by consultees as a central objective in reducing the harm that might be done to children of the marriage'.[43]

This extension of the idea of the child as the victim of physical and sexual harm to include the child as victim of inter-parental hostility and of emotional abuse has produced an influential image which now often underpins action promoted explicitly 'for the sake of the children'. That phrase is one which currently appears to be linked most frequently in internet-based discussion with the question as to whether parents should separate or stay together.[44] Similarly, the 'For the Sake of the Children Program' available to parents in Manitoba and New Brunswick, Canada, provides information at the time of separation and divorce.[45] In England

---

[41] Lord Chancellor's Department, above n. 37, para. 5.1.

[42] Lord Chancellor's Department, *Looking to the Future: Mediation and the Ground for Divorce* Cm 2424, HMSO, London 1993, pp. iii and iv of the Foreword by the Right Honourable the Lord Mackay of Clashfern, my italics.

[43] Lord Chancellor's Department, above n. 37, para. 3.10.

[44] See for example the 72 blogs on the subject on Mumsnet at: <www.mumsnet.com/Talk/relationships/958484-Staying-together-for-the-sake-of-the-children-after-25/AllOnOnePage> (accessed 24.11.2011) or on the Dating Advice site at <www.datingadviceblog.co.uk/2011/06/should-you-stay-together-for-the-sake-of-the-children/>.

[45] See <www.gov.mb.ca/fs/childfam/for_sake_of_children.html> and <www.legal-info-legale.nb.ca/en/for_sake_of_children>.

and Wales the image of children as victims of their parents has also proved to be very important in arguing for reform which is, arguably, predominantly supported for financial or other reasons. An example can be found in the proposals for restricting access to legal aid in family cases as evidenced by the statement in the Consultation Paper in 2010: 'We do not consider that it will generally be in the best interest of the children involved for these essentially personal matters to be resolved in the adversarial forum of a court'.[46]

4. THE GUARDIANSHIP OF INFANTS ACT 1925

The pressures leading ultimately to the wording of section 1 of this Act were in some respects very different but there are similarities. Cretney quotes Edward Jenks, a respected legal academic, as asserting that the Act's 'revolutionary' provisions subjected the institution of the family to 'drastic alteration'[47] and the Lord Chancellor – in terms reminiscent of Lord Shaftesbury – had told the Home Secretary in 1923 that giving the mother legal equality would be 'destructive of all domestic felicity'.[48] Cretney also notes that a letter by Parliamentary Counsel in 1922 referred to another 'preposterous bill' which, he said, 'like many other bills promoted by the Women's Societies, under the pretence of removing slight inequalities between the sexes, strike at the foundations of domestic felicity'.[49]

In part 1 of his article Cretney explains that the mischief aimed at by the women who were newly enfranchised by the Representation of the People Act 1918[50] was to have 'the legal status of her children's parent'.[51] Such aspirations were represented by the leading women's group NUSEC (National Union of Societies for Equal Citizenship) and the first equal parental authority bills were introduced in 1920 with others in subsequent years.[52] Eleanor Rathbone,[53] in *The Disinherited Family,* referred to 'the monstrous legal fiction that a man has a primary right to the sole control of his children whom a woman has borne with great suffering and at the risk of her life'[54] but, whilst the 1925 Act did provide the mother with benefits, it did not give the mother legal equality – a clause which would have done so having been removed after strong opposition. Whilst the case for parental equality was based on principle, the stronger case against

---

[46]   MINISTRY OF JUSTICE, *Proposals for the Reform of Legal Aid in England and Wales,* Consultation Paper CP 12/10, cm 7967, TSO, London 2010, para. 4.20.

[47]   E. JENKS, 'Recent Changes in Family Law' (1938) 44 *LQR* 314; see CRETNEY, above n. 9, 110.

[48]   CRETNEY, above n. 9, 110–111.

[49]   HO45/11936/42909: see ibid., fn 10.

[50]   Provided they were at least 30 years old and householders.

[51]   CRETNEY, above n. 9, 113.

[52]   CRETNEY, above n. 9, 112–113.

[53]   Best known for her success in ensuring family allowances were paid to the mother.

[54]   1924, 91–92, quoted in CRETNEY, above n. 9, 115.

was based on the familiar argument that interfering with the father's primacy would 'sacrifice the peace of the home': this was specifically seen as also sacrificing the 'interest of the children',[55] with the further argument that 'What is at stake... is the well-being of the child itself, and any duality of control must militate against that'.[56]

Reference to the interests of the child to support an argument for parental rights which may or may not be in the best interests of the particular child to be affected is a development with which we are now very familiar. There have been legislative changes more recently – in the UK and elsewhere – which have been presented as 'for the sake of the children' and 'sold' as supported by 'science' which allegedly proves that such reforms are in the child's best interests. However, as many have now pointed out,[57] such science is far from clear and may not prove the wisdom of the changes proposed or implemented. Recent and current examples relate to issues around parental separation and divorce and, particularly in relation to assumptions about the benefits of contact between child and non-resident parent (such that further sanctions for use with errant resident parents are legitimated and present distress to children is downgraded) and about the shared parenting. Complex science, applied in a simplistic way, is proving as useful to campaigns by fathers' groups as did the sentimentalised poems of the Victorians.[58]

The complexity of the issues and pressures accounting for legislation which Cretney's research reveals would suggest we need also to examine legislation which is focused on adults but later extended, with less publicity, for use with lower age groups. Such provisions, not passed for the sake of the children and, arguably, not in a child's best interests include the introduction of anti-social behaviour orders (ASBOs). The Crime and Disorder Act 1998 empowers a court to impose this order if the person has acted 'in a manner that caused or was likely to cause harassment, alarm or distress' to one or more persons outside the

---

55   Sir Charles BIRON, Chief Magistrate, in a Joint Select Committee, 1922, quoted in CRETNEY, above n. 9, 116 and fn. 42.

56   From a draft report prepared by Lord Askwith 1923: see CRETNEY, above n. 9, 116 and fn. 45.

57   See, for example, A. BARNET, 'The Welfare of the Child Re-Visited: In Whose Best Interests? Part 1' [2009] *Family Law* 50; B. FEHLBERG, B. SMYTHE with M. MACLEAN and C. ROBERTS, *Caring for Children after Parental Separation: Would Legislation for Shared Parenting Time Help Children?* Oxford Centre for Family Law and Policy, Oxford 2011; S. GILMORE, 'Disputing contact: challenging some assumptions' [2008] 20 *CFLQ* (*Child and Family Law Quarterly*) 285; F. KAGANAS, 'Contact, conflict and risk' in S. DAY SCLATER and C. PIPER (eds.), *Undercurrents of Divorce*, Ashgate, Aldershot 1999; H. RHOADES, 'Revising Australia's parenting laws: a plea for a relational approach to children's best interests' [2010] 22 *CFLQ* 172.

58   See, for example, J. WALLBANK, '(En)gendering the fusion of rights and responsibilities in the law of contact' in J. WALLBANK, S. CHOUDHRY and J. HERRING (eds.), *Rights, Gender and Family Law*, Routledge, Abingdon 2009.

family.[59] Orders can include various constraining requirements including geographical 'exclusions' and 'non-association' with peers. Originally the government had been unwilling to use ASBOs with children and young people but first reduced the minimum age to 12 and then 10 years of age.[60] Such orders became immediately popular with police and magistrates and the Anti-Social Behaviour Act 2003 incorporated the proposals in *Respect and Responsibility*[61] by widening the scope and use of ASBOs.[62] As a result, by the end of 2004, 52 per cent of orders had been given to 10–17 year olds and research on breaches of prohibitions in the order found that over half of those in their sample group – 46 per cent of whom were under 18 – breached their order, and a third did so on two or more occasions.[63] A breach is dealt with by the criminal courts and, because breaches provided the sentencing courts with such a growing body of work, advice was issued on how to sentence young offenders for breach.[64]

The above development is evidence that after the passage of an Act a provision can alter in character, a development also made clear by Cretney's research on the 1925 Act. In the case of section 1 of that Act the result was, arguably, more protection for children when their lives are before a court. Regrettably, the Legal Aid, Sentencing and Punishment of Offenders Bill 2011 – justified in relation to the restriction on the availability of family legal aid as improving the lives of children[65] – will probably do the opposite. With the near impossibility for most people to access the courts in inter-parental disputes, section 1 of the Children Act 1989 – the welfare principle which was the result of the negotiation for the 1925 Act – will have no scope. That would be a great pity – for the children but also for the mothers who fought so hard for legal recognition of their parenting.

---

59   Crime and Disorder Act (CDA) 1998, ss. 1(1)(a) and 12(3)(c).

60   See E. Burney, *Making People Behave: Anti-social Behaviour, Politics and Policy*, Willan, Cullompton 2005, pp. 97–8.

61   Home Office, *Respect and Responsibility – Taking a Stand against Anti-social Behaviour*, Cm 5778, TSO, London 2003.

62   Sections 85–86 of the Act increased the range of the 'relevant authorities' who can apply for an ASBO to include county councils and Housing Action Trusts as well as the local authority with housing responsibility, the police and registered social landlords.

63   Home Office, *Tackling Anti-Social Behaviour*, National Audit Office 'Value for Money' Report by the Comptroller and Auditor General, HC 99 2006–7, 2006, paras. 5b and 5h of the Executive Summary.

64   Sentencing Advisory Panel, *Consultation Paper on Breach of an Anti-Social Behaviour Order*, SAP, London 2007, para. 78 et seq.

65   Ministry of Justice, *Proposals for the Reform of Legal Aid in England and Wales*, Cm 7967, TSO, London 2010; see also Family Justice Review, *Interim Report* and also *Final Report*, Ministry of Justice, London 2011.

THE ILLEGITIMACY SAGA

Andrew Bainham

Contents

1.   INTRODUCTION

'... Charles II, King of England, enjoys a certain notoriety as the father of a number of illegitimate children; yet it would be absurd to describe him, in defiance of the facts, as "unmarried".'[1]

Stephen Cretney, unlike successive generations of family law students, has never been a devotee of the expression 'unmarried father'. His memorable remark is not merely a question of the correct use of language. Lying behind it is another important truth; the laws of many jurisdictions, including English law, have indeed distinguished between these two different 'species' of fathers, by penalising their offspring to a greater or lesser extent. The 'adulterine bastard', or product of an affair between a father not married to the mother but where he or she was married to someone else, was historically treated less favourably than the child born outside marriage but without this 'aggravating factor'.[2] Some jurisdictions have so resolutely put up barriers to the discovery of extra-marital paternity that only the European Court of Human Rights has forced them to

---

[1]   S. CRETNEY, *Elements of Family Law*, 3rd ed., Sweet and Maxwell, London 1997, p. 176.

[2]   For Cretney's own historical treatment of legitimacy and illegitimacy see S. CRETNEY, *Family Law in the Twentieth Century: A History*, Oxford University Press, Oxford 2003, ch. 15.

reform their repressive legislation.[3] Leaving aside these questions of support for the institution of marriage and the distinction between married and unmarried men, we have also been fond in England of effectively creating sub-divisions within the latter category of 'meritorious' and 'unmeritorious' unmarried fathers.[4]

How the law should react to the now extremely widespread phenomenon of children being fathered by men not married to the mothers concerned,[5] has in Britain always been inextricably linked to the debate about the legal status of legitimacy and illegitimacy. It greatly exercised the English and Scottish Law Commissions in the late 1970s and early 1980s.[6] It is the principal reason why in English law, unlike the law in many other jurisdictions, we still have the legal status of *legitimacy*;[7] though we try as hard as we can to pretend that we have successfully abolished the altogether less desirable notion of *illegitimacy*.[8]

In this short tribute to Stephen Cretney, I will revisit briefly the work of the English Law Commission on illegitimacy, its immediate aftermath and its longer-term legacy. I will suggest that Cretney and his fellow commissioners got it right in 1979. First thoughts are often the best and this is a case in point.

The central concern has always been the position of the child. Yet, as is inevitably the case in all situations involving a child, adult interests and rights are never far below the surface. How those interests can be theoretically and practically disentangled from the child's is one of the most profound questions running through family law. How indeed could a question like illegitimacy, ostensibly about the status of the child, be sensibly detached from the adult claims which might be pressed on behalf of either the father or the mother?

The answer ultimately given by both the English and Scottish Commissions (though not formulated in precisely the same way) and subsequently enshrined in legislation, was that we simply had to distinguish between fathers while removing the remaining legal discrimination affecting children. This was not an

---

3   *Shofman v. Russia* [2006] 1 FLR 680; *Mizzi v. Malta* [2006] 1 FLR 1048.

4   A general solution addressed by the Law Commission in its *First Report on Illegitimacy*, Law Com. No. 118, HMSO, London 1982, where the possibility of defining categories of both meritorious and unmeritorious fathers was mooted but rejected at para 4.29 et seq.

5   The latest available figures record that in England and Wales in 2010, 46.8% of live births took place outside marriage or civil partnership, as compared with 46.2% in 2009 and 39.5% in 2000: Office for National Statistics, *Statistical Bulletin*, 13.07.2011.

6   Law Commission, above n. 4, and *Illegitimacy (Second Report)*, Law Com. No. 157, HMSO, London 1986; Scottish Law Commission, *Illegitimacy*, Scot. Law Com. No. 82, HMSO, Edinburgh 1984.

7   The concept was abolished in the Australian states, for example, as long ago as the 1970s when they passed their Equality of Status legislation.

8   See generally A. Bainham, 'Is legitimacy legitimate?' [2009] 39 *Family Law* 673.

approach which met with universal acclaim. It was pointed out that the relationship between a parent and a child could be seen as a mutual one. Any attempt, therefore, to discriminate between parents must by definition involve discrimination against the children.[9] This presupposes perhaps that it is the genetic connection which makes one a 'parent' and a modern take on this question is that just because one is a 'father', this does not make one a 'parent'.

Is there then a case for continued discrimination between fathers? I will briefly examine this question by focusing on some of the problems such an approach may create, first in the private law and then in the public law. But first it is necessary to return to 1979 and the English Law Commission's first foray into this territory.

2. THE 1979 WORKING PAPER

In his seminal treatment of the history of legitimacy and illegitimacy,[10] Cretney identifies three strands of reform – the gradual acceptance of the process of legitimation by subsequent marriage of the child's parents, mitigating and eventually removing the legal disadvantages of illegitimacy and the more radical removal of the very status of illegitimacy.[11]

When the Law Commission embarked on its work at the end of the 1970s, legitimation had been part of English law for over fifty years though available to the children of adultery for only twenty.[12] Many of the legal disadvantages suffered by the illegitimate had been incrementally removed, though some remained.[13] In its Working Paper published in 1979[14] the Commission identified a field of choice with three possible paths:

(a) that continued discrimination against the illegitimate child was justified and should be preserved;

---

9   I set out my own perspective at the time in A. BAINHAM, 'When is a parent not a parent? Reflections on the unmarried father and his child in English law' (1987) 3 *International Journal of Law and the Family* 208.

10   CRETNEY, above n. 2.

11   As noted by the Law Commission the legally recognised status is in fact *legitimacy* and not illegitimacy but the one flows from the other. The author has suggested that largely for this reason the concentration in the last phase of reform should be on legitimacy and the legislation which still enshrines that concept: BAINHAM, above n. 8.

12   Legitimacy Acts 1926 and 1959.

13   In particular there remained differences in relation to succession rights and procedures for obtaining maintenance orders which, in the case of the illegitimate, still involved recourse to the unsatisfactory affiliation proceedings.

14   LAW COMMISSION, *Illegitimacy* Law Com. WP No. 74, HMSO, London 1979. For a contemporaneous critique see M. HAYES, 'Law Commission Working Paper No. 74: Illegitimacy' (1980) 43 *MLR (Modern Law Review)* 299.

(b) that such discrimination was not justified and that the existing legal disadvantages so far as the child was concerned should be removed; and

(c) that reform should not merely remove the legal disadvantages attaching to illegitimacy, but should abolish that status altogether.

The Commission was quick to reject the first of these models on the basis that the child's status ought not to be affected by the nature of the relationship between his parents. The status quo having been rejected, the better choice between the other two models – removing the disadvantages of illegitimacy or removing the status altogether – was far from obvious to the Commission. The latter would go 'beyond the mere assimilation of the legal positions of children born in and out of wedlock, since that solution…would still preserve the caste labels which help artificially to preserve the social stigma now attached to illegitimacy'.[15]

The position of the father was seen as the key difficulty in 1979[16] and it has remained so ever since. The issue was whether, given the very wide range of factual relationships between the father and the mother and child, the father should gain legal authority in relation to the child only by court order or automatically by virtue of paternity. The Commission considered the extreme example of the rapist and the much more common situation of the casual encounter as incidences in which it could be inappropriate for the father to be vested with legal authority without court intervention. It speculated on the distress and inconvenience which might be caused to lone mothers on whom the onus would fall to take the matter to court if they wished to prevent undesirable interferences by the father. It looked at, but rejected, the New Zealand model under which the mother was sole guardian unless the parties were 'living together' at the date of the child's birth. In general, the Commission thought that consultation was necessary on the question whether the law should attempt to provide for classes of fathers who were effectively deemed 'meritorious' or 'unmeritorious' in terms of automatic status.

Notwithstanding these concerns, the Commission's tentative recommendation was to opt for the radical model. This would have abolished the status of legitimacy and with it illegitimacy; 'for the one cannot exist without the other'.[17] Its view was that this 'would help to improve the position of children born out of wedlock in a way in which the mere removal of remaining legal disabilities attaching to illegitimacy would not.'[18] This was because the illegitimate child

---

[15] Ibid., para. 3.14.

[16] Ibid., para. 3.9 et seq.

[17] Ibid., para. 3.14.

[18] Ibid., para. 3.15. The Commission was also influenced by international obligations and in particular the ECHR and the then comparatively recent decision in *Marck v. Belgium*

suffered a special disadvantage which was not true of the child of a widow or divorcee:

> 'We believe that the law can help to lessen social prejudices by setting an example clearly based upon the principle that the parents' marital relationship is irrelevant to the child's legal position...Mere tinkering with the law would disguise the fact that a new principle has been established.'[19]

Such a change in the law would however also remove the remaining distinction between mothers and fathers and both would have legal rights and duties[20] unless and until a court otherwise ordered. The Commission's tentative view was that the benefits of removal of discrimination from the law outweighed any possible risks posed by giving automatic rights and duties to the father. It did not think either that the question of the father's role in the child's life was one which should be exclusively determined by the mother and concluded that the final decision ought to rest with the courts. Finally, it identified another important advantage which would flow from abolition – simplification of the law and disappearance of many of the complications which had historically bedevilled legal development in this field.[21]

3. THE COMMISSION'S TWO REPORTS AND THE FAMILY LAW REFORM ACT 1987

The Law Commission's consultation process produced widespread agreement that the remaining legal disadvantages affecting the illegitimate should be removed, but no consensus on the question of parental authority for fathers. Indeed, it was evident that even within relevant organisations[22] there were significant divisions of opinion. Accordingly the Commission's conclusion was that there was no consensus supporting the more radical proposal it had tentatively put forward in its Working Paper. It instead opted in its 1982 Report[23] for the more moderate alternative.

These recommendations were substantially enacted in the Family Law Reform Act 1987. The two principal remaining legal disadvantages were removed. First, regarding financial support, affiliation proceedings were abolished. Second, the

---

(1979–1980) 2 EHRR 330 and the European Convention on the Legal Status of Children born out of Wedlock.

19   Ibid., para. 3.15.
20   Now 'parental responsibility'.
21   LAW COMMISSION, above n. 14, para. 3.19.
22   The most prominent of which was the National Council for One Parent Families, formerly the National Council for the Unmarried Mother and Her Child.
23   LAW COMMISSION, above n. 4, paras 4.44–4.51.

rights of the child born outside wedlock to succeed on intestacy were extended beyond parents to the estates of wider relatives. Perhaps most importantly, section 1 of the Act embodied a new rule of construction for future legislation whereby references:

'to any relationship between two persons shall, unless the contrary intention appears, be construed without regard to whether or not the father and mother of either of them, or the father and mother of any person through whom the relationship is deduced, have or had been married to each other at any time.'

One could be forgiven, on a cursory reading of this provision, for concluding that it signalled the abolition of legitimacy and illegitimacy as concepts known to the law. Yet Cretney was one of the first to point out that this would be a premature conclusion. First, the principle governed only future legislation, leaving intact some existing legislation which relied on the concepts. Second, there remained the key distinction between fathers in relation to parental authority. In the first edition of *Elements of Family Law*, published in 1987, he summarised the position as follows:

'The result is that distinctions between children based solely on their parents' marital status remain … and to that extent children are still divided into two categories: those with a "normal" relationship with both parents, and others.'[24]

So what is the answer? Did we and do we (because nothing much has changed since) have legitimacy and illegitimacy after 1987 or not? Cretney's own answer in 1987 was a guarded one:

'Although the Family Law Reform Act removes most of the legal disadvantages of illegitimacy so far as they discriminate against the illegitimate child, it cannot be said that in all respects the question of the parents' marital status has become irrelevant. *It is an interesting question whether, in the result, the concepts of "legitimacy, and illegitimacy" have been abolished.*'[25]

The Scottish Law Commission, which itself reported on illegitimacy in Scots law,[26] took up this question and saw the issue as perhaps turning on the *extent* of any remaining legal differences. When the differently constituted English Law Commission (in particular Cretney's place on the Commission was occupied by Brenda Hoggett, now Lady Hale) produced a second report on illegitimacy in 1986,[27] it did so largely to take into account and to some extent adopt the Scottish approach. Specifically on this question of the survival or not of legitimacy/illegitimacy, the English Commission had this to say:

---

24   CRETNEY, above n. 1, para. 19–14.
25   CRETNEY, above n. 1, para. 19–22 (emphasis added).
26   SCOTTISH LAW COMMISSION, above n. 6, para. 9.2.
27   LAW COMMISSION, above n. 6.

'Should our reports be implemented, as the Scottish Law Commission have observed, "it would be a matter for argument whether it was any longer justifiable to refer to a legal status of illegitimacy...Whether minor differences in the rules applying to different classes of persons justify the ascription of a distinct status is a matter for commentators rather than legislators". In any event, the important differences will not be between the children at all, but between the parents.'

It is worth revisiting briefly the reasons given by those opposed to abolishing the existing distinction between fathers.[28] The heart of the matter was the risk to single mothers as perceived by influential groups such as the National Council for One Parent Families. First, there was concern that if fathers were given automatic 'parental rights' this might lead to a significant increase in the numbers of anxious mothers who would conceal the identities of the fathers to avoid this. Second, there was concern that distress and disturbance might be caused to those mothers who had subsequently married a man who was now in *loco parentis* to the child.[29] Third, it was felt that automatic rights might tempt fathers to harass or blackmail mothers at a time when they might feel exceptionally vulnerable to pressure. Fourth, it was said that it was generally the experience of countries which had abolished discrimination against those born out of wedlock that they had not generally conferred automatic rights on fathers.[30] Finally, it was suggested that practical difficulties might arise where the child was in the voluntary care of the local authority since fathers with parental rights would have a legal right to remove those children.[31]

In the light of these objections, the Commission considered whether it might be possible to define a class of 'unmeritorious' fathers from whom parental rights could be withheld[32] or the alternative of defining a class of 'meritorious' fathers who *could* be awarded such rights.[33] Its conclusion was that neither could be satisfactorily done though two of the mechanisms rejected by the Commission

---

[28]   Law Commission, above n. 4, paras. 4.26–4.27.

[29]   Ibid., para. 4.26.

[30]   Though it is not clear why evidence from those that *had*, particularly Australia and some of the countries of Eastern Europe, was not considered. In Australia any man who can prove he is the father automatically has the equivalent of parental responsibility and there appears to be no evidence that this regime has caused difficulties in practice.

[31]   Law Commission, above n. 4, para. 4.26. This however is a problematic issue as discussed below.

[32]   Ibid., paras. 4.29–4.30.

[33]   Ibid., paras. 4.31–4.42. The Commission also mooted, but quickly rejected, the argument that the rights of all parents, whether married or not, might be restricted in certain circumstances. See para. 4.41. The notion of 'licensing' parents is not new and a modern version of the argument for weeding out or screening potentially harmful or inadequate parents at the time of birth is made most recently in J.G. Dwyer, *The Relationship Rights of Children*, Cambridge University Press, Cambridge, 2006. Any such approach in Europe would be a very clear violation of the ECHR.

in 1982 as capable of identifying meritorious fathers, parental agreements and joint birth registration, have subsequently found favour with the legislature.

A final important aspect of the 1987 reforms relates to terminology. It was strongly felt that even if legal differences remained between fathers the stigmatising terminology of illegitimacy, with its connotations of illegality, should be removed from children. The English Commission's approach to this question was to replace 'illegitimate' with the more morally neutral 'non-marital' and, hence, 'legitimate' with 'marital'.[34] The Scots had however gone for a different approach which avoided applying *any* labelling of the *child* because they saw a risk that new labels would rapidly take on old connotations. This alternative commended itself to the English Commission and, accordingly, legislation now distinguishes, where it is thought to be necessary, between *parents* and not between children.

4. THE POST-1987 ERA

The 1987 settlement is still essentially the law. Such developments as have occurred since have, perhaps unsurprisingly, continued to relate to the father's position and have taken place against a demographic background in which the numbers of children born outside marriage as a proportion of total births have soared.[35]

Within two years of the 1987 reform, the principle of automatic 'parental responsibility' for the father by agreement with the mother had been enacted in the Children Act 1989. That Act also modified the terminology in relation to court orders which, reflecting the new emphasis on responsibility as opposed to rights, were now to be known as 'parental responsibility orders'.[36] Why were agreements, so recently rejected by the Commission, now accepted? In 1985 the Commission had produced a working paper on Guardianship.[37] In this it had expressed the view that judicial proceedings might be unduly elaborate, expensive and unnecessary where a mother did not object to a father obtaining responsibility. The suggestion mooted in that paper was that the mother might in those circumstances be permitted to appoint the father *inter vivos* guardian.[38] There was a consensus among relevant organisations that this was desirable. When the Commission produced its final report on Guardianship and Custody

---

34   Ibid., para. 4.51.
35   OFFICE FOR NATIONAL STATISTICS, above n. 5.
36   See now Children Act 1989, s. 4(1)(c), as amended.
37   LAW COMMISSION, *Guardianship* Law Com. WP No. 91, HMSO, London 1985.
38   The concept of *inter vivos* guardianship was mooted generally in Part IV and specifically in relation to 'natural father' at paras 4.20–4.24: ibid.

in 1988,[39] it therefore recommended that parental responsibility might be shared by an agreement between the mother and father. This would need to be attended by appropriate formalities involving registration in the County Court, but would not entail judicial scrutiny or a court order.[40]

It was a logical progression from the introduction of parental responsibility agreements that in 2002 the trigger for acquisition of parental responsibility by fathers should become the registration of the father as such in the child's birth certificate.[41] The common denominator is the voluntary co-operation of the mother which is certainly required for agreements to share parental responsibility and which, until perhaps recently, has been thought to be a central feature also of the process of joint birth registration.[42] A critical difference between these two reforms was however that, whereas parental responsibility agreements had always been unpopular and of little statistical significance, once parental responsibility was tied to birth registration there was a revolution in the numbers of fathers thereby acquiring it. It is now very much the norm for births outside marriage to be jointly registered and the percentage of unmarried fathers not registered is relatively small and declining.[43]

Indeed, it is official government policy that the number of joint birth registrations outside marriage should be increased or, put another way, that sole birth registration by mothers should be discouraged.[44] This policy is now promoted in section 56 and schedule 6 of the Welfare Reform Act 2009. Space here does not permit a close analysis of these provisions, yet to be brought into force, but some of the central features are worthy of comment in the context of the history set out above. First, it can be said that the for the first time there is an official legislative policy that it is generally desirable for births outside marriage to be jointly registered and for the child to have a relationship with both parents unless

---

[39] Law Commission, *Review of Child Law: Guardianship and Custody* Law Com. No. 172, HMSO, London 1988.

[40] Previously, I erroneously stated (Bainham, above n. 8, 675) that the 1987 Act had introduced both parental rights orders and parental rights agreements. As stated above, while orders were introduced in 1987, agreements were not introduced until 1989 and not effective until implementation of the Children Act in 1991. I am pleased to have this opportunity of correcting the error.

[41] Children Act 1989, s. 4(1)(a) as amended by the Adoption and Children Act 2002 and brought into force on 01.12.2003.

[42] See further A. Bainham, 'What is the point of birth registration? [2008] 20 *Child and Family Law Quarterly* 449.

[43] In 1971 45.5% of births outside marriage in England and Wales were joint registrations. By 2009 this had dramatically increased to 86.6% and nearly two-thirds of those joint registrations (65.7%) were by parents living at the same address: *Social Trends 41*, Office for National Statistics, Newport 2011.

[44] DWP and DCSF, *Joint birth registration: recording responsibility*, Cm 7293, TSO, London 2008.

there is a good reason why not. Second, although there are exceptions to the principle, it is accepted that there should be an *obligation* on the mother to co-operate in this joint registration. For the first time, provision is made for the father to initiate a re-registration with himself registered as the father, but importantly still subject to the mother's co-operation.[45] This is a significant departure for English law which, unlike civil law systems, has never made provision for voluntary recognition or acknowledgment of paternity by men. Third, the exemptions which may be invoked where a mother wishes to resist the statutory obligation of joint registration are redolent of the concerns about the single mother's position which have so dominated debate and reform for over thirty years.[46]

5.   THE CURRENT LAW

It might be thought that by 1987 we had reached a largely satisfactory position. There would henceforth be little need to mention legitimacy or illegitimacy,[47] virtually all the remaining disadvantages between those born inside and outside marriage had been swept away and those that were left were of marginal importance.[48] It might also be felt that the 2002 reform has really taken the sting out of the remaining differentiation of fathers because statistically the norm is now for unmarried fathers to be registered and thereby to acquire parental responsibility, leaving only a rump of the undesirable or unworthy who lack parental responsibility.

I want to suggest that the law is in a rather less satisfactory state than might appear at first blush, and that it does in fact create a number of practical problems. I will look first at some issues affecting fathers and then conclude with some observations on the continuation of the concepts of legitimacy and illegitimacy.

---

[45]   Births and Deaths Registration Act 1953, s. 10B as amended.

[46]   DWP and DCSF, above n. 44, para. 26.

[47]   Though in fact we do and this policy has failed. I have drawn attention to this in two other places: A. BAINHAM, 'Changing families and changing concepts: reforming the language of family law' [1998] 10 *Child and Family Law Quarterly* 1 and above n. 8.

[48]   Distinctions in relation to citizenship could be practically important but have subsequently been swept away by the Nationality, Immigration and Asylum Act 2002, implemented on 01.07.2006. Distinctions remain in relation to the acquisition of titles of honour which can hardly be said greatly to affect the lives of ordinary people.

5.1. FATHERS IN PRIVATE LAW

Where births are not jointly registered and fathers are not named, it is most unlikely that they and the respective mothers will enter into parental responsibility agreements. For those fathers wishing to be involved and to acquire parental responsibility, this means parental responsibility orders. These involve the expense and inconvenience of court proceedings, yet the jurisprudence governing these has developed in such a way that only a small minority of such orders are refused.[49] Essentially the courts have determined, applying a three-fold test of commitment, attachment and motivation,[50] that only in fairly extreme cases will the order be declined.[51] It is therefore surely questionable whether it is a good use of public money to spend it on applications, the vast majority of which are likely to be granted. It would make more sense for the onus to be on mothers to apply to terminate the parental responsibility of men who are in the small minority of those who are likely to be refused parental responsibility under the current law.

Why do some mothers refuse to register births jointly and why do they continue to object to the father being awarded parental responsibility? The traditional reasoning has been that they do so out of fear of violence or interference from those fathers. My own recent experience of representing both mothers and fathers on such applications[52] is that this is usually *not* the reason for the objection.

I suggest that the real reason in many of these cases is psychological. It relates not to the fear of ongoing violence and interference but to the *past relationship* between the parents which may well have involved some domestic violence. The objection by the mother in these cases is not about future fears. It is about her aversion to agreeing to a father being given parental responsibility when she does not regard him as having been responsible and therefore having earned it. Where a court makes a parental responsibility order in such circumstances it does so because, however much advice is given to her about the law, the mother simply cannot bring herself to agree to the father having parental responsibility. The court's role is then to take the weight of the decision from her and take it itself. We see a similar phenomenon in the entirely different context of parents who

---

49   In 2007, for example, 7,570 parental responsibility orders were made and only 149 were refused: *Judicial and Court Statistics 2007*, Ministry of Justice, London, table 5.4.

50   The leading authorities being *Re H (Minors) (Local Authority: Parental Responsibility) (No.3)* [1991] 1 FLR 214 and *Re S (A Minor) (Parental Responsibility)* [1995] 2 FLR 648.

51   Such as deliberate injury of the child with an element of sadism (*Re H (Parental Responsibility)* [1998] 1 FLR 855) or violence and abuse towards the mother (*Re T (A Minor) (Parental Responsibility: Contact)* [1993] 2 FLR 450).

52   Such applications are usually accompanied by applications for contact by the father.

cannot bring themselves to withdraw medical treatment from children and where the court instead takes on this responsibility.[53] The point is that this could be achieved much more easily and less expensively by conferring parental responsibility automatically where paternity is established and by restricting the cases before the court to applications by mothers who are *still* in genuine fear of violence by placing the onus on those mothers to bring the application.

Tying parental responsibility to birth registration, but not making this retrospective, has created a new form of discrimination against children; between those born before and those born after 1 December 2003. The same father may have parental responsibility for the latter but not for the former; despite the fact that his relationship with the elder child may be stronger because he will have known him for longer before the parties separated. Can the mother legitimately claim that parental responsibility should be withheld when it is effectively automatic in the case of the younger child? Such cases are a waste of public money.

5.2 FATHERS IN PUBLIC LAW CASES

The difficulties caused in the public law are arguably more serious. The unregistered father without parental responsibility will not automatically be a party to care proceedings[54] though, if he is contactable and shows an interest in being involved, he should be served with notice of the proceedings[55] and it would normally be expected that he would be joined as a party.[56] Where the mother enters into a section 20 agreement with the authority, the father's agreement is not also required and he has no legal right to terminate the arrangement.[57]

The effect of the law is to marginalise non-marital fathers in care proceedings. Should we be bothered about this? On one view this is a desirable situation. If the background is one of violence or a casual encounter, in which there has been little interest or commitment shown by the father, the child is better off without him.

---

[53]   As perhaps in *Re A (Conjoined Twins: Medical Treatment)* [2000] 4 All ER 961 and most recently in *Re RB* [2009] EWHC 3269 where the father heard harrowing medical evidence during the hearing which caused him to come around to the view that it would be better to allow his son to die than to continue his efforts to keep him alive.

[54]   FPR 2010, r. 12.3(1).

[55]   FPR 2010, PD 12C, para. 3.1.

[56]   *Re B (Care Proceedings: Notification of Father without Parental Responsibility)* [1999] 2 FLR 408. However, in *Re P (Care Proceedings: Father's Application to be Joined as a Party)* [2001] 1 FLR 781 leave to be joined was refused on account of delay.

[57]   Children Act 1989, s. 20(7) and (8).

There are a number of criticisms which can be made of this stance. First, a policy of marginalising fathers in care proceedings clashes with official policy, latterly expressed in the Welfare Reform Act 2009, of encouraging the joint registration of births in as many cases as possible. I have had personal experience of local authorities actively *discouraging* joint registration by the mother and father because the view has been taken that in the best interests of a baby the mother should be assisted to break clear of any involvement with the father.[58] Indeed it is routine, in my experience, where there has been a background of domestic violence in care proceedings, for a parent to sign an agreement not to have contact with the 'problem' parent or bring the child into contact with him/her. The mother may therefore be in breach of such an agreement[59] if she arranges to meet the father to register the birth! Second, and related to this, while in the private law we are busy encouraging as much sharing of responsibility by parents as possible[60], in the public law the objective is very often to break people up. Past domestic violence is often seen as the trigger for this. Third, and perhaps most importantly, the marginalisation of fathers can deny to the child a full exploration of the resources of the *wider paternal family*. The law requires that every opportunity be explored for keeping in children in the birth family.[61] Effectively, this means that viability assessments and, if positive, full kinship assessments should be carried out on those members of the wider family who have come forward or been suggested by the parents and are willing to be considered as potential alternative carers.

Of course it is much easier for the state to write off a violent father and so much less expensive to do so; cheaper again to steam ahead for adoption.[62] But whether this is more in the interests of the child than a painstaking assessment of the causes of the father's behaviour or whether anything can be done by way of treatment, together with an exploration of the paternal family's position, may be doubted.

5.3 LEGITIMACY AND ILLEGITIMACY

Does it matter that we have preserved the concepts of legitimacy and illegitimacy by not repealing those pre-1987 statutes which rely on them? In my view it does.

---

[58] Though local authorities are not always very good at assisting mothers to break clear of violent men despite their insistence that they do so. See *EH v. Greenwich LBC* [2010] EWCA Civ 344.

[59] A serious matter likely to result in the authority restoring the matter to court and seeking an interim care order forthwith.

[60] Most notably reflected in the growth and popularity of shared residence orders.

[61] See particularly Children Act 1989, s. 22C as amended by the Children and Young Persons Act 2008. It is also a central human rights requirement under the ECHR.

[62] As to which see the recommendations for quicker and greater use of adoption in the *The Narey Report on Adoption* (July, 2011), covered extensively in *The Times*, 05.07.2011.

One reason is the degree of confusion which still exists about whether the concepts survive or not. Lord Justice Thorpe, one of our most senior family judges, took the view that they do not when he said ten years ago: 'Illegitimacy with its stigma has been legislated away'.[63] Is it not an indictment of the law in itself that senior judges and senior academics can disagree on whether we have legitimacy and illegitimacy or not? But it gets worse. As I have pointed out elsewhere, when Parliament took the decision to extend the possibility of legal parentage to same-sex partners who are not biological parents, first by adoption[64] and subsequently by assisted reproduction,[65] it found it necessary to transport into this unlikely context the concept of legitimacy and, by implication, illegitimacy; so much for the policy of eradicating the concept from post-1987 legislation. We should perhaps remind ourselves that one of the objectives for the law which the Law Commission identified in its 1979 Working Paper was simplification. Instead we have arrived at a situation in which it is now possible to be the legitimate child of a 'civil partner second female parent' or the illegitimate one of the 'non-civil partner second female parent'.

All of this could have been avoided if we had listened to the good sense of the Law Commission over thirty years ago in its Working Paper. When the Commission itself retreated from its tentative proposals it did so for good reason. The purpose of the Commission's consultation process was to establish whether there was a broad consensus for reform. While there clearly was in relation to removal of the disadvantages of illegitimacy, 'there was a profound division of opinion amongst both legal and non-legal commentators on the parental rights question'.[66] The Commission also rejected, in my view rightly, the notion that illegitimacy could be abolished while 'preserving the existing rules whereby parental rights vest automatically only in married parents.'[67]

Any list of Stephen Cretney's incomparable contributions to Family Law would be a very long one. The 1979 Working Paper, in which he had a major involvement, should figure prominently.

---

63   *Bellinger v. Bellinger* [2001] 2 FLR 1048.
64   Adoption and Children Act 2002, s. 67(2).
65   Legitimacy Act 1976, s. 2A as amended by Human Fertilisation and Embryology Act 2008, Sched. 6, para. 16.
66   LAW COMMISSION, above n. 4, para. 4.49.
67   Ibid., para. 4.44.

MARITAL AGREEMENTS: 'THE MORE RADICAL SOLUTION'

Joanna MILES

Marital agreements are a 'hot topic' in contemporary English family law, having only recently (largely) emerged from shadows cast by various public policy concerns following the Privy Council's decision on post-nuptial agreements in *MacLeod v. MacLeod*[1] and the Supreme Court's judgment on pre-nuptial agreements in *Radmacher v. Granatino*.[2] They are currently being examined by the Law Commission for England and Wales in its project on marital property agreements of all sorts (pre- and post-nuptial and on separation).[3] Now only the *Hyman*[4] principle stands in the way of marital agreements being binding in the ordinary way,[5] leaving both spouses free to invoke the jurisdiction of the matrimonial court in pursuit of some financial resolution different from that agreed.

The relative novelty of pre-nuptial agreements (specifically) as a topic worthy of English family lawyers' attention is demonstrated by its absence from Stephen Cretney's *Principles of Family Law* until its seventh edition in 2002. Until then, successive editions variously devoted parts of chapters or freestanding chapters to maintenance agreements under sections 34–35 of the Matrimonial Causes Act 1973,[6] separation agreements and the *Edgar* case,[7] and consent orders; post-

---

[1]   [2008] UKPC 64.

[2]   [2010] UKSC 42.

[3]   Marital Property Agreements, Law Com CP 198, TSO, London, 2011.

[4]   *Hyman v. Hyman* [1929] AC 601.

[5]   The Supreme Court in *Radmacher v. Granatino* [2010] UKSC 42 was not called on to decide whether pre-nuptial agreements could now be regarded as contractually binding, but various passages in the majority judgment appear to assume that that is the case and Lady Hale and Lord Mance both clearly considered that that was being decided, albeit only obiter. For further discussion, see J. MILES, 'Marriage and Divorce in the Supreme Court and the Law Commission: for Love or Money?' (2011) 74 *Modern Law Review* 430, 439.

[6]   Compare the observation of Wilson LJ (as he then was) in *Radmacher v. Granatino* [2009] EWCA Civ 649 (CA) that section 35 was regarded as something of a dead letter (at [134]): it was nevertheless deemed worthy of full attention in all editions of *Principles*, so the family law profession had at least constructive notice of its existence, even if it had not invoked it for some decades.

[7]   [1980] 1 WLR 1410.

nuptial agreements received only passing mention, and pre-nups none at all.[8] The *Principles'* evolving treatment of marital agreements aside, Cretney's principal writing on marital agreements spans a small corpus of work starting with his contribution to *Consensus ad Idem: Essays in the Law of Contract in Honour of Guenter Treitel*.[9] In concluding his chapter, 'From Status to Contract?', he wrote:

'... the more radical solution – that of allowing financial agreements between spouses to have precisely the same effect as other financial agreements – deserves serious examination. What, precisely, is the public interest in treating maintenance agreements differently from other agreements – perhaps agreements between men and women whose relationship is in substance (albeit not in legal form) indistinguishable from marriage? The public interest in preventing spouses from throwing the cost of maintaining their families [on the state] is now met (so far as it is possible to do so) by specific provisions in the social security legislation. Of course, there must be real concern that the judgmental capacity of parties involved in the trauma of relationship breakdown may have been adversely affected by their emotional and sexual relationship; but recognition of this requires no more than the application of the doctrines of misrepresentation and of undue influence as they have come to be developed. It is not easy to see why any further protection is needed; and it would seem that in this respect, at least, the movement from status to contract might with advantage be carried forward.'[10]

---

[8]   Cretney changed his views about the appropriate 'home' for discussion of marital agreements quite substantially over the course of those seven editions. The topic first appears in its entirety in a lengthy, all-embracing chapter on matrimonial property and financial obligations. It then acquired a chapter of its own on maintenance agreements (3rd ed.) / private ordering of financial matters (4th ed.) – later to be re-titled '*The Limits* of Private Ordering of Financial Matters' (5th ed.) – before becoming split between chapters dealing with the legal consequences of *marriage* (maintenance agreements and their variation under s 35 of the Matrimonial Causes Act 1973) and the financial consequences of *divorce* (consent orders and separation agreements). Only in the 7th edition (2002) were pre-nuptial agreements addressed (quite briefly), in relation to public policy restrictions on contracting in the family context (p. 133*ff*).

[9]   F. Rose (ed.), Sweet & Maxwell, London, 1996 (referred to as 'Consensus' below). The other works which I have read in preparing this chapter are: the casenote on *Xydhias v. Xydhias* – 'Contract not apt in Divorce Deal' (1999) 115 *Law Quarterly Review* 356 ('Xydhias' below); a conference paper delivered to the Annual Family Law Seminar at the University of Staffordshire in February 2003, '"Private Ordering or Not?" How far can we go: Private Ordering and Divorce', ('Stoke' below) later published in revised form in (2003) *Family Law* June edition ('2003 *Family Law*' below); 'The Family and The Law: Status or Contract? (2003) 15 *Child and Family Law Quarterly* 403, the first of his articles to touch on pre-nuptial agreements ('2003 *CFLQ*' below); and most recently his Foreword to S. Gilmore, J. Herring and R. Probert (eds.), *Landmark Cases in Family Law*, Hart, Oxford 2011, ('Foreword' below). The subject matter of this chapter is only footnoted in *Family Law in the Twentieth Century*, Oxford University Press, Oxford 2003, at p. 345, n.165, p. 774, n.210. Cretney also had insight into the process of attempts to settle financial disputes at the point of divorce through his empirical work: G. Davis, S. Cretney and J. Collins, *Simple Quarrels*, Clarendon Press, Oxford, 1994 ('*Simple Quarrels*' below).

[10] Consensus, above n. 9, 281.

Writing about pre-nuptial agreements in 2003, he inquired whether, in that context too, reliance on 'the ordinary principles of misrepresentation and undue influence' would provide 'sufficient protection to the vulnerable and ill-informed'.[11] He conceded that some additional 'special regime of protective formality' might be required. But no more.

He was clearly aware of the controversy of his position, remarking in characteristically amiable and under-stated manner, 'I sense the raising of some eyebrows'.[12] The reader revisiting this body of writing with current debates on the topic in mind will find Cretney's writing distinctive for its strong and early advocacy of autonomy and rejection of paternalism. Notably, perhaps given his tendency to focus on *separation* agreements (specifically), he makes no comment on concerns about the fairness of outcomes produced by other agreements, which may have been concluded many years earlier. This is an omission to which Lady Hale, for one, would take marked exception. But his writing on this topic is all the more important for its apparent dissonance with the 'orthodoxy' applied more or less unquestioningly by many family lawyers.

At the start of his 1996 chapter, he juxtaposed two quotations: H.J.S. Maine's familiar observation about the shift in the understanding of family relationships in 'progressive' societies from status to contract; and a responding dictum of Ormrod J that that evolution in relation to marriage 'is not yet by any means complete', noting in particular the 'extremely difficult' clash between common lawyers' contractual principles and the very different conceptual framework of family law which, in his view (in 1980), was still 'not yet detached... from its ancient roots in the quite different system of the canon law'. We see that tussle between different legal traditions playing out in the various judgments in the *Radmacher* litigation. In particular, Rix LJ in the Court of Appeal may be forgiven for his (commercial lawyer's) perplexity[13] when faced with an agreement said, by his family lawyer colleagues, to be void as a matter of contract law on grounds of public policy but nevertheless to be considered in the exercise of the matrimonial court's discretion, and potentially to attract dispositive weight. At the other end of the debate, Lady Hale's lone voice in the Supreme Court advocates a strongly paternalist (or 'maternalist') approach to marital agreements.

As I have noted elsewhere, the nature of the public policy objection to pre-nuptial agreements has evolved over time, shifting from moralist concerns to protect the institution of marriage from spouses and others who made agreements liable to destabilise an individual marriage to more benevolent, paternalist concerns to protect individual contracting spouses (or would-be spouses) from agreeing

---

[11]   2003 *CFLQ*, above n. 9, 414.
[12]   2003 *CFLQ*, above n. 9.
[13]   [2009] EWCA Civ 649, [64].

terms which, with the benefit of hindsight, might be judged imprudent.[14] As the Privy Council noted in *MacLeod*, the moralist objection has lost its legs, given the abolition of various matrimonial remedies (for example, for restitution of conjugal rights) and the introduction of no-fault divorce.[15] Protective concerns remain prominent in the case law, however. And yet, as Cretney has observed, why should wives (sic., the traditional subjects of concern) be treated akin to minors and the mentally incapacitated when negotiating the nature and extent of their husbands' financial obligations towards them?[16] Prior to 1935,[17] the law was at least consistent in *entirely* depriving wives of contractual competence (even though they had been entitled to hold property at law since the 1880s); that was the context in which the *Hyman*[18] doctrine was expounded.[19] Yet notwithstanding *Radmacher*, that doctrine still prevents spouses from ousting the jurisdiction of the matrimonial court by agreement at any point, long after wives acquired complete contractual capacity: a 'remarkable anomaly' in the world of contractual partnerships.[20]

In 2003, Cretney remarked that 'the paternalism implicit in our refusal to recognise what is widely accepted in continental Europe and the US seems to reflect a view of the relationship between the courts and the family almost as outdated as the rules seeking by legal means to uphold the stability of the family'.[21] His view that the courts should not interfere in spousal contracts on grounds unrecognised by the general law is perhaps partly founded on a belief that we should not over-estimate the power of law – through the courts – to influence relationship-behaviour. In his chapter on divorce reform in Freeman's collection, *Divorce: Where Next?*,[22] he gives a compelling account of his early encounters with family law in practice as an observer of pre- and post-1969 reform divorce courts: on his first visit, he observed the travesty of the law, in its wisdom, holding fast a couple whose marriage had patently broken down; on his second, the dignified dissolution of long-dead marriages of respectable couples who had long since gone their separate ways. Families ought perhaps, for the most part, be left to resolve their own disputes quietly without state interference.

---

14   J. MILES, '*Radmacher v. Granatino:* Upping the ante-nuptial agreement' (2009) 21 *Child and Family Law Quarterly Review* 513, 520.
15   *MacLeod v. MacLeod* [2008] UKPC 64, [39].
16   Xydhias, above n. 9, 359.
17   Law Reform (Married Women and Tortfeasors) Act 1935.
18   [1929] AC 601.
19   Xydhias, above n. 9, 359.
20   2003 *CFLQ*, above n. 9, 413.
21   2003 *CFLQ*, above n. 9, 414.
22   S. CRETNEY, 'Divorce Reform: Humbug and Hypocrisy or Smooth Transition?' in M. FREEMAN (ed.), *Divorce Reform: Where Next?* Aldershot, Dartmouth, 1996 ('Humbug' below).

Cretney is surely right to decry the law's attempts to adjudicate on the conduct of spouses in the manner of the old divorce courts (which were doubtless duped on many occasions by those wily enough to produce the required evidence without arousing any suspicion of collusion, condonation, or indeed fabrication). But we cannot similarly dismiss a role for the courts in ensuring fair allocation of financial resources at the end of a marriage, and nor would Cretney seek to do so. This is a task that requires no divorce-style 'moralising', though it has – in the absence of any clear guidance from Parliament – required judicial appraisal of what 'fairness' demands in this context.[23]

It is the courts' recent work in developing a body of law by which the fair division of assets may be determined that has prompted renewed interest in pre- and post-nuptial agreements in this jurisdiction. As Cretney had argued, the advent of the equal sharing principle was surely destined to be accompanied by the affirmation in *Radmacher* of couples' freedom to displace that principle.[24] After all, no community property jurisdiction deprives its subjects of the power to prefer some other regime, and it cannot be right to leave ex-spouses to the uncertainty of an *ex post hoc* judicial determination of whether theirs was indeed a full economic partnership (fitted for equal sharing) or in fact a looser pairing of economic individuals (for whom equal sharing is anathema) when they are perfectly clear and capable of articulating that for themselves.[25]

Equally, however, in the interests of maintaining family solidarity,[26] our European cousins do limit – even exclude – freedom to contract out of maintenance on divorce.[27] So too *Radmacher* preserves a core of need/compensation-based marital obligation with its concept of 'real need'.[28] This pan-European model would suggest, in answer to Cretney's 1996 inquiry, that there may be good reason to treat *maintenance* agreements differently from other

---

23   See principally *White v. White* [2001] 1 AC 596, *Miller v. Miller, McFarlane v. McFarlane* [2006] UKHL 24; and on 'fairness' where there is a marital agreement, see *Edgar v. Edgar* [1980] 1 WLR 1410 and *Radmacher v. Granatino* [2010] UKSC 42.

24   Though he perhaps went too far to suggest that English law had adopted a deferred community of property: see the criticism by E. COOKE, 'The Future for Ancillary Relief' in G. DOUGLAS and N. LOWE (eds.), *The Continuing Evolution of Family Law*, Jordan Publishing, Bristol, 2009. See also J.M. SCHERPE, this volume.

25   See Consensus, p. 281 and 2003 *CFLQ*, 414, both above n. 9; contrast passages in *Miller, McFarlane* [2006] UKHL 24, [153] and [170] suggesting that this might be left to *ex post hoc* judicial inquiry in ancillary relief proceedings. It should surely be open to parties to 'self-identify' as economically independent entities by executing an appropriate marital property agreement.

26   Not only for the sake of saving the Exchequer, the only legitimate public interest in limiting private autonomy that Cretney could identify: Consensus, p. 281; 2003 *CFLQ*, 413–4, both above n. 9.

27   See the encyclopaedic analysis in J. SCHERPE (ed.), *Marital Agreements and Private Autonomy in Comparative Perspective*, Hart Publishing, Oxford, 2012.

28   [2010] UKSC 42, [81]-[82].

types of agreements – but agreements designed to preclude a default system of property sharing should, prima facie, attract normal binding force.

The key questions are what role the courts should have in policing marital agreements: when should they have power to intervene and on what grounds? And whether the courts should invariably have to give their *imprimatur* to any agreement which parties wish to have binding legal force. These are questions which have acquired added meaning as a result of the vast increase in the conduct of family life outside marriage.[29] Why should spouses be subject to unusual legal interference in their private agreements when cohabitants, who face analogous practical problems and dangers on relationship breakdown, are entirely free of supervision?[30] Is it right that spouses can only be confident that their agreement is binding in law if it has been submitted for judicial approval as a consent order, a procedure not available to them until the point of divorce and so depriving them of the right to define the economic terms of their partnership and any future dissolution from the outset? Should we instead afford *prima facie* binding force to their agreements (whenever made), subject only to normal contractual arguments about misrepresentation, undue influence and so on? Any additional restrictions or protections, whether procedural or substantive,[31] require careful justification.

Of course, most would argue strongly – and the point has been made most eloquently by Lady Hale in *Radmacher*[32] – that additional substantive protection must be available to protect the vulnerable spouse's interests when the vicissitudes of life overtake whatever agreement the parties confidently (if perhaps naïvely) made twenty or more years earlier. But what form should that protection take? Here, the lessons from history – which Cretney has in all his writing so brilliantly delivered – speak clearly of the need to preserve some level of certainty. He describes the 'rude shock' administered by the Court of Appeal in 1952, when its decision in *Bennett v. Bennett*[33] deprived of any binding force agreements making ample provision for wives where the only consideration supplied was a promise (contra *Hyman*) not to invoke the matrimonial jurisdiction. The Maintenance Agreements Act 1957,[34] preserving *Hyman*, restored such agreements' legal force so that wives could sue on them. But the wide power also

---

29 Consensus, above n. 9, p. 281.
30 Of course, the proper answer to that might be not to afford spouses similar freedom, but to increase the mutual responsibilities of cohabitants.
31 As noted earlier, Cretney has not contributed to the debate about substantive safeguards on private ordering, confining his remarks to formality requirements, though his recent remark that 'genuine fairness' must be assured ('Foreword', above n. 9) may hint at substantive concerns.
32 [2010] UKSC 42, [175].
33 [1952] 1 KB 249.
34 See now, with some modification of the original Act, MCA 1973, ss. 34–35.

conferred by that Act on the courts to vary those agreements wherever there has been a relevant change of circumstance means that 'parties are denied precisely the satisfaction of knowing where they stand and the resultant peace and security which they might reasonably consider a high priority'.[35]

Whatever power the court has to interfere ought, therefore, not to be so broad that certainty is to all intents and purposes lost. Strong discretion of the sort advocated by some members of the Court of Appeal in preference to a more structured, principled approach is undesirable.[36] Indeed, it may well be that the continental-style *Radmacher* solution – effectively permitting contracting-out of equal sharing, but preserving liability for (some level of) needs/compensation-based provision – strikes the right balance. Arguments will naturally abound about the extent of needs-based provision that should be supplied in each case. Should it go beyond the somewhat limited objective of ensuring that the needy spouse is not cast on the state when the other can afford to pay? Cretney sees no public interest in seeking greater provision than that. If it does exceed that limited objective, should provision cover only 'real need'[37] (whatever that might mean) in contrast to the old standard of 'reasonable requirements' or 'needs generously assessed' as the contemporary case law has it?[38] But these important details aside, at least the basic principle may be said to be clear. In particular, it is not one articulated exclusively in (meaningless in the abstract) terms of 'fairness' or otherwise hidden behind sweeping endorsement of judicial discretion.

It is important to acknowledge the balance of Cretney's arguments in this area. He has drawn attention to the incoherence of successive governments promoting private ordering of disputes on relationship breakdown while the law persists in purporting to superintend those arrangements.[39] But he has been equally concerned to highlight the dangers inherent in 'dogmatic' promotion of autonomy for its own sake and in notional (rather than real) judicial supervision of the fairness of consent orders.[40] With the benefit of his long historical and political view, and his perspectives as juvenile court-room observer, empirical researcher,[41] legal academic and law reformer, Cretney cautions that the law must

35   Consensus, above n. 9, p. 272.
36   See judgments of Ward and Hughes LLJ in *B v. B* [2008] EWCA Civ 543, [43], and *Robson v. Robson* [2010] EWCA Civ 1171.
37   [2010] UKSC 42, [81]-[82].
38   Somewhat surprisingly, in the first reported post-*Radmacher* case, the respondent conceded that he should pay indefinite maintenance based on generously assessed need or 'reasonable requirements', rather than *Radmacher*'s 'real need': *Z v. Z (no 2)* [2011] EWHC 2878, [30]. I am grateful to Richard Todd QC for drawing my attention to this point.
39   Stoke, 2003 *Family Law*, both above n. 9.
40   Consensus pp. 276–7, Xydhias, 359, both above n. 9.
41   *Simple Quarrels*, above n. 9.

avoid 'humbug and hypocrisy',[42] and law reformers must remember that 'in family law it is all too easy to rely on myth rather than confronting reality'.[43] So while he clearly favours spouses being given the power to conclude *prima facie* binding agreements without the need for what he regards as unnecessarily intrusive judicial oversight in every case (as the consent order procedure requires), he would not wish us to run headlong into a libertarian system free from the option of resort to court where some proper ground for complaint in law exists, and is content to see the range of grounds expanded to some extent in the marital contract context.[44]

And yet elsewhere in current family law and policy we do see what appears to be ideological pursuit of private ordering for its own sake, without ensuring that real access to justice will be available when required. The legal aid reforms,[45] removing from scope most private law family cases including money cases (save where there is specific evidence of domestic violence or child abuse), will expose many more wives (in particular) to the unhappy choice of either attempting to represent themselves in complex financial remedy proceedings or simply settling for whatever meagre portion (if any) is offered to them.[46] It may be questioned how genuine will be the marital agreement in such cases. Likewise the 'family-based arrangements' which the Government also wishes to promote in relation to child support, in preference to application to the state-run calculation and collection agency, an option made less appealing by the introduction of new and quite high application fees.[47] 'Family-based arrangements' sound warm and fuzzy in a way that pre-nuptial agreements never will. But their homely language does little to conceal the fact that they are equally open to the dangers of undue influence, in which the more vulnerable parent feels little option but to cede to the position of the other, who may reasonably gamble on the unlikelihood of the aggrieved parent applying to the agency to assert her claim. These are examples of precisely the sort of dogmatic pursuit of private ordering for its own sake – regardless of the procedural fairness or substantive adequacy of the agreements being reached – which Cretney warns us against. Without a real prospect of the force of law being wheeled in to assert or defend the legal entitlements of the vulnerable party, private ordering may quickly descend into anarchy.[48]

---

42   Humbug, above n. 22.

43   Xydhias, above n. 9, 359.

44   Stoke, above n. 9, p. 17.

45   Legal Aid, Sentencing and Punishment of Offenders Bill.

46   The only hope for such litigants in person will be to seek exceptional funding, an interim order for payment in respect of legal services under clause 47, or practitioners willing to take a chance.

47   DEPARTMENT FOR WORK AND PENSIONS, *Strengthening families, promoting parental responsibility: the future of child maintenance.* CM 7990. TSO, London 2011.

48   And *Simple Quarrels*, above n. 9, outlined some of the difficulties that may be encountered even where legal proceedings are brought, particularly, it may be supposed, by litigants in person.

We can expect that the Law Commission will be more mindful of Cretney's warnings when it formulates its recommendations for reform of the law of marital property agreements. He concluded that it was not open to the judges to abandon the *Hyman* principle; indeed, it is preserved by the decision in *Radmacher*, which effectively subjects all classes of marital agreement to the same *Edgar*-style starting point or presumption.[49] But he did argue that legislation could take that step, following thorough examination of the issues by the Law Commission. However, (as he has reminded us many times) whether government adopts the recommendations and proposes legislation, and whether Parliament passes such legislation, then turns on the curious and unpredictable nature of the statutory family law reform exercise in England and Wales. While the Scottish Parliament has recently dealt with such thorny issues as the grounds for divorce and financial remedies between cohabitants[50] and may soon be invited to consider same-sex marriage,[51] the Westminster Parliament has not dealt with any significant issue directly relating to marriage and its core obligations since the debacle of the Family Law Act 1996. Given the sensitivities likely to be aroused by legislation doomed to be portrayed by social conservatives as somehow 'undermining marriage', it will be a brave government that puts marital property agreements on its legislative agenda.

Without statutory reform, we will be left with *Radmacher*. It is too early in the life of *Radmacher*, with only one significant reported decision applying the case,[52] to pass judgment on the legal framework it creates. It left some loose ends, not least on the matter of whether marital property agreements are now contractually binding. And we will need more case law before we can discern the family bar and judiciary's appetite for the more hard-nosed approach to agreements and the confinement of claimants to 'real need' which the Supreme Court apparently commends.[53] Will we feel that we still have 'the worst of both worlds', marital agreements, whenever made, remaining neither fully binding nor wholly irrelevant?[54] Cretney remarked in 1996 that 'the question of how far contract should be allowed to be decisive remains difficult and controversial'.[55] It still does. But for the time being and despite retaining *Hyman*, it is conceivable that *Radmacher* might turn out to be *quite* a radical solution after all.

---

49   [2010] UKSC 42, [75].

50   Family Law (Scotland) Act 2006.

51   See recent consultation exercise: THE SCOTTISH GOVERNMENT, *The Registration of Civil Partnerships, Same Sex Marriage*, TSG, Edinburgh, 2011.

52   *Z v. Z (no 2)* [2011] EWHC 2878.

53   Early evidence suggests that this may require some considerable adjustment: see concessions made in *Z v. Z (no 2)*, noted at n. 38 above.

54   *Pounds v. Pounds* [1994] 2 FLR 775, 791.

55   Consensus, above n. 9, p. 251.

BUGGERS AND BROOMERS:*
HAVE THEY 'BEEN PRACTISING
LONG ENOUGH'?**

Chris BARTON

Contents

1. INTRODUCTION

The legal gap between civil partnership and marriage has already closed slightly since the implementation of the Civil Partnership Act 2004, and opening marriage to same-sex couples is under favourable consideration by the coalition government. Same-sex cohabitants are neck-and-neck with different-sex cohabitants but neither have reached quasi-marital status despite much 'salami-slicing'.[1] Opinions differ over further legal recognition of different-sex cohabitants, same-sex cohabitants and civil partners. Opening civil partnership to different-sex couples is similarly controversial. Other jurisdictions are hosting their own races and world-wide, the number of reported 'same-sex friendly' jurisdictions increases frequently although reverses are not unknown.[2]

---

*   It has been persuasively suggested that 'jumping the broomstick' could not produce quasi-marital status: it was 'based on accumulated errors and bearing little or no relation to their sources': R. PROBERT, *Marriage Law and Practice in the Long Eighteenth Century: A Reassessment* Cambridge University Press, Cambridge 2009, p. 73. More recently, 'broomer' has been a euphemism for extra-marital cohabitation.

**   Prince Charles' comment on the engagement to marry of Prince William and Miss Kate Middleton: see e.g. *The Sun* 17.11.2010.

[1]   The phrase used by BARONESS HALE, 'Unmarried couples in Family Law' [2004] *Family Law* 419, 423, referring to her time as a Law Commissioner.

[2]   See e.g. developments in California: *Los Angeles Times* 07.09.2011.

Domestic partnership is assumed to embrace, as it were, sexual relations between the couple and it is this factor which has been the biggest driver of opinion. But sexuality is as irrelevant to capacity to civilly partner[3] as it always has been to capacity to wed (or to adopt). Homosexuals have long married, sometimes to other homosexuals. The motive was, and maybe sometimes still is, 'appearances', deceit, or even, sadly, the hope of a 'cure'.[4] Or, like some marriages of heterosexuals, the motive might be 'non-companionate', such as family solidarity, economic support or legal advantage: a marriage blanc. The Burden sisters wanted to civilly partner each other for inheritance tax reasons.[5] One or both of them not being lesbians would no more have disqualified them under the 2004 Act than heterosexuality would have barred them from marriage had they been brother and sister. As siblings they fell within the prohibited degrees for both sorts of yoking. (During the passage of the Civil Partnership Bill 2004 sexual and relational elements were raised as (allegedly) wrecking amendments: Lord Tebbit pressed the Government on why siblings could not be included and John Redwood MP asked whether 'carers, those being cared for and family members living together in their own family units should have the benefit of inheritance tax relief and capital gains tax relief.'[6])

Therefore, by inevitable implication, 'all issues' cohabitation is also denied to all such. But not all capacity bars to formal legal bonding apply to their informal equivalent. Being married is no bar to cohabiting with someone else. Moving on from capacity, there is, *ex hypothesi,* no *lex loci celebrationis* to be followed. So more combinations of couples are permitted to pair informally than may do so formally and both types have increasingly chosen to do so. There was no choice for same-sex cohabitants until the 2004 Act was implemented but now that that injustice, if such it was, has been largely rectified, the issues surrounding informal cohabitation take centre stage. Most of the latter are different-sex cohabitants and further reduction of the legal gap between different-sex cohabitation and marriage seems a more controversial step than the 2004 Act. And will we, should we, ever reach a stage whereby same-sex couples could

---

3   On the other hand '[t]he Bill is about giving civil rights to those who have entered long-term or permanent commitments to each other, not just those who are "having it off"' (Lord Beaumont: *Hansard*, HL Deb 22.04.2004 vol 660 col 660).

4   'It has to be recognized that the mere existence of the condition of homosexuality in one of the partners can result in an unsatisfactory marriage, so that for a homosexual to marry simply for the sake of conformity with the accepted structure of society or in the hope of curing his condition may result in disaster' *The Report of the Departmental Committee on Homosexual Offences and Prostitution* 1957 (hereafter *The Wolfenden Report*), para. 134.

5   *Burden v. UK* [2008] ECHR 357.

6   *Hansard*, Deb HC 12.10.2004 vol 425 col 174. In rejecting this, Jacqui Smith (Deputy Minister for Women and Equality) said '[i]t is rather unfortunate that some Opposition Members have chosen to use an important equality Bill to pursue their campaign about inheritance tax'.

marry, involving the same weddings, legal consequences, annulments and divorces, and that different-sex cohabitants could civilly partner?

We must deal with the numbers of couples involved. Whilst the incidence of homosexuality in society, here and elsewhere, remains a matter of some uncertainty[7] (not to mention controversy[8]), the numbers in England & Wales who are married (c. 24.4 million in 2010[9]), civilly partnered (c. 85,000[10] by 2010) and even cohabiting (some 4.6 million in 2007[11]) are an easier matter. Surprisingly – or even counter-intuitively – there is 'evidence to suggest' a reduction in the numbers of never-wed under-thirties likely to cohabit.[12]

2. COHABITANTS

Over the last forty years or so, the sporadic and disorganized accretion of statute and case law can be classified under three heads: no recognition (e.g. no adult financial provision on separation); lesser recognition (e.g. ouster orders); and full recognition (e.g. child support).[13] The first may still come as an unpleasant surprise, and is the subject of most debate: a sad reflection of the still mainly-pathological nature of family law. Of course the financially-stronger of the two may well welcome the lack of responsibility, having preferred informality for that reason. On the other hand, both parties were once better-placed than their wedded or civilly-partnered neighbour (each member of a same-sex couple used to be able to claim housing benefit and council tax benefit) and the cohabiting woman was – in theory – better protected from rape than her married sister. Even now cohabitation 'contracts' are more likely to stick than marital property 'agreements'.

Should there be an overall policy-led review of the anomalies amongst the four sorts of domestic partnerships? Unfortunately, holistic approaches to family law

---

7   'At one extreme there are people who have never had a homosexual thought in their lives, while at the other are people who feel no arousal towards members of the opposite sex': P. SAUNDERS, Christian Medical Fellowship 20 (2003); <http://admin.cmf.org.uk/pdf/cmffiles/20_homosexuality.pdf>.

8   For example, as to whether or not it is a 'lifestyle choice': see e.g. S. LE VAY, *Queer Science: The Use and Abuse of Research into Homosexuality*, MIT Press, Cambridge, 1996.

9   <www.ons.gov.uk/ons/taxonomy/index.html?nscl=Marriages%2C+Cohabitations%2C+Civil+Partnerships+and+Divorces>.

10 By the end of 2010: in that year, for the first time, more female than male partnerships were entered into: <www.ons.gov.uk/ons/publications/re-reference-tables.html?edition=tcm%3A77–224152>.

11 B. WILSON, 'Estimating the Cohabiting Population' (2009) 136 *Population Trends* 21.

12 Ibid.

13 The development and current state of the differentials are available in many texts and on many websites.

reform have never been our way. This particular matter is, rightly, one of considerable political interest and any suggestions for partial reform, e.g. a narrowing of the chasm between the weaker cohabitant and the weaker spouse, may be drowned out by marriage fundamentalists who may not have studied the details of the proposed changes, nor understood that the proposals would retain a distance between the two family forms. The most recent official effort is the Law Commission's *Cohabitation: The Financial Consequences of Relationship Breakdown*[14] of which Commissioner Cooke has recently written:

> 'We concluded that cohabitants should not be given the same rights as married couples and civil partners in the event of their separation and instead recommended a new scheme of financial remedies. Only those couples who had a child together or who lived together for a minimum period (to be set by Parliament within a suggested range of two to five years) would be eligible to apply. Couples who wished to do so could opt out.'[15]

Of the Coalition's decision not to legislate this Parliament, she added that:

> 'We hope that implementation will not be delayed beyond the early days of the next Parliament, in view of the hardship and injustice caused by the current law. The prevalence of cohabitation, and of the birth of children to couples who live together, means that the need for reform of the law can only become more pressing over time'.[16]

It is unlikely that anyone who has read the Report[17] – or even its Executive Summary – would disagree with this description of its content. Yet 'social commentator' Melanie Phillips said, in anticipation:

> 'This idea that society is changing and therefore the law has to change to keep up with it is wrong, in my view, historically the law has led the progressive dismemberment of marriage by stripping it progressively of meaning... And this is but the latest example of that. The law is based on justice; justice requires that you don't get something for nothing. You don't claim rights if you don't enter into obligations.'[18]

In fact the third sentence, if no other, proved to be inaccurate: any entitlement would have been earned by contributions made during the relationship and would accrue only after a minimum period. Marriage, on the other hand, creates an immediate potential for financial provision orders and on much more generous grounds.

---

[14]   Law Commission, *Cohabitation: The Financial Consequences of Relationship Breakdown* Law Com. No. 307, TSO, London 2007.

[15]   <www.justice.gov.uk/lawcommission/docs/20110906_Statement_on_Govt_response.pdf>.

[16]   Ibid.

[17]   Law Commission, above n. 14, see particularly paras. 8.8–8.24.

[18]   <http://news.bbc.co.uk/1/hi/5032196.stm>.

In its search for a policy, was the Law Commission right to dismiss Part II of the Matrimonial Causes Act 1973, not to mention the – more plausible – idea of a variation of it? Although the Report stated that '[s]ome jurisdictions have applied all or part of their divorce regimes to certain cohabiting relationships',[19] one understands its argument that '[a]pplying the MCA would impose an equivalence with marriage which many people would find inappropriate' as well as being politically unattainable,[20] not to mention the perception that it is anyway unsatisfactory for the couples themselves.[21] Would the same points apply to an amended version of Part II? 'This is not a possibility on which we consulted'?[22] It appears that some consultees did make this point, although 'we do not think that these options, in the form in which they were presented to us, would be workable.'[23]

But would not section 25(2)'s various references to 'marriage' (10) and 'family' (3) – not to mention its opening exhortation to consider 'all the circumstances' – seem well capable of distinguishing between marriage and cohabitation? Marriage fundamentalists could be mollified by an amendment along the lines of the – now rightly abrogated – principle in s. 41(2) of the Family Law Act 1996:

'Where the court is required to consider the nature of the parties' relationship, it is to have regard to the fact that they have not given each other the commitment involved in marriage.'

While this approach is now seen as inappropriate in cases of domestic violence, it may still resonate as regards financial obligation at the end of the relationship. The possibility of reduced financial provision because the applicant did not wed or register years ago, albeit that their family proceeded to function in exactly the same manner as if he or she had, might satisfy politicians fearful of the social right. Are the complications of statutory asymmetry, with its differentials fixed in stone and hard-wired in law until Parliament re-legislates, really necessary to do comparative justice as between divorcing and separating couples? The discretion granted by section 25(2) would allow the court to respond to evolving attitudes to family form. As the Consultation Paper pointed out, 'New Zealand, some Australian states, some Canadian provinces'[24] have chosen to apply some or all of the existing ancillary financial relief law. One accepts that 'the mere fact that one party has financial or other material needs should not in itself justify

---

19   LAW COMMISSION, above n. 14, para. 4.6.
20   Ibid., para. 4.8.
21   Ibid., para. 4.6.
22   Ibid., C 17.
23   Ibid., C 22.
24   LAW COMMISSION, *Cohabitation: The Financial Consequences of Relationship Breakdown: A Consultation Paper* Law Com CP No. 179, TSO, London 2006, p. 127 fn. 1.

the grant of financial relief from the other party on separation'[25] (which is not what the final Report suggested, of course). Yet those needs might otherwise be met by the taxpayer, whether the broken partnership was marital or not.[26] And, in addition to their own virtual disregard of marital status, both the Children Act 1989 and the child support legislation have long recognized that the housing and financing of such minors cannot be segregated from that of their resident parent.

3. SAME-SEX COUPLES

Fornication has not – at least in modern times – experienced as much legal and social disapproval as have the libidinous elements of same-sex relationships. These greater disadvantages were suffered by homosexuals irrespective of whether or not the participants were living together under one roof. Whilst Katherine O'Donovan states that '[h]omosexuality as a special category was created around the 1870's',[27] the Buggery Act of 1533 had long before sent men to the gallows for the 'detestable and abominable Vice' of sodomy. Even after the Offences Against the Person Act 1861 had reduced the penalty, the Criminal Law Amendment Act 1885 had extended the possibility of punishment to 'any act of gross indecency' between two men. On the related issue of lesbianism and the famous rumour that sex between women was not criminalized by the 1861 Act because Queen Victoria told her ministers that there was no such thing, Cretney is more cautious: 'it appears that the possibility of physical homosexual relationships between women was not widely understood at that time.'[28] And before society becomes too complacent and self-congratulatory about not merely discovering 'gays' but tolerating them, we should remember that there are many, many more shades of human sexuality beyond an attraction for a particular gender. Not being apparent by the gender of the chosen partner, such psycho-sexualities have, perhaps until the internet, made it difficult for their adherents to find a symbiotic partner – who may be of either their own, or the other, gender.

But let us move on to 1957 and the Wolfenden Committee's Report which starts with a Kenneth Williams-class *double entendre*: 'We have met on 62 days, of which 32 were devoted to the oral examination of our witnesses'.[29] It is easy, half a century on, to mine that document for what, today, seems almost 'Julian and

---

[25] Ibid., para. 6.76.

[26] See C. BARTON, 'Cohabitants, Contracts and Commissioners' [2007] *Fam Law* 407, 410.

[27] K. O'DONOVAN, *Family Law Matters*, Pluto Press, London 1993, p. 81.

[28] S. CRETNEY, *Same Sex Relationships: From 'Odious Crime' to 'Gay Marriage'*, Oxford University Press, Oxford 2005, p. 3, fn 10.

[29] *Wolfenden Report*, para. 2.

Sandy'[30] stereotyping[31] of male homosexuals, but what ought to come over to the fair-minded reader is the Report's recommended legal tolerance of behavior of which its writers – together with popular view at that time – may well have disapproved. As recently as 1997, Lord Wolfenden was voted 45th in a list of the top 500 lesbian and gay heroes in *Pink Paper*[32] and in this passage 'his' Report may be seen by some as ahead of its time even now:

> 'We have avoided the use of the terms "natural" and "unnatural" in relation to sexual behaviour for they depend for their force upon certain explicit theological or philosophical interpretations, and without those interpretations their use imports an approving or a condemnatory note into a discussion where dispassionate thought and statement should not be hindered by adherence to particular preconceptions.'[33]

Famously, the recommendation that male homosexual acts in private be decriminalized was implemented a decade later in the Sexual Offences Act 1967. The Chairman's son Jeremy, himself homosexual, is reported to have written that years would indeed pass before legislation in view of the 'the hostile response of the British press and politicians'.[34]

But what it did not contemplate was 'coming out' as an individual, still less a pair living openly in a domestic partnership – let alone formally so. Of course such pairings have always existed and, where one or both of the couple was famous enough to warrant an obituary, the relationship might be impliedly, but clearly (unlike the merely eyebrow-raising 'S/he never married'), be brought to wider attention with phrases such as 'lifelong companion'. Here is an excerpt from the post-1967 – but long before 2004 – obituary of the composer, (Lord) Benjamin Britten, referring to the singer, Peter Pears:

> 'Artistically they were the making of each other. Just as socially they proved ideally attuned when they came to share their home in Aldeburgh.'[35]

---

30 The radio programmes, *Around The Horne* and *Beyond our Ken* regularly featured these two men (played by Williams and Hugh Paddick) as 'camp' gays.

31 It was noted that 'there are some in whom a latent homosexuality provides the motivation for activities of the greatest value to society…teachers, clergy, nurses and those who are interested in youth movements and the care of the aged': *Wolfenden Report*, para. 23. (On the other hand, the later, supposedly-corrective, remark that homosexuality may also include 'the dullest oafs' (para. 36) may not appeal either.).

32 Issue 500, 26.09.1997.

33 *Wolfenden Report*, para. 35.

34 Phillip French, *The Observer*, 24.06.2007. Stephen Cretney was one year Jeremy's junior at Magdalene and remembers him as '[a] figure whose *existence* was widely known amongst his University contemporaries' (personal communication, 04.10.2011).

35 *The Times*, 06.12.1976.

Even as recently as the turn of the century famous, and famously durable, same-sex quasi-marital pairs such as that of the restaurateurs Francis Coulson[36] (conscientious objector) and Brian Sack (fighter pilot)[37] were described, ambiguously, as 'partners' to one another. By 2010, the obituary writer of Anthony Grey, 'a pseudonym that he assumed in 1962 when there were real dangers of police attention for any campaigner for gay rights' was able to refer more clearly to 'his partner of 49 years, Eric Thompson'.[38] And by 2011:

> 'They had been together since meeting in London in 1949. For the first 18 years of their relationship, its very existence was illegal, and yet it – and they – survived long enough to enjoy having the state "marry" them, in February 2006, in the first same-sex civil partnership to be conducted in their local register office, in the small market town of Machynlleth, mid-Wales.'[39]

Formal same-sex joinings are now announced in the media *à la* wedding announcements.[40]

Should such pairs differ legally from different-sex couples at the cohabitational level of domestic partnership? Although our law is more interested in acknowledging individual familial relationships rather than the unit as such, this issue first came to light through housing law's interest in the latter. First came *Harrogate Borough Council v. Simpson*,[41] where the survivor of a same-sex relationship claimed succession to her domestic partner's public sector secure tenancy. Her case was that she was a member of the latter's family by virtue of being 'a person who was living with the original tenant as his or her wife or husband.'[42] (Not as 'his or her spouse', one might note). The argument was no more successful then than it was seventeen years later in *Fitzpatrick v. Sterling Housing Association*,[43] the judicial view being that both marriage, or marriage-like, are innately a different-sex matter and that had Parliament intended the provision to apply to same-sex couples it would have said so. Yet as we shall see some people object to any enacting of that very provision on the ground that such innateness is so fundamental that even Parliament should not presume to say differently. Others might see that as a circuitous argument or even that it ignores the wider meaning of marriage as, e.g., 'to combine, connect, or join so

---

36   *The Independent on Sunday*, 06.12.1998.
37   *The Telegraph*, 05.01.2002.
38   *The Times*, 04.05.2010.
39   *The Guardian*, 15.08.2011.
40   'Congratulations to Gillian Hampden-Thompson & Stacey Bielick on their fabulous Civil Partnership', *Yorkshire Post*, 04.07.2009.
41   (1984) 17 HLR 205.
42   Rent Act 1977 Sched. 1, para. 2(2) as inserted by the Housing Act 1988.
43   [2001] 1 AC 27.

as to make more efficient, attractive, or profitable',[44] which is more in tune with the modern notion of partnership rather than that of union. That Martin Fitzpatrick, who gave up his mobile snack bar business to care – wonderfully – full-time for John Thompson for nine years before the latter's death, was held entitled to succeed to John's private sector tenancy, was due to that majority of the Law Lords who held that a same-sex couple could be members of each other's family.

This was on the basis that the purpose of the 1997 Act was to support those who share their lives as a family unit under the same roof, although Lisa Glennon has boldly argued that the decision was 'a deliberate tactic of the majority who wished to lay the doctrinal foundation for a future challenge on human rights grounds whilst also trying to ensure that the decision in 1999 did not outpace social attitudes towards gay and lesbian rights'.[45] It is certainly true (as Glennon points out[46]) that in *Fitzpatrick* Lord Slynn predicted that Convention jurisprudence would evolve on the issue and that he was proved right.

In *Karner v. Austria*,[47] the European Court of Human Rights was faced with a similar same-sex Rent Act story, concerning a man who had nursed his partner, the tenant, as he died of Aids and now sought succession to the tenancy. The Austrian Supreme Court, the *Oberster Gerichtshof* held that its own statutory phrase, 'life companion' (*Lebensgefährte*) was not satisfied, but the European Court held that although protection of the family in the traditional [different sex] sense may be good reason for justifying discrimination:

'In cases in which the margin of appreciation afforded to States is narrow, as is the position where there is a difference in treatment based on sex or sexual orientation, the principle of proportionality does not merely require that the measure chosen is in principle suited for realising the aim sought. It must also be shown that it was necessary in order to achieve that aim to exclude certain categories of people – in this instance persons living in a homosexual relationship – from the scope of application of section 14 of the Rent Act. The Court cannot see that the Government have advanced any arguments that would allow such a conclusion.'[48]

And so, in a comparatively short, 36-paragraph, unanimously-agreed judgment, Lord Nicholls subsequently held in *Ghaidan v. Godin-Mendoza* that *Fitzpatrick* did not survive the 1998 Act. At first sight one might wonder why the tenant's

---

44   <http://dictionary.reference.com/browse/marry>.
45   L. GLENNON, '*Fitzpatrick v. Sterling Association*: A Perfectly Pitched Stall' in S. GILMORE, J. HERRING and R. PROBERT (eds.), *Landmark Cases in Family Law*, Hart, Oxford 2011, p. 269.
46   Ibid., p. 264.
47   (2004) 38 EHRR.
48   Ibid., para. 41.

surviving same-sex partner bothered to appeal, given that at first instance, he was held entitled to an assured tenancy of the flat as a member of his partner's family. In fact he had very practical reasons for wishing to upgrade his position to that of statutory tenant via the 'as husband or wife route': he would not have to compete with other members of that family; he would be liable for the contractual or market rent rather than a fair rent; and the court could not evict him for non-payment of rent without the court being satisfied that such possession order would be reasonable. Quite a potential difference, then, between same-sex couples and different-sex couples. But was it legal? Lord Nichols's reasoning was clear. Article 8 guarantees the right to respect for a person's home and Article 14 guarantees that the rights set out in the Convention shall be secured 'without discrimination' if such would be irrational and unfair. Here Art. 8 is clearly engaged, so Art. 14 applies, and:

> 'A homosexual couple, as much as a heterosexual couple, share each other's life and make their home together. They have an equivalent relationship. There is no rational or fair ground for distinguishing the one couple from the other in this context.'[49]

Are same-sex couples and different-sex couples now wholly legally-symmetrical? Herring is cautious, remarking that the former can claim only 'many of the rights that are available'[50] to the latter. It is suggested that the most important remaining differences that might survive the 1998 and 2004[51] Acts are those procreative issues which must, for unavoidable biological reasons, differ between the two pairings. So far as other child issues are concerned, the position regarding step, adoptive and joint-residential parenthood, plus special guardianship potential, is the same for both couples. There is no time to go into those matters here, although overall it is certainly clear that Tony Blair was badly advised in saying that 'same-sex relationships were invisible in the eyes of the law'.[52]

4. CIVIL PARTNERSHIP

The former prime minister made that remark in celebration of the implementation of the Civil Partnership Act 2004 and perhaps he had in mind that until that time the major difference between same- and different-sex dyads was that only the latter had the option of formalizing their relationship. He proceeded to say that he couldn't 'imagine that any government will reverse them' – a useful test

---

49   [2004] UKHL 30, [17].
50   J. HERRING, *Family Law,* 5th ed., Longman, Harlow 2011, p. 81.
51   Which amended such as the Rent Act 1977 to equate 'persons living together as if they were civil partners' with '… as husband and wife'.
52   *The Independent,* 21.12.2005.

for any apparently-controversial reform. Here, we concentrate upon the differences between civil partnership and marriage. Cretney writes:

> 'It seems likely that the Civil Partnership Act will create a regime according gay and lesbian couples formal and public recognition of their status without apparently outraging that not insignificant part of the population which has deeply held views on what marriage means. It may be that in the years ahead public opinion... will be prepared to accept calling this relationship "marriage".'[53]

Is civil partnership 'Gay marriage'?[54] It is – mainly – pedantry to say that civil partnership involves same-sex rather than different-sex couples, of some practical importance that there are a small number of legal differences, and of considerable satisfaction to some and dissatisfaction to others, that the 'm' word is only analogous, despite the fact that the 2004 Act is the closest thing we have to a codification of marriage law. The legal differences are easily described, from the beginning where the sole means (if not venue) of civil partnership registration is a poor show compared to the range available to the affianced. Yet the common ability to integrate a customized script into the heart of the event, together with the growing perception that the formalities and the reception are all one, may help to satisfy some couples and their guests that the gap is but a 'technical' one, smaller in practice than in theory. Same-sex couples can now register their partnership at any Register Office or Approved Premise, the minimum cost is the same and one day soon both sorts of formalisers will surely prefer to spend any spare money on the marriage rather than the 'wedding'.[55] Clearly, same-sex couples cannot procreate 'mutually': this also separates female couples from male couples with regard to the type of third-party assistance required. With one exception, penetrative sexual expression is radically different for same-sex couples than for different-sex couples and a ministerial/legislative reluctance to confront the matter is the likely explanation for the omissions of non-consummation and adultery from the respective grounds for annulment and dissolution of civil partnership.[56] Perhaps similar worries accounted for the Parliamentary reluctance to concoct a vow, or indeed any ceremony, for the signing, although the lack of the gender-based terms 'husband' and 'wife' may

---

53   *Same Sex Relationships: From 'Odious Crime' to 'Gay Marriage'*, above n. 28, p. 72.

54   E. LEIGH was prepared to withdraw an amendment to the Bill were the Government to admit that 'this ridiculous beast', Hansard HC 09.11.2004 col 731 was about gay marriage: a paradoxical stance given that that was his objection to the Bill.

55   Currently £77 for both weddings and civil partnerships.

56   C. STYCHIN has a more subtle take on these omissions: '[t]he adultery non-provision is reminiscent of the law and economics concern that lesbians and gay men might not 'sign up' to monogamy were they to be given access to same sex marriage, and therefore might not submit to its disciplinary, domesticating function. But the consummation non-provision suggests that it is only within a heterosexual context of penetration that there can be a clear test of what constitutes sexual behaviour anyway, making the determination of same sex adultery problematic', <www.brad.ac.uk/familylaw/seminar1/C_Stychin.pdf>.

please some and not others. Further absentees from the nullity heads are the respondent's pregnancy by a third party – there is anyway no equivalent ground for wives, i.e. that some other woman is pregnant by the bridegroom – and, rather more surprisingly, venereal disease.

But the most practically important differences lie in the tax and benefits area. Although formalization now permits of the same 'tax planning' techniques for both pairs, and all survivors gain from Inheritance Tax advantages, the 2004 Act does not give a civil partner the same survivor pension benefit as a spouse. Private sector occupational pension trustees are still able to discriminate against civil partners, although the Government has stated that it will give civil partners parity with spouses in public sector schemes. Usually, however, members of private pension schemes can nominate anyone they wish to receive their death benefits. And with regard to state benefits, all four of our pairs, be they same-sex, different-sex, informal or formal, are treated the same in calculating entitlement to tax credits in that the incomes of both of them will be taken into account.[57]

Just as those who opposed the abolition of that other CP, capital punishment, rightly feared that the promised alternative of mandatory life imprisonment would quickly be softened, so the fears that civil partnership was, or would become, marriage have been justified. Since the implementation of the 2004 Act the gap has already been narrowed more than once[58], quite apart from the Prime Minister's promise that same-sex couples will be allowed to wed.[59] Ironically, such unity would be most easily achieved by making a few changes to the 2004 Act and subsuming current marriage law within it, given that that Act effectively codifies marriage law. Could a same-sex couple then choose between civil partnership and marriage, if they wished to formalize their relationship? This brings us to the suggestion that different-sex couples should have that very choice, perhaps in a display of solidarity with the other pairing: '[j]ust as it's wrong to discriminate against gay people, it's wrong to discriminate against heterosexual people'.[60] Some might prefer a 'partnership' with its suggestion of equality and some degree of independence from one another, or not want to be, as some see it, stereotyped into separate, sexist, 'husband' and 'wife' categories.

---

[57] See e.g. <www.gayfinance.info/civil-partnerships/civil-partnership.htm> for a detailed account.

[58] Under the Equality Act 2010, and following consultation by the Government Equalities Office, registrations of civil partnerships have been allowed in 'churches' since December 2011 (although it was reported that only six small churches were prepared to host such events, *The Times*, 07.11.2011); see further PROBERT, this volume.

[59] In March 2012 the Government is to commence a consultation process concerning civil marriage for same-sex couples with a view to introducing legislation in the present Parliament: <www.homeoffice.gov.uk/media-centre/press-releases/equal-civil-marriage-same-sex>.

[60] P. TATCHELL, *The Times*, 25.11.2009.

They might be homo- or bi-sexual and believe that civil partnership is thus more openly-appropriate or, in the first case, not wish to imply a sexual relationship or obligation. Perhaps the current legal differences are more in line with their preferred regime, e.g. they might not want to exchange oral vows because they do not wish to impliedly promise life-long union, or because they fear making obligations that they might not keep. Or they might just be tiresomely right-on.

5. CONCLUSION

Treating male and female couples as one, that leaves three dyadic forms which have attracted growing legal attention within the last half-century. We have glanced at their journeys and discussed how much further they might travel towards crypto-marriage recognition or even to marital status itself, plus the possibility that civil partnership might be extended to different-sex couples.

How much closer should cohabitation law be to that of marriage, a matter which concerns so many people? It is – currently – inconceivable that informal pairing will ever be allowed to segue wholly into marriage by name via either longevity or any other policy. Similarly, changing laws to what people wrongly believe them to be[61] is almost as irrational as scrapping them because they are being broken.[62] That leaves lawmakers with the challenge of finding a differential policy to cope with the inevitably-shifting social attitudes to formal and informal couples: an even harder demand on durability than that achieved by such as the Divorce Reform Act 1969, the Matrimonial Proceedings and Property Act 1970 and the Children Act 1989. Those examples are particularly relevant because the debate about cohabitation law is mainly concerned with termination. Yet the closing years of the last half-century have seen a growing interest in the going concern – a fitting tribute to Stephen Cretney's prescience.

---

[61] Surveys persistently demonstrate that 50%-plus of respondents believe, i.e. say they believe, in the 'common law marriage myth' and journalists are still regularly discovering the truth. For an enjoyable survey of media misrepresentations – and the failed attempts at rebuttal – see R. PROBERT, 'Why Couples Still Believe in Common Law Marriage' [2007] *Fam Law* 403.

[62] As recommended by the Transport Secretary Phillip Hammond MP with regard to raising the speed limit to 80 mph: *The Times*, 03.10.2011.

CIVIL RITES

Rebecca PROBERT

Contents

1.   INTRODUCTION

Novels often close with a wedding (or at least, such was the case in an age when marriage was seen as the inevitable conclusion to a romance); for lawyers, however, the formation of a marriage is merely the starting point for discussion of the legal rights and responsibilities that flow from the new status (or, more often, its dissolution). In both his textbooks and his comprehensive *Family Law in the Twentieth Century: A History*, Stephen Cretney accorded significant space to the laws governing not just who could marry whom, but how they could do so.[1]

The depth of the historical perspective in the latter reflects the difference between a description of family law in the twentieth century and an analysis of the history – the roots – of twentieth-century family law. It is impossible to understand the current form of the modern law of marriage without looking back at least to the Marriage Act of 1836 and probably to the Clandestine Marriages Act of 1753. As Willekens and Scheiwe have noted on this subject: 'we cannot understand the present without its past, and the past is not simply past and hence absent – it is still present.'[2]

---

[1]   S. CRETNEY, *Family Law in the Twentieth Century: A History*, Oxford University Press, Oxford 2003, chs 1 and 2.

[2]   H. WILLEKENS and K. SCHEIWE, 'Introduction: The Deep Roots, Stirring Present, and Uncertain Future of Family Law' (2003) 28 *Journal of Family History* 5.

The recent debate in the House of Lords about the registration of civil partnerships taking place on religious premises – or, rather, the extent to which religious denominations would be free to choose not to host such registration – looked primarily to the future rather than to the past. Yet the very idea raises questions about the role that churches play in creating legally binding unions. The first two sections of this chapter accordingly examine first the idea of religious marriage as a civil rite and then the argument that marriage itself is a sacred rite. The final section goes on to consider the debates on where civil partnerships should be registered – and finds, quite unexpectedly, that the arguments have considerable relevance for one very important marriage on which Cretney has also commented.

2.   MARRIAGE IN CHURCH AS A CIVIL RITE

Marriage, as Sir William Scott explained in *Dalrymple v. Dalrymple*, can be viewed from a variety of perspectives:

> 'Marriage in its origin is a contract of natural law; it may exist between two individuals of different sexes, although no third person existed in the world, as happened in the case of the common ancestors of mankind... In civil society it becomes a civil contract regulated and prescribed by law and endowed with civil consequences. In most civilized countries acting under a sense of the force of sacred obligations it has had the sanctions of religion superadded: it then becomes a religious as well as a natural and civil contract; for it is a great mistake to suppose that because it is the one therefore it may not likewise be the other.'[3]

For present purposes, it is the last part of this statement that is the most important: since from 1753 the law prescribed that a couple had to be married in the Anglican church in order for the law to recognise their union as valid,[4] the religious rite was also a civil one.

For most, of course, there was no conflict between the two. The popularity of the Church of England in the eighteenth century is a matter of dispute, but recent research suggests that the prevalent image of non-resident, apathetic parsons and a recalcitrant population is far from the truth. Spaeth has argued that 'the people participated willingly in the official religion of the Church of England: it was not imposed upon them.'[5] According to Jacob, the evidence suggests:

---

3   (1811) 2 Hag. Con. 54; 161 ER 665, p. 669.
4   See R. Probert, *Marriage Law and Practice in the Long Eighteenth Century: A Reassessment*, Cambridge University Press, Cambridge 2009. Prior to this a marriage had to be celebrated before an Anglican priest in order to enjoy legal recognition, but not necessarily in a church.
5   D. Spaeth, *The Church in an Age of Danger: Parsons and Parishioners 1660–1740*, Cambridge University Press, Cambridge 2000, p. 106. See also J. Black, *Eighteenth Century Britain,*

'a deep attachment to Christian faith among a broad cross-section of people, as illustrated by their expectations of the clergy, their active involvement in the worship of their parish churches, the evidence for their personal devotional practices, their concern for the maintenance of Christian morality and peace between neighbours, their Christianly motivated philanthropy... and their substantial investment in repairing, extending, building and beautifying churches.'[6]

But the idea of the Anglican ceremony as a civil rite was important in securing the compliance of non-Anglicans. Most Protestant dissenters had never developed their own marriage rites and so the necessity of compliance with the Anglican form was taken as a matter of course. Indeed, in this period the differences between different sects, and between the various sects and the Church of England, was not always clear-cut. As the evangelist Howell Harris wrote of the London community which he attended in 1742, 'We have Churchmen, Presbyterians, Scottish and English, Lutherans, Calvinists, Independents, Baptists, Quakers, Papists, Jews, Arians, and Armenians, and we all live in sweet harmony.'[7] The Methodist movement that began in the 1740s did not formally separate from the Church of England until the start of the nineteenth century;[8] Warne, for example, reports how in the 1764 Devon returns the 'incumbent of Thurlestone stated that "a few are fond of hearing any Methodist Teacher in his circular ramble, and yet do afterwards continue regular conformists."'[9]

For Catholics, however, the matter was a little different. As Burton explains, 'with them it was not a mere question of objecting to the form of the service, but it was a matter involving the principle that they should under no circumstances take part in the worship or religious rites of another body.'[10] A concession was made that attendance would not be regarded as religious conformity, but as 'a ceremony prescribed by the law of the land for the civil legality of the marriage.'[11] Such an approach had papal sanction, Benedict XIV having held that 'it was quite legitimate for Catholics to obey the civil law in this matter'.[12]

  1688–1783, Palgrave, Basingstoke 2001, p. 133 who notes that there is 'copious evidence both of massive observance of the formal requirements of the churches and of widespread piety'.

6 W.M. Jacob, *Lay People and Religion in the Early Eighteenth Century*, Cambridge University Press, Cambridge 1996, p. 3.

7 Quoted by P. Langford, *A Polite and Commercial People: England 1727–1783*, Clarendon Press, Oxford 1998, p. 245.

8 A. Warne, *Church and Society in Eighteenth Century Devon*, David and Charles, Newton Abbot 1969, p. 106.

9 Ibid., p. 109; see also D. Hempton, *The Religion of the People: Methodism and Popular Religion c. 1750–1900*, Routledge, London 1996, p. 154.

10 E. Burton, *The Life and Times of Bishop Challoner*, Longmans, Green & Co, London 1909, vol. 1, p. 328.

11 Ibid., p. 331.

12 J. Bossy, 'Challoner and the Marriage Act' in E. Duffy (ed.), *Challoner and His Church: A Catholic Bishop in Georgian England*, Darton, Longman & Todd, London 1981, p. 132.

In the event, it would seem that most Catholics did comply with the law. The practice of the elite seems to have been to marry first in the Anglican church and then according to the Catholic rite.[13] The writer and court attendant Fanny Burney married first in an Anglican ceremony and then had a Catholic ceremony a day later at the Sardinian Embassy Chapel. Similarly, Maria Fitzherbert, later to acquire notoriety as the secret and illegal wife of the future George IV, complied with the Marriage Act when marrying her first two husbands, the second marriage being celebrated in the society church of St George's Hanover Square.[14] By contrast, those whose behaviour was less subject to scrutiny might prefer to have the Catholic ceremony first, and the Anglican rite second.[15]

Nor should it be assumed that Catholic couples regarded the Anglican ceremony as a meaningless legal requirement, as the emotional diary entry of one bride – and the apparel thought appropriate for each of the ceremonies – illustrates. The Catholic ceremony having taken place early in the morning:

> 'We had but just time to breakfast, and then I had to dress for the second marriage – my bridal array consisted of a white satin under dress and a patent net over it, with a long veil... my heart beat when we entered the church, nor could I go thro' the second ceremony without feeling even more affected.'[16]

Others took a more jaundiced view of non-communicants marrying in the Church of England. The Rev. Skinner reported celebrating the marriage of a Methodist in 1828 – commenting, perhaps a trifle sourly, that 'the clergy may at least perform their mechanical part of the procession, that is, marry, baptise, and bury'[17] – and noted a colleague's comments that the ceremony of marriage 'had of late been considered rather as a civil rite than connected with the offices of the Church.'[18]

In the decade leading up to the Marriage Act of 1753 the Church of England 'controlled something approaching a monopoly of English religious practice', but by 1830 it 'was on the point of becoming a minority religious Establishment.'[19]

---

[13] M.D.R. LEYS, *Catholics in England, 1559–1829: A Social History*, Longmans, Green and Co Ltd, London 1961.
[14] See J. MUNSON, *Maria Fitzherbert: The Secret Wife of George IV*, Robinson, London 2002, p. 39.
[15] See e.g. R. PROBERT and L. D'ARCY-BROWN, 'Catholics and the Clandestine Marriages Act of 1753' (2008) *Local Population Studies* 78.
[16] See A. FREEMANTLE (ed.), *The Wynne Diaries: The Adventures of Two Sisters in Napoleonic Europe*, Oxford University Press, Oxford 1982, p. 468.
[17] J. SKINNER, *Journal of a Somerset Rector, 1803–1834*, Oxford University Press, Oxford 1971, p. 328.
[18] Ibid., p. 350.
[19] A. GILBERT, *Religion and Society in Industrial England: Church, Chapel and Social Change, 1740–1914*, Longman, London 1976, p. 27.

The number of Methodists,[20] Baptists and Congregationalists[21] increased rapidly, and there was a significant increase in the number of Catholics due to Irish immigration. In the wake of this increase it was understandable that there should be increased dissatisfaction with the requirement that marriages be celebrated in the Anglican church.[22] Eventually the calls for reform resulted in the Marriage Act 1836, which not only allowed approved religious denominations to perform their own marriage ceremonies, but also provided for a purely civil rite of marriage.

3. MARRIAGE AS A SACRED RITE

Some commentators took the view that the new civil ceremony was a distinctly unsatisfactory substitute for the religious rite, a view illustrated in the propensity to describe the 1836 Act as the 'Broomstick Marriage Act'.[23] The *Yorkshire Gazette*, for example, ran an article in 1840 on the proportion of marriages that were still celebrated in the Church of England despite the availability of other options, noting triumphantly that '[w]e always expected that the Broomstick Marriage Act would be treated as a dead letter by the people of the country.'[24] *The Morning Post* similarly headed its article on the rarity of marriages at an Independent chapel with the title 'Broomstickism at a Discount',[25] while *The Age* helpfully provided a guide to the ceremony, on the basis that 'readers, particularly those of the fair sex, perhaps would wish to be informed of the new mode of broomsticking a bridegroom under the new Registration Act', and noted that

---

20 J. OBELKEVICH, 'Religion' in F.M.L. THOMPSON (ed.), *The Cambridge Social History of Britain 1750–1950: Vol. 3 Social agencies and institutions*, Cambridge University Press, Cambridge 1990, noting that Methodists numbered 25,000 in 1770, 94,000 in 1800 and 286,000 in 1830.

21 R. CURRIE, A. GILBERT and L. HORSLEY, *Churches and Churchgoers: Patterns of Church Growth in the British Isles since 1700*, Clarendon Press, Oxford 1997, Appendices 3 and 4.

22 Although it was from the Unitarians – whose apparently increased numbers merely 'reflected a regrouping of the heterodox remnants of the old Presbyterian and General Baptist traditions' (GILBERT, above n. 19, p. 40) – that the demand for reform first emanated.

23 The term 'broomstick marriage', as used in the eighteenth and early nineteenth century, seems to have been used to denote a sham or ersatz ceremony of some kind rather than the physical act of jumping over a broomstick: see further PROBERT, above n. 4, ch. 3. Nineteenth-century claims that couples married in this way may well have been based on a misunderstanding of the term: P. MARSHALL, *Mother Leakey & the Bishop: A Ghost Story*, Oxford University Press, Oxford 2007, p. 244, provides 'a salutary reminder that "oral" traditions can often be shown to have their origins in printed sources.'

24 As reported by *Jackson's Oxford Journal*, 12.09.1840), p. 1. See also *John Bull*, 10.03.1839, p. 12, referring to 'the late Broomstick Marriage Act' and 'Broomstick Marriages', *The Observer*, 09.07.1837, p. 2.

25 *The Morning Post*, 02.12.1839.

with the short exchange of vows required by the statute 'all's over in three minutes.'[26]

The passage of the 1836 Act in fact inspired a number of clergymen to emphasise that marriage was a sacred rite that should still be celebrated according to the ceremonies of the Church of England, regardless of the range of options now available. One, the Reverend Mr Norris of South Hackney, was reported as imploring his listeners 'to cast discountenance and reproach' on any instance of couples marrying in a civil ceremony:

> 'should (what God forbid!) a single instance brave the light of day, and affront the decencies of social life, of such an abandonment to a reprobate mind as shall occasion holy matrimony to be superseded by a coupling together which, upon scriptural principles, can be regarded only as a legalized concubinage, and which our Liturgy... brands as likening those who enterprise it "to brute beasts who have no understanding"...'[27]

The Bishop of London was more moderate, pointing out that the clergy should not take it upon themselves to solemnize marriages between those who had already been united by the Superintendant Registrar, since the law recognized the civil ceremony as a valid marriage, but went on to add:

> 'If such a marriage be without spiritual grace, which the Church connects with matrimony when duly solemnized, the parties have deprived themselves of it by their own act, and we are not to remedy it by an irregular procedure of ours.'[28]

The press was not entirely sympathetic to clerical arguments emphasizing the benefits of marriage in the Church of England.[29] One newspaper referred to the clergy 'advertising, more in the spirit of keen tradesmen, than of spiritual persons, that they should still register baptisms, marriages, and burials, and perform the marriage ceremony as formally' and expressed surprise that they did not regard it as a relief 'that unbelievers may be married elsewhere, rather than compelled to attend the church, there to find themselves spoken of as servants of God and blessed in his name.'[30]

Yet neither criticisms of this kind nor the strictures of the Bishop of London deterred some members of the clergy from seeking to persuade couples to go

---

26 *The Age*, 15.10.1837, p. 333. See also *The Morning Post*, 14.09.1838, suggesting that 'there is less of form in this broom-stick work than in the buying of a pig, or the leasing of a couple of greyhounds.'

27 *Morning Chronicle*, 09.09.1837. See also *The Standard*, 15.08.1837.

28 *Bury and Norwich Post*, 26.10.1842.

29 See e.g. 'The Puseyites on Marriage' *The Bradford Observer*, 18.05.1843.

30 *The Sheffield Independent, and Yorkshire and Derbyshire Advertiser*, 16.09.1837.

through a second ceremony of marriage. In 1854, after the legislation had been in force for almost two decades, the *Bristol Mercury* indignantly reported events at Frome, where a couple who had married at the Zion Independent Chapel had been persuaded to go through a second ceremony in the Anglican church, 'thereby treating the first marriage, to all intents and purposes, as a nullity and thereby, further, declaring illegal and of non-effect a ceremony which the law of England had distinctly legalized.'[31]

The case was widely reported,[32] and may have been in the minds of Members of Parliament when they debated the Marriage and Registration Amendment Bill in 1856. This recognized both the desire of some couples for an additional blessing and the undesirability of casting any doubts on the validity of civil ceremonies. It allowed for a religious marriage service to be held after a civil ceremony but emphasized that 'nothing in the Reading or Celebration of such service shall be held to supersede or invalidate [the Register Office wedding]; nor shall such Reading or Celebration be entered as a Marriage.'[33]

Even after this date occasional examples of second 'marriages' can be found: Cretney alludes to the 'stigma which apparently still attached in some circles to secular marriage', giving the example of an 'extraordinary case' in 1886 in which an Anglican priest 'disregarded a Register Office wedding between the beadle and the pew-opener and "married" the couple on a common licence.'[34]

Given the negative attitudes to civil marriages, together with the continuing importance of religious faith for many, and simple tradition for others,[35] it is unsurprising that the Anglican church continued to be the most popular location for weddings,[36] with civil marriages accounting for only 15 per cent of the total by the end of the nineteenth century.[37] Yet, now that the Church of England no

---

[31] 'Puseyite Re-Marriages at Frome', *Bristol Mercury*, 27.05.1854.

[32] See e.g. *Daily News*, 01.06.1854; *Hampshire Telegraph and Sussex Chronicle*, 03.06.1854; *Bury and Norwich Post, and Suffolk Herald*, 14.06.1854.

[33] Marriage and Registration Amendment Act 1856, s. 12.

[34] CRETNEY, above n. 1, p. 21, fn. 115.

[35] Then as now, there was no necessary correlation between the popularity of Anglican weddings and church attendance: see e.g. K.T. HOPPEN, *The Mid-Victorian Generation, 1846–1886*, Oxford, Oxford University Press, 1998, p. 465, noting that 'Victorian London combined the nation's lowest levels of church attendance with the greatest incidence of Anglican marriages.'

[36] See e.g. *Report of the Royal Commission on the Laws of Marriage 1867–8*, p. vi noting that seven-ninths of marriages were still solemnised in the Church of England; for parish-level studies see e.g. P. WILCOX, 'Marriage, Mobility and Domestic Service in Victorian Cambridge' (1982) 29 *Local Population Studies* 19.

[37] On the debate as to the reasons for the relatively low incidence of civil marriage see e.g. O. ANDERSON, 'The Incidence of Civil Marriage in Victorian England and Wales' (1975) 69 *Past & Present* 50; R. FLOUD and P. THANE, 'The Incidence of Civil Marriage in Victorian England and Wales' (1979) 84 *Past & Present* 146.

longer had a monopoly on the celebration of marriage, it could afford to obtain exemptions from the celebration of certain types of marriages. Accordingly, when legislation was passed in 1857 allowing for judicial divorce, a clause was included to the effect that 'no Clergyman in Holy Orders of the United Church of England and Ireland shall be compelled to solemnize the Marriage of any Person whose former Marriage may have been dissolved on the Ground of his or her Adultery, or shall be liable to any Suit, Penalty, or Censure for solemnizing or refusing to solemnize the Marriage of any such Person.'[38]

One hundred and fifty-five years later, the issues of compulsion, censure and potential penalties were all to be debated in a context that Victorian legislators could not possibly have foreseen: the question of whether the civil partnerships of same-sex couples could be registered on religious premises, and of the wording appropriate to insulate from challenge those religious denominations that did not wish to host such ceremonies.

4. THE RITE OF REGISTRATION

When the Civil Partnership Act was passed in 2004, it specifically provided that the registration of a civil partnership could not take place on religious premises. In 2010, however, this prohibition was removed, although it was made clear that there would be no obligation on religious organizations to host civil partnerships.[39] After extensive consultation, and a debate in the House of Lords that was both passionate and informed, the relevant provisions were brought into force by the Marriages and Civil Partnerships (Approved Premises) (Amendment) Regulations 2011.[40]

There is an oddity in the final result. While the Equality Act 2010 removed the prohibition on civil partnerships taking place on religious premises, it did not alter the prohibition on registration being accompanied by any religious service.[41] Yet, as the Lord Bishop of Oxford pointed out in the debates, 'denominations wishing to offer services of blessing following civil registration can already invite people to come to the church or synagogue after the registration and have that element there.'[42] The conceptual distinction between the civil rite of registration (albeit one taking place on religious premises) and the sacred element of blessing has seemingly been maintained.

---

[38] Divorce and Matrimonial Causes Act 1857, s. 57.
[39] Civil Partnership Act 2004, s. 6A(3A) as amended by the Equality Act 2010, s. 202(4).
[40] SI 2011 No 2661.
[41] Civil Partnership Act 2004, s. 2(5).
[42] *Hansard*, HL Deb 15.12.2011 col 1420.

In practice, though, this distinction will almost inevitably be blurred. While the Regulations restate the formal position that '[t]he proceedings conducted on the approved premises may not be religious in nature', the Explanatory Note adds that 'this prohibition applies only during the proceedings themselves.' Given that the actual procedure for registering a civil partnership is pared down in the extreme – it is, indeed, the mere act of registration, shorn of any accompanying ceremony – the prohibition will be of extremely short duration. (At the most it might prevent a hymn being sung during the signing of the register.) This sleight of hand does at least avoid the absurd necessity of requiring the newly partnered couple to leave the premises after registration and return (perhaps by a different door) for a blessing at a later stage, but it might have been more straightforward to have removed the prohibition on the proceedings being religious in nature altogether.

The debate in the House of Lords, however, focused on whether religious denominations or churches that did not want to host civil partnership ceremonies had been sufficiently insulated against legal challenge. At first sight the legislation would appear to be clear. The Equality Act 2010 had amended the Civil Partnership Act by inserting the clause:

'For the avoidance of doubt, nothing in this Act places an obligation on religious organisations to host civil partnerships if they do not wish to do so.'[43]

The subsequent Regulations similarly stated that:

'Nothing in these Regulations places an obligation on a proprietor or trustee of religious premises to make an application for approval of those premises as a place at which two people may register as civil partners of each other'.[44]

Concern was nonetheless expressed that 'churches and denominations could be squeezed by combining the obligations of the Equality Act, the Human Rights Act, the European Convention on Human Rights, and EU law.'[45] The clarity of legislation does not of course guarantee that there will be no legal challenge to it, since the challenge may be to the very form of the legislation.[46] It was feared that the very universality of the Church of England would mean that pressure might be put upon incumbents of parish churches to allow the registration of civil

43   Equality Act 2010, s. 202(4), inserting s. 6(A)(3)(3A) into the Civil Partnership Act 2004.
44   Marriages and Civil Partnerships (Approved Premises) (Amendment) Regulations 2011, reg. 2B.
45   Hansard, HL Deb 15.12.2011 col 1411 (Baroness O'Cathain).
46   See e.g. Wilkinson v. Kitzinger & ors [2006] EWHC 2022 (Fam), challenging the equally clear provision in Civil Partnership Act 2004, s. 215.

partnerships there.[47] The Lord Bishop of Blackburn suggested that a more appropriate way of insulating the Church of England from legal challenge would be to expressly exclude it from the scope of the regulations, leaving it to the General Synod to decide whether Church of England churches and chapels should be approved for the registration of civil partnerships.[48]

Lord Lester, however, reassured those expressing such fears that the clear view of the lawyers advising both the government and the church was that a religious denomination that refused to have its premises approved for the registration of civil partnerships could not be held to be discriminating in a way that was unlawful under the Equality Act.[49] He quoted at length from the opinion given to the Church of England by its legal advisors:

> 'section 29 of the Equality Act... makes it unlawful for "a person... concerned with the provision of a service to the public or a section of the public" to discriminate on various grounds, including sexual orientation, "against a person requiring the service by not providing the person with the service". A Church which provides couples with the opportunity to marry (but not to register civil partnerships) is "concerned with" the provision of marriage only; it is simply not "concerned with" the provision of facilities to register civil partnerships. That would be a different "service", marriage and civil partnership being legally distinct concepts. If Parliament were in due course to legislate for same sex marriage, as recently suggested by the Prime Minister, we would of course be in new territory. But that is a separate issue which would have to be addressed in the course of that new legislation.'

It was, however, the former Lord Chancellor, Lord Falconer of Thoroton who dealt with the human rights argument in most detail. He noted the argument that had been advanced by one QC to the effect that section 3 of the Human Rights Act, in requiring the provisions of the 2004 or 2010 legislation to be read in accordance with the European Convention on Human Rights, might 'give rise to the possibility that it could be construed away or read down.' He went on, however, to note that such an argument was 'hopeless', pointing out that the QC in question had also, and rightly, set out:

> 'the basic law in relation to reading down under Section 3. He says that the only limitation on Section 3 of the Human Rights Act, on interpretive obligation, according to the House of Lords decision in *Ghaidan*, is that in reading words into the legislation, or in deleting offending words, the courts have to be satisfied that such emendation could not be said to "go against the grain" by overriding some cardinal

---

47 *Hansard*, HL Deb 15.12.2011 col 1437–8.
48 *Hansard*, HL Deb 15.12.2011 col 1428.
49 *Hansard*, HL Deb 15.12.2011 col 1433.

feature of the legislation in question, or otherwise raise generally policy issues that a court cannot properly seek to resolve by a process of judicial rewriting.'[50]

It perhaps escaped the notice of the other peers that only six years earlier Lord Falconer had himself advanced a creative use of the Human Rights Act when arguing that it was clear that there was no prohibition on the Prince of Wales marrying in a civil ceremony. His suggestion then was that:

'the Human Rights Act has since 2000 required legislation to be interpreted wherever possible in a way that is compatible with the right to marry (article 12) and with the right to enjoy that right without discrimination (article 14). This, in our view, puts the modern meaning of the 1949 Act beyond doubt.'[51]

It might nonetheless be thought that the law governing the ways in which members of the royal family could marry did also raise 'policy issues that a court cannot properly seek to resolve by a process of judicial rewriting'. The new regulations may well have been drafted in a form that is apt to prevent any challenge to churches that do not wish to seek approval for the registration of civil partnerships. But it should equally be recognized that the law on royal marriages was far less clear, and that relying on how the relevant legislation might be interpreted in case of challenge was hardly the best way of proceeding. Back in 2005 Cretney led the call for a simple piece of legislation to confirm the possibility of members of the royal family marrying in a civil ceremony.[52] It is to be hoped that any future legislation changing the rules of succession to the crown addresses this small but crucial point.

5. CONCLUSION

History takes one in odd directions. In this case my research began in the middle – my interest excited, as so often, by one of the footnotes in Cretney's *History* – and moved back to the eighteenth century before seeing the resonances with modern debates. And – having deliberately decided not to write on the topic of royal marriages for fear of repeating myself[53] – it was a pleasing irony that the arguments advanced by Lord Falconer should immediately evoke the events of 2005.

---

[50]   *Hansard*, HL Deb 15.12.2011 col 1418.
[51]   Written Ministerial Statement, *Hansard*, HL 24.02.2005 col WS87.
[52]   S. CRETNEY, 'Royal Marriages: the Law in a Nutshell' [2005] *Family Law* 317, 321.
[53]   R. PROBERT, *The Rights and Wrongs of Royal Marriage: How the law has led to heartbreak, farce and confusion, and why it must be changed*, Kenilworth, Takeaway 2011.

History – and particular Cretney's rich research into the making of family law – also shows us that what is taken for granted may be a compromise rather than being based on any clear principle. One cannot help but feel that all of the initiatives described above reflect a very English fudge. With demands being voiced for both same-sex marriage and opposite-sex civil partnerships through the Equal Love campaign, an increasing number of UK residents going overseas to marry and regular stories in the media about the cost of modern weddings, perhaps we need today more than ever a serious discussion about respective interests of church, state and people in the celebration of marriage.

TOWARDS A MATRIMONIAL PROPERTY REGIME FOR ENGLAND AND WALES?

Jens M. Scherpe

Contents

1. INTRODUCTION: COMMUNITY OF PROPERTY IMPOSED BY JUDICIAL DECISION?

When one thinks about creating a matrimonial property regime, the first step from a technical point of view is very simple: either the marriage has an immediate effect on the property relations of the spouses – or it does not. However, even this very first and seemingly simple decision will not only determine the proprietary effect of marriage but also reflect the general view of the respective jurisdictions on the meaning and function of marriage.[1]

---

[1] For a more detailed analysis of matrimonial property regimes see e.g. J.M. Scherpe, 'Marital Agreements and Private Autonomy in Comparative Perspective' in J.M. Scherpe (ed.), *Marital Agreements and Private Autonomy in Comparative Perspective*, Hart Publishing, Oxford 2012; E. Cooke, A. Barlow and T. Callus, *Community of Property. A regime for England and Wales?*, Nuffield Foundation, London, 2006; E. Cooke, 'The Future for Ancillary Relief' in G. Douglas and N. Lowe (eds.), *The Continuing Evolution of Family Law*, Jordan, Bristol, 2009; W. Pintens, 'Ehegüterstände in Europa', *Zeitschrift für Europäisches Privatrecht*

All European civil law jurisdictions have adopted a 'default' matrimonial property regime, i.e. a regime that will apply unless the parties agree otherwise in a marital agreement.[2] The jurisdiction of England and Wales with a certain defiant pride, has not so far adopted a matrimonial property system as such.[3] Instead it relies on a system that, by affording the court a very wide discretion on divorce, allows – at least in theory – for a fair outcome for each individual case. While this acknowledges that each marriage is different and that therefore fairness might require tailor-made court orders, such an approach very deliberately sacrifices the legal certainty that matrimonial property regimes can provide to achieve the overarching aim of a 'fair' outcome.

Two quotations very aptly describe the approach to the financial consequences upon divorce, in England and Wales.

The first one is by Lord Denning and goes back to 1981:

> 'The Family Court takes the rights and obligations of the parties all together and puts the pieces into a mixed bag. Such pieces are the right to occupy the matrimonial home or have a share in it, the obligation to maintain the wife and children, and so forth. The court then takes out the pieces and hands them to the two parties – some to one party and some to the other – so that each can provide for the future with the pieces allotted to him or to her. The court hands them out without paying any too nice a regard to their legal or equitable rights but simply according to what is the fairest provision for the future – for mother and father and the children.'[4]

(ZEuP) 2009; K. BOELE-WOELKI, B. BRAAT and I. CURRY-SUMNER (eds.), *European Family Law in Action IV: Property Relations between Spouses*, Intersentia, Antwerp 2009; W. PINTENS, 'Matrimonial Property Law in Europe' in K. BOELE-WOELKI, J. MILES and J.M. SCHERPE (eds.), *The Future of Family Property in Europe,* Intersentia, Antwerp 2011; see also in the same volume K. BOELE-WOELKI and M. JÄNTERÄ-JAREBORG, 'Initial Results of the Work of the CEFL in the Field of Property Relations Between Spouses'.

2   Marital agreements and the private autonomy of the spouses have been discussed extensively in J.M. SCHERPE (ed.), *Marital Agreements and Private Autonomy in Comparative Perspective*, Hart Publishing, Oxford 2012, and this contribution will focus on the default matrimonial property regimes only. On marital agreements see also N. DETHLOFF, 'Contracting in Family Law: A European Perspective' in BOELE-WOELKI, MILES and SCHERPE, above n. 1; S. HOFER, D. SCHWAB and D. HENRICH (eds.), *From Status to Contract? – Die Bedeutung des Vertrages im europäischen Familienrecht*, Gieseking, Bielefeld 2005; for practitioners' views on international marital agreements D. SALTER, C. BUTRUILLE-CARDEW, N. FRANCIS and S. GRANT, *International Pre-Nuptial and Post-Nuptial Agreements*, Jordan Publishing, Bristol 2011.

3   Neither have the other common law jurisdictions of Europe, Northern Ireland and the Republic of Ireland. Some common law jurisdictions outside of Europe, however, seem to at least to have taken a deliberate step towards such regimes, i.e. by implementing legislation defining matrimonial property, on which see 3.1. below.

4   *Hanlon v. Law Society* [1981] AC 124, 147.

The more recent quotation is by Lord Nicholls and stems from the decision in *White v. White*:

'Everyone would accept that the outcome on these matters, whether by agreement or court order, should be fair. More realistically, the outcome ought to be as fair as is possible in all the circumstances. But everyone's life is different. Features which are important when assessing fairness differ in each case. And, sometimes, different minds can reach different conclusions on what fairness requires. Then fairness, like beauty, lies in the eye of the beholder.'[5]

It is the decision of the House of Lords in the latter case that marks the beginning of the recent developments in financial provision. In his well-known and sagacious case commentary in the Law Quarterly Review, Stephen Cretney very provocatively suggested that combined effect of *White v. White* and *Lambert v. Lambert*[6] was to impose a community of property regime on England and Wales.[7] This was expressly (and rightly) rejected first by Bennett J in *Sorrell v. Sorrell*[8] and later by Baroness Hale in *Miller v. Miller; McFarlane v. McFarlane*.[9] But even in rejecting Cretney's provocative suggestion, Baroness Hale felt compelled to state England and Wales 'do not yet have a system of community of property, whether full or deferred'.[10] It is the 'yet' which makes this statement remarkable. The further development, apparently also foreseen by Baroness Hale, certainly proved that Cretney had a point and that England and Wales are indeed moving towards a matrimonial property regime (although not necessarily a community of property one as such). As so often, Cretney, with his vast experience and enormous knowledge, had a keen sense for what was to come and was therefore able critically to comment on a development before it really started, providing an impetus and a warning at the same time.

This contribution will explore the development towards a matrimonial property regime that he heralded.

---

5   *White v. White* [2001] 1 AC 596, 599.
6   [2002] EWCA Civ 1685.
7   S. CRETNEY, 'Community of property imposed by judicial decision' (2003) 119 *LQR (Law Quarterly Review)* 349. Any reference in the following to 'English law' should of course be understood to refer to the law of England and Wales.
8   *Sorrell v. Sorrell* [2005] EWHC 1717, [96].
9   *Miller v. Miller; McFarlane v. McFarlane* [2006] UKHL 24, [151].
10   Ibid.

2. WHAT IS A MATRIMONIAL PROPERTY REGIME?

Matrimonial property regimes regulate the property relations of the spouses during marriage and in the event of divorce. The regimes of continental Europe can be divided into two groups according to the effect the marriage itself has on the property relations of the spouses: community of property regimes and separation of property regimes. Space precludes a comprehensive description and the following is merely a broad-brush categorisation outlining the bare structures of the default regimes, i.e. those that apply in the absence of a matrimonial property agreement.

2.1. COMMUNITY OF PROPERTY REGIMES

There are two main default matrimonial property regimes in Europe based on a community of property.

The Dutch universal community of property is the only matrimonial property regime where upon marriage all the assets of the spouses become joint property; at first glance this might seem like a 'gold-digger's paradise', but unsurprisingly matrimonial property agreements are very common.[11]

The community of acquest is the prevalent matrimonial property regime in continental Europe and is the default property regime in the Romanic jurisdictions and Eastern Europe. Here the community of property is a limited one as it only consists of the marital acquest. While the exact definition of what is considered to be the acquest varies from jurisdiction to jurisdiction, in broad terms it can be said that everything that is acquired during the marriage becomes part of the communal property, with the exceptions of assets received through gift or inheritance.

In the event of a divorce, in all these regimes the communal property is to be divided equally[12] and the courts have no discretion to divide the matrimonial property in any other way at this stage.[13]

---

[11] K. BOELE-WOELKI and B. BRAAT, 'Marital Agreements and Private Autonomy in the Netherlands' in SCHERPE (ed.), above n. 2.

[12] Of course in practice it is more complicated than that, as payments made/benefits derived from the separate assets etc. need to be equalised before the division of the communal assets, cf. SCHERPE, above n. 1, pp. 449 et seq., esp. 451.

[13] While Poland and Serbia allow for a limited discretion, apparently in practice the courts do not very often depart from equal sharing; cf. PINTENS, 'Matrimonial Property Law in Europe', above n. 1, 26.

2.2. SEPARATION OF PROPERTY REGIMES

The matrimonial property regimes based on a separation of property can be divided into two main groups, namely the deferred community of property (prevalent in the Nordic Countries) and what has been called 'statutory compensation' systems.[14]

In the latter group, in which we can find, for example, the German accrual of gains community and the Swiss participation in acquests, no communal property is ever created – but on divorce, spouses can have statutory claims for an equal share of the acquest/gains accrued during the marriage. Notably, property acquired before the marriage and through gift or inheritance during the marriage (although not necessarily the increase in value of such separate property) is excluded from the sharing. Again, there is no discretion for the judge to divide the matrimonial property otherwise.[15]

This is different in the deferred community of property jurisdictions, the Nordic Countries. While here on divorce all assets owned by the spouses become communal property and in principle are to be divided equally, the courts retain the power to divide the communal property differently when an equal division would be inequitable. Even though this power is used sparingly, it will for example be used if the assets of one spouse were largely acquired before the marriage or through gift or inheritance during the marriage, and particularly if the marriage was of short duration.

2.3. THE (LIMITED) FUNCTION OF MATRIMONIAL PROPERTY REGIMES IN THE EVENT OF DIVORCE

While matrimonial property regimes can have an important function during the marriage, particularly in community of property jurisdictions, the focus here will be on its function in the event of a divorce.[16]

Unlike in England and Wales, where the financial relief upon divorce is fully at the discretion of the judge, the continental matrimonial property regimes generally aim at providing a spouse with a 'guaranteed share' in matrimonial

---

[14] Ibid., pp. 29 et seq.

[15] On the German community of accrued gains see A. DUTTA 'Marital Agreements and Private Autonomy in Germany' in SCHERPE (ed.), above n. 2. See also the answers to questions 57 et seq. for Germany by N. DETHLOFF and D. MARTINY and for Switzerland by I. SCHWENZER and A. BOCK, all in BOELE-WOELKI, BRAAT and CURRY-SUMNER (eds.), above n. 1.

[16] For the function of matrimonial property regimes during marriage see the references in n. 1 above and J.M. SCHERPE, 'Foreign Marital Agreements: the Approach of the English Courts' [2010] *Private Client Business* 181.

assets and thus providing certainty with regard to the proprietary relations of the spouses. From an English point of view it is often argued that this certainty comes at the expense of fairness, as the matrimonial property regimes generally do not allow the individual circumstances of the case to be taken into account.

But looking at the matrimonial property regimes in isolation does not convey the full picture of the financial consequences of divorce. Property division according to the matrimonial property regimes is only one of the 'pillars'[17] upon which the financial consequences of divorce rest, albeit of course an important one. In addition to the division of matrimonial property, claims for maintenance, pension sharing, allocation of the use of the marital home etc. can be made. The remedies available under these other 'pillars' are generally discretionary. In some jurisdictions, the additional remedies often even are of a proprietary nature, such as the French *prestation compensatoire*[18] and the Spanish *pension compensatoria* which allow for lump sum payments or even property redistribution.[19] Notably, the 'pillars' in principle are independent of each other and pursue different policy aims.[20]

While the matrimonial property regimes are designed such that they provide adequate and fair outcomes in the vast majority of cases, the continental jurisdictions nevertheless strive for an overall fair outcome in *all* cases. But they do not do so by taking a 'holistic view' and offering one 'package' as England and Wales does, but by relying on several 'pillars'. In order to judge the ability of a jurisdiction to provide for a 'fair' outcome the overall result of the remedies of all 'pillars' must therefore be considered, of which the division of property according to the matrimonial property regime is only one. In English terms this 'pillar' could perhaps be described as the 'sharing pillar' (although of course the underlying policy for sharing of matrimonial property is also meant to compensate and to cover needs). Where the division of assets according to the matrimonial regime leads to hardships or 'unfair' results, the other 'pillars' are to step in – by, for example, providing a high lump sum as *prestation compensatoire* as in France or higher ongoing maintenance payments to cover needs and compensation.

---

17   This term was used by DUTTA, above n. 15, and J.M. SCHERPE and A. DUTTA, 'Cross-border enforcement of English ancillary relief orders – Fog in the channel, Europe cut off?' [2010] *Family Law* 385.

18   W. PINTENS, 'Marital Agreements and Private Autonomy in France and Belgium' in SCHERPE (ed.), above n. 2.

19   J. FERRER-RIBA, 'Marital Agreements and Private Autonomy in Spain' in SCHERPE (ed.), above n. 2.

20   For a more detailed analysis of the 'pillar' approach see SCHERPE, above n. 1, esp. pp. 474 et seq.

Hence having a matrimonial property regime does not necessarily mean sacrificing fairness or even the court's discretion; and even where the matrimonial property regime does not allow for discretion, the other 'pillars' will still be available and allow for discretionary remedies. But in any event, a matrimonial property regime provides a greater degree of certainty with regard to the spouses' proprietary relations than a system of unfettered discretion. Indeed, one could argue that the uncertainty which is inevitably the result of a system based on discretion is unfair in itself.

3. ARE ENGLAND AND WALES REALLY THAT DIFFERENT?

As mentioned and exemplified by the two quotations in the introduction, the financial consequences of divorce in England and Wales, embodied in Part II of the Matrimonial Causes Act 1973, are largely discretionary; the overarching principle is to achieve fairness; and sharing, need and compensation have been identified as the guiding rationales/strands of fairness.[21] On the face of it, this approach, which seems deliberately to eschew any form of systematic approach, appears very different from the way the financial consequences of divorce are dealt with in the continental European jurisdictions. However, when examined closely in the light of the recent jurisprudence in England and Wales, the differences perhaps are not as big as they seem.[22]

3.1. DEFINING MATRIMONIAL PROPERTY AND A PRESUMPTION OF EQUAL SHARING

As described briefly above, the continental matrimonial property regimes are based on the notion that marriage is a partnership of equals and that certain assets should therefore be shared equally.[23]

Apart from the Netherlands, there seems to be a further consensus with regard to which assets are to be shared in the event of divorce as part of the matrimonial

---

21 Cf. *Miller v. Miller; McFarlane v. McFarlane* [2006] UKHL 24; *White v. White* [2001] 1 AC 596.

22 But see COOKE, above n. 1.

23 Only Greece is an exception, as here there is a rebuttable presumption that the spouse contributed 1/3 to the other spouse's accrued gain, and if the presumption is not rebutted than the assets will be divided accordingly. See the answers to Questions 57 et seq. for Greece by A. KOUTSOURADIS, S. KOTRONIS and F. HATZANTONIS in BOELE-WOELKI, BRAAT and CURRY-SUMNER, (eds.), above n. 1; PINTENS, 'Matrimonial Property Law in Europe', above n. 1, p. 32; SCHERPE, above n. 1, p. 459.

property division, namely only those that can be considered 'fruits' of joint labour, as generated by the joint endeavour of the spouses in their respective roles in the marriage. Assets acquired before the marriage or during the marriage through gift or inheritance are thus generally exempt from the definition of matrimonial property and hence from equal sharing according to the statutory rules.

In England and Wales a similar approach was taken in the seminal decision of *Miller v. Miller; McFarlane v. McFarlane*.[24] Despite the perceived or actual differences in the details of the categorisation of assets by Baroness Hale and Lord Nicholls, both categorised the assets into two groups for which the division of assets in principle follows different rules. Both also agreed that assets owned before the marriage or acquired during the marriage through gift or inheritance could (or should) be treated differently from other assets with regard to the sharing. Indeed, a total of nine references to the 'fruits' of the marriage/matrimonial partnership/the couple's labours[25] and three to the 'joint/common endeavours' of the spouses[26] can be found in this decision, underlining this distinction.

For 'matrimonial property'[27] arguably a presumption of equal sharing was established, or at least that a 'computation stage' is required[28] and that the assets are to be classified as either matrimonial or non-matrimonial. Subsequent case law has picked up on this distinction, and indeed in some cases 'non-matrimonial property' was not shared equally (or at all).[29] At the very least a strong tendency to treat differently assets acquired before the marriage or during the marriage through gift or inheritance can be observed, and the English courts seem to be making the distinction between matrimonial and non-matrimonial assets according to criteria similar to those that can be found in the continental European jurisdictions: by excluding assets that are not deemed to be 'fruits of the marriage'.

However, one obvious distinction between most continental European jurisdictions and England and Wales with regard to the definition of matrimonial property remains: irrespective of when and how it was acquired, the matrimonial

---

24 [2006] UKHL 24.
25 Ibid., [17], [19], [20], [21], [85], [141], [149] and [154] (twice).
26 Ibid., [22], [91] and [143].
27 Lord Nicholls' terminology seems to have been followed by subsequent case law, see e.g. *K v. L* [2011] EWCA Civ 550; *AR v. AR* [2011] EWHC 2717 (Fam); *N v. F (Financial Orders: Pre-Acquired Wealth)* [2011] EWHC 586 (Fam); *Jones v. Jones* [2011] EWCA Civ 41.
28 *Charman v. Charman (No 4)* [2007] EWCA Civ 503, [67].
29 Above n. 27; see also *B v. B (Ancillary Relief)* [2008] EWCA Civ 543; *McCartney v. Mills McCartney* [2008] EWHC 401; *AR v. AR* [2011] EWHC 2717 (Fam); *K v. L* [2011] EWCA Civ 550; *N v. F (Financial Orders: Pre-Acquired Wealth)* [2011] EWHC 586 (Fam); *Jones v. Jones* [2011] EWCA Civ 41.

home will always be regarded as part of the matrimonial property in England and Wales, while this is not the case in many continental jurisdictions. This can be explained by the special social and financial importance of real estate in this jurisdiction.[30] In most continental jurisdictions the housing situation is quite different and hardships are generally dealt with through the preferential allocation of the use of the matrimonial home rather than property (re-) allocation.[31] Interestingly, statutory extensions of the shareable/matrimonial property to property that is not 'fruits of the marriage' but functionally connected to it and that therefore are comparable England and Wales can for example also be found in Austria,[32] New Zealand[33] and Singapore.[34] In any event, the variations in the definition of matrimonial property do not detract from the commonality of an underlying assumption that matrimonial property as defined by the respective jurisdiction is to be shared equally in the event of divorce.

3.2. DISCRETION FOR NEEDS AND COMPENSATION

That said, in England and Wales the rule on sharing of matrimonial property is not absolute, and non-matrimonial property is also not completely exempt from the sharing. The courts retain their discretion, and the main reason for exercising it is to achieve fairness by considering the strands of needs and compensation.

While this is not an established rule or approach yet, English law seems to be moving toward the following approach to the division of property upon divorce:

---

[30] Cf. J. MILES and J.M. SCHERPE, 'The Future of Family Property in Europe' in BOELE-WOELKI, MILES and SCHERPE (eds.), above n. 1, p. 428 and COOKE, BARLOW and CALLUS, above n. 1, esp. pp. 28 et seq.

[31] See e.g. for Germany ss. 1568a, 1568b BGB (German Civil Code); on this see DUTTA, above n. 15, pp. 165 et seq.; for Spain and Catalonia Art. 96 Código Civil (Spanish Civil Code)/ Art. 220–20.2 and 3 Codi civil de Catalunya (Civil Code of Catalonia); on this see J. FERRER-RIBA, above n. 19, pp. 365 et seq.

[32] S. FERRARI, 'Marital Agreements and Private Autonomy in Austria' in SCHERPE (ed.), above n. 2, pp. 52 et seq. on ss. 81 et seq. Ehegesetz (Marriage Act) – 'assets inextricably linked with the matrimonial assets'.

[33] M. BRIGGS, 'Marital Agreements and Private Autonomy in New Zealand' in SCHERPE (ed.), above n. 2, pp. 261 et seq. on s. 8 Property (Relationships) Act 1976 – 'family home whenever acquired'; 'family chattels whenever acquired'; 'property acquired in contemplation of the marriage'; 'property intended for the common use or common benefit of both spouses'.

[34] W.K. LEONG, 'Marital Agreements and Private Autonomy in Singapore' in SCHERPE (ed.), above n. 2, p. 314 on s. 112(10) Women's Charter – 'any asset acquired before the marriage by one party or both parties to the marriage (i) ordinarily used or enjoyed by both parties or one or more of their children while the parties are residing together for shelter or transportation or for household, education, recreational, social or aesthetic purposes; or (ii) which has been substantially improved during the marriage by the other party or by both parties to the marriage'.

- *Matrimonial assets* are to be shared upon divorce unless considerations of fairness demand otherwise. Such considerations can include the (short) duration of the marriage and 'stellar' contributions.
- *Non-matrimonial assets* are not to be shared unless considerations of fairness demand otherwise. Such considerations can include the duration of the marriage and the contributions made to the overall welfare of the family, particularly past and future child-care and related sacrifices, as well as other relationship-generated advantages and disadvantages and, more generally, the needs of the spouses.

Hence when fairness and particularly the rationales of needs and compensation require it, the court will exercise its discretion, divide the assets differently and also make additional orders for maintenance etc. where appropriate. But the burden of proof for this now lies on the spouse wanting to depart from what could be described as a 'rule' for sharing.

A similar approach is taken in some other common law and even some civil law jurisdictions. So for example Austria, New Zealand, Scotland, several US jurisdictions and Singapore, in common with England and Wales, have an approach whereby the division of the matrimonial property is, in principle, discretionary. However, this discretion is guided either by express statutory provisions or by case law that has firmly established that the matrimonial property is to be divided equally, absent special circumstances, although the discretion to decide otherwise is retained.[35] Irrespective of whether the rule for the division of property is established by statute or case law, a deviation from the sharing rules in these jurisdictions therefore requires specific justification, so essentially the rules establish a rebuttable presumption. Likewise, in the Nordic countries equal sharing of (all) assets is the statutory rule, but the courts also retain discretion to order differently and will do so particularly in cases of assets acquired before the marriage or through gift or inheritance during the marriage, and if the marriage was a short one.

---

[35] See, e.g. the statutory presumptions in Arkansas and North Carolina (Arkansas Code Ann §9–12–315(a)(1)(A)(2009):'All marital property shall be distributed one-half to each party unless the court finds such a division to be inequitable.'; North Carolina Gen Stat Ann §50–20(c)(2009): 'There shall be an equal division by using net value of marital property and net value of divisible property unless the court determines that an equal division is not equitable'. Cf. I.M. ELLMAN, 'Marital Agreements and Private Autonomy in the United States' in SCHERPE (ed.), above n. 2, pp. 407 et seq., esp. fn 10) and Scotland (s. 10(1) Family Law (Scotland) Act 1985; cf. K. NORRIE, 'Marital Agreements and Private Autonomy in Scotland' in SCHERPE (ed.), above n. 2, pp. 293 et seq.) and the statutory rule on equal sharing in New Zealand (s. 11(1) Property (Relationships) Act 1976, cf. BRIGGS, above n. 33, pp. 260 et seq.); see also for Austria FERRARI, above n. 32, pp. 53 et seq. and for Singapore LEONG, above n. 34, p. 316 and W.K. LEONG, *Elements of Family Law in Singapore*, LexisNexis, Singapore 2007, pp. 697 et seq.

All these jurisdictions therefore combine rule-based and discretion-based approaches and it could therefore be said that they have a 'rule-based discretionary' approach to the financial consequences of divorce.[36]

It is worth repeating that in the other European civil law jurisdictions the financial remedies/'pillars' that aim to deal with the needs of a spouse[37] and compensation for relationship-generated disadvantages are also largely awarded at the discretion of the judge.[38] Furthermore, as the examples of Austria and the Nordic Countries particularly show, even a 'real' matrimonial property regime and discretion with regard to the property division upon divorce are not mutually exclusive – on the contrary, they can be combined. Hence one could argue that the approaches between the continental European jurisdictions and England and Wales are not as different as they appear at first glance, particularly when considering the recent developments in this jurisdiction with regard to matrimonial property agreements.

3.3. THE 'PILLARISATION' OF FINANCIAL RELIEF?

As explained (too) briefly above, the continental European jurisdictions generally follow a 'pillar' approach to financial relief upon divorce, with separate claims/ remedies based on matrimonial property, for maintenance, pension sharing, allocation of the use of the matrimonial home and, for example in France and Spain, also additional, essentially proprietary, claims such as the *prestation compensatoire* and *pension compensatoria* respectively.[39] England and Wales, on the other hand, in principle take a 'holistic' or 'package' approach and there are no such clear dividing lines.

This 'pillar' approach is mirrored in the European private international law instruments, so that, for example, different European regulations apply to the division of property and maintenance.[40] Without such clear distinctions,

---

36 SCHERPE, above n. 1, pp. 467 et seq. However, the statutory rule establishing equal sharing in the Nordic Countries is much stronger than a mere (rebuttable) presumption and is generally not departed from to achieve 'fairness' or to compensate for marriage-related disadvantages. Therefore perhaps the approach in the Nordic countries is better described as a 'discretion-based rule' approach (i.e. primarily based on a rule with discretion in some circumstances), although admittedly, in practice, the distinction might merely be semantic.

37 What constitutes 'needs' of course varies from jurisdiction to jurisdiction and depends on a variety of factors; see SCHERPE and DUTTA, above n. 17; see SCHERPE, above n. 1, pp. 479 et seq.

38 See SCHERPE, above n. 1, pp. 475 et seq.

39 FERRER-RIBA, above n. 19; PINTENS, above n. 18.

40 See e.g. Council Regulation (EC) 4/2009 on jurisdiction, applicable law, recognition and enforcement of decisions and cooperation in matters relating to maintenance obligations [2009] OJ L7/1 and the proposal for a Council Regulation on jurisdiction, applicable law and

England and Wales will find it very difficult to opt into or apply these regulations.[41] Moreover, orders made in England and Wales without such clear distinctions between the 'pillars' of property division and maintenance might be more difficult to enforce on the continent.[42] So at least for orders with a 'foreign element' which might need to be enforced on the continent, and for maintenance generally, lawyers in England and Wales will have to think 'pillarised'.[43]

Perhaps more crucially, the recent Supreme Court decision in *Radmacher v. Granatino*[44] has arguably already created a 'pillar' approach to the financial consequences of divorce. While confirming that marital agreements cannot oust the jurisdiction of the courts, it was held that a

> 'court should give effect to a nuptial agreement that is freely entered into by each party with a full appreciation of its implications unless in the circumstances prevailing it would not be fair to hold the parties to their agreement.'[45]

The court then went on to explain that, of the three strands of fairness identified in *White v. White*[46] and *Miller v. Miller; McFarlane v. McFarlane*,[47] the court is most likely to consider a departure from equal sharing as fair, whereas needs and compensation were held to be the strands which most readily could render it unfair to hold the parties to a marital agreement. This is very similar to the approach taken in continental European jurisdictions and their 'pillar' systems, where contracting out of the property division (i.e. the sharing) generally is possible, but there are considerable restrictions to opt out of the other 'pillars'.[48]

---

the recognition and enforcement of decisions in matters of matrimonial property regimes, COM(2011) 126/2 and the Proposal for a Council Regulation on jurisdiction, applicable law and the recognition and enforcement of decisions regarding the property consequences of registered partnerships, COM(2011) 127/2.

41   As evidenced by the Council Decision of 30 November 2009 on the conclusion by the European Community of the Hague Protocol of 23 November 2007 on the Law Applicable to Maintenance Obligations (2009/941/EC) [2009] OJ L331/17. See also COOKE, above n. 1, esp. pp. 216 et seq.

42   See e.g. Bundesgerichtshof (XII ZB 12/05, FamRZ 2009, 1659; MDR 2009, 1225; NJW-RR 2010, 1); ECJ *de Cavel (N. 2)* Case 120/1979 [1980] ECR 731. See also SCHERPE and DUTTA, above n. 17.

43   Otherwise, to utilise the obvious pun, they might find themselves in the pillory (and indeed potentially liable to their clients for the extra costs generated).

44   *Radmacher v. Granatino* [2010] UKSC 42. See also the case notes by J. MILES, 'Marriage and Divorce in the Supreme Court: for Love of Money?' (2011) 74 *MLR (Modern Law Review)* 431 and J.M. SCHERPE, 'Fairness, freedom and foreign elements – marital agreements in England and Wales after *Radmacher v. Granatino*' [2012] 24 *CFLQ (Child and Family Law Quarterly)* forthcoming.

45   Ibid., [75].

46   *White v. White* [2001] 1 AC 596.

47   *Miller v. Miller; McFarlane v. McFarlane* [2006] UKHL 24.

48   See SCHERPE, above n. 1, esp. pp. 501 et seq.

The Supreme Court therefore has effectively identified and singled out the sharing of (matrimonial) property as a separate (and waivable) part of the financial provision upon divorce, thus almost elevating it to a separate 'pillar' amongst the strands of fairness. In the recent case of *Z v. Z (No. 2)*,[49] Moor J followed that approach and accepted the exclusion of sharing by a (French) matrimonial property agreement and made an order based on needs only.

If such a separation of the strands is deemed possible where there is a matrimonial property agreement, it should also be possible to make a similar separation with regard to the sharing of matrimonial and non-matrimonial property without an agreement. If this approach is followed, the English law of financial relief could in fact become 'pillarised' and become much closer to the approach taken to the financial consequence of divorce on the continent.

4. CONCLUSION: TOWARDS A REGIME OF RULE-BASED DISCRETION

When Cretney suggested that the courts in England and Wales imposed a community of property, he qualified this to be a deferred community limited to acquisitions of the spouses during marriage, and also forecast that assets acquired by inheritance or gift would not necessarily be part of the community.[50] But even he could not foresee the rapid development the law of ancillary relief would take at the beginning of this century.

Having had the benefit of seeing the case law develop, it is now possible to state that England and Wales might indeed be on the cusp of developing a kind of matrimonial property regime, but it is not really a community of property of acquests, deferred or otherwise. Marriage as such still does not fundamentally change the property relations of the spouses, and neither does the divorce as such. Thus at no point is an actual community of property, even a community limited to the acquest, established in English law.

Yet upon divorce the courts of course have the power to redistribute the property, so in that sense English law is closer to that of jurisdictions based on a separation of property and a participation in the other spouse's property upon divorce. But this does not necessarily entail an equal sharing of *all* assets. As Cretney predicted,[51] property owned before the marriage and acquired during the marriage through gift or inheritance is treated differently from 'matrimonial

---

49   [2011] EWHC 2878 (Fam).
50   CRETNEY, above n. 7, 349.
51   Ibid.

property'. While the law of England and Wales still eschews a formulaic approach, there seems to be a clear tendency towards (and perhaps even a presumption of) only sharing the matrimonial property equally – with said property being 'defined' in accordance with the specific requirements of this jurisdiction and thus always including the matrimonial home.

But at the same time, the courts in England and Wales do of course retain the discretion assigned to them by the Matrimonial Causes Act 1973 to distribute the property otherwise. Still, other jurisdictions (including not only the Nordic Countries and Austria but also the common law jurisdictions of Australia, Singapore and New Zealand) have proved that a rule-based approach and a discretionary approach can be combined into a 'rule-based discretionary' one, and it appears that England and Wales are on the verge of adopting such an approach as well – through precedent rather than express legislation.

The 'rule' concerns the division of matrimonial assets and mainly addresses the sharing strand of fairness. Elements of compensation and needs are, as in most jurisdictions, mainly dealt with by discretionary remedies, which can also take the form of property reallocation, irrespective of whether the property is matrimonial or not. The law of financial relief in England and Wales thus effectively might become 'pillarised', and the 'rule' could be categorised as a (nascent) form of a matrimonial property regime.

There is no reason to assume that a 'rule-based discretionary' approach would not be workable and appropriate in England and Wales as well. It provides greater certainty for the spouses and at the same time does not sacrifice the central feature and aim of English law, namely the ability to administer fairness under all circumstances and for all couples.

HOLDING ONTO THE PAST?

Adoption, Birth Parents and the Law in the Twenty-First Century

Sonia Harris-Short

Contents

1. INTRODUCTION

Writing in his seminal work on the history of family law in the twentieth century, Stephen Cretney observes that for lawyers:

> '[adoption] is concerned above all with the legal rights of the birth and adoptive parents on the one hand and the adopted child on the other. Because the legal effect of adoption – in effect, an irrevocable transfer of a child from one family to another – is so dramatic lawyers have tended to regard it as a process necessarily different in kind from other legal processes for dealing with the care of children.'[1]

This essay explores, with some concern, the extent to which in the push towards achieving 'more adoptions more quickly', any recognition that the 'dramatic' legal effect of adoption demands a legal process in which the rights and interests

---

[1]   S. Cretney, *Family Law in the Twentieth Century: A History,* Oxford University Press, Oxford 2003, pp. 597–598.

of the birth parents are given the most careful and anxious consideration by the courts is being eroded.

The legal nature and social purpose of adoption has of course changed dramatically over the course of the twentieth century necessitating legal change.[2] From a 'private or amateur' activity that sought to provide solutions for childless couples and young women trapped within a social context that rendered them unable to care for their own children,[3] adoption has been transformed into an integral part of the State's child protection machinery.[4] This has, or at least should have, fundamentally changed the way adoption is understood.[5] From an essentially voluntary, consensual and mutually beneficial arrangement, adoption is now most typically a coercive process, in which the State has become a central player and in which its actions are often vigorously contested and opposed by the birth parents.

Within this transformed social context, it is perhaps the position of the birth parents, and the birth mother in particular, that has changed most dramatically. From a willing participant in the process, she has become intensely vulnerable to the coercive power of the State. As we look to the future and further anticipated reforms to adoption,[6] it is instructive to pause for a moment and look back, with the help of Cretney, to the history of the legal regulation of adoption in English family law. That history reveals some salutary lessons. It is of course important that the different needs and priorities caused by the changed social function of adoption are properly understood and accounted for. However, in looking back at the history of adoption it is striking how two key principles have endured: the legitimate place of the rights and interests of the birth parents in decisions about a child's adoption and the importance of independent scrutiny of those decisions by the courts. And although the social context in which adoption operates has changed dramatically, it will be contended that rather than diminishing their significance, these two fundamental principles entrenched in English law for almost a century are now more important than ever.

---

2   See C. BRIDGE, 'Adoption law: a balance of interests' in J. HERRING (ed.), *Family Law: issues, debates, policy,* Willan, Cullompton 2001, pp. 198–199.

3   Ibid., p. 198.

4   To some extent the social care function of adoption has always been present. See CRETNEY, above n. 1, pp. 596, 616, 624 and 627.

5   See N. LOWE, 'The changing face of adoption – the gift/donation model versus the contract/ services model' [1997] 9 *CFLQ (Child and Family Law Quarterly)* 371 and N. LOWE et al., *Supporting Adoption – Reframing the Approach,* BAAF, London 1999.

6   In November 2011 David Cameron promised an overhaul of the care and adoption system. See discussion below. In December 2011 reforms were announced to the way in which potential adoptive parents are assessed. See: <www.guardian.co.uk/society/2011/dec/22/adoption-system-changes?INTCMP=SRCH>.

2. LOOKING TO THE FUTURE: MORE ADOPTIONS MORE QUICKLY – AGAIN!

Since the turn of the century adoption has rarely been off the political agenda. The Adoption and Children Act 2002 (ACA 2002) was driven by the Labour Government's desire to increase the use of adoption as a route to permanence for looked-after children.[7] This legislation was hailed as the most radical overhaul of adoption law in 25 years and was accompanied by new Adoption Standards and performance targets aimed at increasing by 40 per cent the number of children adopted from care by 2004–05.[8] These targets initially met with some success. From a low of 4,617 adoptions in 1998 the number rose to a highpoint of 5,486 in 2002.[9] However, the number has subsequently declined again with the total number of orders made in 2010 falling to 4,472, a 4.1 per cent decrease since 2009.[10] This failure to sustain a rise in the number of adoptions, particularly of looked-after children, has attracted the attention of the Coalition Government, with David Cameron calling for an overhaul of the care and adoption system to 'improve chances for vulnerable children.'[11] The Prime Minister's intervention followed the appointment in July 2011 of Martin Narey, former chief executive of Barnado's, as a ministerial adviser on adoption.[12]

The extent to which Martin Narey will be driving future government policy on adoption is unclear but his views, as expressed in a special report commissioned by *The Times* and published as part of its pro-adoption campaign, are concerning.[13] Narey is unequivocally pro-adoption. Setting the tone for his report he notes, 'no-one disputes that adoption offers the most stable and secure environment for a child who can no longer live with his or her own parents.'[14]

---

[7]   See, in particular, CABINET OFFICE, PERFORMANCE AND INNOVATION UNIT, *The Prime Minister's Review of Adoption*, 2000. Available at: <http://webarchive.nationalarchives.gov.uk/+/www.cabinetoffice.gov.uk/strategy/downloads/su/adoption/adoption.pdf>.

[8]   DEPARTMENT OF HEALTH, *Adoption – A New Approach. A White Paper*, Cm 5017. HMSO, London 2000.

[9]   OFFICE OF NATIONAL STATISTICS, *Marriage, divorce and adoption statistics*, Series FM2 no 34, 2009, table 6.2a. Available at: <www.statistics.gov.uk/downlaods/theme_population/FM2no34/FM2_No34.pdf>.

[10]   OFFICE OF NATIONAL STATISTICS, *Statistical bulletin. Adoption in England and Wales 2010*, 2011. Available at: <www.ons.gov.uk/ons/taxonomy/index.html?nscl=Adoptions>.

[11]   Family Law Week, 'Local authorities challenged to do better on adoption.' See, <www.familylawweek.co.uk/site.aspx?i=ed88746>.

[12]   <www.education.gov.uk/childrenandyoungpeople/families/adoption/a00192226/martin-narey-appointed-as-ministerial-advisor-on-adoption>.

[13]   M. NAREY, *The Narey Report: A blueprint for the nation's lost children*, The Times, London July 2011. Tim Loughton, the Children's Minister, has already distanced the government to some extent from the report making it clear that it is not government policy. See: <www.communitycare.co.uk/Articles/14/07/2011/117160/childrens-minister-rejects-key-ideas-from-his-adoption-tsar.htm>.

[14]   Ibid., p. 2.

The 'saving children' rhetoric is strong, it being observed, 'we are talking about something entirely positive, rescuing children from abject neglect and giving them a family who will love and value them.'[15] He thus concludes, in words strongly reminiscent of Tony Blair's, 'we need to see many more adoptions and of much younger children in the UK.'[16]

It is not the purpose of this essay to question the undoubted fact that, for many abused and neglected children who find themselves in the care of the State, adoption provides the much-needed love and security of a 'forever family'. However, adoption is but one of a range of possible options for achieving permanency for looked-after children and it will not always be the most appropriate. Research on outcomes for adopted children is generally positive, but the results are much more nuanced than Narey suggests. Where a child is voluntarily relinquished by the birth mother and placed with the adoptive parents at birth outcomes are usually very good, indeed as good if not better than outcomes for children remaining in birth families.[17] However, even here there are some concerns about the psycho-social wellbeing of adopted children.[18] Moreover, the outcomes for children adopted out of care are much less convincing, with significant disruption rates, particularly for children aged over five at placement, and mixed results in studies focusing on psycho-social wellbeing and behavioural adjustment.[19] The evidence as regards outcomes for adopted children as compared with looked-after children in institutional care or long-term foster care is also somewhat equivocal. There is some evidence to suggest that the greater permanence and sense of security offered by adoption may result in generally better outcomes for adopted children.[20] However, recent research published by Biehal et. al. is more circumspect.[21] In line with previous studies, disruption rates for children in foster care compared unfavourably with rates for adopted children. However, as the researchers point out, like is not being

---

15   Ibid., p. 3.
16   Ibid.
17   J. CASTLE, C. BECKETT and C. GROOTHUES, 'Infant adoption in England. A longitudinal account of social and cognitive progress' (2000) 24 *Adoption and Fostering* 26.
18   Ibid., 26–27.
19   J. TRISELIOTIS, 'Long-term foster care or adoption? The evidence examined' (2002) 7 *Child and Family Social Work* 23; C. DANCE and A. RUSHTON, 'Predictors of outcome for unrelated adoptive placements made during middle childhood' [2005] 10 *Child and Family Social Work* 269; D. HOWE, D. SHEMMINGS and J. FEAST 'Age at placement and adult adopted people's experience of being adopted' [2001] 6 *Child and Family Social Work* 337; and M.H. IZZENDOORN and F. JUFFER, 'Adoption is a successful natural intervention enhancing adopted children's IQ and school performance' (2005) 14 *Current Directions in Psychological Science* 326.
20   TRISELIOTIS, above n. 19, 31.
21   N. BIEHAL, S. ELLISON, C. BAKER and I. SINCLAIR, *Characteristics, Outcomes and Meanings of Three Types of Permanent Placement – Adoption by Strangers, Adoption by Carers and Long-Term Foster Care*, DCSF-RBX-09–11, available at: <www.adoptionresearchinitiative.org.uk/briefs/DCSF-RBX-09–11.pdf>.

compared with like as children in long-term foster care are generally placed at an older age with much greater exposure to pre-care adversity and, as is well-recognised in the literature, age at placement is a key predictor of placement stability in all placement types.[22] Moreover, the researchers found no significant difference in the children's emotional and behavioural outcomes, participation and progress in education, and perceptions of belonging and permanence.[23] As the researchers note, in one sense these were positive findings in that children in stable long term foster care were doing as well as those who had been adopted. However, the results also expose some of the ongoing vulnerabilities of adopted children and raise questions about whether adoption really is an inherently superior form of alternative care for looked-after children.

The fact that the evidence suggests somewhat mixed outcomes for children adopted from care does not mean adoption cannot be a successful intervention for many looked-after children. It does, however, counsel caution against treating adoption as a panacea, particularly when we are considering adoption as an option for older children with challenging backgrounds and for whom the legal transplant model of adoption may be particularly problematic. The child's route to permanence should always be firmly based in the welfare of the particular child. The difficulty when adoption becomes idealised as it is in the Narey report is that it can become the holy grail, an objective to be pursued at all costs. With such emphasis placed on the importance of achieving 'more adoptions more quickly' there is a tendency to ignore potentially valuable alternatives,[24] marginalise the legitimate rights and interests of the birth parents and to minimise the importance of the procedural and substantive safeguards provided by the courts. There is evidence that this tendency is currently garnering ever stronger support amongst both policy makers and the courts.

3.   PROTECTING THE LEGITIMATE RIGHTS AND INTERESTS OF THE BIRTH PARENTS

At the heart of the law's approach to adoption has always been the need to mediate between a triad of interests: the birth parents, the adoptive parents and the child. Striking a balance between these often-competing interests is never easy but it has always been a key function of the law, and thereby the courts, to ensure the rights and interests of all the parties to an adoption are given due and

---

22   Ibid. See also DANCE and RUSHTON, above n. 19, 279 and J. SELWYN, L. FRAZER and D. QUINTON, 'Paved with Good Intentions: The Pathway to Adoption and the Costs of Delay' (2006) 36 *British Journal of Social Work* 561.

23   Ibid.

24   Narey, for example, expresses concern about the growing use of special guardianship. See above n. 13, pp. 32–33.

proper consideration. The importance of this task is underlined by the often intense vulnerability of all those involved and the importance of the decisions at stake.[25] For the adoptive parents, adoption can see the realisation of a desperately held dream to be a parent. The loss of that dream can be devastating. For the child, adoption not only promises a 'forever family' but the potential loss of the birth family and a change of legal status with life-long legal and social consequences. And for the birth parents, adoption represents one of the most drastic and far-reaching exercises of State power still possible in a liberal society: the permanent and irrevocable termination of their very parenthood. It is because of the dramatic impact of adoption on the existing parent-child relationship that from the outset the law has rightly been particularly concerned with the vulnerability of the birth parents and ensuring that their rights and interests are given the most anxious and careful consideration before an adoption order is made.[26]

3.1. LOOKING BACK: LESSONS FROM THE PAST

The first piece of legislation in which adoption was legally recognised and sanctioned was largely motivated by the desire to provide some degree of legal security and protection to the adoptive parents, in particular from birth parents who it was feared might seek the return of the child when the child became economically useful.[27] However, the Tomlin Committee, whose recommendations lay behind the Adoption Act 1926, was also deeply concerned with the position of the birth parents. At a time when adoption was essentially a voluntary contractual arrangement between the birth parents and the adoptive parents, this concern focused on ensuring that the birth parents had given a truly informed and voluntary consent to the adoption.[28] The courts were thus charged with ensuring the parents had understood the nature and effect of the adoption order and that consent was not being given under duress.[29] There was particular concern for the vulnerability of the birth mother, with the courts acting as an 'effective safeguard' against the possibility that the mother had been compelled by social and economic pressures to surrender her child.[30]

---

[25] As to the characteristics and typical problems of families involved in care proceedings see J. Masson, J. Pearce and K. Bader et al., *Care profiling study,* Ministry of Justice Research Series 4/08, London 2008.

[26] See also A. Bainham, *Children – The Modern Law,* 3rd ed., Jordan Publishing: Bristol, 2005, pp. 266–267.

[27] Cretney, above n. 1, p. 601. See also S. Cretney, 'From Status to Contract?' in F.D. Rose (ed.), *Consensus Ad Idem, Essays in the Law of Contract in Honour of Guenter Treitel,* Sweet & Maxwell, London 1996, p. 253.

[28] Ibid., p. 256.

[29] Ibid.

[30] Ibid.

By the time of the Adoption Act 1949, the protection of the birth mother had been somewhat eroded. Addressing the concern of prospective adopters regarding possible future interference by the birth parents, the 'shroud of secrecy'[31] had begun to descend over adoption with the removal of the need for the birth parents to know the identity of the prospective adopters before a valid consent could be given.[32] More fundamentally, there was increasing acceptance that parental consent could be dispensed with under certain prescribed circumstances, albeit important protections remained in place. The courts had always been able to make an adoption order without the birth parents' consent but the courts used this power sparingly, restricting its use to cases where the child had been abandoned or the parent was mentally incapable of giving consent.[33] In 1949, Parliament removed the general discretion vested in the court to dispense with consent, replacing it with the more-defined ground that parental consent could be dispensed with where it was being unreasonably withheld.[34] The Adoption Act 1949 thus laid the groundwork for the freeing procedure that was to become a central feature of the Adoption Act 1976.[35]

Again, however, the rights and interests of the birth parents were not swept away by these changes. In the wake of the 1949 legislation debate focused on the extent to which the child's welfare should be taken into account in determining whether or not the consent of the parent was being unreasonably withheld.[36] This debate was settled by the House of Lords in *Re W (An infant)*,[37] it being held that whilst a reasonable parent in deciding whether or not to consent to an adoption would have regard to the child's welfare, it would not be the only or paramount consideration: the reasonable parent would also take into account his or her own wishes and feelings in the matter. Throughout the twentieth century the position was thus maintained both in the legislation and by the courts that the rights and interests of the birth parents had a legitimate place in decision-making about adoption.

The role of the courts in overseeing adoption and protecting the rights and interests of potentially vulnerable parties, particularly the birth parents and the child, was also recognised as indispensable throughout the twentieth century. Given the nature of the state's intervention into the existing family when an adoption order is made, the importance of the court's role as independent arbiter

---

31   BRIDGE, above n. 2, pp. 198–199.
32   CRETNEY, above n. 27, p. 258.
33   Ibid., p. 260.
34   CRETNEY, above n. 1, p. 614.
35   CRETNEY, above n. 27, p. 259.
36   Ibid., pp. 260–261.
37   *Re W (An Infant)* [1971] AC 682. See also *Re H; Re W (Adoption: Parental Agreement)* (1983) FLR 614 and *Re C (A Minor) (Adoption: Parental Agreement: Contact)* [1993] 2 FLR 260.

may seem self-evident. Indeed, Cretney describes the role of the court as the 'only constant in the development of the adoption process over the past 70 years.'[38] Under the Adoption Act 1926 the role of the courts was fairly minimal. With adoption seen as essentially a civil contract between the birth parents and the adopters, the primary function of the court was to recognise and uphold the 'adoption contract' between the parties if satisfied as to the truly voluntary consensual nature of the arrangement.[39] However, even in these embryonic stages of the law's regulation of adoption the court was perceived as having a much wider protective function. In 1920 the Hopkinson Committee recommended that legal effect should be given to adoption agreements provided only that the '"sanction of some responsible judicial or other public authority" were given.'[40] Throughout the twentieth century it was thus the court which was charged with the key duty of safeguarding the child's welfare and ensuring the rights and interests of the birth parents were properly accounted for.[41] The potential for abuse of the adoption process was an ever-present consideration. Whilst adoption has always had an altruistic dimension, it has never been able to completely shake the perceived threat of a 'darker' side. The courts were thus seen as an important bulwark against the legalised trafficking of children, the potential exploitation of vulnerable mothers and social engineering by the State.[42] In 1937, the Horsburgh Committee recommended greater state regulation of adoption agencies and a clearer role for the courts in scrutinising agency adoptions.[43] With adoption agencies now acting as agents of the State in pursuing the placement and adoption of children away from their birth families, the need for regulation, accountability and independent scrutiny of their actions in individual cases may seem greater than ever.

3.2. LOOKING FORWARD: MARGINALISING THE BIRTH PARENTS AND THE COURTS

The ACA 2002 marked a clear move to a more 'child-centred' approach to adoption with the result that the rights and interests of the birth parents have become increasingly marginalised in the decision-making process.[44] The ACA 2002 provides that whenever a court or adoption agency is coming to a decision relating to the adoption of a child, the child's welfare must be the *paramount*

---

[38] CRETNEY, above n. 27, p. 268.
[39] Ibid., p. 252.
[40] Ibid., p. 254.
[41] Ibid., p. 268.
[42] See, for example, CRETNEY, above n. 1, pp. 606–609.
[43] There were particular concerns about the agencies concealing the identity of the adopters from the birth mother, encouraging unregulated *de facto* adoptions and later sending children abroad: CRETNEY, above n. 1, p. 608.
[44] See generally S. HARRIS-SHORT and J. MILES, *Family Law: Text, Cases & Materials* 2nd ed., Oxford University Press, Oxford 2011, pp. 901–907.

consideration.[45] This constitutes a significant departure from the previous legislation in which the child's welfare remained only the *first* consideration.[46] The decision to make the child's welfare paramount was controversial. Under the Adoption Act 1976 the courts had the flexibility to take into account factors other than the child's welfare, including the rights and interests of the birth parents, when making decisions about adoption. The paramountcy principle, at least as traditionally understood in English law, precludes such an approach.[47] In interpreting the child's welfare, sections 1(4)(c) and 1(4)(f) of the ACA 2002 direct the decision-maker to have regard to the wishes and feelings of the birth parents and the importance of their relationship with the child. This is, however, quite different from giving separate and independent consideration to the distinct rights and interests of the birth parents.[48]

Concerns about the welfare test enshrined in the ACA 2002 are compounded by the legislation's new test for dispensing with parental consent. Section 52 of the ACA 2002 now provides that parental consent can only be dispensed with if the court is satisfied that the parent or guardian cannot be found or is incapable of giving consent or the welfare of the child requires consent to be dispensed with. At the time the legislation was passed there was some debate as to whether the use of the word 'requires' could be interpreted to allow the court to take into account the rights and interests of the birth parents.[49] That debate has most probably been silenced by the Court of Appeal in *Re P (a child)*.[50] It was argued before the Court of Appeal that consent could not be dispensed with on the basis of a simple welfare test because the word 'requires' was intended to convey: 'a sense of the imperative; something which was a necessity; and a demand which was the antithesis of something voluntary or optional.'[51] In support of this position counsel pointed to the need to strike an appropriate balance between the rights of the birth parents and the rights of the child as demanded by the Strasbourg case law,[52] arguing that an 'enhanced' welfare test must be applied in order to give proper regard to the parents' Article 8 rights.[53] Applying this 'enhanced' test to cases where there was a feasible alternative which would constitute a less drastic interference with the rights and interests of the birth

---

45   ACA 2002, s. 1(1)-(2).
46   Adoption Act 1976, s. 6.
47   *J v. C* [1970] AC 688, 710–711.
48   S. Harris-Short, 'The Adoption and Children Bill – a fast track to failure?' [2001] 13 *CFLQ* 405, 419–420.
49   S. Choudhry, 'The Adoption and Children Act 2002, The Welfare Principle and the Human Rights Act 1998 – A Missed Opportunity' [2003] 15 *CFLQ* 119, 122–124.
50   [2008] EWCA Civ 535.
51   Ibid., [75].
52   In particular, *Johansen v. Norway* (App No 17383/90, ECHR) (1997).
53   Above n. 50, [99]-[101].

parents, adoption would be difficult to justify.[54] The Court of Appeal, emphasising the legislation's clear focus on the child's welfare, firmly rejected this approach, holding that the application of the extended welfare test in s. 1(4), in particular the requirement that the court is to have regard to the child's welfare throughout his or her life, was sufficient to ensure proper regard was had to the rights and interests of the birth family.[55] Consequently, although the Court of Appeal does note that the word 'requires' suggests the adoption must be 'imperative' or 'demanded' rather than 'merely optional or reasonable or desirable',[56] the likely practical effect of the Court of Appeal's decision is that once adoption is deemed to be in the best interests of the child, parental consent will be dispensed with without further thought or consideration.

As has been argued elsewhere, making the child's welfare determinative throughout the adoption process is difficult to reconcile with the demands of Article 8 and the Strasbourg jurisprudence on taking a child into care and his/her subsequent adoption.[57] A number of recent cases have emphasised the importance of the court complying with its obligations under Article 8 of the ECHR when making a care order, particularly when the care plan is to place the child for adoption. In the case of *EH v. Greenwich London Borough Council and others; Re A (children) (non-accidental injury)*,[58] the Court of Appeal reiterated that, in accordance with the demands of Article 8, the local authority's core obligation when intervening into family life is to work to support the family and ensure that rehabilitation has 'a reasonable prospect of success.'[59] On the facts, the local authority were strongly criticized for not providing the mother with the rigorous support work she needed in order to give rehabilitation a realistic chance, the local authority having decided at an early stage to place the children permanently outside the birth family.[60] Lord Justice Wall was particularly trenchant in his criticism of the local authority observing, '[s]ocial workers are perceived by many as the arrogant and enthusiastic removers of children from their parents into an unsatisfactory care system, and as trampling on the rights of parents and children in the process. This case will do little to dispel that perception.'[61] This concern with the birth parents' Article 8 rights has not, however, been reflected in the post-2002 case law on adoption.

---

54   Ibid., [83]-[84].
55   Ibid., [127]-[128].
56   Ibid., [125].
57   Harris-Short, above n. 48 and 'Making and Breaking Family Life: Adoption, the State and Human Rights' (2008) 35 *Journal of Law and Society* 28. As to the obligations on the State under Article 8 of the ECHR when taking a child into care see, *Haase v. Germany* (2005) (App No 11057/02, ECHR), [90]-[92].
58   [2010] EWCA Civ 344.
59   Ibid., [14].
60   Ibid., [55].
61   Ibid., [109].

The courts have consistently adopted a strong and often exclusively child-centred approach when interpreting the ACA 2002 on a range of issues. The courts have thus held that the child's welfare will be a relevant consideration on an application for leave to revoke a placement order[62] and in determining whether to strike out an appeal.[63] Despite warning against stacking the odds too highly against the birth parents, the Court of Appeal has also held that the child's welfare will be the paramount consideration on an application for leave to defend an adoption order.[64] It is perhaps revealing that in the course of its judgment the Court of Appeal notes, 'the [o]bject of the 2002 Act was to simplify the adoption process and to reduce delays in children being placed for adoption and adopted.'[65] The Court of Appeal's commitment to what it perceives as the overriding priorities now entrenched within the ACA 2002 is equally clear from its decision in the case of *C v. X, Y, Z County Council*.[66] The case concerned the question of whether the fact of the child's birth and planned adoption should be disclosed to the birth father against the wishes of the birth mother. It was argued on behalf of the child that regardless of the mother's wishes there was a duty on the local authority, underpinned by sections 1(4)(c) and 1(4)(f) of the legislation, to make enquiries about the child's father and the wider birth family and that 'compelling reasons' would therefore be required to prevent disclosure taking place.[67] The Court of Appeal dismissed the argument holding that there is no duty to make enquiries if disclosure would only delay the adoption with no discernable benefit for the child.[68] Furthermore, the Court stressed that there is no requirement as a matter of policy for any preference to be given to the birth family.[69] In the words of Thorpe LJ, the ACA 2002 does not compel the adoption agency to 'inform and assess all and sundry' – which in this case included the child's father.[70] Taken together these authorities reveal a strong judicial commitment to a more child-centred approach to adoption, an approach which has resulted in the rights and interests of the birth parents being squeezed out of consideration at every stage of the decision-making process.

---

[62] *Re M (children) (placement order)* [2007] EWCA Civ 1084.

[63] *Re M (placement order)* [2010] EWCA Civ 1257.

[64] *Re P (a child) (adoption order: leave to oppose making of an adoption order)* [2007] EWCA Civ 616, [26] and [30]-[32].

[65] Ibid., [53].

[66] [2007] EWCA Civ 1206.

[67] Ibid., [23]. Previous authorities held that the child's father should generally be informed and his views considered before the child was placed for adoption unless there were strong countervailing factors. See *Re L (Adoption: Contacting Natural Father)* [2007] EWHC 1771.

[68] Ibid., [3]-[21].

[69] Ibid., [15].

[70] Ibid., [78]. It should be noted that the Court of Appeal has subsequently held that there is no reason to suppose that in adopting this more robust approach to non-disclosure the Court of Appeal intended to depart from previous authorities. See *M v. F and others* [2011] EWCA Civ 273.

The current policy agenda dictating 'more adoptions more quickly' has also led to calls for the role of the courts in adoption decision-making to be restricted. Masson, for example, has suggested that alongside the need for care proceedings to be 'made smaller', the adoption process needs to be simplified 'either through restricting the role of the court or the role of the adoption panel'.[71] Masson recognises that there are arguments in favour of the courts retaining the jurisdiction to decide on the principle of adoption, most notably that the courts being fully aware of all the relevant evidence regarding the child's needs from its involvement in the care proceedings will be best placed to make the decision.[72] However, she also raises some concerns regarding the uncertainty created by placing these decisions in the hands of judges with differing views on the benefits of adoption.[73] Cretney has also questioned whether there is still any meaningful role to be played by the courts in the adoption process. Although he notes that an adoption order has always been regarded as requiring 'real adjudication'[74] and that the court has always played a 'useful, indispensable purpose in contested cases',[75] he also asks whether such adjudication is still necessary now that adoption occurs in the context of an 'elaborately structured system of investigation, counselling and decision-taking.'[76]

Although recent case law impacting on the rights and interests of birth parents is disappointing, any further marginalisation of the role of the court in adoption proceedings would constitute another significant blow to the vital procedural and substantive protections to which the birth parents are entitled. Although adoption typically now occurs at the end of lengthy care proceedings in which the child's welfare and the parenting of the birth parents have been subjected to the most careful scrutiny, the fact that a care order has been made does not provide an answer to the need for careful adjudication of the decision to proceed with adoption. The two issues are different; fundamentally so. As was recognised in the Houghton Report, adoption is different from all other decisions regarding the care and placement of the child.[77] It has lifelong, permanent and irrevocable, legal and social consequences.[78] Adoption thus represents a drastic intervention by the State into the parent-child relationship.

---

[71]   J. MASSON, 'Adoption, Future Legal Issues' (2010) 34 *Adoption & Fostering* 80, 83. The Government has announced it intends to remove the role of the adoption panel: MINISTRY OF JUSTICE and DEPARTMENT OF EDUCATION, *The Government Response to the Family Justice Review: A system with children and families at its heart*, 2012, Cm 8273, 16.

[72]   Ibid.

[73]   Ibid.

[74]   CRETNEY, above n. 27, p. 256.

[75]   Ibid., p. 268.

[76]   Ibid.

[77]   CRETNEY, above n. 1, p. 707.

[78]   For Cretney's account of these juristic differences see S. CRETNEY, *Principles of Family Law*, 4th ed., Sweet & Maxwell, London 1984, p. 445.

Moreover, it cannot be assumed that the motivations of those who act on behalf of the State are entirely benign. There is a clear political agenda underpinning the concern of successive governments with adoption, providing as it does a 'privatised' solution to the problem of looked-after children. Through the medium of adoption all responsibility for the care and upbringing of looked-after children, financial and otherwise, is shifted from the State back to the private sector. From the State's perspective, adoption thus provides the ideal solution to the increasing number of children needing permanent alternative care away from their birth parents. A very traditional 'privatised' view of adoption in which the adoptive parents stand in relation to the child as if the child had been born their own legitimate child and the State is able to withdraw completely from any further role in the child's life clearly underpins the Narey report.[79] The State's interest in preserving and promoting a traditional legal transplant model of adoption, particularly in a world of unprecedented cuts in public-spending, is not necessarily consistent with the interests of the individual child and is almost certainly adverse to the interests of the birth parents. Against the backdrop of these political pressures, the adjudicatory role of the court as independent arbiter in adoption proceedings, safeguarding and promoting both the welfare of the individual child and the rights and interests of the birth parents against the machinations of the State, has never been more important.

4. CONCLUSION

As we look to the future, we can expect to see further reforms to the law on adoption in the fairly immediate future. There is a strong perception that the care system is in crisis with adoption providing the most effective solution for looked-after children caught within it. In order to maximise the 'transformational impact' of adoption,[80] it is argued that children need to be placed much more quickly and at a much younger age.[81] This has led to strong calls for more robust and decisive decision making by social workers, child welfare professionals and the courts before, during and after care proceedings.[82] Concern about exacerbating delay in securing permanent placements for looked-after children has also been one of the key drivers behind the gradual marginalisation of the rights and interests of the birth parents in decision-making about adoption. There are, however, necessary limits as to how far this process can go. The law

---

[79]   NAREY, above n. 13, pp. 17 and 26. Cf. LOWE, above n. 5 and B. LUCKOCK and A. HART, 'Adoptive family life and adoption support: policy ambivalence and the development of effective services' (2005) 10 *Child and Family Social Work* 125.

[80]   NAREY, above n. 13, p. 2.

[81]   Ibid.; see also MASSON, above n. 71, 80 and BIEHAL et al., above n. 21.

[82]   NAREY, above n. 13, pp. 4–12 and FAMILY JUSTICE REVIEW, *Final Report*, Ministry of Justice, London 2011, pp. 13–17.

starts from the position that the parent-child relationship means something: it is worthy of *a priori* protection. We do not countenance the removal of children from their birth parents simply because others could do a better job. In the words of Baroness Hale:

'Taking a child away from her family is a momentous step, not only for her, but for her whole family, and for the local authority which does so. In a totalitarian society, uniformity and conformity are valued. Hence the totalitarian state tries to separate the child from her family and mould her to its own design. Families in all their subversive variety are the breeding ground of diversity and individuality. In a free and democratic society we value diversity and individuality... As Justice McReynolds famously said in *Pierce* v. *Society of Sisters*..., "The child is not the mere creature of the State".'[83]

In the current climate, these words have particular potency for parents facing the permanent and irrevocable termination of their very parenthood. The lessons of history tell us two things. First, the special position of the birth parents has always been recognised and protected in the English law of adoption. Second, responsibility for ensuring the legitimate rights and interests of the birth parents are properly weighed in the decision-making process is rightly entrusted to the independent authoritative adjudication of the courts. Our trust in the courts fulfilling this function may have been shaken in recent times. However, as the political momentum gathers towards further reform of adoption, now more than ever it is vital that we do not lose sight of these two most fundamental principles.

---

[83]   *Re B (Children) (Care Proceedings: Standard of Proof)* [2008] UKHL 35, [20].

INHERENTLY DISPOSED TO PROTECT CHILDREN
The Continuing Role of Wardship

Nigel LOWE

Contents

1. INTRODUCTION

My first conversation with Stephen Cretney was about wardship, which in itself makes it appropriate to be the subject of my contribution to this volume. But an additional reason is that wardship has that wonderfully quirky history that makes English law so fascinating, as is illustrated in Cretney's incomparable work *Family Law in the Twentieth Century: A History*.[1] It is also an opportune moment to look at wardship 20 years after the implementation of the Children

---

[1] S. CRETNEY, *Family Law in the Twentieth Century: A History*, Oxford University Press, Oxford 2003, pp. 583–92.

Act 1989, given that that Act intended to reduce, if not remove, the need to invoke it both in private and public law.[2]

Although the 1989 Act was indeed a decisive watershed for wardship, as Waite J memorably commented in *Re X (Minors)(Wardship: Disclosure of Documents)*:

> 'It would be rash to start writing obituaries today for a jurisdiction which has survived with protean tenacity down the centuries.'[3]

The object of this chapter is to demonstrate that that comment is as true now as it was in 1991, when it was made.

2. THE NATURE AND ORIGIN OF WARDSHIP AND THE INHERENT JURISDICTION

2.1. THE NATURE OF WARDSHIP

Wardship places the child under the protective care of the court such that *throughout the wardship* (that is, from the moment the child becomes a ward[4] until its discharge)[5] as Cross J put it in *Re S (Infants)*: '[n]o important step in the child's life can be taken without the court's consent.'[6]

In exercising its care over its ward the court can draw upon both its inherent powers and its statutory powers. These inherent powers are extremely wide. In *Re Z (A Minor)(Identification: Restrictions on Publication)* Ward LJ said:

> 'The wardship or inherent jurisdiction of the court to cast its cloak of protection over minors whose interests are at risk of harm is unlimited in theory though in practice the judges who exercise the jurisdiction have created classes of cases in which the court will not exercise its powers.'[7]

---

2   See Lord Mackay LC, when introducing the Bill (*Hansard*, HL Deb, 06.12.1988, vol. 502, col 493).

3   [1992] Fam 124, 137G.

4   By s. 41(2) of the Senior Courts Act 1981 a child automatically becomes a ward upon the making of the wardship application, i.e. it is triggered by an administrative rather than a judicial act.

5   By r. 12.41(1) of the Family Procedure Rules 2010, a child ceases to be a ward upon the determination of the wardship application 'unless the court orders that the child be made [commonly understood as continuing the wardship] a ward'. Where the court so orders the child only ceases to be a ward upon a court order to that effect or upon the ward attaining his or her majority: Senior Courts Act 1981, s. 41(3) and FPR 2010, r. 12.41(2).

6   [1967] 1 All ER 202, 209.

7   [1997] Fam 1, 23.

Although whether the powers can truly be said to be theoretically unlimited has been questioned,[8] there is no doubt that the inherent powers are the widest that the court enjoys to protect children. It is the combination of placing the child under the protection of the court and its consequent access to the inherent powers that makes wardship not only unique but the greatest form of protection for a child that the English (there is no equivalent in Scotland) Family Justice system can offer.

Although wardship was the normal means by which the inherent jurisdiction could be accessed, even before the 1989 Act it was clear that the jurisdiction could be invoked and exercised independently.[9] Indeed Lord Mackay LC commented in his 'Joseph Jackson Memorial Lecture' that:

> 'in the Government's view wardship is only one use of the High Court's inherent parens patriae jurisdiction. We believe therefore, that it is open to the High Court to make orders under its inherent jurisdiction in respect of children other than through wardship.'[10]

It was on this view that the Children Act 1989 was predicated (see further below).

2.2. THE NATURE OF THE INHERENT JURISDICTION

Although it is accepted that the High Court's inherent jurisdiction is equally exercisable whether the child is a ward or not,[11] it is important to emphasise that the inherent jurisdiction and wardship are not the same. In particular, unlike wardship, the exercise of the inherent jurisdiction does *not* place the child under the court's protection. Conversely, whereas only children can be made wards of court, the wider inherent jurisdiction is not so constrained.[12] Accordingly, notwithstanding the commonality of the powers and the tendency in both the 1989 Act and the Family Procedure Rules 2010 to obscure the distinction by using the term 'inherent jurisdiction' to refer to both wardship and the residual

---

[8] See N. Lowe, 'The Limits of Wardship Part 2 – the extent of the court's power over a ward' (1989) 1 *Journal of Child Law* 44.

[9] See e.g. *Re L (An Infant)* [1968] P 119, 156–7, per Lord Denning MR, *Re N (Infants)* [1967] Ch 512 and *S v. McC; W v. W* [1972] AC 24, 47–50, per Lord MacDermott.

[10] (1989) 139 NLJ 505, 507.

[11] See e.g. *MA v. DB (Inherent Jurisdiction)* [2010] EWHC 1697 (Fam).

[12] It has been developed, for example, to protect vulnerable adults, see *Re PS (Incapacitated or Vulnerable Adult)* [2007] EWHC 623 (Fam).

jurisdiction,[13] it is probably best to regard wardship as one manifestation of the inherent jurisdiction.

2.3. AN HISTORICAL EXCURSUS

Although wardship dates from feudal times,[14] the key development was the recognition in the nineteenth century[15] that its origin lay in the concept that the Sovereign as *parens patriae* had a duty to protect his subjects, particularly those such as children who were unable to protect themselves and that this duty had been entrusted to the Lord Chancellor and through him to the Court of Chancery. An important consequence of this recognition was that it came to be established[16] that the wardship jurisdiction was not dependent upon the existence of property belonging to the infant. Accompanying these developments was the Court of Chancery's development, largely behind the closed doors of wardship proceedings, of the child's welfare principle. As Kay LJ put it in *R v. Gyngall*, wardship:

> 'is essentially a parental jurisdiction and that description of it involves that the main consideration to be acted upon in its exercise is the benefit or welfare of the child. The term "welfare" in this connection must be read in its largest possible sense, that is to say, as meaning every circumstance must be taken into consideration, and the Court must do what under the circumstances a wise parent acting for the true interests of the child would or ought to do.'[17]

In short, the court enjoyed wide inherent powers to protect its ward based on the court's view of what was in the child's best interests.

Although these developments had sown the seeds for expanding the use of wardship and notwithstanding that the jurisdiction had been made more accessible by procedural reforms first in 1949 (enabling children to be made wards solely to protect them) and then in 1971 (transferring jurisdiction to the Family Division and to the consequent ability to begin wardship in District

---

13   Section 100 is headed 'Restrictions on use of wardship jurisdiction' but the substance of the section applies as much to the inherent jurisdiction as to wardship. In contrast, FPR 2010, Part 12, ch. 5 is entitled 'Special Provisions About Inherent Jurisdiction Proceedings' but most of the consequent rules only apply to wardship. Rule 2.3 defines 'inherent jurisdiction as meaning 'the High Court's power to make any order or determine any issue in respect of a child, including in wardship proceedings, where it would be just to do so unless restricted by legislation or case law'.

14   See N.V. Lowe and R.A.H. White, *Wards of Court*, 2nd ed., Barry Rose, London 1986, ch. 1.

15   *Johnston v. Beattie* (1843) 10 Cl & Fin 42.

16   *Re Spence* (1847) 2 Ph 247.

17   [1893] 2 QB 232, 248.

Registries), until the 1970s, it remained a little used jurisdiction invoked for the most part in relation to children of wealthy families.[18] In 1951 there were just 74 wardships and even in 1971 there were only 622. But all this changed such that by 1991 there were 4,961 wardship applications – a 6,700 per cent increase on the 1951 figure.

The key reason for this exponential increase was the use of wardship by local authorities, which found that the jurisdiction offered a way round the restrictions and difficulties presented by the then child care legislation both as a means of committing children into their care and of keeping them there. By the late 1980s over half of all wardship applications were made by local authorities. But there were other uses of the jurisdiction too, by relatives, who, until 1985, had no other means of initiating court proceedings either to seek to look after the child or to have contact, and by parents, particularly in relation to international child abduction. Finally, there were always the novel cases where the availability of High Court expertise, as well as the jurisdiction's wide powers and the court's supervisory control was clearly an advantage; as for example when dealing with the future of the UK's first commercially arranged surrogate child.[19]

3. THE MOVES TO RESTRICT THE USE OF WARDSHIP

In many ways the growth of wardship was an indicator of the inadequacies of the family justice system and in particular of its public law provisions. There was concern, too, at the escalating costs of wardship and indeed of the basic unfairness of some children being given a Rolls Royce service. In the mid 1980s the Social Services Committee considered[20] that in the local authority context the expansion had gone far enough and called upon the Family Division judges to exercise restraint in accepting wardship applications. The *Review of Child Care Law* subsequently made important proposals for overhauling the public law provisions,[21] the effect of which was estimated[22] potentially to halve the number of wardship applications. This Review was followed by the Law Commission's review of the private law[23] and the eventual radical overhaul of English child law through the Children Act 1989.

---

[18] See LORD CROSS, 'Wards of Court' (1967) 83 *LQR (Law Quarterly Review)* 200.

[19] *Re C (A Minor)(Wardship: Surrogacy)* [1985] FLR 846.

[20] See their Second report for the Session 1983–4 *Children in Care* vol. 1, HC 360–1, para. 82.

[21] DHSS, *Review of Child Care Law*, HMSO, London 1985.

[22] See DHSS, *Report of the Working Party on Costing the Review of Child Care Law* DHSS, London 1986, para. 5.12.

[23] LAW COMMISSION, *Review of Child Law: Guardianship and Custody* Law Com. No. 172, HMSO, London 1988.

3.1. THE CHILDREN ACT 1989

With a view to curbing the public law use of wardship, the 1989 Act makes wardship and local authority care incompatible. If a ward of court is committed to care, the wardship ceases,[24] and while a child is in care he cannot be made a ward of court.[25] Furthermore, both the former statutory and inherent powers to commit wards into local authority care and to make supervision orders have been respectively repealed and revoked.[26] Although these restrictions do not prevent the High Court from exercising its inherent jurisdiction to decide a specific question in relation to a child in care, the jurisdiction cannot be exercised 'for the purpose of conferring upon any local authority power to determine any question that has arisen, or which may arise, in connection with any aspect of parental responsibility for the child.' Local authorities wishing to invoke wardship or the inherent jurisdiction need court leave to do so and that can only be given if the court is satisfied that (a) the result cannot be achieved under any statutory provision, and (b) there is reasonable cause to believe that if the inherent jurisdiction is not exercised the child is likely to suffer significant harm.[27]

3.2. RE T

Although the 1989 Act is silent on the use of wardship in the private law context, its clear policy was to reduce the need to resort to wardship in *both* the public and private law arenas.[28] The full import of this was made clear in *Re T (A Minor)(Child: Representation)* in which Waite LJ referred to wardship being 'an exceptional status under the modern law as it must now be applied'.[29] In that case the issue was whether a child could bring proceedings on her own behalf without the need for a guardian ad litem. It was found that the Rule[30] providing that she could applied equally whether or not the child was a ward. Accordingly, there was no justification for continuing the wardship nor in particular to appoint through that jurisdiction a guardian for the child. In discontinuing the wardship, Waite LJ observed that, while it survives as an independent jurisdiction, the 'courts' undoubted discretion to allow wardship to go forward in a suitable case is subject to their clear duty, in loyalty to the scheme and

---

24   Children Act 1989, s. 91(4).
25   Ibid., s. 100(2)(c) and the Senior Courts Act 1981, s. 41(2A).
26   Ibid., s. 100(1) and (2)(a).
27   Ibid., s. 100(4).
28   See DEPARTMENT OF HEALTH, *The Children Act 1989 Guidance and Regulations*, Vol. 1, 'Court Orders', HMSO, London 1991, para. 3.98, which commented '[b]y incorporating many of the beneficial aspects of wardship, such as the 'open door' policy, and a flexible range of orders, the Act will subsequently reduce the need to have recourse to the High Court.'
29   [1994] Fam 49.
30   Then FPR 1991, r. 9(2A), now FPR 2010, r. 16.6.

purpose of the Children Act legislation, to permit recourse to wardship only when it becomes apparent that the child's welfare demands it and there is no other available remedy'.

4. THE CURRENT USE OF WARDSHIP

The impact of the 1989 Act on the use of wardship was both immediate and dramatic. Whereas in 1991 there were 4,961 wardship applications, in 1992 there were just 492 but interestingly, there were similar numbers in 1998 (431) and in 1999 (418).[31] Applications further declined to 268 in 2010 but rose to 194 in the first half of 2011 and it is this continued residual use that will now be explored.[32]

4.1. USE IN PUBLIC LAW CASES

Given the restrictions imposed by the 1989 Act it might have been thought that the use of wardship in public law cases had effectively been ended, but it is clear that it has not. In fact the Act did not prohibit local authority use of wardship (or the inherent jurisdiction) per se but only as a means of obtaining a care order, maintaining court control over children in their care, or keeping children in their care. There is therefore no embargo on authorities seeking to use wardship[33] in relation to a child being accommodated by them, nor indeed in any case where the authority is not itself seeking care but is nevertheless concerned about the child's well-being. An early post-Act example was *Re R (A Minor)(Contempt)*,[34] where a local authority warded a 14-year-old child accommodated by them to protect her from a relationship with a 33-year-old man. More recently, in *Re S (Wardship: Peremptory Return)*,[35] the local authority, having initiated care proceedings, successfully invoked wardship to ensure the child's return to the jurisdiction in circumstances where the 1980 Hague Abduction Convention was inapplicable because the removal had been lawful and, as a result, no other remedy was available.

---

31   See N.V. Lowe and G. Douglas, *Bromley's Family* Law, 10th ed., Oxford University Press, Oxford 2007, p. 898 and HHJ Mitchell, 'Whatever Happened to Wardship? Part I' [2001] *Family Law* 130.

32   Figures obtained by a Freedom of Information Request to HM Courts and Tribunals Service.

33   This requires obtaining court leave, discussed above. It is also open to the local authority to apply (again, with leave) for a prohibited steps or specific issue order, though on this, note Thorpe LJ's comment in *Langley v. Liverpool City Council* [2005] EWCA Civ 1173 that he had yet to encounter a case 'in a which a local authority has decided that it can achieve the end that its child protection duties require by applying for a prohibited steps order'.

34   [1994] 2 FLR 185. Quaere whether a prohibited steps order could have been made in this case instead.

35   [2010] EWCA Civ 465.

A commonly cited example of the use of wardship is where, though not itself seeking care, the local authority is concerned about the medical treatment of a child. Past examples have included concerns about a child's sterilisation and contested cases involving emergency medical treatment of children in care.[36] But this may have to be re-examined in the light of *A Local Authority v. SB, AB &MB*[37] in which, upon a local authority application to withdraw care proceedings, the court declined to make the child a ward in the context of concerns about the lack of parental co-operation with a hospital over the child's medical treatment, upon the basis that, upon withdrawal, there was no issue for the court to decide.

Another example is *Re F (Mental Health Act: Guardianship)*[38] in which a 17-year-old with a mental age of between 5 and 8 had been accommodated by a local authority because of chronic neglect (her seven siblings were taken into interim care for the same reason). Her parents sought her return. Care proceedings were not possible because of the child's age and the local authority instead obtained a guardianship order under the Mental Health Act 1983. It was held that wardship was the more appropriate remedy because the 1983 Act was not a child-centred jurisdiction and the child lacked the benefit of independent representation. Furthermore, on the particular facts, wardship enabled a single judge to consider the interests both of the child in question and her seven siblings.

Wardship was also successfully invoked in proceedings concerning children who, though happily placed with foster carers, could not, according to Regulations[39] then in place, remain there since the foster-father had previously been formally cautioned for actual bodily harm to another foster child (subsequently adopted by him and his wife). Following the foster parents' intervention in care proceedings at which the mother was still seeking her children's return, it was held in *Re RJ (Fostering: Person Disqualified)*[40] that although the Regulations did not prevent *the court* from making a residence order, in this case the preferable course was to discharge the interim care orders, ward the children and grant interim care and control to the foster parents. In this way the status quo could be preserved pending the full hearing and, by not granting even interim residence orders which would have vested parental responsibility in the foster parent, any perception of prejudice the mother might

---

[36] See respectively, *Re B (A Minor)(Wardship: Medical Treatment)* [1981] 1 WLR 1421, *Re O (A Minor)(Medical Treatment)* [1993] 2 FLR 149 and *Re R (A Minor)(Blood Transfusion)* [1993] 2 FLR 757.

[37] [2010] EWHC 1744 (Fam).

[38] [1996] 2 FLR 43.

[39] Viz the Children (Protection From Offenders)(Miscellaneous Amendments) Regulations 1997, SI 1997/2308, which aimed to prevent paedophiles from becoming foster parents.

[40] [1999] 1 WLR 581.

have could be avoided. At the subsequent hearing (*Re RJ (Fostering: Wardship)*)[41] it was held that, given the exceptional circumstances, the appropriate long-term solution was to continue the wardship and to grant care and control to the foster carers. This solution was considered advantageous, because: (a) giving ultimate control to the court would be reassuring to the foster carer (who would otherwise have shared parental responsibility with the mother had they been granted residence orders); (b) it was only by this means that the local authority could remain involved in what had become a private law case; and (c) it would allow the children's guardian to continue to be involved.

In *Re W and X (Wardship: Relatives Rejected As Foster Carers)*,[42] proceedings had been brought in respect of children living with their maternal grandparents after the death of a sibling. It was common ground that the threshold criteria had been satisfied but the local authority's preferred option was to leave them with the grandparents subject to a care order. However, because the authority had previously rejected the grandparents as foster parents, Regulations[43] meant that this option could not be adopted since the children would have to be removed from them immediately the care order was made. It was held that this inability to pursue what was perceived to be the best option was a *lacuna* in the legislation which wardship could properly remedy since it neither infringed the letter nor the spirit of section 100 given that the court were not seeking to control the local authority. Moreover, the children's placement warranted long-term external control which could not be achieved by a care order but only through wardship. The children were accordingly warded in addition to making supervision orders and residence orders in favour of grandparents.

The above cases demonstrate the court's willingness to use wardship to overcome restrictions imposed by Regulation on local authorities' freedom to put children in foster placements which would otherwise operate to the detriment of the particular children concerned. But two further cases are illustrative of a potentially wider use. In *Re M and J (Wardship: Supervision and Residence Orders)*[44] a mother and stepfather conceded the threshold criteria in care proceedings and agreed to the psychologist's recommendation that one boy should live with his father and the other with his maternal grandmother. The local authority did not agree with this recommendation but did not seek alternative orders. Charles J took the 'exceptional course' of making a residence order and a supervision order coupled with wardship orders in respect of each child, and an order for contact. The justification for wardship was to manage the inevitable future tensions that would arise within the

---

41   [1999] 1 FLR 618.
42   [2003] EWHC 2206 (Fam).
43   Viz the Fostering Services Regulations 2002, SI 2002/57.
44   [2003] EWHC 1585 (Fam).

family which he found that by themselves the authority may not have been able to handle. In *E v. London Borough of X*,[45] E, who had come to England from Ghana, was being temporarily accommodated following the breakdown of E's relationship with a woman she believed to be her mother. E made herself a ward of court but after a section 37 investigation, the other woman denied she was the mother and alleged that E was 20. The local authority was asked to make an age assessment which found E to be 'at least 20'. E then sought an order in wardship that she was 17. The court acceded to her request, ruling it was not prevented from doing so by section 100(2); found her to be 17 and continued the wardship until E's majority 'in the light of the uncertainty as to her present circumstances should she be obliged to leave her present lodging', it appearing to the court to be 'desirable' for it to 'retain oversight of her welfare for the 10 months or so of her minority'.

4.2. USE IN PRIVATE LAW CASES

Notwithstanding the strictures of *Re T* (above) against invoking wardship save where it is the only legitimate means of securing a child's welfare, its immediacy of protection, the width of the court's powers and the continuing court protection have proved useful in diverse situations.

The most common use is in connection with international child abduction. Although there are no longer any jurisdictional advantages in invoking wardship,[46] and while many of the powers that were formerly unique to it are now more generally available, wardship remains useful because of the immediate and all round protection that it offers. Because of the automatic embargo against the child's removal from England and Wales without court leave arising immediately upon warding the child, and the consequent triggering of mechanisms both to impose port alerts and to trace children, the jurisdiction is a useful device to prevent abduction[47] and to deal with children who have been

---

[45]   [2005] EWHC 811 (Fam).

[46]   According to Munby LJ in *Re A (Removal Outside Jurisdiction: Habitual Residence)* [2011] EWCA Civ 625, the correct approach is first to consider whether the Council Regulation (EC) 2201/2003 (the revised Brussels II) applies and if it does not then jurisdiction must be taken upon the basis of the provisions of the Family Law Act 1986. In practice this means that jurisdiction will not normally be taken in respect of a child, even if a British subject and *a fortiori* if the child is not, if he or she is neither present nor resident in England and Wales: *Re A*, above, *H v. H (Jurisdiction to Grant Wardship)* [2011] EWCA Civ 796 and *Al Habtoor v. Fotheringham* [2001] EWCA Civ 186.

[47]   Though, as Munby J pointed out in *S v. S* [2008] EWHC 2288 (Fam), it cannot be used as means getting a judge to direct the Secretary of State to release the dependant of a failed asylum seeker from administrative detention, or by the court putting pressure on the Secretary of State by making a declaration about the child's health. For a general discussion of the advantages of wardship in this context, see R. WHITE, A.P. CARR, N. LOWE and A.

abducted into the country.[48] It can also be sometimes advantageous to use wardship to obtain the return of children wrongfully taken abroad.[49]

In this latter connection there has been a raft of cases involving children being taken to the Indian sub-continent for arranged or sometimes forced marriages. In *Re KR (Abduction: Forcible Removal By Parents)*,[50] a 16 year-old Sikh girl living in England was taken to the Punjab by her parents for an arranged marriage. Her elder sister issued wardship proceedings and, following what has been described[51] as 'an imaginative order, replete with recitals' which secured the co-operation of the Indian authorities, the ward was returned. In *B v. A and B*[52] a child was made a ward of court in a dispute between a mother and the paternal grandmother over allegations that the grandmother had removed the child from her in Pakistan at a time when the mother had no visa to return to England. The court ordered CAFCASS to investigate the circumstances. Most recently, in *Re S (Wardship: Stranded Spouses)*[53] in concluding that a mother had been forcibly separated from her child and removed and abandoned in another jurisdiction, the court made an urgent plea to the immigration authorities that consideration be given as to what arrangements can be put in place to assist mothers to return to this jurisdiction in similar circumstances. Following this plea guidance has now been issued[54] including the advice that the best vehicle for these types of cases is wardship, the proceedings of which should be managed, if possible, and heard by a judge of the Family Division.

MacDonald, *White, Carr and Lowe: The Children Act in Practice*, 4th ed., Butterworths, London 2008, 12.20–23.

[48]   See e.g. *Re H (Abduction: Non Convention Application)*[2006] EWHC 199 (Fam), *Re S (A Child)* [2008] EWCA Civ 951, in which a child was warded after being abducted to India and then returned. On appeal an order to allow disclosure of phone numbers (together with the name and addresses) on the mother's mobile phone was reversed because of concerns for the safety of the mother and child who were in protective custody and *H v. D* [2007] EWHC 802 (Fam) in which children were warded after complicated 1980 Hague Abduction Convention proceedings in which the children's return to Venezuela was refused.

[49]   See e.g. *B v. D (Abduction: Inherent Jurisdiction)* [2008] EWHC 1246 (Fam) in which children living temporarily in Portugal were warded although the mother could have applied to the Portuguese court for a return order under the 1980 Hague Abduction Convention.

[50]   [1999] 2 FLR 542. See also *SB v. RB (Residence: Forced Marriage: Child's Best Interests)* [2008] EWHC 938 (Fam), an 11 year old girl was made a ward of court after her mother agreed to marry her to a 20 -year old in Bangladesh. C.f. *RB v. FB & MA* [2008] EWHC 1669 (Fam), a 15 year old Pakistani girl with British nationality who had never been to the UK but was due to arrive for an arranged marriage was warded (quaere whether there was jurisdiction to do so). Note also *P v. P* [2006] EWHC 2410 (Fam), wards returned from Nepal in compliance with the order.

[51]   HHJ Mitchell, 'Whatever Happened to Wardship? Part II' [2001] *Fam Law* 212, 215.

[52]   [2005] EWHC 1291 (Fam).

[53]   [2010] EWHC 1669 (Fam).

[54]   *Re S (Wardship)Guidance in cases of Stranded Spouses* [2011] 1 FLR 319.

Apart from abduction, wardship has been found useful in other international situations. In *Re M (Child's Upbringing)*,[55] for example, a boy born in South Africa to Zulu parents was brought, with their consent, to England by a white woman who later applied to adopt him. The parents objected to the adoption and the child was warded. The adoption application was refused and the child was ordered to be returned to his parents but the wardship was continued. The boy's return proved unsuccessful and he returned to England living with the applicant under a wardship order. In *Re K (Adoption and Wardship)*[56] a Bosnian Muslim orphan baby was brought to England by an English couple initially to receive medical treatment. The couple were later granted an adoption order. However, because they had failed to reveal to the court that the child had relatives who wished to look after her, the adoption was set aside. Nevertheless the court decided that she should remain with the couple because of her psychological bond with them. The wardship was therefore continued with the couple being granted care and control and access being granted to the relatives.

Wardship continues to have a role in domestic disputes. The court's wardship powers are wider than those under section 8 of the Children Act 1989 and where advantage needs to be taken of this it would be proper both to invoke and to continue the jurisdiction. In *Re W (Wardship: Discharge: Publicity)*,[57] for example, in which a father having been granted care and control of four sons aged between 10 and 15 in earlier wardship proceedings had unilaterally changed their schooling and acquiesced in them talking to the press about their 'fight to stay with Dad', had his request to discharge the wardship refused. It was held that the continuation of the wardship was justified because no comparable protection could be achieved under the 1989 Act since it was impossible to make a prohibited steps order which could anticipate how the father might act and because a prohibited steps order might not be appropriate to prevent the publishing of information about the children. Furthermore, the continuing nature of the wardship meant that the Official Solicitor could remain involved and act as a buffer between the parents. The case could also be reserved to the same judge.

There are also examples where the court's overall control of its wards has been thought advantageous particularly in the context of ongoing protracted familial dispute. In *Re P (Surrogacy: Residence)*[58] in the context of a dispute over a surrogacy agreement (the mother concealing the birth) it was held appropriate, when making a residence order in favour of the biological and commissioning

---

55 [1996] 2 FLR 441.
56 [1997] 2 FLR 221. See also *Re R (Inter-Country Adoption)* [1999] 1 FLR 1014.
57 [1995] 2 FLR 466.
58 [2008] 1 FLR 177.

father and his wife with contact to the surrogate mother and her husband, that the child and his surrogate sibling be made wards of court to enable a level of court supervision of the situation in the absence of any input by the local authority. Such an arrangement also enabled the children's guardian, who had played a vital role in the contact arrangements, to remain involved in the case.

More recently, in *T v. S (Wardship)*[59] in which, faced with unabated and continuing disputation between the parents, from which the child seemed unemotionally scarred, the court continued the wardship so as to manage the disputes at least in the short term. By also granting care and control, rather than making residence orders, a more neutral status could be created, thereby lowering the tension between the parents.

The court's overall control of its wards might also be thought advantageous in the case of an abandoned child, where no-one looking after him has parental responsibility.[60] Alternatively, it can be appropriate for a court to assist with taking responsibility in cases of grave anxiety. In *Re C (a baby)*, a child developed meningitis which left her brain-damaged and unable to survive without artificial ventilation and likely to suffer increasing pain and distress with no hope of recovery. Sir Stephen Brown P commented: '[i]t appeared appropriate that the courts should take responsibility for this child and relieve the parents in some measure of the grave responsibility which they have borne since her birth.'[61]

5.   CONCLUSION

As indicated at the outset, Waite J's caution in 1991 against writing obituaries for wardship has proved prescient since as the above summary shows, the jurisdiction remains alive and uniquely useful in diverse situations both in the public and private law contexts and both domestically and internationally. Indeed there has been a spate of recent reported cases (there are eight 2010/2011 cases cited in this contribution) some of which could lay the foundation for further development.[62] Although its continued existence is undoubtedly a peculiarity that does not easily stand with a comprehensive statutory scheme, the jurisdiction continues to provide an invaluable underlying additional means of securing certain children's interests who would otherwise not be protected. Long may wardship live!

---

59   [2011] EWHC 1608 (Fam).
60   The jurisdiction can also provide an effective means of protecting and managing a child's property interests in the event of the parents' death.
61   [1996] 1 FLR 43.
62   Notably those, such as *T v. S* (above n. 59) and *Re M and J* (above n. 44), in which wardship was used to manage acute familial conflict.

THE LAW OF SUCCESSION:
DOING THE BEST WE CAN

Elizabeth Cooke

Contents

1. INTRODUCTION

The law of succession is almost a neglected area within family law. Few law degrees offer it as an option; only a few academics regard it as their specialisation, although there is a wealth of practitioner material. Nevertheless, this area of the law has been blessed with the full Cretney treatment. Stephen Cretney's work on the development of succession law in England and Wales over the past century or so, and his critical comment on the shortcomings of the law and of efforts made to reform it, provide a unique insight not only into the detail of the law but also into the mysteries of the many attempts made to get it right.

And there have been so many, from 1925 onwards. At a conference in September 2011 at the University of Trier[1] I took part in a discussion on testamentary freedom. Most of those present were civil lawyers, for whom the common lawyer's tripartite division of succession law into wills, intestacy and family provision seems distinctly foreign – family provision especially. The civil law view of inheritance involves defined and substantial shares for close family

---

[1] The conference was on comparative law, organised by the Gesellschaft für Rechtsvergleichung; see <www.gfr.jura.uni-bayreuth.de/de/index.html>.

members which cannot be overridden by will, and they have nothing resembling the discretionary jurisdiction of the courts in England and Wales to override the provisions of a will or the effect of the rules of intestacy in the interests of certain family members and dependents. We discussed *Ilott v. Mitson*,[2] which concerned the award of family provision, under the Inheritance (Provision for Family and Dependants) Act 1975, to the long-estranged daughter of a lady who left all her property to charities. It was suggested to me by a German professor that the fact that the family provision legislation has been amended so often demonstrates that it is not very good. I responded, with truly British restraint, that on the contrary this is an area of law that has to be sensitive to changing family structures and social mores, and so requires amendment from time to time, and that it is an achievement of our legal system that it has indeed been amended and successfully kept up to date.

A fuller answer would have referred the questioner to Cretney's work on succession law, which shows how very difficult it has been to keep the law up to date and how imperfectly and belatedly that has been achieved. Cretney's painstaking research and unrelenting eye for detail reveal to us the characters, quirks and coincidences involved in the process. It demonstrates that law reform involves not only matching the rigidity of law with the fluidity of human experience, but also the manipulation of law and of process by individuals whose motivation is often complex and whose circumstances often conspired against them. That anything at all has been achieved is perhaps a cause for wonder.

The whole story of the process throughout the twentieth century is told in 'The Ending of Relationships by Death: The Financial Consequences', chapter 12 of *Family Law in the Twentieth Century*.[3] In this short celebration I have chosen to focus on three of Cretney's articles, each of which discusses the enactment of one of the series of statutes that have reformed the law, step by step; I have chosen three where it is possible now to complete the story, or at least to add the next instalment. The first gives a unique portrait of a vanished era; the second involves a most entertaining instance of the way that history repeats itself; and the third represents a dilemma that remains unsolved despite the best efforts of the Law Commissioners of 1989 and of their successors today.

---

[2] [2011] EWCA Civ 346.

[3] S. CRETNEY, *Family Law in the Twentieth Century*, Oxford University Press, Oxford 2003, pp. 478–515.

2. THREE EPISODES IN THE SAGA OF REFORM

2.1. RECALLING A LOST WORLD

The 1925 legislation represented, to a considerable extent, a fresh start for the law of succession, with the old rules distinguishing personal and real property being swept away. For the first time, testamentary freedom was unrestricted, a situation that lasted until the enactment of the Inheritance (Family Provision) Act 1938, which enabled the courts to override, in very limited circumstances, the provisions of a will but not the operation of the intestacy rules. But for situations where there was no will, the Administration of Estates Act 1925 set up the entitlements of family members on intestacy in a way that gave pre-eminence, for the first time, to the surviving spouse. The widow or widower took the first £1,000, and a life interest in the residue;[4] that meant that the surviving spouse would have taken the whole of all but the largest intestate estates.

But the system inaugurated in 1925 made no allowance for inflation. £1,000 was then a tidy sum, but the inflation of the following decades eroded it until it was no longer adequate, in many cases, for a surviving spouse to be sure of being able to remain in the family home if he or she did not own it already or did not take it by survivorship. Cretney's article 'Intestacy Reform: The Way Things Were, 1952' tells the story of the appointment of the Morton Committee to resolve this problem and the enactment of its recommendations in the Intestates' Estate Act 1952.[5]

In doing so, it gives us a wonderful picture of the legal and political world of the late 1940s and early 1950s. In its generously populated footnotes we can see and hear the pin-striped gentlemen whose working methods and professional culture are almost unimaginable to my children's generation, with their fierce memoranda couched in icy courtesy,[6] and their occasional kindly admission that women might have a place alongside them. For there was one woman on the Morton Committee: Mrs Dorothy Rees MP, put forward as 'a sensible and practical woman'[7] (we have to hope that the men were too). The Committee was

---

[4]   The spouse's entitlement was to a life interest in half the residue if there was issue, and in the whole if there were other relatives but no issue.

[5]   S. CRETNEY, 'Intestacy Reforms – The Way Things Were, 1952' (1994) 9 *Denning Law Journal* 35.

[6]   For example, the letter sent by Parliamentary Counsel responsible for the drafting on the Inheritance (Family Provision) Act 1938 to a member of the Lord Chancellor's department in 1941: 'I never ceased to say at every opportunity throughout the time whilst I was dealing with it that it appeared to me to be wrong both in conception and in drafting. Consequently no attacks upon it are likely to offend my *amour propre*': ibid., 39, fn 335.

[7]   Ibid., 37–38. There seems to have been even more reluctance to have someone from Wales.

obviously rather briskly chaired;[8] the idea that a sample of wills might not be the best evidence of what might be an appropriate reform of the intestacy rules did not occur to the Committee, nor did the possibility of taking any other steps to ascertain public attitudes.[9]

The Morton Committee recommended the raising of the level of the statutory legacy, and inaugurated the system of two levels: one (then £5,000) for where there are surviving issue as well as a spouse, and a higher one (then £20,000) for where there is no issue but there are other close relatives. That system remains in place today; the legacy levels since 2008 have been £250,000 and £450,000. As I write this paper, almost on the eve of the publication of the Report, *Intestacy and Family Provision on Death*,[10] the Law Commission is about to recommend that where there is no surviving issue the surviving spouse should take the whole of an intestate estate absolutely, so that only one legacy level is required.

But the Morton Committee made no recommendation for keeping that figure up to date.[11] Was there perhaps a touching faith that inflation would not happen again? At any rate, no provision was made. Later the Lord Chancellor was given power to change the rate by order[12] – but nothing was done to ensure that he or she would in fact change it. As Cretney notes,[13] the power was used only 5 times between 1966 and 1993; after that there was a sixteen-year gap until 2009.[14] It was the responses to the Ministry of Justice's consultation on the statutory legacy in 2005, which led to that last increase, that also prompted the Law Commission's latest project.[15] The Law Commission is now recommending a mechanism for periodic updating, with a view to keeping the statutory legacy at least approximately in tune with rising prices. It recommends that the legacy be updated at least every five years by reference to the retail prices index, together

---

8   Ibid., 40: 'the Chairman did not encourage excessively lengthy discussion'.
9   The lack of necessary correlation between what goes in wills and what should be in the intestacy rules, and the desirability of evidence of public attitude, were both obvious to the Law Commission in the 1980s, as Cretney points out (above n. 5 fn. 47), and in its most recent project: see LAW COMMISSION, *Intestacy and Family Provision Claims on Death*, Law Com. CP No. 191, HMSO, London 2009, paras. 1.38–1.41.
10   LAW COMMISSION, *Intestacy and Family Provision Claims on Death* Law Com. No. 331, TSO, London 2011.
11   Indeed, there seems to have been some concern to keep its terms of reference narrow; CRETNEY, above n. 5, footnotes 34 and 80.
12   Family Provision Act 1966, s. 1(1).
13   S. CRETNEY, 'Reform of Intestacy – the best we can do?' (1995) *LQR (Law Quarterly Review)* 77, 82, text at fn. 41.
14   Family Provision (Intestate Succession) Order 2009, SI 2009 No 135, art. 2.
15   See MINISTRY OF JUSTICE, *Administration of Estates – Review of the Statutory Legacy: Response to Consultation*, London 2008.

with a power for the Lord Chancellor to carry out a more thorough or more frequent review when he chooses to do so.[16]

Another problem formed part of the Morton Committee's remit: whether the provisions of the Inheritance (Family Provision) Act 1938 might be extended to intestacies. It did so recommend, and the title of the Intestates' Estates Act 1952 reflects the importance of that reform. The major reason for the recommendation was the perception that the passing of the majority of the estate to a surviving spouse on intestacy, where the deceased had children from a previous marriage was problematic;[17] yet the extension of family provision was hardly an effective way to address this long-standing difficulty because, of the deceased's children, only minors, unmarried daughters, or disabled adult sons, could apply.[18]

So of the two problems so conspicuously left unsolved by the Morton Committee, one – the need to keep the statutory legacy up-to-date – has now been addressed by the Law Commission in a way designed to be future-proof. The other, as we shall see below, remains a conundrum.

2.2. THE REFORM OF THE FORFEITURE RULE AND THE UNEXPECTEDNESS OF PRIVATE MEMBERS

Before reverting to more mainstream issues in intestacy and family provision, we can pause to look at the enactment of the Forfeiture Act 1982, which ameliorated the rigours of the forfeiture rule that prevents a killer from inheriting from his victim. Its enactment came as a surprise to its sponsors. Cretney's account[19] is a fascinating revelation of the vagaries of the Parliamentary process, and of the ingenuity of those who have learned how to use those vagaries in a good cause.

Members of Parliament, as we all know, may enter a ballot in order to determine the order in which they may introduce a Private Member's Bill. It may be a surprise to realize that not all those who enter the ballot have a bill in mind; and that means that the 'winners' – those who come in the first few places on the ballot – may have to find a bill quickly, on their own initiative or at the urging of the lobbyists who will certainly pursue them when their success is known. In

---

16 LAW COMMISSION, *Intestacy and Family Provision on Death,* Law Com. No. 331, TSO, London 2011, paras. 2.114–2.130, and Schedule 1 to the draft Bill annexed to the Report.

17 Not, of course, 'from another relationship', as we would put it now; this was 1951.

18 CRETNEY, above n. 13, footnotes 72 and 90.

19 S. CRETNEY, 'The Forfeiture Act 1982: the Private Member's Bill as an Instrument of Law Reform' (1990) 10 *OJLS (Oxford Journal of Legal Studies)* 280, and chapter 3 of *Law, Law Reform and the Family,* Clarendon Press, Oxford 1998, pp. 73–90.

1982, Cretney tells us, W Homewood MP came quite a way down the ballot; he approached Leo Abse MP to ask for ideas, and the latter suggested to him that he might introduce a Bill designed to resolve the difficulties experienced with the forfeiture rule – and in particular its harshly punitive operation against those who had killed in circumstances where they were scarcely culpable, for example after prolonged domestic violence. Abse's idea was simply to give some exposure to the issue, in the hope that it might be raised another day by the Government itself or referred to the Law Commission.

The Bill was prepared by Abse 'practically on the back of a cigarette packet' (his own words).[20] No-one expected it to be enacted. Once it became clear that it did indeed have a chance, it was re-drafted by Parliamentary Counsel so as to render it acceptable.[21] It owed its success to the absence of debate and indeed, the evidence gathered by Cretney would indicate, absence of thought by those who supported it. It ensured that in all cases falling short of murder,[22] the courts have a discretion to disapply or modify the forfeiture rule. There is also provision to ensure that social security benefits are not forfeited where that is inappropriate.[23]

One reason why law reform is so difficult is that it is difficult to think of everything. In 2001 the case of *re DWS (deceased)*[24] caused some consternation. There, R murdered his parents, both of whom died intestate. Clearly the forfeiture rule prevented R from inheriting. But R had a son, T. Did he take his grandparents' estates, as would have happened had R pre-deceased T in accordance with the terms of the statutory trusts?[25] Or did it pass to the next branch of the family (the grandfather's sister)? Or did it pass to the crown as *bona vacantia*? The Court of Appeal held that T could not inherit, because the statutory trusts had to be construed literally; he only took in substitution for his parent if that parent had predeceased him. Instead the estate passed to the grandfather's sister, who was also his executor.

There was a view that this was inappropriate, since the sins of the father were in effect being visited upon the child. The Law Commission was asked to undertake a project designed to address that problem and other imperfections in the operation of the forfeiture rule. In 2003 it published a Consultation Paper[26] and

---

20   S. Cretney, *Law, Law Reform and the Family*, Clarendon Press, Oxford 1998, p. 81, fn 52.
21   Ibid., at 83; Cretney refers us at fn 58 to *Hansard*, HL Deb, vol 431 col 716.
22   Murder was not excluded in the original draft, but an amendment was accepted.
23   The Bill as enacted did not achieve this, and it was left to later social security legislation to amend the Forfeiture Act 1982 to make this aspect of it work: Cretney, above n. 20, p. 89.
24   [2001] Ch 568 (CA).
25   Administration of Estates Act 1925, ss. 47(1)(i) and 46 (1)(ii).
26   Law Commission, *The Forfeiture Rule and the Law of Succession* Law Com. CP No. 172, HMSO, London 2003.

in 2005 it published a short Report, *The Forfeiture Rule and the Law of Succession*,[27] in which it recommended a 'deemed predecease' rule to resolve this problem, in cases of forfeiture and also of disclaimer, whether the estate concerned was testate or intestate.

Nothing happened for five years. The recommendations were accepted by Government, and eventually the clauses of the draft bill formed part of the Civil Law Reform Bill of 2010; but that Bill was not enacted, as a result of the calling of a general election. It was not clear that the recommendations then had any chance of implementation. But history repeated itself. Greg Knight MP came fifth in the private members' ballot for 2010; he consulted the Law Commission for advice about a suitable Bill for him to take forward; and of the suggestions made he chose the draft Bill annexed to the 2005 Report on Forfeiture.

The Government's role in the passage of Private Members' Bills varies,[28] but in this case support was given. The Law Commission's role, too, is not prescribed in these circumstances; we provided behind-the-scenes support, which was acknowledged in Parliament.[29] The Bill was the subject of a remarkably long debate on second reading in the House of Commons;[30] in due course it became the snappily titled Estates of Deceased Persons (Forfeiture Rule and the Law of Succession) Act 2011 and by the time this volume is published will have been brought into force on 1 February 2012.

2.3. 'THE STEP-MOTHER' PROBLEM

We cannot know how many people's lives have been affected by the forfeiture rule or by the reforms just discussed. Very few, probably, compared with those affected by an unsolved problem in law reform which, for brevity and with apologies for the gendered term, I call the step-mother problem. The problem, of which the members of the Morton Committee and their contemporaries were

---

27 LAW COMMISSION, *The Forfeiture Rule and the Law of Succession* Law Com. No. 295, HMSO, London 2005.

28 As Cretney explains: CRETNEY, above n. 20, p. 73 and fn 3.

29 *Hansard*, HL Deb 13.05.2011 vol 727 col 1119. One significant outcome of that involvement was that the Bill was amended – and thereby greatly abbreviated – by the removal of clauses designed to impose a trust so as to ensure that where the grandchild (for example) was a minor, the inheritance would be held in such a way as to ensure that the killer would not benefit from it whether directly or indirectly. It was agreed by all concerned that this was unnecessary and indeed impracticable. See *Hansard*, HC Deb 21.01.2011 vol 521 col 1134, and HL Deb 13.05.2011 vol 727 col 1118.

30 Time spent on debate on Private Members' Bills is not always directly related to a real need for debate; see the comments of Joan Walley MP in *Hansard*, HC Deb 21.01.2011 vol 521 col 1127.

aware, is this: X marries and has children. His first wife dies and all her property passes to him. He remarries; he then dies intestate. His much younger second wife, Y, takes all or most of his estate under the intestacy rules.[31] Y lives her own life, and perhaps re-marries; whether or not she does so, if she dies intestate her estate will not pass to X's children at all. Equally she may make a will that leaves nothing for X's children. Thus their father's second marriage and his death intestate have deprived X's children of his property and their mother's.

That was the problem in the form in which the Morton Committee contemplated. When we look at the problem today we have to note that it arises equally when X's children were born of a cohabiting relationship prior to X's marriage to Y, or when X's children were the issue of an extra-marital affair. We cannot discriminate between the children born in those different cases.

So what can we do about it? It has been noted above that the extension of the ambit of family provision to intestate estates could not do the trick in 1952 because family provision was available to so very few adult children. That limitation disappeared in 1975 with the enactment, on the Law Commission's recommendations, of the Inheritance (Provision for Family and Dependants) Act 1975. But it is easy to see that that does not solve the problem for X's children either; all adult children can now apply, to challenge the provisions of a will or the effect of the intestacy rules, but the provision that can be ordered for them is limited to what is required for their 'maintenance'. As Cretney puts it, citing *Re Coventry*,[32] 'although maintenance does not mean just enough to enable a person to get by, it does not extend to provision for everything which may be regarded as reasonably desirable for the applicant's general benefit or welfare'. The provision made for the applicant in *Ilott v. Mitson* fell far short of what might be regarded as a reasonable inheritance for an only child.[33] So the fact that X's children might expect provision, or that their mother might have wanted her property to pass to them, or that indeed most people might feel troubled by the outcome of the scenario described here, does not avail them. If they are able to earn their own living then, absent special circumstances, they are unlikely to recover anything.

---

31 The Law Commission's research indicates that only 10% of intestate estates exceed the £250,000 statutory legacy applicable when the deceased left issue (and only 2% exceed the higher level): LAW COMMISSION, above n. 9, para. 3.11. The figures are drawn from research carried out jointly by the Law Commission, HM Revenue and Customs and the Probate Service; the data are set out in Appendix C to the consultation paper.

32 [1980] Ch 461.

33 Or at least, far short of what that only child might have regarded as reasonable; Mrs Ilott was awarded £50,000 out of her mother's estate of £486,000; see [2011] EWCA Civ 346.

The Law Commission picked up the problem and ran a bit further with it in the project that led to its Report, *Family Law: Distribution on Intestacy*.[34] But they rejected any specific provision to solve the step-mother problem, preferring to leave the courts to do what they could in family provision.[35] As we have noted, that does not solve the problem. And it is this conclusion on the step-mother issue, along with some other persistent conundrums, that Cretney interrogates in his 1995 article 'Reform of intestacy: the best we can do?'[36] – and indeed that has exercised the Law Commission in its latest efforts towards the reform of succession law.

The step-mother problem arises from the entitlement, on intestacy, of the surviving spouse; he or she takes so much that the deceased's children rarely have anything to share. The Law Commission in 1989 recommended that in fact a surviving spouse should take the whole estate on intestacy, in the light of the evidence that they gathered of the proportion of estates where that was what happened anyway. That conclusion met with considerable opposition and, unlike the other recommendations in the report,[37] was not implemented.

Informed by that experience, but also by the evidence we were able to obtain of public opinion today, the Law Commission's report *Intestacy and Family Provision on Death* concludes that an intestate estate should still be shared between the surviving spouse and the children, insofar as it exceeds the statutory legacy.[38] But we have made no further recommendation to resolve the step-mother problem. Why?

---

[34]   Law Commission, *Family Law: Distribution on Intestacy* Law Com. No. 187, HMSO, London 1989.

[35]   Ibid., para. 45: '... the circumstances of second (or subsequent) marriages vary so much that only discretionary provision would be able to take into account all the relevant factors.'

[36]   Cretney, above n. 13. Two of those other persistent problems have been re-examined in Law Com. No. 331. One (Cretney, at 90 and 97) is the ineligibility of a 'child of the family' to apply for family provision in cases where the deceased was not married, which would be resolved by our recommendation at para. 6.41 of Law Com. No. 331. The other (Cretney, at 91) is the fact that any death benefit received from the deceased's pension fund cannot form part of the net estate for the purposes of family provision. Our consultation led us to the conclusion that the advantages of changing that position would be rather less than might be supposed and would be outweighed by the disadvantages of complexity; see Law Commission, above n. 10, paras. 7.99 et seq.

[37]   The other recommendations are set out in Law Com. No. 187 (Law Commission, above n. 34) at paras. 62 and 63, and summarised in Law Com. CP No. 191 (Law Commission, above n. 9) at para. 1.16 as follows:
(1) a surviving spouse of an intestate should in all cases take the whole estate;
(2) the statutory rules of 'hotchpot' should be repealed;
(3) a spouse should inherit on intestacy only if he or she survived the deceased for 14 days; and
(4) cohabitants of two years' standing should be able to apply for family provision.

[38]   But we have recommended a simplification of the system by giving the surviving spouse an absolute entitlement to half the balance above the statutory legacy, rather than a life interest in it.

There are two options.

One is to frame the intestacy rules so that there is a different entitlement in cases where there is a second spouse, or children who are not the children of a surviving spouse. As Cretney pointed out,[39] a number of jurisdictions do this. We discussed in our Consultation Paper[40] the 'conduit theory' that lies behind these different legislative structures; the theory is that a parent is a reliable conduit of wealth to his or her own children but not to step-children. We were uneasy, when we drafted our Consultation Paper, about the prospect of introducing a version of conduit theory into English law. It is based on assumptions that may well not be true, and it would run the risk of causing hardship to second spouses. Consultees agreed with us and with Cretney's own view: intestacy rules structured on the basis of conduit theory would be too complicated and not a sufficiently clear reflection of public opinion about second families.[41]

The other option is to rely upon family provision to sort things out for X's children, as both the Morton Committee and the Law Commission in 1989 concluded. In re-examining it, therefore, the Law Commission in its 2008–11 project endeavoured to find a way for the family provision system to be reformed so that it could actually deliver a solution.

But that can only be done by removing the restriction to 'maintenance' as the standard of provision. Removing that restriction requires us to construct another standard, and that is where ingenuity seems to falter. Either we leave the matter open to the undirected discretion of the judge – and I think it would be universally agreed that that would be unacceptable – or we substitute a standard which could *only* be framed by reference to the parent/child relationship, whether it is a fixed share (of X's estate? Or of what X received from his first wife?), or some more subjective measure of what a child *ought* to expect. That sends us straight to the forced heirship tradition; and if there is one fixed point in public opinion on succession in this jurisdiction, it is that forced heirship is unacceptable and testamentary freedom is paramount.[42]

Could that objection be met by applying a new rule *only* to intestate estates? We think not; if there is an entitlement based on a relationship, then it cannot be dependent upon the parent's marital status. And even if the rule did apply only

---

[39] CRETNEY, above n. 13, 93.

[40] LAW COMMISSION, above n. 9, paras. 3.98 to 3.111.

[41] LAW COMMISSION, above n. 10, paras. 2.67–2.82.

[42] This runs deeply through all the available evidence of public opinion; CRETNEY, above n. 13, at footnotes 56, 57, 63, 64; and see Law Com. No. 331 (LAW COMMISSION, above n. 10), at para. 6.14.

to intestate estates, would it apply only to those children whose parent died while married to someone who was not their parent? We have already noted that conduit theory is not a universal rule of human behaviour; practitioners are well aware of the many cases where parents have disinherited their own children, and to introduce an entitlement only for those who have a step-parent might well leave others at a considerable disadvantage. There are wicked mothers as well as wicked step-mothers.

And finally there is a practical problem. If X's children are to have an entitlement in family provision, when are they to claim it. On X's death? That forces them into litigation with Y, with whom they might well otherwise be on perfectly good terms, and who indeed might require X's estate for her own support. Could they therefore claim instead on Y's death, if she does indeed prove not to be a conduit? That might be so far into the future as to be of little or no comfort. And would the entitlement be available whether or not Y made a will? If so, is that consistent with her own property rights and testamentary freedom? Or with the intestacy rights of Y's later surviving spouse? And how would the property be identified so far into the future?

We have no satisfactory answers to these questions and we have concluded that the step-mother problem cannot be solved through the family provision system.

That does not mean that it is insoluble. It may well be soluble, but only by X and Y.[43] With testamentary freedom comes testamentary responsibility.

3.   CONCLUSION

Perhaps there is nothing new under the sun. Generations of law reformers have done the best they can, writing – on a slate that is never clean – words that will be outdated by the time their children read them but that nevertheless have to be written, and written by quirky and imperfect human beings struggling with their own individuality as well as with a constantly-changing world. And some problems cannot be solved by law reform.

---

[43]   We have to say X and Y both, because some of the permutations cannot be addressed by X's will alone. If X's estate is large enough to provide an appropriate entitlement for both Y and his children, then of course he can achieve this by will; but otherwise, although X might leave his estate to his children, he and they may be unable to defeat a family provision claim by Y. Accordingly, where X's estate is not large enough to make provision both for Y and for the children, X may leave his property to Y and she may feel it right to make provision for X's children in her own will or by a lifetime gift later.

So the answer to the question I was asked in Trier, set out more fully, is that the law of family provision and of succession generally has to march along with social change, and that its amendment to enable it to do so is right and good. That said, it is a wonder that that amendment is ever managed at all. Cretney's work demonstrates how truly astonishing it is that that has actually been achieved in the face of the complexity of life and of human nature.

DIVORCE, INTERNET HUBS AND STEPHEN CRETNEY

Jonathan HERRING

Contents

1.   INTRODUCTION

Any fan of Stephen Cretney's writing, and there are so very many of them, will know its hallmarks: the witty turn of phrase, the depth of analysis, the care over detail, and the footnotes...ah the footnotes, is there any legal academic whose footnotes rival his? I cannot think of one. But the article on which I will focus contains none.

2.   PRIVATE ORDERING AND DIVORCE

It is his lecture given to the Centre for the Study of the Family, Law and Policy at Staffordshire University in February 2003, which was printed in *Family Law* as *Private Ordering and Divorce – How Far Can we Go?*[1] In just six pages he writes one of the best recent articles on divorce.

---

[1]   S. CRETNEY, 'Private Ordering and Divorce – How far can we go?' [2003] *Family Law* 399.

The article starts with a definition of his key concept:

> '"Private ordering" is based on this philosophy that individuals should have the right to organise their lives as they wish, free from intervention by the state and by the courts, and that, accordingly, they should have the right to create legal obligations, enforceable by the courts, either in substitution for what the state prescribes as the default option, or to provide for situations in which the state makes no regulatory provision.'[2]

Just one sentence is required to capture the theme of the article. Yet, as he is quick to point out, the concept contains contradictions, which he proceeds to bring out during the article.

Typically, we are off to the nineteenth century by the second paragraph. But that is not merely to provide background. One of his great qualities as a legal historian was to be able to use the past to throw light on the present. While students today would be quick to locate the 'right to be left alone' in Article 8 of the European Convention on Human Rights, Cretney identifies it as a 'fundamental principle of English constitutional law' which goes back many centuries.[3] In a characteristic turn of phrase he explains the reasons for it:

> 'The fact that the gentleman in Whitehall (or the lady in the social services department) may well know what is best for a family does not, of itself, provide an excuse for interference.'[4]

He notes that this principle, particularly in family law, has been eroded in the course of the twentieth century. He uses the example of criminal law, which has extended its role in the family: the areas of marital rape and domestic violence are examples he provides. We have seen also, he notes, an increase in the state offering services to families and compulsion facing those who do not take the services up. A remarkable example is the Family Law Act 1996 which tells us that not only is marriage to be supported but that couples are to 'take all practicable steps whether by marriage counselling or otherwise to save the marriage.'[5]

Cretney is, however, far too fine a scholar to see the course of history as simply one of increased state involvement in family life. As he points out:

> 'we have come to accept a hugely increased role for the state in our everyday lives. But at the same time we are confronted by the increasing belief that the courts – the state's

---

2   Ibid., 399.
3   Ibid., 399.
4   Ibid., 399.
5   Family Law Act 1996, s. 1.

enforcement agencies – are not appropriate bodies to deal with family relationships and that these are not apt for submission to judicial monitoring.'[6]

He could not have foreseen how by the time of the *Family Justice Review*[7] this statement would be so taken to heart in Government policy.

Turning to his central issue, divorce, Cretney traces the remarkable shift from the view of marriage as a legal status in which the state had a vital interest, 'transcending and operating independently of the will of the parties'[8], to the more modern law on divorce following the 1969 Divorce Reform Act and the special procedure, which he argues shows 'not much evidence…of the majesty of the law, not much evidence of adjudication.'[9] He sees with the current divorce law 'the triumph of private ordering'.[10] We 'now believe that the decision on whether or not a marriage is over is primarily one for the parties'.[11]

He then comes to the central question for his paper:

'Is it right that, in cases in which the parties are agreed about dissolution and its consequences, we should insist that the process is one that should, in form, be handled by the courts?'[12]

He acknowledges the argument that the courts' role in part is to supervise and formally record a matter of civil status. However, he notes that the word 'court' is associated with prison and punishment. Of course family courts are not normally punitive, but he is talking about the public perception of what courts do. He asks:

'Is it sensible to convey the message – as, perhaps, our insistence on treating divorce and its consequences as a matter for judicial activity rather than private ordering does – that if your relationship breaks down you should go to court in the same way as if you break your leg you go to hospital?'[13]

He concludes that we should consider whether we need the court in the uncoupling process or whether to accept 'divorce avowedly based on consent: divorce would be available to a couple who make and register an agreement in a

---

6   CRETNEY, above n. 1, 400.

7   FAMILY JUSTICE REVIEW, *Final Report*, MoJ, London, 2011.

8   CRETNEY, above n. 1, 400.

9   Ibid., 401.

10   Ibid., 403.

11   Ibid., 403.

12   Ibid., 404.

13   Ibid., 404.

prescribed form.'[14] He is clear that he still thinks that couples should have access to apply for orders under the Children Act 1989 and that provision needs to be made for couples who are not prepared to consent. Having gone this far, his ultimate conclusion is surprising:

'By accepting there is, today, virtually no one who is ultimately denied a divorce if he or she wants one we have effectively removed the only really powerful lobby for change. So I am forced to accept that we should leave the law governing the ground for divorce untouched.'[15]

He makes it clear that that is his conclusion only because he thinks it would be politically unacceptable to produce administrative, no fault divorce. His preference would be for divorce based on consent, which would be registered in a prescribed form.

3.   THE FAMILY JUSTICE REVIEW

Things have moved on more quickly than Cretney could have predicted. The Supreme Court in *Radmacher v. Granatino*[16] has opened up the possibility of allowing couples to reach their own agreement and that is a major theme in the Family Justice Review:

'Generally it seems better that parents resolve things for themselves if they can. They are then more likely to come to an understanding that will allow arrangements to change as they and their children change. Most people could do with better information to help this happen. Others need to be helped to find routes to resolve their disputes short of court proceedings.'[17]

I am deeply concerned about that argument, but I will not present my concerns here.[18] My focus will be on the proposals in the Family Justice Review in relation to divorce, which, in result, if not motivation, seem to fit with the argument Cretney proposes. It is worth setting out the proposals on divorce at length:

'a.   Where a person seeks a divorce they should go first to the information hub, where they will be able to access an online divorce portal. This would explain the process and possible grounds for divorce and give access to the necessary application forms. The person initiating divorce would complete the application online. The system should have in built checks to prevent the now frequent administrative

---

14   Ibid., 405.
15   Ibid., 405.
16   [2010] UKSC 42.
17   Above n. 7, para. 104.
18   J. Herring, 'Relational autonomy and family law' in J. Wallbank, S. Choudhry and J. Herring (eds.), *Rights, Gender and Family Law* Routledge, Abingdon, 2010.

errors. The individual would also be prompted to consider arrangements for children, financial and religious issues and be directed to further information and support services as appropriate. The applicant would not be expected to provide details of arrangements for children or money, as for all other separating couples. Where there are disputes over children or money parties would make an application under the relevant section of the Children Act 1989 or the Matrimonial Causes Act 1973.

b. The online form would then be submitted to a centralised court processing centre. The application would not be processed unless it was accompanied by a fee or a remissions form and verification, and approved identification documents, such as an original copy of the marriage certificate.

c. The application would be received by a court officer who would check that the application had been filled out correctly, acknowledge receipt and serve the application on the other party. The other party would then return the forms to the processing centre indicating whether or not they contested the divorce or whether they wished to make a cross application.

d. *Where the ground for divorce is uncontested* the court officer would issue both parties with a decree nisi. Parties then would be able to make further arrangements and resolve any outstanding issues with regard to their divorce. As now, after six weeks the applicant would be able to apply for the decree to be made absolute. After a further three months the respondent would be able to apply for the decree to be made absolute. If the applicant does not apply for the decree to be made absolute, the respondent may apply 3 months from the earliest date on which the applicant could have applied. The ability to apply for an expedited decree should remain.

e. *Where the ground for divorce is contested*: if the other party wishes to contest that the marriage has irretrievably broken down, they should indicate this when returning the divorce application. The processing officer would transfer the application to the applicant's local court for judicial consideration. The judge would then examine the case and determine whether the decree nisi should be issued.'[19]

It should be emphasised that the Family Justice Review considered only the process, and not the ground for divorce.[20] Of course, it is hard to disaggregate the procedure of divorce and the basis on which a divorce is granted. A ground that requires proof of facts, for example, is not readily consistent with a procedure that is essentially administrative.

The Review sees the current system as inefficient:

'There is scope to increase the use of administrators in the courts to reduce burdens on judges and create a more streamlined process in the 98% of cases where divorce is

---

19   FAMILY JUSTICE REVIEW, above n. 7, Appendix H.
20   Ibid., para. 4.164.

uncontested. The current process requires judges to spend time in effect to do no more than check that forms have been filled in correctly, with accurate names and dates. This is a waste. To change it would not make any difference to the ease or difficulty of obtaining a divorce. It would just make more judge time available for more important things.'[21]

The driver for the proposed reform is efficiency and the hope that the change in procedure will release 'perhaps 10,000 judicial hours'.[22]

The proposed reforms are very much in line with the proposals in the Cretney article. Non-contested divorce will become 'form filling', albeit online. However, it is striking that the motivation behind the Family Justice Review is cost-saving, while Cretney's approach was a principled one, based on his view of private ordering. A most revealing comment on the role played by costs in the thinking of the *Review*, is the question of whether there should be change in the terminology used concerning the stages of divorce:

> 'The terms decree nisi and decree absolute are outmoded. It had been intended to change them as part of the changes to the Family Procedure Rules. Remarkably this could not be done on grounds of the IT cost.'[23]

4. SOME BAD ARGUMENTS FOR COURT-BASED DIVORCE

So, if a principled and a pragmatic approach can agree on administrative divorce, at least in non-contested cases, is there anything that might be said to urge caution against the proposal? I will argue in the remaining section that there is. Although, ultimately, they do not lead me to oppose the proposal in the *Family Justice Review*, they do lead me to urge great caution and argue for a more thought-out response to divorce.

Let me start with three arguments which are commonly made against allowing mutual divorce by administrative process, which do not convince me.

First, there is a concern, which Cretney mentions in his article,[24] that requiring mutual consent gives one party a weapon in the bargaining process. One party to the marriage can argue that unless their view is adopted in discussions over finances or the children they will withhold consent. However, Cretney responds

---

[21] Ibid., para. 4.166.
[22] Ibid., p. 180.
[23] Ibid., para. 4.168.
[24] CRETNEY, above n.1, 304.

to this thus: 'is it not equally true that the fear of escalating legal costs is at the moment such a weapon?'[25] That must be right. It is hard to believe that the bargaining positions of the parties will be radically affected by the withholding of consent to divorce.

Second, there is the argument that changes in divorce law cause an increase in divorce. It is easy to ridicule such a claim. As Tolstoy tells us, 'Happy families are all alike; every unhappy family is unhappy in its own way.'[26] The causes of divorce are no doubt multiple, but it is hard to believe that for many it is a reading of the Matrimonial Causes Act 1973 which is the last straw, or indeed any of the straws at all. As Martin Richards puts it:

'Those who argue for harder divorce seem to have an exaggerated view of the power of the law to control people's domestic living arrangements. Their model seems to be that of a sluice gate which stands between the married and the divorced. The wider this sluice is opened, the more of the married that will become divorced. Such a view suggests that it is only the difficulty of getting out that keeps people married.'[27]

But, we should not be too quick. After all, there is no doubt the law could affect the divorce rate: a country which did not permit divorce would have no divorce.

The argument can be made on the statistics. Baroness Deech thinks the issue is clear:

'In fact it is now proven that it is the law and its administration that push the rate up. It has been shown that the introduction of so-called no fault divorce… has had the effect of increasing divorce by 2 per 1,000 married people in the long term. This was based on analysis of 18 European states between 1950 and 2003. Reforms based on no-fault were said to account for 20% of the increased rates across Europe in the late twentieth century'[28]

Most commentators are far less convinced by this link.[29] Indeed it must be questioned whether it could be *shown* that the introduction of no fault divorce

---

25   Ibid., 403.

26   L. Tolstoy, *Anna Karenina*, Penguin, London 2011, p. 1.

27   M. Richards, 'Private Worlds and Public Intentions – the Role of the State at Divorce' in A. Bainham and D. Pearl (eds.), *Frontiers of Family Law*, Chancery Law Publishing, London, 1993, p. 15.

28   She quotes ('Divorce – A Disaster' [2009] *Family Law* 1048, 1050) L. Gonzalez and T. Viitanen, *The Effect of Divorce Laws on Divorce Rates in Europe* Sheffield University, Sheffield 2006.

29   B. Stevenson and J. Wolfers, *Marriage and Divorce Changes And Their Driving Forces*, National Bureau of Economic Research Working Paper 12944, 2007; T. Kneip and G. Bauer, 'Did unilateral divorce law raise divorce rates in Western Europe?' (2009) 71 *Journal of Marriage and Family* 592.

has an effect. As even the most junior social scientist knows, correlation cannot be necessarily equated with cause. Major social forces, including the changing role of women, decreased formal religious observance and, greater economic prosperity, will all play their role. As John Eekelaar has suggested, if changes in the law have played any role in increasing the divorce rate it is at the margins.[30]

A more fundamental objection to Deech's view is that it assumes divorce is bad, carrying high costs. I do not doubt for a moment the severe costs in financial and emotional terms of relationship breakdown, but I am not sure that Deech's solutions of making divorce 'more difficult' will result in any improvement. She advocates a year's delay before divorce. This is similar to the proposal in the 1996 Family Law Act which had at least a year's delay, during which the couple were intended to determine whether they were fixed in their decision to divorce and how they wished to live their life after divorce. Cretney famously suggested it was more likely that the couple would not do what was intended and would rather spend their time 'in the far more pleasurable activity of conceiving – necessarily illegitimate – babies.'[31] More worryingly the time may be spent continuing an abusive relationship. Even if divorce is bad, some marriages are even worse.

A third argument is that no-fault divorce demonstrates a lack of moral standards. Deech argues that the move towards no-fault divorce is part of a general attitude towards:

> 'a society where there are no constraints on private morality, no judgmentalism, no finger wagging or name calling, only acceptance of anything that anyone does, short of the criminal law, in the name of the pursuit, if not of individual happiness, then at least individual choice[32]

I will avoid the temptation to digress into an explanation of why that is over-simplification of what is happening (would the obese, the conservative evangelical Christian or the smoker agree?), or into a debate over whether it is undesirable. Keeping on issue, is there not something in her complaint that it is more difficult to terminate a contract of employment or a tenancy than a marriage?

The response to that argument can be found in Cretney's article. It is wrong to assume that the court is the only or even the most appropriate place to provide a statement about marriage, or even if it is, that the divorce procedure is the most appropriate way to say things about divorce. Some of the most interesting, and

---

[30]   J. EEKELAAR, 'Evaluating Legal Regulation Of Family Behaviour' (2010) 1 *International Journal of the Jurisprudence of the Family* 17.

[31]   S. CRETNEY, 'The Divorce White Paper – Some Reflections' [1995] *Family Law* 302, 303.

[32]   DEECH, above n. 28, 1049.

important, things said about marriage by the judiciary are to be found not in the law on divorce, but in some of the recent developments of the law on financial orders. The principles of equality of contribution by spouses, the importance of non-discrimination and the acknowledgement of inequalities caused by marriage are all to be found there, rather than in the divorce petition. No one can read decisions like *White v. White*[33] or *Miller; McFarlane*[34] and conclude that the law does not take marriage seriously and is not willing to send some very clear moral messages.

5.   SOME BETTER ARGUMENTS FOR COURT-BASED DIVORCE

If the arguments just considered are not found convincing, are there any better ones? I suggest there are two.

5.1. DIVORCE, EMOTION AND SOLEMNITY

Lawyers tend to overlook the psychological issues surrounding divorce. In Cretney's words 'punitive and even savage emotion'[35] can be produced on divorce. Divorce law is dealing with people who are often feeling chaotic emotions and powerful passions. There is loss, injury, grief and pain. To strive for the bitterness-free, allegation-free divorce that some seek, is sometimes unrealistic. As Joanne Brown and Shelley Day Sclater have argued:

> 'the ideal of the harmonious divorce is more likely to emerge (if at all) when the emotional conflict that psychoanalysis alerts us to is somehow acknowledged if not contained...This is what the divorcing couple may also benefit from: the dispute resolution process acting as a container for some of their conflict and thus perhaps increasing their own trust in reparation, new beginnings, and a new sense of self. Crucially, however, our ability to mourn and to repair losses depends upon an acknowledgement of conflicted emotions consequent upon separation.'[36]

A law which fails to acknowledge their emotions, or, even worse, papers over them with a pretence that everyone is happy about what is happening, is doing no service to those who are divorcing. We should acknowledge the feelings of

---

[33]   [2000] UKHL 54.
[34]   [2006] UKHL 24.
[35]   CRETNEY, above n.1, 404.
[36]   J. BROWN and S. DAY SCLATER, 'Divorce: a psychodynamic perspective' in S. DAY SCLATER and C. PIPER (eds.), *Undercurrents of Divorce*, Ashgate, Aldershot 1999, p. 153.

'damage, death, failure, guilt' and anger that divorce typically creates.[37] The current law fails to address these emotions adequately. To quote Day Sclater and Brown again:

> 'Small wonder, perhaps, that so many divorcing people carry around such a profound and enduring sense of injustice which the legal system seems powerless to address. We cannot assume, therefore, that because the law moves away from allegations of fault and discourages litigation that divorcing people will easily be able to follow suit. On the contrary they may continue to be preoccupied with questions of blame, responsibility and culpability.'[38]

Law, lawyers and judges struggle to respond to emotion. Witnesses are berated for being too emotional and emotional harms and losses are found impossible to address, or to address adequately, in either criminal law or the law of tort.[39]

So what does this have to do with the proposals to amend the law on divorce in the Family Justice Review? First, I am concerned that the completion of an internet form assessed by an administrator to complete a divorce lacks the solemnity that should mark the end of a marriage. We could, when a person dies, arrange for an economical and efficient way of disposing of the body. We do not. The death of the person is marked as a serious moment, respecting what has been lost and looking forward to the future. Allowing divorce by an internet form, appears to trivialise a loss for the couple. Of course the current law may be seen as little more than an administrative procedure by post. Is it any different that it is by the internet? Is it somehow undignified to obtain a divorce by a form which will presumably be slightly shorter than that required for a credit card?

Second, there is the notion of a Responsible Divorce. In Helen Reece's wonderful book, *Divorcing Responsibly*, she argues that the Family Law Act 1996 reflected 'post-liberal conception of autonomy'. The choice to divorce was to be respected, but it must be a choice that was exercised with care and with thought.[40] Now, there were all kinds of problems with the Family Law Act 1996 proposals, but I do see a role for the law in highlighting to individuals the seriousness of the decision they are making. It is one of the main reasons to require formalities, in the making of wills or entering a civil partnership, for example. Of course these do not guarantee that people will not make the decision flippantly, but they mark to people that this is a decision of especial significance. They should take care.

---

[37]   Ibid., p. 154.
[38]   Ibid., p. 155.
[39]   For further discussion see J. HERRING, 'The Serious Wrong of Domestic Abuse and the Loss of Control Defence' in A. REED and M. BOHLANDER (eds.), *Loss of Control and Diminished Responsibility*, Ashgate, Aldershot 2011.
[40]   H. REECE, *Divorcing Responsibly*, Hart, Oxford 2003, ch. 2.

Once again, I question whether the filling in of an internet form satisfies this concern.

Third, the message sent by divorce as an online procedure is that it is simply a private matter. Of course it is not. Ruth Deech has argued:

> 'The material costs comprise inter alia legal aid for proceedings, welfare for one-parent families, extra housing because one unit is now two, the running of the family courts (about 100 in London alone) and judges, lawyers, accountants, conciliators, additional illness arising from the divorce stress, which is documented, absence from work and children's extra needs because more of them are taken into care, and in general divorced households receive more in benefits than they pay out in tax. The overall cost of family breakdown has been variously estimated at either £20 billion p.a.[41] or up to £40 billion'[42]

This may be slightly overegging the case. Many of these costs would arise even if the law on divorce was draconian and fault-based. Indeed we may have even greater costs caused by the misery of couples forced to live together. Nevertheless, marriage is seen as a public act and receives a degree of public recognition and support which is presumably, in part, a recognition of some kind of public benefit. Nowadays few would put it as strongly as the US Supreme Court once did:

> '[Marriage]... is an institution, in the maintenance of which in its purity the public is deeply interested, for it is the foundation of the family and of society, without which there would be neither civilization nor progress.'[43]

Yet, even if somewhat perilously, it seems to have some special status in our society. Its demise too is of public significance, which should be acknowledged by some kind of public act. The current judicial pronouncement is very limited, but is some kind of formal public acknowledgement. An administrator working through the internet does not play that kind of public role.

In summary, what will be lost by an administrative internet-based system for divorce? A degree of solemnity; a respect for the emotions felt by those involved; and a signalling of a fact of public significance. I do not know how to weigh such matters up against the cost-saving which so dominated the thinking of the Family Justice Review. More importantly, and here I return to a point made by

---

41   DEECH, above n. 28, 1051: she quotes *Breakdown Britain*, Social Justice Policy Group, London 2006, vol. 2, p. 68.

42   Ibid.; J. KIRBY, *The Price of Parenthood*, Centre for Policy Studies, London 2005; *When Relationships Go Wrong: Counting the Cost of Family Failure*, Relationships Foundation Cambridge, 2009.

43   *Maynard v. Hill*, 125 U.S. 190, 211 (1888).

Cretney in his article, maybe the court is not the best place for doing this. Maybe religious groups should offer 'divorce services'; maybe secular groups could offer some kind of equivalent. If the law moves out, as on balance I agree it should, I think there needs to be something to fill the gap.

5.2. DIVORCE AND MARRIAGE

The argument here is that administrative divorce can undermine a central benefit of marriage or civil partnership. Intimate relationships typically involve risks. Within them one party often sacrifices their own interests for the interests of the other, or of the relationship. These sacrifices can be in the long-term be a worthwhile part of the relationship, but at any given time one party may have gained less from the marriage than the other. As one economist puts it:

'At the time of formation, the marriage contract promises gains to both parties. Yet the period of time over which these gains are realized is not symmetrical. As a rule, men obtain gains early in the relationship, and women late. This follows from women's relative loss in value. Young women are valued as mates by both old and young men. When they choose to marry a particular man they give up all their other alternatives. And over those early years, as women are wont to complain, they give that man "the best years of their lives." At the back end, when their value on the marriage market falls relative to their husbands, they expect to be repaid for their sacrifice. The creation of this long-term imbalance provides the opportunity for strategic behaviour whereby one of the parties, generally the man, will perform his obligations under the marriage contract only so long as he is receiving a net positive marginal benefit and will breach the contract unless otherwise constrained once the marginal benefit falls below his opportunity cost.'[44]

This kind of argument sounds strange to non-economists. It speaks of intimate relationships in terms that seem alien. Yet it is true that intimate relationships generate unequal advantages or disadvantages. Ensuring protection from being taken advantage of, is something the law needs to be concerned with. However, it may not be the law on divorce which is the most useful tool to combat this. Forcing an unwilling husband to remain with his wife so that she can gain her benefits from the marriage is likely to be counter-productive!

---

[44]   L. COHEN, 'Marriage: The Long Term Contract' in A. DNES and R. ROWTHORN (eds.), *The Law and Economics of Marriage and Divorce* Cambridge University Press, Cambridge 2002, pp. 24–5.

Katherine Baker captures some of these themes in this, to me, more attractive argument, describing the right to marry in these terms:

'the right to be considered as part of a unit, to have another person's needs, wants and desires determine one's own needs, wants and desires. It is a right rooted not in self-expression or autonomy but almost in their opposite. It is a right rooted in the human flourishing that comes from relationship. After all, what seems sacred, or at least awe-inspiring and worthy of protection is not that two people make the promise, but that they actually keep it, by being able to subordinate the "I" to the "We."'[45]

This is a worthy view of marriage or civil partnership, but it is not obvious why a strict divorce law is needed to achieve it. The argument is that the relationship may be stronger if the parties are able to commit to it and make sacrifices safe in the knowledge that the relationship cannot be readily terminated by the other party.[46] If the relationship can be ended without good reason then it is a vulnerable institution and people are less likely to invest in it.[47] Betsey Stevenson argues:

'People invest in their marriages to the extent that they expect them to stay intact, or the extent to which their partners can credibly commit to sharing the fruits of such investments. Weakening the marriage contract by making it easier for someone to exit the marriage changes the incentive to invest in the marriage.'[48]

This is an attractive argument, but not, I suggest, ultimately convincing. People commit to a relationship with a specific person, not to an institution. The trust is in the other person and not in a legal regime. People, generally, do want their marriages or civil partnerships to last for ever. But that does not mean they want the law to force them to do so. Where the relationship goes wrong the investment has foundered. Compelling or seeking to compel the relationship to continue will in fact undermine the values of mutual love and respect, which we hope underpin marriages and civil partnerships. At best this kind of argument provides one strong reason in favour of requiring a redistribution of property on divorce. It does not justify enforced marriage.

---

[45] K. BAKER, 'Family, the law, and the constitution(s)', available at SSRN: http://ssrn.com/abstract=1106423, p.16.

[46] E. SCOTT, 'Marital Commitment and the Legal Regulation of Divorce' in DNES and ROWTHORN, above n. 44, p. 35.

[47] Ibid.

[48] B. STEVENSON, 'The Impact Of Divorce Laws on Marriage-Specific Capital' (2007) 25 *Journal of Labour Economics* 75, 92.

6.   CONCLUSION

Cretney's 2003 article has considerable contemporary significance in the debates surrounding the Family Justice Review. Its call for private ordering and a questioning of the assumption that courts should be involved in divorce finds much resonance with some of the proposals in the Review. In fact, it provides a far stronger argument, in favour of transforming divorce into an essentially administrative procedure, than the argument in the Review, which seems so obsessed with cutting costs. Many will be convinced that if divorce is reformed along the lines Cretney and the Review suggest this will be a long-overdue improvement. This article, while not disagreeing with that, warns that there will be gaps produced by making divorce simply an administrative procedure. Something will be lost and more thought needs to be given to how our society responds to marriage breakdown. In particular, the solemnity, acknowledgement of public interest and respect for the parties' emotions and encouragement of investment in marriage need more thought. I think, as Cretney implied, that these may best be found outside of the court structure. Our society has not yet developed them. A role, dare I say it, for the Big Society?

THE CO-RESPONDENT'S ROLE IN DIVORCE REFORM AFTER 1923

Sue Jᴇɴᴋɪɴsᴏɴ

Contents

1. INTRODUCTION

'Adultery has been thought more conclusively disruptive to marriage than any other single cause and has always afforded the main ground for marital relief.'[1]

1923 saw the gender equalisation of the adultery grounds for divorce under the Matrimonial Causes Act 1923[2] which resulted in an increase in the number of petitions from wives.[3] Prior to this, male adultery had to include an additional aggravating factor: the adultery needed to be incestuous,[4] or a wife could petition if her husband had been guilty of bigamy, cruelty or two years desertion. Opposition to this reform focused at least in part on concern that this would lead to an increase in collusive divorce. Stephen Cretney's *Family Law in the Twentieth Century*[5] details the debates during this period in detail.

---

[1] R. Gʀᴀᴠᴇsᴏɴ and F. Cʀᴀɴᴇ (eds.), *A Century of Family Law 1857–1957*, Sweet and Maxwell, London 1957, p. 323.

[2] Matrimonial Causes Act 1923 s. 27.

[3] A. Hᴀʟsᴇʏ, *British Social Trends Since 1900*, Macmillan, London 1988, p. 80. In 1916–1920 33% of petitions were filed by wives and by 1921–1925 this had risen to 59%. By 1969 the percentage of petitions filed by wives had stabilised at about 63%.

[4] Matrimonial Causes Act 1857, s. 27.

[5] S. Cʀᴇᴛɴᴇʏ, *Family Law in the Twentieth Century: A History*, Oxford University Press, Oxford 2003.

This equalisation led to the period 1923–1969 becoming the heyday of the female co-respondent. Throughout this period marriage continued to be considered the bulwark of sexual order and social purity, yet by the 1969 Divorce Reform Act the primacy of the individual had come to dominate the debate, and the gap between private desire and legal rules was unbridgeable by the existing law. The divorce numbers had continued to rise,[6] but they remained small compared to today, and the matrimonial offence continued to be central. Public and judicial concern about the collusive contortions used by those with access to the relevant information, and the role of the co-respondent, was in part responsible for the reform.

It was in the sphere of collusion that the co-respondent had the most influence, in particular by way of the notorious 'hotel bill divorce'. Since a wife's adultery was still regarded more severely than a husband's, a couple might agree that he should appear to be the one at fault. Booking into a hotel with a woman not his wife – and being found with her the following morning by the chambermaid bringing tea – would be circumstantial evidence of adultery.[7] Although its actual level is impossible to establish, it was a cause of concern, and it increasingly brought the law into disrepute by highlighting the hypocrisy and deceit of the existing divorce practice, which allowed couples to comply formally with the law whilst, at the same time, achieving the desired outcome, a divorce. The divorce rate and the legal contortions couples resorted to was a grave concern to the courts, Government, Church, and public alike and played a significant part in ultimately hastening change. Eventually the Divorce Reform Act 1969, and the expansion of the facts available to illustrate irretrievable breakdown, while not eliminating the co-respondent, reduced her role from the almost essential to the optional and rarely used one of today.

The formal and informal debates around divorce clearly illustrate the continuing gendered, biased, nature of divorce law throughout the period. The Matrimonial Causes Act had been reluctantly enacted and failed to address the true issues of inequality that the patriarchal structure of the family had so effectively institutionalised. The legal history of adultery as exemplified by the co-respondent illustrates the further transformation of the institution of marriage throughout the twentieth century – from an economic unit to a sight of individual fulfilment.

---

6   There were 2,700 divorce decrees in 1923 and 51,000 in 1969: HALSEY, above n. 3, p. 80.
7   This was gradually relaxed until a hotel bill rather than a statement from a chambermaid was sufficient, see *Pilgram v. Pilgram* (1939) PRO J77 3896 for an example of a husband supplying a wife with the necessary evidence of adultery: 'Dear Edith, after over 12 years' separation I feel the time has come to relieve this most unhappy position. So I am enclosing herewith a hotel bill. It may be that either of us at some future time will wish to marry again but in any case, should you decide to move on this matter, it will I am sure you will agree, allow us both to live a much happier and better life than is possible under the present circumstances'.

2. THE REPORTING OF SCANDALOUS DETAILS

For some time there had been concern about the harmful effect on public morality of the press interest[8] in matrimonial cases: indeed, in spite of efforts to curb it, the tabloids interspersed 'spicy' divorce reporting with equally prurient reports of rape cases until 1969 and beyond. During and after the passage of the Matrimonial Causes Act 1923 there was a constant stream of stories of matrimonial troubles reported in great detail in the press, with the inevitable emphasis on the adulterous liaisons echoing the eighteenth century's 'titillating erotica'.[9]

The social stigma attached to divorce on account of its links to adultery meant ruin in some professions. In *GMC v. Spakman*, after Mr. Pepper had been awarded a decree on the grounds of his wife's adultery with Dr Spakman, plus one thousand pounds damages, the doctor, like others before him, was struck off the medical register for 'infamous conduct'.[10] It was believed that the threat of undignified and prurient publicity prevented even more infidelity. The President of the Probate, Divorce and Admiralty Division commented that: 'The adulterous have a horror of the public opprobrium to which they are exposed and the sense of shame and repugnance at the public consequences of the conduct was a most wholesome state of affairs'.[11] In a society more reticent and private than today such a fear was seen to be an efficient form of social control, making people think twice before embarking on an affair. It may be, however, that such publicity merely ensured that extramarital liaisons were conducted with greater discretion. Just as the divorce statistics do not reflect the true success or failure of marriages, neither can the impact of public exposure on those seeking to end their marriages be accurately gauged.

The Gorell Commission[12] had come down firmly on the side of censorship and in 1912 had made it clear that if the newspapers failed at self-censorship then legislation would be necessary. Indeed, by 1923 the Bishop of Durham was 'haunted and depressed' by the rapid decline of sexual morality amongst the people'[13] as evidenced daily in the newspapers. Eventually, pressure resulted in the Judicial Proceedings (Regulations of Reports) Act 1926, which restricted

---

8   The *Times* 17.04.1926.
9   P. WAGNER, 'Trial Reports as a Genre of Eighteenth Century Erotica', (1983) 5 *British Journal of Eighteenth Century Studies* 117, 121.
10   *GMC v. Spakman* (1943) TLR 58 234, 321.
11   Quoted by CRETNEY, above n. 5, p. 104.
12   *Royal Commission on Divorce and Matrimonial Causes* Cd 6478, HMSO, London 1912.
13   *Hansard*, HL Deb 24.04.1923 vol 53 col 854.

press reporting.[14] The legislation was flawed because the newspapers continued to be allowed to print the judgments of cases, often including a great deal of, for the time, scandalous and intimate detail. Further undermining its effectiveness, the Act failed to stop the press from conducting and indeed paying for, direct interviews with the various parties including the alleged co-respondent.[15] Further, it had no effect on reporting proceedings in the Magistrates' Courts where the vast majority of matrimonial proceedings took place.

It was however a start towards the recognition of the private nature of family proceedings and that the legitimate interest of the press was limited. While it was deeply unpleasant to feature in a divorce case with extensive social and employment ramifications, there continued to be a frequent need for third party involvement, in order to provide the necessary evidence of adultery.

3. EXPANDING THE GROUNDS FOR DIVORCE

The absurdity of concentrating on this one area of matrimonial disharmony resulted in genuine hardship and unhappiness, whilst at the same time causing the legal system to become increasingly distant from the realities of people's lives. The ideal of a life-long indissoluble marriage was being questioned, and organizations like the Divorce Law Reform Union[16] found support growing[17] and their message more and more sympathetically received. Sometimes the judiciary appeared exasperated with the cases they were dealing with and all who participated were aware of the fiction, indeed the legal pantomime, to which they found themselves privy.[18] This was despite the harsh judgment in *Walton v.*

---

[14] Section 1(b) made it unlawful to print or publish any particulars other than name, address, legal argument and 'concise statement of the charges, defence and counter charges in support of which evidence is given'.

[15] For example *Daily Express* 09.04.1938. The co-respondent disclosed the 'vile orgies' Major and Mrs Griggs had indulged in at Cannes: Mr Justice Buchnall commented that 'it was difficult to imagine a case with more vile features'.

[16] There were various organisations and pressure groups seeking reform of the marriage laws including The Progressive League and the Marriage Law Reform Society, with amalgamations and splits throughout the period. The Divorce Law Reform Union was both the most influential and well documented. Their publication *The Journal* is a useful barometer of the reformer's agenda, their supporters referred to as 'sufferers and sympathisers' (*The Journal* 1919 to 1922).

[17] Before the First World War the DLRU had 400 members; by 1919 it had 1,700 members: CRETNEY, above n. 5, p. 216.

[18] *Stuart v. Stuart and Holden* [1930] P 77. Hill J felt he was unable to exercise his discretion in favour of an adulterous petitioner because 'it would encourage people, first of all to concealment, and then to perjury, everyone who is guilty himself of seeking relief from the other spouse would be encouraged to run the risk of first of all making no disclosure, in the hope the court would be hoodwinked, and secondly of successfully perjuring himself. I think that would be making a most mischievous use of the court's power to use its discretion'.

Walton and Hazel where the King's Proctor had intervened, uncovering the petitioner's own adultery after the decree nisi was granted. Giving judgment, the primacy of the perceived public interest in preventing consensual divorce is clear in Mr. Justice Hill's remark:

'After his wife left him this lady with whom he is now living came to look after his children. He was not driven to misconduct with her by any conduct of his wife… it would in my opinion, be against public policy that people entitled to divorce should take the law into their own hands. It would no doubt be in the interests of the parties themselves, but the injury to public morality would far outweigh that benefit and I must therefore rescind the decree and dismiss the petition.'[19]

While there was a fear that failing to release parties from a marriage would encourage 'illicit unions' and the irregular families that might result, judicial discretion to excuse the admitted adultery of a petitioner was exercised increasingly but inconsistently. This was despite *Apted v. Apted and Bliss*,[20] which, although a hard decision[21] refusing the petition, identified the circumstances under which discretion could be used.[22] The 'broad rules' approved, and emphasized, the public interest in preserving virtually all marriages. Yet the scandal of 'hotel divorces' continued to make a mockery of the courts and the law, and was frequently identified as a device for securing a consensual divorce in such cases as *Aylward v. Aylward*[23] where a decree was refused because:

'I have to consider evidence of this kind, in a state of things, which undoubtedly exists in regard to artificial proceedings for dissolution of marriage by consent of the parties. The respondent seems to be a respectable man, not the sort of man to commit adultery with some chance person. Doubtless he stayed at the hotel with a woman with the object of seeking a decree nisi, but I see no reason to suppose that the respondent "committed adultery with a woman unknown". The woman at the hotel might have been, for all I know, some near relative of his own. I pronounce no decree in this case.'

The changes in social climate, with the gradual emergence of a women's movement coupled with ideas of companionate marriage, meant that the existing divorce law was increasingly inadequate. Ingenious deceptions were proliferating,

---

19 (1920) 36 TLR 228.
20 [1930] P 246.
21 'The effect of the judgment was to perpetuate the form of marriage which had failed, to commit four lives to further sexual irregularity': J. WOSLEY-BOWDEN, *Mischief of the Marriage Laws*, Williams and Norgate Ltd, London 1932, p. 182.
22 *Walton v. Walton and Hazel* (1920) 36 TLR 228, 257: 'every relevant fact must be asserted and every interest involved should be considered. A governing consideration was the interests of the community at large in maintaining the sanctity of honest matrimony'.
23 (1928) 44 TLR 456.

promoting extensive discussion. A.P Herbert's *Holy Deadlock,* a novel about the divorce process, is alleged to have been used as a template for Wallis Simpson's divorce from her husband Ernest which prompted the abdication crisis in 1936.[24] Evelyn Waugh published *A Handful of Dust* in 1934 and there was beginning to be a serious discussion about the fundamental basis of marriage and hence divorce.

Despite the recommendations to liberalise divorce by the Gorell Royal Commission in 1912[25] it took the arrival of A. P. Herbert in Parliament as independent member for Oxford to bring about the 1937 Matrimonial Causes Act. As a committed reformer, with a 'demon in him about divorce reform',[26] he was both willing to compromise in order to achieve reform and determined to force the opposition to face the reality of the situation. Both Herbert and the Divorce Law Reform Union believed that the existing law, far from upholding morality, forced people into immorality.

Herbert's determination was helped by a governmental position of 'benevolent neutrality'[27] allowing the first small step to be taken away from the matrimonial offence doctrine. The government was aware of the need for reform but in a foretaste of 1969[28] was unwilling to put forward such controversial legislation itself; it was felt that divorce was an issue of individual conscience and not party politics. The government chose instead to rely on the dedication and commitment of Herbert. However, one clause that it did oppose was that attempting to get rid of the six-month gap between nisi and absolute decrees. As it was essential that the Government's neutrality be maintained,[29] the clause was abandoned. Indeed a new clause[30] was inserted in order that supporters of the Bill were not seen to condone collusion. So instead of requiring evidence of collusion before refusing a decree, the onus was reversed and the court could require evidence of an absence of collusion before granting a decree.

Herbert had optimistically believed that the extended grounds for divorce would make subterfuge and collusion a thing of the past,[31] but the role of the co-respondent continued to be both central and fundamental for those seeking to sever their uncongenial matrimonial bonds. The Act did however establish a

---

24   B. Inglis, *Abdication*, London, Hodder and Stoughton 1966, p. 352.

25   Royal Commission on Divorce and Matrimonial Causes 1912, above n. 12.

26   R. Pound, *A P Herbert, a Biography,* Michael Joseph, London 1976, p. 125.

27   S. Kent, *In on the Act*, Macmillan, London 1979, p. 79.

28   The Divorce Reform Act 1969, a private member's initiative.

29   The Cabinet provided a law officer to help at the Committee stage and provided the services of Parliamentary Counsel to the reformers. See Cretney, above n. 5, p. 238 for a detailed account.

30   Matrimonial Causes Act 1937, s. 4.

31   A. Herbert, *The Ayes Have It,* Methuen, London 1937.

chink in the moral armour of the matrimonial offence and a recognition that marriage could end for misfortune, with the introduction of divorce on the basis of insanity[32] as well as misconduct.

The grounds provided in the Matrimonial Causes Act 1937 substantially lasted until 1969. The law was consolidated, but little of significance changed, and enlargement of the grounds for divorce came from the courts and judicial initiatives, in particular by continuing to extend definitions of cruelty.[33] By stretching the interpretation of cruelty to incorporate incompatibility, the line between the normal wear and tear of married life and cruelty was being moved.[34] The significant cases were *Gollins v. Gollins*,[35] which held an intention to harm was not an essential prerequisite to cruelty, and *Williams v. Williams*,[36] where insanity was not a defence to a charge of cruelty. The courts further enlarged the divorce grounds by making constructive desertion slightly easier to establish[37] and most significantly, as already mentioned, by extending the court's role as exerciser of discretion in adultery cases. This meant that statute and case law were conflicting: while statute law continued to be framed entirely on the marital offence, judicial interpretation of the statutory framework was gradually beginning to operate on the principle of breakdown.[38]

4. THE IMPACT OF THE SECOND WORLD WAR

The hasty wartime marriages and long separations necessitated by the Second World War resulted in a post-war divorce boom of alarming proportions and almost caused the collapse of the existing legal machinery.[39] The huge backlog of divorces provoked fears that those unable to resolve their matrimonial position would resort to infidelity and 'a slime of unfaithfulness will creep over our land'.[40] The requirement for all divorces to be adjudicated, whether contested or not,

---

32   Matrimonial Causes Act 1937, s. 2(d).
33   L. ROSEN, 'Cruelty in Matrimonial Causes' (1949) 12 *Modern Law Review* 325; J. BIGGS, *The Concept of Matrimonial Cruelty*, Athlone Press, London 1962.
34   ROSEN, above n. 33.
35   [1964] AC 644.
36   [1964] AC 698.
37   Conduct that effectively 'drove out' a wife continued to need to be beyond the normal 'wear and tear' of marriage: *Buchler v. Buchler* [1947] P 25. It became possible to establish desertion when parties were living under the same roof after *Powell v. Powell* [1922] P 278. See also C. CHAPMAN, *The Poor Man's Court of Justice*, Hodder and Stoughton, London 1925.
38   P. WEBB, 'Breakdown versus Fault' (1965) 4 *International and Comparative Law Quarterly* 194.
39   The low of 7,800 divorces in 1941 was followed in 1947 by the alarming figure of 60,300 divorces: HALSEY, above n. 3, p. 80.
40   *Hansard*, HC Deb 10.05.1946 vol 422 col 447 (Mr Skiffington Lodge).

however much of a fiction, ensured the courts were increasingly clogged and unable to cope.

During the war, concern about servicemen's morale and its effect on their fighting ability had led to the introduction in 1942 of the Army Legal Aid Scheme which had opened up divorce to many whom cost had previously barred from divorce. This was subsequently expanded to the civilian population in 1949 with the Legal Aid and Advice Act offering wider access to divorce than the entirely inadequate Poor Persons Procedure,[41] with its very severe means and merit test, had done. The provision of legal aid was recognition that state funding was essential for full and equal access to justice. Again there was a substantial rise in the divorce rate as those who had previously been financially excluded began to seek divorce, with the consequent rise in the numbers of co-respondents.[42] Although legal aid was means tested, there was a high eligibility rate and 80% of the population was covered to some extent.[43]

5. 1950s DEBATES

The 1950s saw a stabilizing of the divorce rate:[44] perhaps there was felt to be a need to return to a stable and more traditional way of life, after the dislocation and upheaval of war. Still, family work dominated the legal aid budget and judges were increasingly reluctant to waste public money where a divorce was inevitable, yet for the parties the ancillary matters continued to mean that questions of guilt and innocence were crucial and adversarial cross petitions were inevitable.[45]

In 1951 Mrs White introduced a Matrimonial Causes Bill, which would have allowed divorce after seven year's separation. The Bill's principal stated aim was to enable the many illicit unions to be regulated and was, as with previous legislation, surprisingly vigorously promoted with a marriage morality argument[46] which sought a new and appropriate divorce law for modern

---

[41] A. BARRISTER, *Justice in England,* Gollanz Ltd, London 1938.

[42] From a high of 60,000 decrees in 1947 to a low of 23,000 decrees in 1958.

[43] M. MACLEAN, 'Access to Justice in Family Matters in Post-War Britain' in S. KATZ, J. EEKELAAR and M.MACLEAN (eds.) *Cross Currents: Family Law and Policy in the US and England,* Oxford University Press, Oxford 2000, p. 536.

[44] In 1952 2.8% of marriages ended in divorce, yet by 1960 this figure had fallen to 2% (L. STONE, *Road to Divorce: England 1530–1985,* Oxford University Press, Oxford 1990, p. 436).

[45] The 'heart' of divorce has often been the ancillary matters, for which the guilt and innocence labels were critical. A 'guilty' wife continued to lose both the majority of any maintenance entitlement and custody of her children.

[46] *Hansard,* HC Deb 09.03.1951. vol 485 col 927: 'Many thousands of men and women are living apart in a state which is not marriage in any full sense of the word, but in which they are unable to form another union or to establish a normal home life.' (Mrs White).

marriages which were increasingly based on love as opposed to economic considerations. Such a change would have destroyed the doctrine of the matrimonial offence and was opposed. Yet, in an increasingly secular society the fault basis was becoming recognized as a charade, with an understanding that it was impossible for the courts to apportion blame accurately, although concern still centred on the evil of 'guilty' spouses being able to divorce their unwilling and 'innocent' partners.

Divorce for many continued to be surrounded by stigma, although this declined throughout the 1950s. Adultery by a wife was still a property offence, a form of theft, for which damages continued to be claimed. As the twentieth century progressed, the acceptability of a pecuniary value being placed on a woman's chastity was being questioned:

> 'That the process should be made use of and payments accepted by men, some of whom are of position and decent family, is still less edifying. That such a custom continues to be tolerated in otherwise good society is of course due to the survival of ideas of ownership in women, as any domestic animal.'[47]

Yet for others the satisfaction the injured could receive from formal recognition of another's guilt and quasi-criminal conduct justified the continued use of such awards: 'why should a man who breaks up a home of another, escape the proper consequences of criminal conduct.'[48] The heads of damage were several, the pecuniary, which could be substantial if a wife was a business partner,[49] the consortium value of a lost wife, compensation for injury to a husband's feelings and honour, and even hurt to his family. It was not necessary to prove the co-respondent knew his lover was married, merely that he should have done.[50] However a woman who pretended not to be married and entered a casual sexual encounter was held to be valueless and damages would be reduced accordingly:

> 'Where a man commits adultery with a woman he takes a risk, but where a woman held herself out to commit adultery as if she were not a married woman, then the

---

47   O. ROTHERFIELD, *The Garden of Thorns*, Hutchinson, London 1933, p. 243.
48   H. MERRIVALE, *Marriage and Divorce*, Allen and Unwin, London 1936, p. 58.
49   *Scott v. Scott and Another* [1957] 1 All ER 63, 64. Where the wife was a shrewd business woman, the co-respondent appealed against the amount of damages, Denning L.J. commented 'of course it is well settled in law that damages against the co-respondent are not to punish him for his wrong doing, but are compensation to the husband for the loss of his wife, in the case of a wife who was a good business woman, for the loss of her business capacity used in his interests'.
50   *Lycett-Green v. Lycett-Green and du Pay* [1956] 3 All ER 97, 98. His Honour Judge Granville Smith 'I think in the circumstances it would be shutting one's eyes to the way of the world if I held that he had no reason to know. The present is quite different from the case of a man who meets a woman, who is behaving like a prostitute. In those circumstances he may come forward and say 'I have no idea, what she was, for I do not know her'.

damages, if any, should be reduced to next to nothing because she would be a women whose loss could not matter to her husband.'[51]

If a man was careless as to whether a woman was married or not then he must take the consequences.[52] The almost farcical situation continued whereby the petitioner, when seeking damages, was required to establish that his erring wife was, prior to the seduction, a virtuous woman and ideal wife, while the co-respondent, in order to minimise the award against him, would be seeking to establish the exact opposite.[53]

Mrs White's Bill threatened to undermine this property relationship, i.e. that most married men had a valuable asset, which if used or stolen by another man could lead to damages from the 'trespasser'. Her Bill was a Private Member's Bill without Government backing and hence was always vulnerable. Although receiving surprising support inside the Commons[54] it was entirely withdrawn in return for the establishment of a Royal Commission with a wide remit to look at all areas of divorce and marriage. Yet the Government's underlying motive for procrastination, and its unwillingness to take responsibility for such a controversial legislative proposal as divorce reform, was clear to some MPs:

'Could my Right Honourable friend give an assurance that this Commission, which cannot possibly report for some years and which in any event binds no-one to anything, will not be made a pretext for murdering the Bill passed in this House on Friday with a decisive majority and widespread public approval?'[55]

The resulting Morton Commission[56] finally reported in 1956. The Report was unable to recommend substantial reform and resulted in the near stagnation of an increasingly discredited system and effectively closed down secular discussion of divorce reform for a further decade. The majority report held on to the belief that marriage was a binding legal duty and marriage remained an institution rather than a relationship. Adultery continued to be an offence against the institution and required suitable compensation. The majority of the Royal Commission sought to retain the matrimonial offence and there were various splits and subgroups with different views over how best to address the existing problems of the grounds for divorce, but all justified their position as being in the best interest of couples, children and the community. All articulated concern

---

51   *Watson v. Watson and Watts* (1905) 21 TLR 320.

52   *Langrick v. Langrick and Funnell* [1920] P 90.

53   *Scott v. Scott and Another* [1957] 1 All ER 63.

54   *Hansard*, HC Deb 09.03.1951 vol 485 col 926.

55   *Hansard*, HC Deb 14.03.1951 vol 485 col 1537 (Colonel Lipton). It is not clear whether Irene White believed the Royal Commission would produce a more liberal divorce law; as is shown subsequently, it did not.

56   Royal Commission on Divorce and Matrimonial Causes Cmd 9678, HMSO, London, 1956.

for the decline of the traditional marital family, which continued to be the perceived cornerstone of society. Yet while recognizing that the existing law undermined the institution of marriage, it was believed that this could be remedied by a more vigorous upholding of the law[57] and by people taking a more realistic view of their marital obligations. The success or otherwise of individual marriages continued to matter less than the maintenance of the institution.

The majority of the Committee believed that a proper divorce law was 'to give relief where wrong had been done'[58] and that the increasing divorce rate reflected higher wifely expectation[59] which in one crucial respect should be met: it was suggested the 'the woman named' should become a financially liable co-respondent.[60] There was a fear that if divorce was available on the separation ground alone, women would start to poach each other's husbands: 'we have in mind the type of women who would find it much more profitable to entice a husband away from his wife and family if she could be sure that ultimately divorce could be forced on the wife'.[61] There was great concern about a national state of 'divorce mindedness' and the effect of the increasing expectations of individualism on 'moral fibre': divorce was seen as a legacy of wartime immorality despite its declining rate,[62] and some people gave evidence to the effect that divorce should be entirely abolished if the rate began to rise.

The evidence the Commission heard was often anecdotal and unscientific but held to be appropriate. The Commission was criticized for its lack of scientific rigor and the limited evidence they chose to hear. The Commission was accused 'with some justification of reaching conclusions by intelligent guesswork'.[63] McGregor commented:

'It is a matter of opinion whether the Morton Commission is intellectually the worst Royal Commission of the twentieth century, but there can be no dispute that its report is the most unreadable and confused...'[64]

In contrast to the Commission's view, Rowntree's and Carrier's[65] research recognized the need to democratise the divorce process and to allow the opportunity to divorce for those that had been previously excluded. While

---

57   Ibid., para. 47.
58   Ibid., para. 69.
59   Ibid., para. 45.
60   Ibid., para. 462.
61   Ibid., para. 69.
62   C. Haste, *Rules of Desire, Sex in Britain,* Random House, London 1994, p. 144.
63   O. Kahn Freund, 'Divorce Law Reform' (1956) 19 *Modern Law Review* 573.
64   O. McGregor, *Divorce in England,* Heinemann, London 1957.
65   G. Rowntree and N. Carrier, 'The Resort to Divorce in England and Wales 1857–1957' (1958) 11 *Population Studies* 189.

McGregor was appalled at the Morton Commission's backward-looking focus and lack of useful and constructive suggestions towards a fairer and more open system of divorce, other commentators were more impressed, for instance: 'the report is a document of great social importance, reflecting the wide terms of reference of the Commission and the infinite care with which their terms have been carried out'.[66]

In the final analysis, the Report had virtually no recognition that divorce was not an entirely one-sided, fault-based, social and individual catastrophe. It was therefore left to the judiciary to continue to mitigate the harshness of the existing law. They did this throughout the 1950s, most significantly by the doctrine of the discretion statement, developing and accelerating its use. This ensured that adultery remained the most popular ground for divorce with a corresponding need for third-party involvement. The use of the discretion statement to identify and effectively pardon the petitioner's own marital offence meant the distinction between guilty respondent and innocent petitioner was becoming more and more blurred. Yet in an increasingly affluent society, where couples had homes and assets to redistribute on divorce, the distinction remained critical, because ancillary outcomes remained predicated on the guilt and innocence paradigm.

6.   1960s REFORM

With the dawning of the 1960s and changing social attitudes this state of affairs was becoming unacceptable and several attempts were made to make the law both fairer and more realistic. In 1963, Leo Abse attempted a further assault on the matrimonial offence with the Matrimonial Causes Act 1963, motivated by concern for the many illegitimate children living in stable illicit unions.[67] These were children who suffered both social stigma and financial penalties. Abse reminded the House that illegitimate children had very restricted inheritance rights and that a magistrates' court affiliation order was needed to claim maintenance from a father.[68] His Bill would have allowed divorce after seven year's separation and included a clause allowing adultery to be retained as a ground if a couple attempted reconciliation but the reconciliation subsequently failed.[69] Collusion became a discretionary bar giving the Bill the nickname a 'kiss

---

[66]   GRAVESON and CRANE, above n. 1, p. 147.
[67]   L. ABSE, *Private Member,* Macdonald, London 1973, p. 160: 'the subsequent children (of those unable to divorce) of illicit unions possessed like all children of sensitive antennae, were too often bought up in an atmosphere of guilt, embarrassment and shame'.
[68]   *Hansard,* HC Deb 08.02.1963 vol 671 col 1818.
[69]   Matrimonial Causes Act 1963, ss. 1 and 4.

and make up' Bill.[70] Under the threat of being 'talked out' the divorce and separation clauses were dropped, Abse bitterly commenting that in order to preserve some limited benefits of the Bill he had had to sacrifice the important proposed separation grounds:

'Because I must put this before my pride and my passionate belief in the morality of this clause, with a heavy heart my sponsors and I have no alternative but to yield to this duress imposed upon us. I am aware that this may cause deep disappointment and grief, as it does to me, to many thousands who hoped Parliament would release them from their present plight.'[71]

The Matrimonial Causes Act 1965 was a consolidating piece of legislation, and the co-respondent remained significant for the ancillary relief matters. It continued to allow a guilty wife's property to be settled on her husband and children,[72] as well as for damages to be awarded,[73] which even at this late date were still felt to be a deterrent to adultery.

The Church remained opposed to a radical departure from the matrimonial offence doctrine despite the numerous examples of injustice and evidence of divorce by consent already existing.[74] But it was clear that the established Church would soon be unable to retain its position on the indissolubility of marriage and needed to look forward to a role as a religious adviser to an increasingly secular state, not back to the days of indissoluble marriages and ecclesiastical courts. Action was needed to restore and maintain the Church's influence over policy. In 1963 the Archbishop of Canterbury, Arthur Ramsey, announced that he was initiating a Committee to look at and advise him on divorce and how to decrease the gap between its principles and practice. The group met eighteen times and soon agreed on the very unsatisfactory nature of the current law, and that the Church had a responsibility to address these complex issues. The Archbishop's group remained opposed to divorce by consent and believed all cases needed investigation by the courts as representative of the State.[75] They concluded that

---

70   For problems of condonation prior to MCA 1963 see *Henderson v. Henderson and Crillin* [1944] AC 49. Here the agreement of the wife never to see the co-respondent again, recanted after sexual intercourse with her husband, was held to mean that the previous adultery was condoned by him and divorce impossible on those facts.

71   *Hansard*, HC Deb 03.05.1963 vol 676 col 1562.

72   Section 17.

73   Section 41. Criminal conversation, which was neither criminal nor a conversation.

74   The position of the Church was however mellowing: 'But it is clear to us all that the result of these clauses being law will be to increase the likelihood of reconciliation between estranged parties particularly by removing the fear of losing status in possible divorce proceedings by following a course of action which would appear humane, kindly in nature and often having the express purpose of preventing the final break-up, or restoring some chance of reconciliation' (*Hansard*, HL Deb 22.05.1963 vol 250 col 393, Bishop Leicester).

75   *Putting Asunder: A Divorce Law for Contemporary Society*, SPCK, London 1966.

irretrievable breakdown as ascertained by a court was a more Christian approach than the present discredited system:

> 'The procedure needed would, in some respects, be akin to an inquest instead of the present accusatorial process, the judge would be enquiring into the alleged death of a matrimonial relationship and into its alleged causes, in order to see whether he could rightly order the remains to be buried. The legal presumption would be that the relationship was alive until such time as cogent evidence to the contrary had been provided, in other words the onus would be on the petitioner.'[76]

The recommendation was that pleadings should be expanded, parts of which could be confidential. As far as the co-respondent was concerned, it was suggested 'that such persons… should be served and made liable for costs only in cases where adultery is alleged to be a major cause of breakdown. Otherwise the concept of the co-respondent would no longer be appropriate'.[77] There was also recognition of the complexity of human relationships, and 'forensic social workers'[78] were proposed to establish the blame, (which continued to be required to resolve ancillary disputes). Yet it was beginning to be recognized that the blame was not likely to be entirely one sided:

> 'If we concentrate our attention wholly on the actions that are designated matrimonial offences we inevitably fail to do justice to the complexity of emotions and the interacting pressures which finally drives one to act and the other to treat the action as a ground for a divorce petition.'[79]

This was a startling shift by the Church (even if one motivated by self-preservation) and gave new impetus to the divorce reform debate.

Following publication of *Putting Asunder,* the recently established Law Commission,[80] under the Chairmanship of Sir Lesley Scarman, started work on matrimonial causes. There was a visible gap between the law and the reality of people's lives, created by the unrealistic nature of the existing law.[81] *The Field of Choice* was published in 1966 and was a catalytic document, encouraging the move towards reform by obtaining public support: 'it clarifies social vantage points and indicates which of the available lines of approach are practical, it sifts and narrows down controversial views to debatable points and presents them to the public and legislature'.[82] Co-respondents, however, continued to be important

---

76   Ibid., para. 5, p. 117.
77   Ibid., para. 12.
78   Ibid., para. 12.
79   Ibid., para. 17.
80   Law Commission Act 1965.
81   *Hansard*, HC Deb 17.12.1968 vol 774 col 2037 (Mr Jones).
82   B. Lee, *Divorce Law Reform in England,* Peter Owen, London 1974, p.73.

as establishers of adultery[83] and there was continuing importance placed on fault as far as ancillary matters were concerned.

It was the question of whether breakdown of marriage was something that could be established by a trial that was the biggest difference between the two groups, the Law Commission recognizing that a judicial inquest would be expensive, and impractical, and would create another humiliating and distressing charade, perhaps more private, but essentially the same as the existing system.[84] However 'irretrievable breakdown' as the ground was in reality simple window dressing as one of the five facts had to be established to prove the breakdown, effectively giving the old matrimonial offence and the co-respondent a new lease of life. The Law Commission ultimately persuaded the Church group of the impracticality of investigation and for the first time it was proposed that a 'guilty' spouse should be able to seek a divorce.

Subsequently the hybrid 1969 Divorce Law Reform Act was passed, retaining the matrimonial offence in the 'facts' required to establish irretrievable breakdown. Like previous matrimonial legislation,[85] it was within a rhetoric of facilitating more successful marriages and legally recognized families,[86] demonstrating a touching faith in the stabilizing influence of reconstructed families. So after 1969 co-respondents retained their place, as evidence of adultery[87] although not necessarily named. Scorned spouses continued to be facilitated by the law to embroil third parties in their disintegrating relationships (despite damages being no longer available).[88] The retention of co-respondents continues to emphasize a failure to understand the true complexities of a disintegrating marital relationship.

---

83 Above n. 75, para. 27.

84 Law Commission, *The Field of Choice* Law Com. No. 15, HMSO, London 1966, paras. 58, 59.

85 At second reading Mr Jones raised examples of separations as long as 53 years: 'these empty marriages as they accumulate add increasing harm to the community and injury to the ideal of marriage itself' (*Hansard*, HC Deb 17.12.1968 vol 774 col 2037).

86 R. Deech, 'Divorce Law and Empirical Studies' (1990) 106 *LQR (Law Quarterly Review)* 229. See also A.P. Herbert's introduction to the Matrimonial Causes Act 1937: *Hansard*, HC Deb 20.10.1936 vol 317 col 2079.

87 MCA 1973, s. 1(2)(a).

88 The last significant case was *Pritchard v. Pritchard and Sims* [1967] 3 All ER 601. Lord Diplock commented that pecuniary damages were no longer appropriate and were reminiscent of a slave market, yet an award of £2,000 was substituted for the original £7,500, which was held by the Court of Appeal to have been a punitive sum for, amongst other things, the husband's loss of consortium with his wife and hurt to his feelings. Damages were formally abolished in the Law Reform (Miscellaneous Provisions) Act 1970, s. 4.

SIMPLE QUARRELS?
Autonomy vs. Vulnerability

Gillian Douglas

Contents

1. INTRODUCTION

One of the most enduring conundrums which remain to be resolved in family law is how to balance the competing interests of the parties when determining financial and property settlements on divorce. In particular, there are two key factors which may conflict with each other: autonomy and vulnerability. Stephen Cretney made two major contributions to the law on this question: first, as a Law Commissioner, where he led reform proposals which resulted in the enactment of the Matrimonial and Family Proceedings Act 1984; and secondly, after he returned to academia, as a collaborator, with Gwynn Davis and Jean Collins, in an empirical study on how such cases are dealt with in everyday legal practice, *Simple Quarrels* published in 1994.[1] This chapter examines the significance of these contributions to the development of both legal policy and our understanding of the law in operation.

---

[1] G. DAVIS, S. CRETNEY and J. COLLINS, *Simple Quarrels: Negotiating Money and Property Disputes on Divorce*, Clarendon Press, Oxford 1994.

2. SIMPLE QUARRELS – COMPLEX ISSUES?

It is rather remarkable that a legal regime devised at the end of the 1960s to deal with a highly controversial issue – obtaining and dealing with the consequences of divorce – should have survived into the 21st century relatively untouched despite the enormous social, economic and cultural changes which have taken place in the meantime. The well-known history of the failed attempt in the Family Law Act 1996 to update the ground and procedure for ending a marriage sheds light on why reform has not taken place in relation to that issue, but the reluctance of politicians even to engage[2] with calls for reform of the system of 'ancillary relief' or, as it is now known, 'financial remedies',[3] is less understandable. However, it could be argued that there are two basic reasons. First, it is simply too difficult to strike the balance between considerations of autonomy and vulnerability in a way which would be acceptable across the political spectrum and particularly as between men and women. But secondly, the very nature of the wide discretionary jurisdiction of the courts can be seen to enable any couple to achieve, if not a settlement tailor-made to meet all their requirements, an off-the-peg solution which can be altered to take account of their basic situation. The law can thus be said to cater for both rich and poor. This is important because, unlike when Cretney was at the Law Commission or undertaking his socio-legal research, the reported case-law has now become almost entirely dominated by the concerns of the very wealthy, creating a 'fantasy family law' of potentially little relevance to the mass of high-street solicitors still attempting, in the face of the death of legal aid, to provide some kind of service to their clients who, otherwise, may be reaching outcomes, as unrepresented divorcees, ever more removed from either legal principle or economic common sense.

3. AUTONOMY *VS.* VULNERABILITY

The conflicting issues of autonomy and vulnerability apply to divorce settlement across two separate dimensions – the relationship of the parties with the state, and their relationship with each other. Autonomy, for instance, may refer to the ability of the parties to shape their own settlement (before, during or at the end of the marriage)[4] free from state interference, an issue of major significance given the emphasis on private ordering in family legal policy which has manifested

---

[2] It is true that Lord Irvine, when he was Lord Chancellor, did establish an Ancillary Relief Advisory Group made up of judges, practitioners and academics (including Stephen Cretney) (see their *Report to the Lord Chancellor*, LCD, London 1998) but as the group recommended against any radical reform, no action was taken and subsequent governments have left it to the courts – and latterly the Law Commission – to wrestle with the issues.

[3] Family Procedure Rules 2010 SI 2010/2955, r. 2.3(1).

[4] Law Commission, *Marital Property Agreements* Law Com. CP No. 198, TSO, London 2011.

itself most recently in the calls to recognise marital property agreements and the decision of the Supreme Court to create an effective presumption in their favour in *Radmacher v. Granatino*.[5] But autonomy also applies to the ability of each of the spouses to be, or become, financially independent of each other after the marriage is ended and to sever the marital tie not just legally but economically. This is the 'clean break' principle which was originally expounded by Lord Scarman in *Minton v. Minton*:

> 'There are two principles which inform the modern legislation. One is the public interest that spouses, to the extent that their means permit, should provide for themselves and their children. But the other – of equal importance – is the principle of "the clean break." The law now encourages spouses to avoid bitterness after family break-down and to settle their money and property problems. An object of the modern law is to encourage each to put the past behind them and to begin a new life which is not overshadowed by the relationship which has broken down.'[6]

Calls to increase the courts' power to order such a clean break formed part of the backdrop to the Law Commission's reconsideration of the regime enacted in the Matrimonial Proceedings and Property Act 1970, consolidated in the Matrimonial Causes Act 1973, which Cretney led in 1980/81.

The vulnerability of a spouse – most often the wife – also has a dual dimension. On the one hand, women continue to face greater economic hardship than men due to their continuing role as primary carers of children and to the structural inequalities in the labour market which mean that, 40 years after the Equal Pay Act 1970, they still 'enjoy' only 79 per cent of men's average gross hourly earnings.[7] But a woman's vulnerability may also stem from her relationship with her spouse – both because of the emotional dynamic operating between them and by virtue of the choices (or constraints) that applied during their relationship. If a couple 'choose', or have no effective choice other than, to prioritise the husband's earnings or career over the wife's, how far should that decision influence their divorce settlement? How far should an *ex*-spouse, in other words, make good the economic shortfall facing the other, when the divorce terminates any legal obligation of support? And how fair is it to place that burden on the ex-spouse when it stems from the broader societal inequality of women as much, if not more than, the couple's own financial decision-making?

---

5   [2010] UKSC 42. For discussion, see J. MILES, 'Marriage and Divorce in the Supreme Court and the Law Commission: for Love or Money?' (2011) 74 *MLR (Modern Law Review)* 430.
6   [1979] AC 593, 608.
7   'European Commission campaigns to reduce gender pay gap', <http://ec.europa.eu/unitedkingdom/press/press_releases/2010/pr1017_en.htm> accessed 23.09.2011, citing Eurostat, 'Pay gap between women and men in unadjusted form in EU Member States – 2008'.

Cretney's activities at the Law Commission engaged with all of these issues and his subsequent academic research brought a further dimension to them, by revealing the extent to which the financial remedies jurisdiction itself may serve to disempower and thus render vulnerable *both* parties to the divorce.

4. THE LAW COMMISSION'S VIEWS ON THE FINANCIAL CONSEQUENCES OF DIVORCE

4.1. THE DISCUSSION PAPER

In 1980, the Law Commission published a 'Discussion Paper' on the financial consequences of divorce, in response to a request to provide advice to the Lord Chancellor.[8] The abolition of marital fault as the basis for the grant of a divorce, had led to departure from the earlier principle that, as the Law Commission put it:

> 'The right and duty of maintenance was related to the performance of reciprocal matrimonial obligations; a husband who was at fault should continue to support his wife, but conversely it would be unjust to require a husband who had "performed substantially all his matrimonial obligations to continue to provide maintenance for a wife who had substantially repudiated hers."'[9]

The replacement of fault with the concept of irretrievable breakdown provable on evidence of one or more of five 'facts' meant, as the Law Commission said, that 'if either party wants a divorce, sooner or later he will be able to obtain one.'[10] Yet at the same time, section 25 of the Matrimonial Causes Act 1973 imposed an obligation on the court, known as the 'minimal loss principle',[11] to exercise its powers so 'as to place the parties, so far as it is practicable and having regard to their conduct, just to do so, in the financial position in which they would have been if the marriage had not broken down and each had properly discharged his or her financial obligations and responsibilities towards the other.' Moreover, in the leading case of *Wachtel v. Wachtel*[12] the Court of Appeal had applied the shift away from fault to the issues of financial provision and property adjustment (notwithstanding the reference to having regard to the parties'

---

[8]   Law Commission, *The Financial Consequences of Divorce: The Basic Policy* Law Com. No. 103, HMSO, London 1980.
[9]   Ibid., para. 13, citation omitted.
[10] Ibid., para. 15.
[11] J. Eekelaar, *Family Law and Social Policy*, 2nd ed., Weidenfeld and Nicholson, London 1984, p. 109.
[12] [1973] Fam 72. For discussion of the case and its legacy, see G. Douglas, 'Bringing an End to the Matrimonial Post Mortem: *Wachtel v. Wachtel* and its Enduring Significance for Ancillary Relief' in S. Gilmore, J. Herring and R. Probert (eds.), *Landmark Cases in Family Law*, Hart, Oxford 2011.

conduct in section 25). The result was that a husband who was divorced without himself having committed a matrimonial offence and who may not have wished to end the marriage at all, could find himself required to give up part (or all) of 'his' capital and to make continuing – potentially life-long – periodical payments to his ex-wife.[13]

This situation, compounded by the lack of any power of the courts to compel an ex-spouse to forgo ongoing financial support and receive a share of capital alone (via a 'clean break') created a sense of grievance which gave rise to the creation of a lobbying campaign group, the 'Campaign for Justice in Divorce', one of a number of groups, such as Families Need Fathers, who have been formed to protest at what they see as the partisanship of the law and the bias of decision-making in favour of women as either wives or mothers.[14] Eventually, the Lord Chancellor referred the issue to the Law Commission. It is quite clear from their Discussion Paper that they did not wish to undertake a review of legislation which, after all, had only been in force for about a decade and which had become highly politicised. They therefore stated that they were taking a limited approach to the exercise, producing a 'discussion paper' rather than the normal working paper, and focusing only on the issues arising between husband and wife, within the sphere of private law, and declining to consider the position of children, or how the law operated in other jurisdictions. They also adverted to the much wider – and political rather than legal – questions underlying the controversy they had been dragged into, raising the spectre of the implications that a shift away from private liability would have for social security expenditure and indeed, the very nature of marriage,[15] which were, no doubt, intended to give Conservative ministers serving under Margaret Thatcher's first administration some pause for thought.[16]

The Law Commission analysed the fundamental problem as being the retention of the 'minimal loss' principle which, in their view, caused much of the bitterness felt towards the law.[17] They then responded to the arguments put by those

---

13   LAW COMMISSION, above n. 8, paras. 24, 25.
14   On which see R. COLLIER, 'The Fathers' Rights Movement, Law Reform, and the New Politics of Fatherhood: Some Reflections on the UK Experience' (2009) 20 *University of Florida Journal of Law & Public Policy* 65.
15   LAW COMMISSION, above n. 8, para. 3.
16   Uncannily echoing current economic gloom, the situation was dire in 1980 when the Law Commission were deliberating. As Hugo Young described in his biography of Margaret Thatcher, 'monetarism went through its first crisis during the second half of 1980, the middle of a seemingly unending deterioration in every relevant indicator... "As gloomy a picture as it is possible for anyone to paint", said the chairman of the CBI economic committee in his July survey of business opinion, "and I fear things will get worse before they get better."' H. YOUNG, *One of Us*, Macmillan, London 1989, p. 205.
17   LAW COMMISSION, above n. 8, para. 29. It is striking that they refer to 2,439 men being sentenced to imprisonment in 1978 for wilful refusal or culpable neglect to pay maintenance.

seeking to challenge the principle of potentially life-long support for the ex-spouse, providing in particular statistical evidence about the continuing inequality of women in the workplace which, they concluded, 'suggests that for many women, and especially for married women, opportunities are still largely non-existent and equality a myth.'[18] In spelling out the sectored nature of women's employment, their reliance on part-time work, their continuing responsibility for the bulk of child care and their greater vulnerability to becoming unemployed in the economic down-turn, the Discussion Paper has a depressingly up-to-date feel.[19]

Having set out the problem and the context, the Law Commission then presented various models[20] for reforming the law, pointing out their strengths and weaknesses without expressing a view on which would be most appropriate. These ranged from simple repeal of the minimal loss principle to its replacement by the relief of need (for many couples, the only relevant criterion) or the clean break (reflecting a growing trend in private ordering, as shown in *Minton v. Minton*), or even the introduction of a mathematical formula (in order to achieve certainty). Responses to their paper were summarised and evaluated in their follow-up Report in 1981.[21]

4.2. THE RESPONSE AND RECOMMENDATIONS

The Law Commission reported that responses to the Discussion Paper confirmed their view that the minimal loss principle was no longer appropriate as the governing objective of the jurisdiction, being 'rarely possible of attainment... [and] in the great majority of cases, undesirable that it should be attained.'[22] But, as they had pointed out in the Discussion Paper, simply repealing it without

---

There are no comparable current data for committals to prison for failure to make periodical payments to a spouse, but in 2010/11, only 40 men were committed to prison for non-payment of *child support*: CMEC, *Child Support Agency National Statistics June 2011* <www.childmaintenance.org/en/publications/statistics.html> (accessed 23.09.2011), p. 23. The decline probably has more to do with changing attitudes to enforcement than to a lesser feeling of 'bitterness' towards the law.

[18] LAW COMMISSION, above n. 8, para. 50. At para 5 they report that women's average earnings were 'still only' 73% of those of men – thirty years subsequently, as noted above, the figure has crawled up to 79%.

[19] For discussion of the socio-economic context currently facing women who separate or divorce, see S. HARRIS-SHORT, 'Building a house upon sand: post-separation parenting, shared residence and equality – lessons from Sweden' [2011] 23 *Child and Family Law Quarterly* 344.

[20] LAW COMMISSION, above n. 8, Part IV.

[21] LAW COMMISSION, *The Financial Consequences of Divorce: The response to the Law Commission's Discussion Paper, and recommendations on the policy of the Law*, Law Com. No. 112, HMSO, London 1981.

[22] Ibid., para. 17.

providing an alternative would result in an 'uncontrolled discretion [which] would inevitably exacerbate the divergence of practices between different tribunals, as well as leaving individual judges and registrars with no real guidance about the important issues of policy involved.'[23] They rejected any significant reduction in the scope for discretion and therefore proposed that an evolutionary change in the law should be achieved by 'adding certain provisions designed to give a clear indication of how the discretion… should be applied to the facts of individual cases.'[24]

Accordingly, they recommended that priority be given to the needs of the children of the family, considering that 'there would be important advantages if the legislation were clearly to embody the principle that the interests of the children should be seen as a matter of overriding importance.'[25] In so recommending, they provided an early indication of the shift in focus which we have since seen in family law away from the adult couple as *spouses,* onto the children and to the adults' role as *parents.* This shift provides a partial[26] means of reconciling the legal principle that divorce terminates the adults' mutual obligations to support each other with the reality that economic circumstances may require ongoing financial ties between them. As the Law Commission put it,

'adequate recognition would be given to the value of the custodial parent's role, while discouraging the belief that such payments may be regarded as an automatic life-time provision intended for the benefit of the custodial parent (usually, of course, the wife) perhaps for many years after the children have ceased to live with her.'

And they added,

'Secondly, it is (we understand) often the case that the allocation of a larger proportion of the overall maintenance provision for the children's benefit makes the maintenance obligations more acceptable to the payer (usually, of course, the father).'[27]

The re-casting of the obligations between the adults as based on their shared parenthood rather than their former marriage not only provided a mechanism for making the payment of support apparently[28] more palatable to the father whilst going some way to minimising the mother/ex-wife's economic vulnerability in the future, but it also legitimised the corresponding new focus

---

23   LAW COMMISSION, above n. 8, para. 69, quoted in LAW COMMISSION, above n. 21, para. 18.
24   LAW COMMISSION, above n. 21, para. 23.
25   Ibid., para. 24.
26   Partial only, because, as discussed below, not all divorcing couples have children.
27   LAW COMMISSION, above n. 21, para. 24.
28   Child support compliance rates have not, historically, suggested that this makes a huge difference to fathers in practice, whatever is said rhetorically.

on the desirability of encouraging financial independence and thus promoted the goal of achieving the future autonomy of the parties.

Thus, their second recommendation was to encourage the courts to consider the possibility of limiting the duration of any continuing financial support, through a requirement specifically to consider whether a periodical payments order for a limited term only would be appropriate[29] and to empower the courts to dismiss the wife's claim for periodical payments without her agreement.[30] The Law Commission also recommended that the courts

> 'should be more clearly directed to the desirability of promoting a severance of financial obligations between the parties at the time of divorce; and to give greater weight to the view that in the appropriate case any periodical financial provision ordered in favour of one spouse (usually the wife) for her own benefit as distinct from periodical payments made to her to enable her to care for the children – should be primarily directed to secure wherever possible a smooth transition from marriage to the status of independence.'[31]

This emphasis upon viewing payments for the ex-spouse as directed towards meeting her claims as child-carer rather than in her own right has since been endorsed by the Supreme Court in *Radmacher v. Granatino* where, in giving weight to the pre-nuptial agreement reached by the parties, it upheld the limitation by the Court of Appeal of the husband's award to support and housing only whilst the children were growing up.[32]

However, not all marriages produce children, and not all divorcees are carers of children. Many divorcees, particularly those stereotyped in the original justification for the minimal loss principle (to prevent husbands casting aside their first wives in favour of younger 'trophy' wives at no financial cost), are women of middle or older years, with limited or no earning capacity and, because of the societal factors noted above, with limited or no independent financial resources to fall back on after divorce. The provisions eventually enacted in the Matrimonial and Family Proceedings Act 1984 arguably provided sufficient leeway to the courts to steer a fairly cautious path in navigating the new encouragement of self-sufficiency. They subsequently held that the new law had not introduced a *presumption* in favour of a clean break,[33] and were particularly wary of exercising the power to direct that a spouse not be entitled to apply for

---

29 Ibid., para. 27.
30 Ibid., para. 29. Which power the courts then lacked, according to *Dipper v. Dipper* [1981] Fam 31.
31 Ibid., para. 30.
32 [2010] UKSC 42, [112], [119].
33 *SRJ v. DWJ (Financial Provision)* [1999] 2 FLR 176.

the extension of a fixed term order, lest unforeseen events place her in financial difficulties.[34]

The legislation introduced as a result of the Law Commission's report amended, but not in any fundamental way, the scheme set out in the original 1970 legislation. The broad powers, and broad discretion, entrusted to the courts, have been criticised particularly for the lack of certainty and predictability of outcome that they engender, leaving it difficult for practitioners to advise, and for judges to achieve consistency.[35] The Law Commission recognised this problem, but eschewed radical reform, not least because of the absence of any robust evidence into its working or effect.[36] Indeed, they made a strong plea for proper monitoring of the law, a thorough investigation into the overall cost of divorce to the state, and research into the procedures used to promote private ordering.[37] When he returned to academic life, Cretney was able to fill part of this evidence gap by collaborating on a path-breaking study into the workings of the law, published as *Simple Quarrels*.

5. THE FINANCIAL REMEDIES JURISDICTION IN ACTION

The frustration expressed by the Law Commission regarding the dearth of information pertaining to the workings of the family justice system was neither new at that time, nor relieved subsequently. We continue to know remarkably little about the operation or outcomes of a jurisdiction which affects hundreds of thousands of people every year. There are huge constraints upon researchers in gaining access to either data or to populations. Even leaving aside the legitimate concerns of ensuring confidentiality for litigants, information held by the courts is poorly managed and frequently of limited use in answering the questions that policy-makers may ask.[38] Information on the 'dark figure' of those who do not go to court is even harder to obtain. It is not surprising then that scholars have tended to undertake detailed qualitative rather than quantitative studies in which what is lacking in statistical validity is more than compensated for by the richness of the data. *Simple Quarrels* was one of the first such studies, pursuing 80 cases from start to finish through the legal process, observing all appointments

---

34   Matrimonial Causes Act 1973, s. 28(1A), See the discussion of the case law by E. Hamilton, 'Extending the Extendable Term' [2005] *Family Law* 466.

35   A point made in *Simple Quarrels*, above n. 1, itself.

36   Apart from W. Barrington-Baker, J. Eekelaar, C. Gibson and S. Raikes, *The Matrimonial Jurisdiction of Registrars*, Social Science Research Council, London 1977.

37   Law Commission, above n. 21, paras. 7–12 and 46.

38   Family Justice Review, *Interim Report*, Ministry of Justice, London 2011, paras. 3.123–3.143.

and hearings, scrutinising documentation and interviewing both parties and their lawyers and the district judge. Nearly 20 years after publication and notwithstanding significant changes in the procedures under which cases are now handled[39] and the erosion and imminent ending of legal aid for these, it remains one of the most important sources of information on what it may be like to experience this jurisdiction, as either client or lawyer.

Its essential significance was summed up by the authors themselves:

'Much of what is written on [the resolution of financial and property disputes on divorce]... is concerned with statute and case law – that is to say, with reports of court decisions which are thought to clarify or refine statute in some way. The focus, then, is upon adjudication. These reported cases offer a guide to practitioners who are attempting to settle cases, and to judges when they have to try them. But these case reports offer comparatively little insight into the routine reality of the divorce process, either for practitioners or the parties. Reading them, one might be tempted to think that divorce is all about getting decisions from a court. This is not so. For most divorcing couples, a decision of the court is as remote a prospect as the summit of Mount Everest viewed from base camp.'[40]

Simple Quarrels corrected this misleading picture by emphasising that not just the emotional but also the legal ending of a marriage is a process[41] made up of many different steps, actions and decisions punctuated by (frequently lengthy) periods of inactivity. The study highlighted the vulnerability of both parties, as 'one off' players in the system, to disempowerment through lack of understanding and the overwhelming pressure to settle rather than go to trial. It also illuminated the potential for the stronger spouse (either emotionally or financially) to exploit the system to his or her advantage, and despite both parties being legally represented:

'Some [solicitors] positively refuse to argue a case which they believe to be unreasonable. But others go along with their client's demands and, perhaps as a reflection of the vulnerability of the other party, perhaps as an indication of the feebleness of the opposing solicitor, can find that their client's intransigence is

---

39   Fundamental changes were made by the Family Proceedings (Amendment No 2) Rules 1997, SI 1997/1056 after the successful introduction of the Ancillary Relief Pilot Scheme; these have been consolidated with a further emphasis on settlement-seeking and proportionality, by the Family Procedure Rules 2010.

40   DAVIS, CRETNEY and COLLINS, above n. 1, p. 253.

41   This view of divorce as an inevitable process rather than a one-off event was also the key insight of the Law Commission recommendation for divorce to be obtained as a 'process over time' (LAW COMMISSION, *The Ground for Divorce* Law Com. No. 192, HMSO, London 1990), later enacted in the Family Law Act 1996 and subsequently abandoned.

rewarded… we can see that the protections which are supposed to be conferred by the legal process can be overridden.'[42]

Moreover, many cases in their sample were settled with inadequate information as to the parties' financial circumstances,[43] again playing into the hands of the party better able to withstand a delay in concluding the proceedings, with the result that settlements were not 'fine-tuned' but '*compromise-driven…* [so that] the endowments apparently conferred by statute and case law may be overridden.'[44]

Simple Quarrels may well have influenced the major procedural reforms to the ancillary relief system which took place at the beginning of the last decade but its message that it is important to distinguish between the promotion of settlement, and achieving effective case management,[45] has probably not been heard by hard-pressed court managers and judges, facing a financial squeeze on resources and ever-higher numbers of litigants in person. The latter, in particular, pose an increasing challenge to judges and lawyers who as *Simple Quarrels* certainly demonstrated, may have come into the profession at a time when the parties were regarded as very much taking a back-seat (literally) in the proceedings, including directions hearings and even in-court mediation appointments:

'One indication of the domination of the proceedings by solicitors and barristers was solicitors' habit, observed in several cases, of leaving the parties in the waiting area when they first outlined the case to the District Judge.'[46]

'In the course of negotiations conducted on court premises the parties may figuratively and literally disappear. The literal disappearance arises because they are typically confined to separate cubicles, each accompanied by a solicitor's clerk… All the work is done by the barristers, who huddle together in a corridor or landing and attempt to reach an agreement.'[47]

'The implicit hierarchy of the courtroom… is reflected in the proximity of the various actors to the District Judge: the nearer, the more powerful… Typically, the advocates (whether barristers or solicitors) sat in the front row, while the parties… sat in the row behind. These seating arrangements convey, in unmistakable fashion, the relative standing of those present.'[48]

---

42   DAVIS, CRETNEY and COLLINS, above n. 1, p. 81.
43   Ibid., pp. 114–116. The current requirement to disclose standardised information through Form E may have improved this situation but there is no research to confirm this.
44   Ibid., p. 117.
45   Ibid., p. 169.
46   Ibid., p. 182.
47   Ibid., p. 208.
48   Ibid., p. 229.

Ironically, as one of their cases demonstrated, a litigant in person may be advantaged by such arrangements:

> '... in the hearing on the Watkins ancillary relief application Mr Watkins was unrepresented while Mrs Watkins rejoiced in the presence of both her solicitor and her barrister. Seeing this, the District Judge invited Mr Watkins to sit alongside the two lawyers. Mrs Watkins, looking thoroughly miserable and disengaged from the whole proceedings, remained at the back of the room...'.[49]

6.   CONCLUSION

The amendments to the Matrimonial Causes Act enacted as a result of the Law Commission's work in the 1980s appear to have successfully de-politicised the law on financial relief (although no doubt the subsequent enactment of the Child Support scheme and more latterly debates over shared care have provided an alternative focus for those embittered by relationship breakdown and its consequences). Criticism became a technical matter for lawyers and judges[50] and as Cretney himself pointed out, with no powerful lobby for change or some glaring injustice demanding legislative redress, there is now little incentive for politicians to bring forward complex legislation likely to tie up the parliamentary process when there are more pressing demands on their time.[51]

But it does not follow that change may not be required. *Simple Quarrels* showed that the jurisdiction did not work as well as it might as often as it should. Even if the picture painted in the book (and not necessarily fully endorsed, it seemed, by Cretney himself)[52] was rather more negative than other accounts (particularly those by Mavis Maclean and John Eekelaar in their wider exploration of family justice in action)[53] it offers a note of caution to those, including this writer, who are sceptical of the recent drive towards upholding the value of autonomy, in the guise of the promotion of contracts such as pre-nuptial agreements. In particular, it puts into perspective the fear that the more vulnerable party will be pressured into signing disadvantageous agreements, for it shows how poor bargains may

---

49   Ibid.
50   See, for example, the strictures delivered by the Court of Appeal in *Charman v. Charman (No 4)* [2007] 1 FLR 1246, [106]-[126].
51   S. Cretney, 'Private Ordering and Divorce – How Far Can We Go?' [2003] *Family Law* 399.
52   See the correspondence between Cretney and Davis in the pages of [1994] *Family Law* at 409 and 465.
53   See J. Eekelaar, M. Maclean and S. Beinart, *Family Lawyers; The Divorce Work of Solicitors*, Hart, Oxford 2000; J. Eekelaar and M. Maclean, *Family Law Advocacy: How Barristers Help the Victims of Family Failure*, Hart, Oxford 2009; and M. Maclean and J. Eekelaar, 'What Judges Do: Decision Making in the Lower Courts' [2011] *Family Law* 152.

also be reached at the end of the marital relationship, under a system intended to protect the weaker party from precisely this result.

Cretney himself seems to have taken this lesson from his research and subsequent case law developments, and to have become less confident than when he was a Law Commissioner that broad discretion can help achieve justice and square the competing claims of autonomy and vulnerability. Writing in 2003 he said:

> 'I myself have come to believe that… the least disadvantageous way of reconciling the claims of certainty, predictability and personal autonomy would be to allow husband and wife the liberty, which we concede to those who live together outside marriage, to decide for themselves the terms of their own partnership.'[54]

Given his wisdom and judgment in striking the balance between 'evolution' and 'revolution' in his Law Commission work and his acuity in analysing and evaluating the system in practice, such a declaration demands the attention of all who seek to promote the pursuit of real justice within the family jurisdiction.

---

54   S. CRETNEY, 'The family and the law – status or contract?' [2003] 15 *Child and Family Law Quarterly* 403, 413.

SHAPESHIFTERS OR POLYMATHS?

A Reflection on the Discipline of the Family Mediator in Stephen Cretney's World of Private Ordering

Neil ROBINSON

Contents

1. NEARLY FIFTY YEARS OF MEDIATION

The last essay I wrote for Stephen Cretney was in 1976 as an Oxford undergraduate with no particular ability in family law; in a recent speech in Cambridge I had the task of envisioning the Family Justice System of September 2020.[1] During that – nearly – half century of developments, mediation has moved from a footnote to a future centre stage in the family justice pantheon. How far does it pass muster as a professional discipline? How sure can we be that the Family Justice System of the future is in safe hands? Or, as law student turned mediator, have I merely exchanged one 'poverty of method and analysis'[2] for another?

Cretney has always had a sympathetic, though characteristically thoughtful and questioning, view of family mediation.[3] In 1984 he wrote that 'it would be surprising if the English system were not *progressively adapted* to make use of the positive contribution which conciliation can make'.[4] For him, it was already part of the family law whose principles he so helped to elucidate. By 1997 he was writing in the Preface to the first edition of Lisa Parkinson's *Family Mediation* textbook that 'one can be realistically optimistic that mediation will be able to demonstrate its true potential in helping to achieve the objectives stated in the very first section of the Family Law Act 1996.'[5] This support follows inevitably from his interest in private ordering (the subject of his paper to Staffordshire Law School's Centre for the Study of the Family, Law and Social Policy in 2003,[6] an occasion when I also delivered a paper on the subject of the development of mediation).

But even since 2003, the ground has continued to shift. We now have the Pre Application Protocol,[7] part of the new FPR which, if properly and consistently implemented, creates an *expectation* of mediation being attempted before litigation; a wealth of research indicating dissatisfaction with the courts resolving anything but the most intractable family conflicts;[8] a Family Justice Review which sees mediators as the *case managers* for all family cases pre-court;[9] and of

---

[1]   N. Robinson, 'Blue Sky – Now or Never?' the Henry Brown lecture to the Resolution ADR Conference, Murray Edwards College Cambridge, 23 September 2011; [2012] *Family Law*.

[2]   S. Cretney, on the writer's 1976 undergraduate essay on the 1969 Divorce Reform Act.

[3]   Indeed, he has remained a good friend to mediation, including, inter alia, a lengthy term of office as a patron of Bristol Family Mediation (www.bfmbristol.co.uk).

[4]   S. Cretney, *Principles of Family Law*, 4th ed., Sweet & Maxwell, London 1984, p. 204.

[5]   S. Cretney, preface to the first edition of L. Parkinson, *Family Mediation*, Sweet and Maxwell, London 1997. It's worth quoting, not without irony, a further part of that Preface, that, following the 'enactment and keenly anticipated implementation of the Family Law Act 1996…, mediation is intended to become a central feature of the marriage uncoupling process…The time for mere words has passed and the time for effective action is here.' Of course, the failure to implement the rest of the Act alongside mediation has damaged any intellectual cohesion that might have prevailed; see Herring, this volume.

[6]   S. Cretney, 'Private Ordering – or not?' University of Staffordshire, 1 February 2003.

[7]   Family Procedure Rules 2010 SI 2010/2955; Pre Application Protocol Practice Direction and Rule 3.1.

[8]   J. Hunt, 'Parental experiences of the family justice system an overview of the research', Ministry of Justice 2010; even the 'winners' are mostly dissatisfied!

[9]   *Family Justice Review: Final Report*, The Stationery Office, London November 2011.

course a Legal Aid, Sentencing and Punishment of Offenders Bill which will cut the heart out of the provision of informed advice and support for the most needy. And at the time of writing, the Government's response to the Family Justice Review in February 2012 is to promise a doubling of public funding for family mediation. The broadening of aspiration for mediation is truly extraordinary, from minority occupation to the assumption that it should be attempted in most family cases – 'Great Expectations'[10] indeed!

This essay is likely to pose more questions than it answers, since each venture into 'simple' family quarrels, whether as academic, advocate, adjudicator or mediator, is likely to be 'a new beginning, a raid on the inarticulate/With shabby equipment always deteriorating/ In the general mess of imprecision of feeling'.[11] Or, as Cretney put it, less poetically, 'Even after all these years, there remain many questions to be asked.'[12]

2. WHO IS TO FACILITATE THE PRIVATE ORDERING?

'The least disadvantageous way of reconciling the claims of certainty, predictability and personal autonomy would be to allow husband and wife the liberty... to decide for themselves the terms of their own partnership.'[13]

Cretney wrote his preface to the first edition of Lisa Parkinson's *Family Mediation* in September 1997, at the time of the first great sea change in the take up of mediation, the implementation of the 'Funding Code referral' mechanism whereby those requiring Legal Aid for litigation were required, subject to exceptions, to attend a meeting with a mediator.[14] We are now at the second great sea change, the Pre Application Protocol of April 2011, whereby the opportunity offered to the publicly-funded party is now extended to all potential litigants (again, subject to exceptions, and also subject to substantial demographic

---

10   The title of speeches by the Under Secretary of State Jonathan Djanogly to both Resolution and FMA Conferences in September 2011 – see *Resolution Review* Nov/ Dec 2011. In his bi-centenary year, we might remember Dickens was being ironic.

11   T.S. ELIOT, 'East Coker' from 'Four Quartets', Faber, London 1943.

12   CRETNEY, above n. 5. He continued: 'It is a sadness to me that some proselytizers for mediation seem unwilling to accept this.' Lisa Parkinson (2011) comments in a personal communication: 'This common academic warning against the unquestioning espousal of mediation as a universal panacea is a danger that mediators themselves have constantly warned against'.

13   S. CRETNEY, 'The family and the law – status or contract?' [2003] 15 *Child and Family Law Quarterly* 403, 413.

14   This brought about a rise in the numbers of legally aided mediations (the only statistics we have) from 400 to 14,000 pa from 1998–2005, followed by a somewhat surprising plateauing out. (Press Release by LSC 20 Feb 2000).

inconsistencies arising in part at least from the unclear drafting of the Protocol and its Form FM1).

The third great leap forward is likely to be the implementation of the Family Justice Review, moving from 'are expected to attend a meeting about mediation' to 'should attempt mediation.'[15]

Family Courts as an effective dispute resolution process have been found wanting, whether in relation to issues involving children[16] or in 'simple quarrels' about finance, where the descriptions by Cretney and his colleagues of crude negotiation at the courtroom door[17] still sound as true as they did 19 years ago.

Others in this volume critically appraise whether 'private ordering', either as espoused by Cretney or as more unthinkingly promoted by Government, is something to be aspired to at the conclusion of a marriage. But if we were for a moment to accept that, in principle, it is better for most fractured families to order their affairs than for others to do it for them, we are left with what Lisa Parkinson calls the 'Family Separation Paradox' – that parents are expected to communicate and co-operate to order their affairs at the point when they (or one of them) has concluded that the co-operation and communication that underpin married or cohabiting relationships no longer exist. It is reasonable therefore to assume that many people will need some help. That help is likely to be mediation.[18]

Cretney's own, not uncritical, discussion of private ordering, both in *Simple Quarrels* and in his 2003 lecture in Stoke, and the issues raised by both Gillian Douglas and Jonathan Herring in this book, would be a good starting point for all engaged in the 'dogmatic pursuit of private ordering.'[19] But these challenging analyses hardly mention the safeguards that might be provided by professional Dispute Resolution, suggesting that the process and practice of mediation has really not entered the academic consciousness – evidence of an even greater academic/ practitioner divide than that recognised in the field of family law more generally? If what some of us believe underpins the FJR proposals on Dispute Resolution is a moral step forward, how might academics, teachers, philosophers, regulators and DR practitioners work better together to ensure positive change does really come about?

---

[15]   *Family Justice Review*, above n. 9, p. 35.

[16]   HUNT, above n. 8.

[17]   G. DAVIS, S. CRETNEY and J. COLLINS, *Simple Quarrels: Negotiating Money and Property Disputes on Divorce* Clarendon Press, Oxford 1994, p. 229.

[18]   I use 'mediators' and 'mediation' throughout this essay in the knowledge that much of what I say might equally well be applied to other forms of (A)DR such as collaborative law.

[19]   HERRING, this volume.

3. WHERE DO MEDIATORS NOW SIT IN THE PANTHEON OF FAMILY LAW PROFESSIONALS?

Baroness Deech[20] claimed in 1994 that 'control over divorce' was 'about to pass from lawyers to less qualified professionals';[21] Cretney's concern at the same time was that in future its management will be informed by 'social work ideologies'.[22] Yet in 2012 the proposed home page of the embryonic Jordans Family Law Directory has four disciplines of presumably equal standing leading off its core – Family Barristers, Family Solicitors, Family Law Experts, and Family Mediators.[23] (My own 2020 vision of the Blue Sky Academy contained lawyers, mediators, academics – researchers and teachers – philosophers and others, all of equal standing and with equal funding.[24])

The family cases that remain appropriate for judicial decision/ state intervention might be said to fall into three categories:

1. where there is a public interest in protection of children or adults from harm (whether public law or domestic abuse);
2. where there is a public interest in the creation of a precedent by the resolution of a point of principle; and
3. where all avenues for co-operative resolution have been exhausted.

Given that the first two categories must remain within the courts, it is this third area that creates the challenge.

This requires very substantial further research, training, expertise and experience, and dialogue, along with services that complement the dispute resolution process (for example, properly available high-quality therapeutic and mental health services to assist those 'stuck' individuals and couples caught up in chronic litigation). But if we know that litigation generally damages children, teaches adults to fight, and is ill-appreciated by adults then the responsibility must lie with those involved in dispute resolution and the development of the

---

[20] R. DEECH, 'Comment' (1994) 24 *Family Law* 121.
[21] 'Unaware, perhaps, that many family mediators were dually qualified. One of the main training organisations, the Family Mediators Association, already had five years' experience in training equal numbers of family lawyers and qualified social workers to co-mediate on all issues, encouraging them to draw and learn from each other's areas of experience and expertise while also developing their new role as mediators': Lisa Parkinson, personal communication.
[22] S. CRETNEY, 'Looking Further into the Future,' Central Hall, Westminster, 7 June 1995. Both were cited by S. ROBERTS, 'Decision Making for Life Apart' (1995) 58 *Modern Law Review* 714.
[23] Private communication; due to go live Spring 2012.
[24] ROBINSON, above n. 1.

wider Family Justice Service to ensure services of the highest quality, provided by leaders in their existing professions – that is, dispute resolution practice is the practice to aspire to.

If mediation is to be more than 'an imperfect procedure that employs an imperfect third party to help two imperfect people conclude an imperfect agreement in an imperfect world'[25] then we need some clarity about what it is, how it is taught, and how effective it is and might be.

4.   WHAT MAKES A GOOD MEDIATOR?

Mediators are often said to be on a life-long transition from their profession of origin. The mediator acquires an eclectic knowledge base from many disciplines, in none of which he or she may be 'specialist'; their specialism is that of mediator or practitioner in Appropriate Dispute Resolution, and one of their skills the ability to access the appropriate expertise or knowledge base for the issue before them. Might the mediator therefore best be seen as a shapeshifter or chameleon, or, better, as a polymath?

As Lisa Parkinson has said, 'mediation draws from parent disciplines, but it is a discipline in its own right.'[26] In 2000, she considered that the 'qualities needed for family mediation' in relation to foundation training included:

- Warmth
- Ability to engage with people and empathise with them
- Respect for individuals
- Non-directive
- Bringing a positive and optimistic approach to conflict and disputes
- Balance – ability to relate to conflicting views and manage power imbalances
- Self-knowledge
- Good communication skills
- Firmness
- Understanding – of emotions and needs
- Patience
- Sense of humour
- Intelligence and analytic skills
- Common sense
- Maturity

---

25   L. MARLOW, *Divorce Mediation – a practice in search of a theory*, Harlan Press, 1997.
26   L. PARKINSON, 'Training for Family Mediation', Family Mediators Association Journal November 2011.

- Personal integrity
- Professional discipline and objectivity
- Ability to co-mediate
- Humility
- Stamina and energy
- Imagination and intuition – not constrained by a rigid model or formula[27]

She added: 'It is really rather difficult for one person to embody all these qualities!'

So, to take one set of skills and knowledge as an example, to what extent does the mediator have to be a family law expert?

Whatever the failings of an adversarial Court system, this is not the same as saying that *family law* has failed separating families. Family mediation is often said to take place 'in the shadow of the law' and although those ordering their affairs privately are not bound to follow the current judicial thinking, such guidelines may provide a more acceptable framework for doing so than often appears in the adversarial process.[28] The mediator needs this knowledge to clarify and demystify, to set parameters for exploring options and finding common ground; the lawyer needs this knowledge, for example, to explore ambiguity to get the best for the individual client. Indeed, sharing legal information in the context of co-operative resolution is a skill that may be as difficult to acquire for the experienced family lawyer as the non-lawyer.

So we state in foundation mediation training that the quality, standard and depth of knowledge of the family mediator should be no less than that of any other Family Justice practitioner, lawyer or otherwise.

It is the function, role and environment that differ in the distinction between information/guidance and advice, not the quality/ depth of that knowledge, that is, whether one is working in a partisan or impartial role. The same arguments

---

[27] L. Parkinson, Family Mediation Foundation Course materials reproduced and edited by permission. Parkinson has written far more extensively about this and so many other matters in her second edition (*Family Mediation* 2nd ed., Jordans, Bristol 2011). Mediation sceptics may well find therein the 'full and scholarly account' they seek, and the 'analytical skills, understanding…and…intellectual honesty' about both its 'practicalities and theoretical underpinnings' praised by Cretney in his preface to the first edition.

[28] Of course, this masks a subtler point about the freedom or otherwise to come to mutually acceptable proposals that may not be in the interests of one or both or, worse, do not protect children. But then, almost every aspect of this reflective essay indicates how much further we have to go to create a *jurisprudence* of conflict resolution to match that of the centuries old adversarial system it aspires to replace in most cases.

about acquiring a particular knowledge base and then subsuming it to the benefit of a co-operative process might be applied to all areas of mediation expertise.

Some, but not all, of the qualities outlined by Parkinson may be learned. And some, but not all, are susceptible to objective regulation and scrutiny. In 2008, the American Bar Association, tasked with finding some objective criteria for the effectiveness of mediation and the training of the next generation, could only conclude that there were four key factors that impacted on successful outcomes:

1. Preparation
2. Case by case customisation
3. Analytical techniques
4. Persistence[29]

And so the mediator perhaps best presents as a polymath, a fuser of an eclectic skills and knowledge base, not as master of no trades, but as a combination of insights from different disciplines drawn to the service of a particular process and outcome. And the challenge is to make the transition to something 'more than' lawyer or psychotherapist, that is, to distil a new profession rather than dilute an old one. Is this not an argument for the model of mediation that provides access to a multi-disciplinary community of mediators, who both work in co-mediation pairs and as sole practitioners within a wider grouping?

5. IS THERE A RECOGNISABLE ACADEMIC DISCIPLINE OF FAMILY DISPUTE RESOLUTION? WHAT ARE THE IMPLICATIONS FOR TRAINING?

5.1. THE UNDERGRADUATE AS POTENTIAL PEACEMAKER

'Any system of conciliation has to confront problems about the qualifications and skills of the individuals involved in the process, and about such detailed matters as confidentiality and privilege.'[30]

So how early in the process of legal education should these problems be addressed? My limited enquiry into the current experience of law undergraduates at Cambridge suggests only limited lip service is still given to the theory and practice of mediation (although at Staffordshire University, by contrast, there is

---

29   Quoted by J. WADE, LEADR, Bond University 12 March 2009 – 'The Edges of Orthodoxy – you did *what?*'
30   CRETNEY, above n. 5, p. 203; and see generally L. PARKINSON, 'Conciliation: Pros and Cons' [1983] 13 *Family Law* 22, 183.

some greater acknowledgement). How far might the family law syllabus be transformed if we took private ordering seriously?

Speculatively, I might identify the following as worthy of attention at undergraduate level:

- Theory, philosophy and history of non-violent conflict resolution;
- History of resolution of family disputes in English and comparative law – adversarial versus inquisitorial versus private ordering; emerging trends in the resolution particularly of disputes relating to children;
- Case law, practice and sanctions relating to the development of mediation jurisprudence;[31]
- Specific law relating to mediation, e.g. privilege and confidentiality;
- An introduction to the psychosocial background of mediation and to different models of resolution – transformative, narrative, therapeutic etc.;
- A critical look at the current place of mediation in proposals for reform of the family justice system;
- Specific areas of family law relating to the subject matter of dispute resolution – not least the limits of judicial discretion, the 'no order' and welfare principles; concepts of and challenges to shared parental responsibility and shared parenting;
- A contextualising of family relationships and conflicts in the arts and sciences, with insights from poetry and literature, anthropology and neurology.

The argument against 'learning mediation' at degree level is presumably that it is a second profession to which one makes a transition. Yet the danger is that, like their clients, lawyers 'learn to fight' before they learn to place their considerable skills at the service of those who try to solve co-operatively the most entrenched of human problems.

5.2. FAMILY CONFLICT RESOLUTION IN VOCATIONAL TRAINING

If the LPC and BPTC courses are really about 'Preparation to Practice', then must they not include some awareness and practice of mediation and of mediation advocacy? Yet only five pages of the current 450-page LPC civil

---

[31]   For example, *Halsey v Milton Keynes General NHS Trust* [2004] EWCA (Civ) 576; amongst other things, *Halsey* provides a valuable context: 'the value and importance of ADR have been established within a remarkably short time. All members of the legal profession who conduct litigation should now routinely consider with their clients whether their disputes are suitable for ADR' [11].

litigation handbook is devoted to ADR, and of that, only one paragraph to mediation, where it is described as 'interchangeable with conciliation'. Faced with a mock allocation questionnaire to complete, and coming to the question about 'arranging a mediation appointment', my informer tells me that her tutor told everyone 'just say no'.

At the least, we need an understanding at the vocational training level that advocates of whatever persuasion are as likely to find themselves in the forum of mediation as that of the Court room, and that this advocacy will draw on the same legal expertise but a very different kind of participation in resolution (an area where, in my experience of both the civil and family fields, lawyers are equally woefully inadequate). Many of those experienced barristers and solicitors, not to say judges and academics, I have had the privilege to train or supervise would recognise that the multi-skilled approach taken in mediation (rapport, facilitation, guidance and limited evaluation) often presents greater challenges than their professions of origin.

Viewed from my perspective of '2020' vision, a common training in law and other disciplines which might then lead to a tri-partite choice of career as solicitor, barrister or mediator is not so far-fetched – but, if we can go this far, given the current threats to both Bar and high street practice, why not a common training in partisan advice-giving and representation, advocacy, and impartial facilitation? An experienced family lawyer who had recently trained as a family mediator told me that not only had she started to acquire the skills of a mediator, but also that both her advocacy of mediation as a partisan lawyer and her advocacy within mediation as a lawyer had been considerably enhanced.

5.3. FMA FOUNDATION COURSE – 'THE ECLECTIC MIX'

It takes eight days to train a family mediator. Or rather, the Foundation Course for family mediation is eight days long, but assumes a transition from an existing professional background, and a follow up of 'life-long learning'. In that sense, whilst bearing in mind that the equivalent course in France consists of 560 hours of study,[32] a better comparison might be the training to become a new family arbitrator with Resolution (under four days), or a Deputy District Judge (a five day residential course). Of course, in the latter case this is only a very small part of the supervision, appraisal and ongoing training that is required, along with all that comes with the profession from which the transition is being made. This is by no means the universal approach; to be a Judge of the People's Court in Russia, for example, one need only be 25 years old and have undertaken discrete training.

---

[32] PARKINSON, above n. 26.

Similarly, the career path to mediation in other countries need not be via an existing professional discipline.

A glance at a foundation syllabus would show that it contains, amidst a majority of time given over to experiential learning, role play, self, peer and trainer assessment, sections on at least the following:

- law, practice and research relating to the children of separating parents, including child protection;
- research into domestic abuse;
- systems of referral and assessment;
- gender and equality;
- neuro-linguistic programming;
- marketing and setting up in practice;
- psychosocial elements;
- principles, processes and skills;
- family law and practice.

5.4. A REGULATED PROFESSION?

Regulation does not sit comfortably with an 'alternative' and still emerging profession, especially not one often characterised as creative, humane, and innovative. At least one of family mediation's UK founders sees parts of the profession as already over-regulated.[33] Yet it is right that government and others should require some greater clarity and consistency for prospective clients as to the standards of service they can expect. The Family Justice Review recommends that 'a clear plan must be developed to maintain and reinforce standards of competence and to ensure the effective regulation of mediation as numbers of mediators increase.'[34]

There are very significant issues currently both as to the form and identity of regulation and also the forms of measurement of 'competence'. A credible case could be made out for publicly funded mediation already being over-regulated and stultifying in its reliance on paper evidence and NVQ-style 'competencies'. Yet many seem to consider that this is the model of regulation and minimum standards we should all be aiming for.[35]

---

[33]   H. Brown, 'Creating confidence in mediators and the process: an exploration of the issues' Paper to CIARB's Mediation Symposium 2010.
[34]   *Family Justice Review*, above n. 9, para. 4.102.
[35]   M. Stevenson, 'Learning to be a Mediator: the Importance of Standards' [2011] *Family Law* 1152, challenged by A. Cox [2011] *Family Law* 1413.

Faced with a feared (and unrealised) deluge of mediation clients in March 2011, the MOJ and Family Mediation Council devised a set of 'minimum requirements' falling short of the existing competence assessment processes which effectively involves 10 hours of co-working and a day course on the Mediation Information and Assessment Meeting (MIAM). Lisa Parkinson again: 'If market forces become more powerful than professional standards, mediation itself is jeopardised.'[36]

5.5. ACCREDITATION AND COMPETENCE

'Mediation is a professional skill that cannot be learned without training and close supervision for a significant time.'[37]

As those using family lawyers and Courts to their cost (literally) have discovered, there has to be a higher standard of ethics and creativity to which all can aspire – examples might be found within the Code of Practice and Good Practice Guides of Resolution, but not, I would suggest, in the involvement of independent regulators whether in relation to lawyers or in the form of the disastrous intervention of OFSTED in the 'development' of CAFCASS.

In a recent essay, Barbara Wilson tackles this creative tension between ensuring and developing high standards through regulation and evidence and through creativity and individuality. Her challenges as to 'what makes a successful mediator' encourage movement from 'toolbox mentality' to 'lifelong learning and fallibility'.[38] She encourages moving from a 'discipline that is still dominated by various prescriptive models of practice and strong ideological discourses' to a more sophisticated understanding of expertise.[39]

6. SOME 2020 VISION AND BLUE SKY THINKING

6.1. INTEGRATED FAMILY JUSTICE PRACTITIONERS IN THE BLUE SKY ACADEMY OF 2020

Through the filter of my 2020 vision, the Integrated Family Justice Practitioners who replace solicitors and barristers and form part of the Academy of Advanced and Accredited Appropriate Dispute Resolution Practitioners (AAAADRP) will

---

[36] PARKINSON, above n. 26.
[37] *Family Justice Review*, above n. 9, para. 4.100.
[38] B. WILSON, 'Naughty Departures: Expertise, Orthodoxy and the Role of Theory in the Practice of Mediation' in P. Deleuran (ed.), *Conflict Management in the Family Field and in other Close Relationships – Mediation as a way Forward*, DJOF Publishing, Copenhagen 2011.
[39] WILSON, above n. 38.

be trained in both Dispute Resolution skills and advocacy skills such as would complement both mediation and inquisitorial litigation from the outset, at university, on Legal Practice Courses, in training contracts, and thereafter. Mediation training is life-long learning.

6.2. A HIGHER STANDARD?

But there is something missing – a level of higher accreditation that recognises both a career path and excellence. As solicitors, we tend to see this either in business terms (partnership, directorship) or as the badge of honour that comes with representing the super rich and getting them to the Court of Appeal as part of the 'fantasy family law' that Gillian Douglas writes of.[40] As barristers, we aspire to become QCs or to the bench.[41] As long as we measure success in these terms rather than the skills needed to assist in the facilitation of private ordering, we will not value sufficiently where the really hard work is to be done. As facilitator, I call on a far wider range of skills than as specialist child care lawyer or even judge. But we will also need a standard of practice and of training that transcends the competent or accredited. In my own service, our core belief is expressed in the following way:

> 'People in conflict can, and should, be given every opportunity to work together to resolve their disputes co-operatively, for their own sakes and for the good of their children and society. A *core expectation of Courts* should be that the potential for co-operative resolution has been definitively assessed. The greater the level of conflict, the greater the imperative to find a mediated solution, the greater the rewards of doing so, and the greater differential in outcome'.[42]

We draw on Lord Justice Thorpe's statement that: '[i]n principle, any dispute, at any stage of litigation, is potentially suitable for mediation, with appropriate judicial oversight.'[43]

We need to challenge ourselves far more as mediation services. The core values of such a service might be:

Humanity – by which I mean putting clients and their children at the centre, and making the relationship between the facilitator/ mediator and the participants paramount.

---

[40] Her chapter in this book would be required reading for a mediator seeking to reflect on the issues of 'autonomy vs vulnerability' that dominate mediation thinking as much as case law.

[41] ROBINSON, above n. 1. In my 2020 vision, Integrated Family Justice Professionals can still become QCs, or 'Quality Collaborators'.

[42] See www.themediationcentre.co.uk.

[43] See THORPE LJ in *Al-Khatib v Masry* [2004] EWCA Civ 1353, [2005] 1 FLR 381.

Innovation – by which I mean that if the mechanism for resolution of a particular conflict has not yet been established, we will establish it.

Excellence – by which I mean that regulation and minimum standards are not enough, and that we should create 'Centres of Excellence' where hard cases can be sent with confidence, and specialist training and internships developed.

6.3. DEVELOPING MEDIATION – A HIGHER LEVEL OF TRAINING

The basic model of mediation principles and process has proved itself to be remarkably robust. But there is a need to encourage more sophisticated working practices. My series of articles for *Family Law* developing the mediation model addressed this.[44] A level of specialist training, creating a bridge to such new models by building on expertise, would be a starting point.

7. WORKING IN PARTNERSHIP

Another bridge to this higher standard lies in the building of community, one that functions at the level of regulation and membership of leading bodies but also relies on *relationships*, from Professional Practice Consultation to peer groups and case discussion, from Pods to Linked-In, from specialist training to master class.

It is in areas where there are close partnerships between mediators and lawyers, closer understandings between mediators, judges and other family justice professionals through Local Family Justice Councils, that the Pre-Application Protocol is working.[45] Our experience at The Mediation Centre is that, with now around 100 referrals a month, our referrals have gone up by 52 per cent. Our 'conversion' from referral to mediation has remained around 27 per cent (LSC national figure for 2010 23 per cent) and proportion of successful outcomes increased from 81 per cent to 88 per cent; we attribute this as much to understandings between professionals and the Courts as to the quality of our own service.

---

44   N. Robinson, 'A new model of Court Directed Mediation' [2006] *Family Law* 139; 'Developing Family Mediation' [2008] *Family Law* 926; 'Innovative Approaches to ADR' [2008] *Family Law* 1048; 'Civil and family models' [2009] *Family Law* 253; 'Interdisciplinary ADR committees' [2009] *Family Law* 539; 'Partnerships with Cafcass and Courts' [2009] *Family Law* 734.

45   Nevertheless, a Family Justice Service and Dispute Resolution Services shorn of legal advice and advocacy, and existing in the desert of appropriate legal advice and guidance resulting from the Legal Aid Bill, are bound to fail.

But what of the practitioner/ academic chasm? Once we have established that the mediation room is a better forum for private ordering than the courtroom, it only remains to ensure that the best people are encouraged to train to be part of the service provided, and that practitioners work in partnership with academics to assure the best possible service. 'In the beginning is the conversation…' is the maxim on our home page, and it is this conversation between practitioners and academics for which we need to find the time.

8. SOME TENTATIVE CONCLUSIONS

So – charlatans or shapeshifters? Or eclectics and polymaths? If mediation, like jazz, is spontaneous invention within a theoretical framework, we might recognise this, say, in the jazz pianist, who draws on a range of traditions and influences to create something new and of the moment, both intellectually rigorous and improvised, audience and client-focused – 'Ein Eklektiker, der handwerklich über die Möglichkeiten verfügt'.[46]

An aspiration to be a professional eclectic or Renaissance person is no excuse for lack of knowledge or experience, or laziness either on the part of mediation apologists or those who seek to challenge their effectiveness. We need academic studies of effective mediation and its outcomes that are worthy of a profession that seeks to supplant the courts in dealing with the majority of family disputes that require some third-party involvement to resolve them.

And if the 'progressive adaptation' of *Principles of Family Law* is indeed one from adversarial to inquisitorial, from families 'learning to fight better' to acquiring the skills to problem solve, from public interest to private ordering, from advocacy to informed facilitation, then we need a shared understanding of both theory and practice arising from continued 'conversations' between academic and practitioner that are worthy of Stephen Cretney.[47]

---

[46] G. SIMCOCK, cover notes to 'Good Days at Schloss Elmau' [2011 ACT records] 'An eclecticist, who re-arranges possibilities like a craftsman'.

[47] 'ββδ: Good, but i) more detailed use of case law, and ii) generally more methodical and analytical approach, would improve' Stephen Cretney on my last attempt at an essay for him in 1976.

FAMILY LAW – WHAT FAMILY LAW?

John Eekelaar

Contents

1. INTRODUCTION

Readers of Stephen Cretney's *History*[1] will know that Private Members' Bills have occasionally contributed to the development of family law in England and Wales. Perhaps the most significant was the Bill promoted by Sir Alan Herbert, which became the Matrimonial Causes Act 1937.[2] The Legitimacy Act 1959 also originated in such a Bill, introduced by John Parker MP,[3] as did the Marriage Act 1994, introduced by Gyles Brandreth MP.[4] But as Cretney explains, there is a subtle relationship between these instruments and government, which is fundamental to their chances of success in becoming law.[5] If the Bill is introduced in the House of Commons under the 'Ten Minute Rule', it is unlikely to become

---

[1] S. Cretney, *Family Law in the Twentieth Century: A History*, Oxford University Press, Oxford 2003.
[2] Ibid., pp. 233 et seq.
[3] Ibid., pp. 553–4.
[4] Ibid., pp. 30–31.
[5] Ibid., pp. lvii-lviii.

law, but, as in the case of the Legitimacy Act 1959, can be significant in building up pressure for legislation.

In June 2011, Baroness Cox of Queensbury introduced the Arbitration and Mediation Services (Equality) Bill in the House of Lords. Among its provisions were the following:

> cl.4. Any matter which is within the jurisdiction of the criminal or family courts cannot be the subject of arbitration proceedings.

On the face of it, this could seem like an attempt to deal with, or head off, problems associated with one type of alternative dispute resolution of family matters. Any attempt to use arbitration procedure, under which an arbitral award could be enforced as an order of court under the Arbitration Act 1996, section 66, would be ineffective. However, a much sterner purpose appears from clause 7:

> cl. 7
> (1) A person is guilty of an offence if that person –
> (a) falsely purports to be exercising a judicial function or to be able to make legally binding rulings, or
> (b) otherwise falsely purports to adjudicate on any matter which that person knows or ought to know is within the jurisdiction of the criminal or family courts.

While the exact scope of this provision is debatable,[6] and the word 'arbitrate' is not used, it probably applies to anyone attempting to arbitrate on a matter within the jurisdiction of the family courts. If so, not only would the Bill make such arbitrations ineffective, it would seek to stop them altogether, as if the process was some social evil. Clearly more is going on than merely dealing with concerns about alternative dispute resolution. The first clause of the Bill suggests what it may be. This provides that

> Cl. 1
> A person must not, in providing a service in relation to arbitration, do anything that constitutes discrimination, harassment or victimisation on grounds of sex.
>
> ... discrimination on grounds of sex includes but is not restricted to –
> (a) treating the evidence of a man as worth more than the evidence of a woman, or vice versa,
> (b) proceeding on the assumption that the division of an estate between male and female children on intestacy must be unequal, or

---

6   This is discussed in more detail in J. EEKELAAR, 'The Arbitration and Mediation Services (Equality) Bill' [2011] 41 *Family Law* 1209.

(c) proceeding on the assumption that a woman has fewer property rights than a man, or vice versa.

Although not apparent on the face of the Bill, these provisions are aimed at determination of family disputes under Islamic law (or *shari'a*). Of course, since no arbitrations at all could be legally carried out in family (or criminal) matters if clauses 4 and 7 were enacted, clause 1 would only apply to arbitration in other areas of law, which are likely mostly to be commercial.

The Bill was introduced under the House of Lords' equivalent of the Commons' 'Ten Minute' Rule. The Guidance on Private Members Bills published by the House of Lords states that even if the Bill passes the House of Lords, once the Bill goes to the Commons:

> 'Because of the restrictions on the time for private member's Bills in the Commons, members of the House should be aware that a Lords private member's Bill can be blocked in the Commons by a single MP. In particular, a Bill which is opposed by the Government or Opposition front benches stands little or no chance of proceeding in the Commons. A short, uncontroversial Bill is more likely to succeed.'

So the objectives of the sponsors of the Bill may have been primarily to provoke debate about issues that are of concern to some members of the public, and perhaps achieve legislation later. Why therefore should there be concerns about the involvement of religious authorities in the resolution of the family conflicts of members of their religion?

2. BACKGROUND TO THE BILL

The tensions appearing in European countries in their response to immigration, especially from Islamic societies are well-known. The appalling massacre in Norway by Anders Behring Breivik on 22 July 2011 is a dramatic manifestation of this. At the political level, the German Chancellor, Angela Merkel, said in October 2010 that the policy of 'multiculturalism' in Germany had failed. The issue is politically controversial in other European countries, including the United Kingdom.[7] In 2008, the Archbishop of Canterbury's suggestion that Islamic law (*shari'a*) might need to be treated as a system supplemental to and running in parallel with the state law[8] attracted considerable criticism.[9]

---

[7]   See N. MEER and T. MODOOD, 'The Multicultural State We're In: Muslims, 'Multiculture' and 'Civic Re-balancing' of British Multiculturalism' (2009) 57 *Political Studies* 473.

[8]   R. WILLIAMS, 'Civil and Religious Law in England: A Religious Perspective' (2008) 10 *Ecclesiastical Law Journal* 262.

[9]   For one example, see D. MACEOIN, *Sharia Law or 'One Law for All'?*, Civitas, London 2009.

Many European societies are constituted of groups which seek to follow norm systems that differ in varying degrees from state law. They include Christians, Jews, and Muslims but also others, such as Sikhs, Hindus and Buddhists. Furthermore, there can be distinct strands within these groups. In the United States this is particularly notable with regard to Christian groups, and there is growing unease over the present relationship between religious norms and state law.[10] With regard to Muslims in Britain the position is exacerbated by at least three features. One is the colonial background of British Muslim communities. Patterns of settlement have tended to emphasize cultural distinctions within them, and have to some extent perpetuated localized structures used under colonial rule. This has created expectations that these structures should the retained in the United Kingdom.[11] Another feature is the strongly patriarchal character Islamic family law is perceived to possess. However, it shares this with the other Abrahamic faiths, though of course they vary in degree. Cretney's *History* describes how the deep and pervasive discrimination against women in English law, heavily influenced by Christianity, only began to be attenuated from the last quarter of the nineteenth century, and continued well into the twentieth.

But Islamic family law has to contend with the added fears generated by terrorist attacks and worries that some Muslims are bent on destruction of 'the west'. It is therefore relevant that in 2003 Baroness Cox[12] co-authored a book entitled *The West, Islam and Islamism: Is Ideological Islam compatible with liberal democracy?* This opens by stating its aim as being 'to encourage reconciliation and mutual understanding between Islam and the West',[13] and that it is dealing with Islamic 'fundamentalism' so as not to alienate moderate Muslims. It refers to the authors' establishment of the International Islamic Christian Organisation for Reconstruction and Reconciliation.[14] The remainder of the book however focuses

---

[10] For an excellent discussion, calling for a re-appraisal of the current constitutional balance in the US, see P. HORWITZ, *The Agnostic Age*, Oxford University Press, Oxford 2010.

[11] See J. BOWEN, 'How could English Courts recognize Shariah?' (2010) 7 *University of St. Thomas Law Journal* 411, 413–418; J. BOWEN, 'Europe' in M. COOK (ed.), *The New Cambridge History of Islam*, Cambridge University Press, Cambridge 2010 ch. 4.

[12] Formerly Caroline Cox, Baroness Cox was made a peeress in 1983 by Margaret Thatcher. With a degree in sociology and a medical background, she has been active in promoting humanitarian relief, particularly in areas under political oppression, and assistance to the disabled, for which she has drawn much admiration. She established the Humanitarian Aid Relief Trust (HART) which 'supports the forgotten people of Europe, Africa and Asia: the oppressed and the persecuted, and often those who are neglected by other organisations, largely out of sight of the world's media. Its aid is designed to relieve suffering and sow the seeds of longer-term solutions; its advocacy is designed to raise awareness of problems – and solutions – at home and abroad.' The range of activities is impressive. Baroness Cox is also patron of SPUC Evangelicals, a part of the Society for the Protection of the Unborn Child.

[13] C. COX and J. MARKS, *The West, Islam and Islamism: Is Ideological Islam compatible with liberal democracy?*, 2nd ed., Civitas, London 2006, p. viii.

[14] That organisation appears to have dissolved in 2008. www.cdrex.com/international-islamic-christian-organisation-for-reconciliation-and-reconstruction-ltd-5036558.html.

entirely on Islamic extremism and its threat to 'western' societies, characterising it as an ideology (like Marxism) based on 'claims of revealed truth and infallibility' found in a religious text deemed to be 'perfect'. The authors write:

> '(Mohammed's) mosque, and its descendants, was and is the very centre of the all encompassing political, social, military and religious motivation of Mohammed and his followers as they set out, and continue to set out, to conquer the world for Allah and Islam … This role is still played by mosques in the modern world.'[15]

And, later:

> 'There are now many thousands of people, both in Islamic countries and in most of the free countries of the world, who are working together to further the cause of Islamism and to undermine Western societies.'[16]

I make no pretence at evaluating the strength of these claims. However, it illustrates a perspective that is unlikely to be congenial to Islamic processes. In 2009, Baroness Cox invited the controversial anti-Islamic Dutch politician, Geert Wilders, to the United Kingdom, but the visit was blocked by the then Government. It seems reasonable to conclude that the Arbitration and Mediation Services (Equality) Bill was intended to promote further debate about the role of Islam in Britain with the goal of limiting its influence.

3. DO ISLAMIC RELIGIOUS BODIES IN ENGLAND AND WALES PROVIDE ARBITRATION?

3.1. NATURE OF THE ISLAMIC SHARIA COUNCIL AND MUSLIM ARBITRATION TRIBUNAL

Under the Arbitration Act 1996, section 66(1):

> 'an award made by the tribunal pursuant to an arbitration agreement may, by leave of the court, be enforced in the same manner as a judgment or order of the court to the same effect.'

It is therefore important to establish whether decisions of Islamic bodies in family matters fall under that provision.

---

15   Cox and Marks, above n. 13, p. 87.
16   Ibid., above n. 13, p. 129.

The Islamic Sharia Council (ISC) was established in 1982 in order to pronounce Islamic divorce and deal with its consequences. According to its website[17] it claims to have handled some 7,000 cases since 1982, mostly divorce. It has been claimed that in England and Wales at least 85 'courts' make rulings (fatwa) according to *sharia* law under the ISC's auspices.[18] The website does not, however, claim that the decisions of these bodies are enforceable under the Arbitration Act. Indeed, it states at a number of places:

> 'The ISC conducts Islamic divorces only: it does not conduct cases as part of the UK legal or judicial systems: for advice regarding a civil divorce, please consult a qualified legal representative. (See for example www.islamic-sharia.org/how-it-works/how-the-isc-works-2.html).'

The document, 'ISC Procedure for Talaq (when husband is the petitioner)' issued by one such body states in very bold letters: 'For civil divorce, a solicitor must be consulted as this is an Islamic Divorce, and The Shari'a Council does not deal with legal matters'.

John Bowen, who has observed the proceedings of some of these bodies, points out that their members regard themselves as 'scholars' and mediators, not judges, and that their primary role is to grant divorces according to Islamic law. He writes:

> 'If the dispute leads to divorce, the mediator will suggest arrangements for child care, the disposition of the bridal gift (*mahr*), and support for the wife and the children – all according to his interpretation of *sharia*. Sometimes the couple signs an agreement based on the scholar's recommendations'.[19]

This may be more proactive than family mediation is supposed to be, and closer to the way judges oversee Family Dispute Resolution (FDR) proceedings as they seek to facilitate agreement. Samia Bano, who has also observed the councils, refers to mediation taking place within 'reconciliation' meetings, and reports:

> 'the term "religious judge" was not used by any of the religious scholars as it was deemed likely to confuse clients as to the legality of their verdicts under English law. In fact the scholars were all keen to underline the fact that their verdicts were not legally binding under English law but served to uphold "the moral authority of the Muslim community".'[20]

---

[17] <www.islamic-sharia.org>.
[18] MACEOIN, above n. 9, p. 69.
[19] J.R. BOWEN, 'Private Arrangements: 'Recognizing Sharia' in England' *Boston Review* March/April 2009.
[20] S. BANO, 'Islamic Family Arbitration, Justice and Human Rights in Britain' (2007) *Law, Social Justice and Global Development* <www2.warwick.ac.uk/fac/soc/law/elj/lgd/2007_1/bano> accessed 8.11.2011.

Gillian Douglas and colleagues have interviewed officials of some of these bodies as part of a study of the operation of tribunals in Catholicism, Islam and Judaism. They remark that the primary purpose of the ISC bodies is to make re-marriage possible within the tenets of Islam. The bodies did not deal with 'ancillary' matters, but

> 'the guidance and mediation offered by the Council on what should happen to the mahr or dower agreed on at the time of the marriage may be an important safeguard of (the woman's) financial position, with the Council offering sometimes strong persuasion to the husband 'to be generous' even if a traditional interpretation of Islamic rules might suggest otherwise'.[21]

3.2. ARE THEIR PROCEEDINGS ARBITRATIONS UNDER THE ARBITRATION ACT?

In October 2008, the Parliamentary Secretary of State in the Ministry of Justice, Bridget Prentice MP, stated that arbitration did not apply to family law. Responding to a Parliamentary Question, she replied:

> 'We do not issue any guidance on the validity of fatwas or other rulings by a religious authority because there is no need for such guidance. Shari'a law has no jurisdiction in England and Wales and there is no intention to change this position. Similarly, we do not accommodate any other religious legal system in this country's laws. Any order in a family case is made or approved by a family judge applying English family law.
>
> If, in a family dispute dealing with money or children, the parties to a judgment in a Shari'a council wish to have this recognised by English authorities, they are at liberty to draft a consent order embodying the terms of the agreement and submit it to an English court. This allows English judges to scrutinise it to ensure that it complies with English legal tenets.
>
> The use of religious courts to deal with personal disputes is well established. Any member of a religious community has the option to use religious courts and to agree to abide by their decisions but these decisions are subject to national law and cannot be enforced through the national courts save in certain limited circumstances when the religious court acts as arbitrator within the meaning of the Arbitration Act 1996. Arbitration does not apply to family law and the only decisions which can be enforced are those relating to civil disputes.
>
> Religious courts are always subservient to the established family courts of England and Wales'.[22]

---

21   G. Douglas, N. Doe, S. Gilliat-Ray and R. Sandberg, 'Marriage and Divorce in Religious Courts: A Case Study' [2011] 41 *Family Law* 956, 959.

22   *Hansard*, HC 23.10.2008, vol. 481 col 562W.

However, nothing in the Arbitration Act prevents family matters being subject to arbitration. Nevertheless, it may be difficult to enforce some types of arbitral award as an order of a civil court. For example, the Children Act 1989 requires the court, when making a determination regarding the upbringing of as child, to treat the child's welfare as the paramount consideration. It is arguable, though, that when a court implements an arbitral award, it is not making such a determination. A party to an arbitral award would certainly not be thereby prevented from seeking the benefits of the courts' family jurisdiction, for that jurisdiction cannot be ousted by agreement. However, that depends on a party wishing to escape the arbitral award, and the court having jurisdiction in the matter.

But even if, technically, family matters might be the subject of arbitration under the Arbitration Act 1996, it would need to be decided whether the decisions of ISC bodies were arbitrations. Neil Addison has written that any body that applies *shari'a* principles must be engaged in arbitration and not mediation because 'mediation does not involve the application of legal rules, whether religious or otherwise, it involves a search for a mutually acceptable compromise' so if any organisation 'is applying shariah principles to a dispute, then it is engaged in arbitration and not mediation.'[23] But mediation can be, and usually is, carried out within a legal framework, sometimes referred to as 'in the shadow of the law', and there is no reason to believe that this cannot be true if conducted within the principles of *shari'a*.[24] But are the processes in fact arbitrations, and not mediation? Arbitration must be preceded by a written arbitration agreement between the parties to be bound by the arbitral award.[25] Samia Bano[26] has described an applicant to the ISC as receiving 'a form requesting the agreement of the applicant to abide by any decision.' It is unlikely that completing this form amounts to an agreement between the parties. Even if it did, the agreement to 'abide' by the decision is not equivalent to an agreement to be 'bound', in the sense of 'legally bound' by it, especially in view of the disclaimer by the ISC mentioned earlier that it does not deal with legal matters.

The Muslim Arbitration Council (MAT) claims to 'operate within the legal framework of England and Wales', and its website refers to forced marriage, domestic violence and family disputes as being among the Tribunal's cases. However it does not claim that its decisions in those matters will be enforced under the Arbitration Act.

---

23   Foreword to MACEOIN, above n. 9, pp. xi-xii.
24   P. FOURNIER, *Muslim Marriage in Western Courts: Lost in Transplantation,* Ashgate, Farnham 2010, gives many examples of such negotiation.
25   Arbitration Act 1996, ss. 5, 6, 66(1). R.M. MERKIN and L. FLANNERY, *Arbitration Law,* Informa Law, London 2004, pp. 168–9.
26   BANO, above n. 20.

4. SCOPE OF THE ARBITRATION AND MEDIATION SERVICES (EQUALITY) BILL

If the processes of these Islamic bodies are not arbitrations, the Bill's attempt to exclude them from potential enforcement under the Arbitration Act 1996 would be otiose. But even if they were arbitrations, the Bill might have limited effect because it only rules out arbitrations on matters that are within the jurisdiction of the criminal or family courts. Many family disputes between Muslims may fall outside that jurisdiction because many marriages contracted by Muslims in the United Kingdom are not legally recognized. In his *History* Cretney observed, enigmatically, that the fact that in 1999 only 189 Islamic and 926 Sikh marriages were recorded 'may raise questions.'[27] In 2007 only 197 Muslim marriages were recorded, out of a total of 79,169 religious marriages (there were 156,198 civil marriages that year).[28] Of course, Muslims may marry in a civil ceremony, either instead of or in addition to a religious ceremony, and many probably do. But many may not, and if the marriage is not legally recognized, then, apart from issues concerning children, which are governed by the Children Act 1989, matters such as dissolution of the marriage, and ancillary relief, would seem to fall outside that jurisdiction, as would child support, which operates outside the court system. Property issues fall within the Chancery Division.[29] Uncontested probate is dealt with in the Family Division, but the Chancery Division deals with contested wills, and there is concurrent jurisdiction between them regarding family provision claims. But that is not conclusive, because courts may make ancillary relief orders when making a nullity decree. Whether a marriage between Muslims which the parties deliberately refrained from registering because they wished to avoid acquiring civil status would fall within the family jurisdiction as being 'void' rather than 'non-existent' is debateable.[30]

Whether the activities of the Islamic bodies would contravene the Arbitration and Mediation Services (Equality) Bill depends on how those matters are resolved. If we assume that the matters dealt with do fall within the jurisdiction of the family courts, an offence would be committed by a person who 'falsely purports to be exercising a judicial function or to be able to make legally binding rulings' or 'otherwise falsely purports to adjudicate on any matter which that person knows or ought to know is within the jurisdiction of the criminal or family courts'. It seems that the bodies do not claim to exercise judicial functions,

---

27 CRETNEY, above n. 1, p. 35.
28 OFFICE FOR NATIONAL STATISTICS, *Marriage, Divorce and Adoption Statistics 2007*, Series FM2, Table 3.4.
29 See the discussion in LAW COMMISSION, *Cohabitation: the Financial Consequences of Relationship Breakdown* Law Com. No. 307, HMSO, London 2007, para. 4.110 et seq.
30 See R. PROBERT, 'When are we married? Void, non-existent and presumed marriages' (2002) 22 *Legal Studies* 398; *G v. M* [2011] EWHC 2651.

or, probably, to make legally binding rulings, but they may be thought to 'adjudicate' in some way, if only by giving guidance on the application of Islamic law to the case of the parties in dispute. If that is so, the Bill would have a very wide reach. On the BBC programme *Women's Hour* on 29 June 2011 Baroness Cox said that the intention was to prevent the operation of two systems of law within the United Kingdom, so that no family issues would be determined according to *shari'a* (or any other) norms other than the civil law. The implication seems to be that this would cover the activities of the ISC, whether or not it claimed that the decisions were enforceable under the Arbitration Act. This also seems to be the aspiration of some commentators.[31]

5. FAMILY ARBITRATION

We need now to confront the question: why should family arbitration, including arbitration, if it is arbitration, by Islamic bodies, be regarded with such hostility? It could argued that all family arbitration allows the state to evade its responsibility to ensure the proper and fair application of its laws. It is privatized justice, on the cheap, with no quality control, and carries special risks for children and the vulnerable. But it could be attractive to a state anxious to reduce the costs of the justice system, and one which may even regard law as having little or no place in resolving family conflict.[32] These objections might be partly met by allowing family arbitration to be carried out only by trained and approved arbitrators.

But that strategy has only limited value in the case of religious arbitration. There the main objection is that the case could be determined according to norms over which the state has no control. While there are good reasons to allow the parties to choose the law applicable to their case in commercial matters, and to allow the courts to apply a foreign law (subject to safeguards) even in family cases where there are grounds for accepting the involvement of a foreign jurisdiction, or the applicability of foreign law,[33] the same reasons do not seem to apply in a case arising entirely within the courts' jurisdiction. Since states claim authority over all people within the geographic area of their jurisdiction, and reinforce this

---

[31]   See for example C. PATTERSON, 'Two legal systems, and two choices. Which do we want?' *The Independent Viewspaper* 03.08.2011, concluding: 'Most Muslims … don't want Sharia courts, or Sharia law, or Sharia "zones". We have given far, far too much power to the people who do.' Since it is unclear in what sense power has been 'given' to such bodies, the implication seems to be that legislation should restrict the power they presently exercise.

[32]   I have argued that there is evidence that this view is taken by policy-makers under the Coalition government: see J. EEKELAAR, '"Not of the Highest Importance": Family Justice under Threat' (2011) *Journal of Social Welfare and Family Law* 311.

[33]   As in conflicts of laws cases.

through a coercive apparatus, they also have responsibility to ensure the equal application of its laws and its international obligations to those people.

This last argument could be met by requiring family arbitration to be conducted according to English law. This approach has been adopted in Ontario. In 2002, a conservative religious group, the Canadian Society of Muslims, proposed to establish a 'Shari'a Tribunal' to deal with family disputes under the Ontario Arbitration Act, which allowed disputes to be decided in accordance with laws chosen by the disputants.[34] This generated much debate, and in 2004, the Canadian Council of Muslim Women (CCMW) stated that 'CCMW sees no compelling reason to live under any other form of law in Canada, as we want the same laws to apply to [Muslim women] as to other Canadian women.'[35] Also in 2004, the Boyd Report, commissioned by the Ontario Attorney-General, recommended that religious arbitration be allowed, with some safeguards. This was opposed by a newly formed 'No Religious Arbitration Coalition' (which included the CCMW), and their position was accepted by the Government. The result was that, while religious bodies may still carry out arbitration in family matters under the Arbitration Act, they must do so according to the 'law of Ontario or of another Canadian jurisdiction'.[36] Furthermore, regulations require family law arbitrators to undergo training in the law of Canada, that cases are screened for 'power imbalances and domestic violence, by someone other than the arbitrator' and that a written record be kept of the proceedings.

Ayalet Shachar has criticized the Ontario solution, writing:

> 'A less heavy-handed approach might have required religious tribunals themselves to determine, through their actions and deeds, whether to enjoy the benefits of binding arbitration – including the boon of public enforcement of their awards – if they *voluntarily* agreed to comply with statutory thresholds and default rules defined in general family legislation. These safeguards typically establish a 'floor' of protection, above which significant room for variation is permitted.'[37]

Under Shachar's approach, persons who desire their dispute to be determined according to their religious beliefs would have this option, and the religious authority would be supported by the state enforcement mechanisms provided that the determination fell within certain parameters laid down by the state. Shachar further explains of her proposal:

---

34   For an account, see A. SHACHAR, 'Privatizing Diversity: A Cautionary Tale from Religious Arbitration in Family Law' (2008) 9 *Theoretical Inquiries in Law* 573.

35   See CANADIAN COUNCIL OF MUSLIM WOMEN, *Position Statement on the Proposed Implementation of Sections of Muslim law [Sharia] in Canada* (2004), available at <www.ccmw.com/resources/res_Position_Papers.html> accessed 09.11.2011.

36   Family Statute Law Amendment Act 2006, s. 2.2(1).

37   SHACHAR, above n. 34, 601 (emphasis in original).

'if a resolution by a religious tribunal falls within the margin of discretion that any secular family-law judge or arbitrator would have been permitted to employ, there is no reason to discriminate against that tribunal solely for the reason that the decision-maker used a different tradition to a reach a permissible resolution.'

The longer-term hope is that this approach would lead to the adaptation of the communal norms themselves. Of course, the religious authorities may decline the opportunity of state enforcement of their decisions on this basis. Information is not yet available as to the extent to which religious authorities conduct arbitration under the reformed procedures. It is at least possible that resolutions according to versions of Islamic law continue, or may even have increased, without the potential of being enforced by the civil courts.

6. CONTRACTUAL APPROACHES

A different ground for supporting the application of non-state norms in family law might be sought through the (civil) law of contract.[38] The juristic basis of Islamic marriage is contractual. It might therefore be possible to extract from the religious context the elements of a contract enforceable by the civil law. For example, in *Uddin v. Choudhury*[39] the Court of Appeal enforced an agreement by a husband to pay *mahr* (a dowry) to his wife on the breakup of a Muslim marriage, not recognized by English law. This seems to have been done by characterizing the agreement as a contract under principles of contract law. There is therefore scope for certain obligations that arise within a religious and family context to be enforced in the courts under the civil law.[40]

However, it is arguable that, in family cases, the principles of contract do not apply in the 'normal' way.[41] But this qualification applies within the context of the exercise of the family jurisdiction, which, as has been seen, may not apply to

---

[38] See S. CRETNEY, 'The Family and the Law: Status or Contract?' [2003] 15 *Child and Family Law Quarterly* 403, 413, saying that he had 'come to believe that, rather than imposing a statutory system of community of property, the least disadvantageous way of reconciling the claims of certainty, predictability and personal autonomy would be to allow husband and wife the liberty, which we concede to those who live together outside marriage, to decide for themselves the terms of their own partnership.' This perspective won favour in the Supreme Court in 2010 when the Court upheld a prenuptial agreement in *Radmacher v. Granatino* [2010] UKSC 42.

[39] [2009] EWCA Civ 1205.

[40] For development of this argument, see BOWEN, 'How could English courts recognize Shariah?' above n. 11.

[41] In *Radmacher v. Granatino* (n. 38 above) the majority of the Supreme Court recognised 'the difficult question of the circumstances in which it will not be fair to hold the parties to their agreement. This will necessarily depend upon the facts of the particular case, and it would not be desirable to lay down rules that would fetter the flexibility that the court requires to reach a fair result' [76].

many Muslim marriages (and did not in *Uddin v. Choudhury*). But should it matter whether the case arises in the context of, for example, an application for ancillary relief, or for enforcement of a contract? If the qualification does apply, how much more difficult is it to know whether it is fair to hold someone to the religious norms they apparently accepted at some earlier point in their lives, or where they may still accept the religion, but contest its interpretation in their particular case. So, while contract law may well have a role to play in the legal enforcement of minority norms, it could be a difficult one.

Similar issues arise if the parties seek an order under the family jurisdiction on the basis of an agreement that reflects non-state norms. Here it is the parties' *agreement* that the court is asked to enforce (say, by a consent order), or to take into account when making its own order. The fact that the agreement reflects non-state norms is incidental. It is possible that the outcome of proceedings before ISC bodies often take the form of such agreements. Samia Bano writes of the reconciliation process in such proceedings:

> 'Furthermore the interviews and observation data revealed that husbands used this opportunity to negotiate reconciliation financial settlements for divorce and in many cases access to children. Settlements which in effect were being discussed under the shadow of law. Quite clearly these women were in a weak bargaining position and their autonomy and choice was to some extent being limited if they were to be granted a Muslim divorce ... Thus in operation, there are subliminal and covert forms of power and coercion rendering the parties unequal and the process unfair.'[42]

The problem of mediator influence and inequality of power between the parties in the case of family mediation generally is well-known and this is probably more marked in a religious context. While courts are strongly motivated to accept such agreements, they are not bound to do so. The Arbitration and Mediation Services (Equality) Bill enhances the possibility of *ex post* scrutiny of agreements by providing:

> cl. 5. A court may issue a declaration setting aside any order based on a mediation settlement agreement or other negotiated agreement if it considers on evidence that one party's consent was not genuine.

However, it may be desirable to encourage caution over such agreements at an earlier stage. Courts might be required, when making consent orders, to satisfy themselves that the parties have taken independent legal advice, at least in the case of family mediation by religious bodies. In this way parties to such agreements should have been made aware of whatever rights they might have to invoke the civil law in their case.

---

[42]   Bano, above n. 20.

7. WHAT FAMILY LAW?

We should now take a look at the wider picture and consider how the state might approach the family laws of minority communities.

One way might be for the state to try to totally prevent their application. This seems to be the approach of the Arbitration and Mediation Services (Equality) Bill to the extent that it appears to seek to prevent adjudication of family issues other than by the state. I have elsewhere described this as a 'delegation' model, because the state treats the minority families as its delegates, required to carry out its view of what people's family rights and duties should be. That approach is inimical to diversity, and finds its extreme form in totalitarian systems.[43]

The potentially oppressive features of the model can be mitigated insofar as the state's legislative processes, and human rights norms, allow minority values to influence state law, and allow state law to recognize or give exemptions to specific minority practices.[44] This could be represented as incorporating an element of multiculturalism into state law itself. But the scope for such modifications is limited. Any attempt by state institutions to *decide* issues according to minority norms could lack legitimacy for the minorities. This is unlikely to be overcome by claiming that such decisions are determinations of fact (as in a conflict of laws case), and not law. First, the distinction may not make the decision any more acceptable to the minority. Second, in a conflict of laws case, the law the court applies its own private international law, according to which the foreign law is treated as fact. The court's conclusion on that fact is unlikely to carry much weight in the foreign jurisdiction. By contrast, in a case that arises solely within its jurisdiction, the decision is indeed one of law, which will carry weight in the jurisdiction. The problem would not be easily remedied by appointing authorities from minority groups to the judiciary,[45] given the variety of minority legal orders. The non-state norms could therefore be applied inappropriately.[46] Finally, and decisively, state law is subject to parliamentary sovereignty, tempered by human rights provisions: the courts' loyalty is ultimately to those sources, not those of the minority legal order. Courts should therefore decline any invitation

---

[43] J. EEKELAAR, 'From Multiculturalism to Cultural Voluntarism: A Family-based Approach', (2010) 81 *The Political Quarterly* 344 and 'Self-Restraint: Social Norms, Individualism and the Family' (2012) 13 *Theoretical Issues in Law* 75.

[44] For example, English law has long allowed marriages effected according to the practices of Jews and Quakers to have legal consequences. Polygamous marriages could be given limited recognition, for example, for inheritance or tax purposes.

[45] Although this has been suggested for South Africa with respect to Islamic law: see W. AMIEN, 'A South African case study for the recognition and regulation of Muslim family law in a minority Muslim secular context' (2010) 24 *International Journal of Law, Policy and the Family* 361.

[46] This is demonstrated by FOURNIER, above n. 24, pp. 66–70.

to make a determination in family matters by a direct application of non-state norms.

The opposite strategy would be to allow minority authorities to apply their norms and to recognize their decisions as having the force of law.[47] A number of states adopt this model, known in the Ottoman empire as the 'millett' system. But it has serious problems.[48] These include the heterogeneity of minority groups, possible conflict between recognition of such laws and the state's commitment to human rights norms, accentuation of boundaries between minority groups and wider society, and reduction of incentives for the state to assume responsibilities to individuals within those communities. A modified version of this strategy, put forward by Ayalet Shachar,[49] which she calls 'transformative accommodation', was regarded with favour by the Archbishop of Canterbury.[50] This proposed a form of 'joint governance' whereby agreement would be reached between the state and minority groups over issues around which individuals could choose either to follow the minority legal order or that of the state. The hope is that both the state and the groups (but particularly the latter) will be encouraged to adapt their norms by way of accommodation with the other in order to minimize the risks of individuals choosing to transfer out of their system to the alternative regime. However, apart from its complexity, the scheme raises similar problems to the millett system. The state would need to identify which authorities to deal with; problems would arise where one individual wished to opt in and another did not; and it could be intimidating for individuals to make a formal decision to 'opt out' of their religious system.

7.1. CULTURAL VOLUNTARISM

I have therefore argued for an approach that I call 'cultural voluntarism' (CV), which has the following features:[51]

1. It draws on the belief that, since individuals can experience considerable benefits from the operation of intra-group support mechanisms that give groups a certain solidarity and self-sufficiency, and that these can be important to people's sense of self-identity, there are good reasons for states

---

47   I have called this the 'authorisation' model: above n. 43.

48   It has been twice rejected at government level for the United Kingdom: see S. POULTER, *Ethnicity, Law and Human Rights: The English Experience*, Oxford University Press, Oxford 1998, pp. 210–12.

49   A. SHACHAR, *Multicultural Jurisdictions: Cultural Differences and Women's Rights*, Cambridge University Press, Cambridge 2001.

50   WILLIAMS, above n. 8.

51   This is expanded in EEKELAAR, above n. 43.

to allow individuals within groups space to follow their own family, and inter-family, practices.

2. However, it also recognizes that groups can be dominated by power elites. Therefore the approach opposes recognizing norms of minority legal orders as having legal force, or conferring power on the groups to make and apply norms with the authority of law. Courts should only apply the civil law, including any exemptions demanded by human rights norms, except insofar as subject to acceptable compromises between the parties. This is important because that law is subject to the democratic processes of criticism and reform, and the state is obliged to observe its international commitments for the benefit of all within its jurisdiction.

3. Individuals should be made aware whether the civil law applies to their case, and access to it protected and facilitated. Muslims should be encouraged to register their marriages without thereby disabling them from access to their religious authorities.

   Individuals in minority groups will thus have access both to the norms of their system and of the state. Resort to one need not be to the exclusion of the other.

4. The state should intervene even without invocation where this presently occurs with regard to families, for example, in child protection cases. Maleiha Malik has described this as a process of 'severance', where the state decides on a case by case basis which parts of the minority legal order it is willing to allow to function and which to override.[52]

5. Subject to intervention under the idea of severance, under CV the state would allow individuals to follow the norms of their group should they so wish, giving effect to the outcomes of transactions made according to those norms *insofar as this complies with civil law norms*. For example, contractual obligations or property transfers could be recognised even if they arise in a religious or other cultural context. Of course, in all such cases the entire cultural and religious *context* would be relevant to the application of the civil law. In effect, CV promotes diversity *among individuals* within the general community rather than diversity of *groups*.

8.   CONCLUSION

I have argued that the family law applied and enforced through the courts in cases arising solely within their jurisdiction should always be that of the state, subject only (within limits) to modifications of their civil rights agreed between

---

[52]   M. MALIK, *Minority Legal Orders in the United Kingdom: Multiculturalism, Minorities and the Law*, British Academy, London, 2012.

the parties.[53] Decisions in family matters made in religious arbitration (or any other form of religious determination) should not be directly enforceable by state institutions. However, the law should give space for individuals to follow alternative family law norms should they choose to do so, and if such a decision were carried out, for example, by the transfer of property, or making of a contact, its effects could be recognized if compliant with the general law. Family courts could make orders based on agreements reached under religious law but only if the agreement was genuine and followed independent legal advice, and was consistent with overriding policy goals (for example, the best interests of the child). State law would be available at all times to anyone who chose to invoke it, and access to it should be safeguarded and encouraged. It would also intervene without invocation in cases of clear harm or its risk, decided on a case-by-case basis.

The state need not ignore reports that norms uncongenial to its values are being applied within its jurisdiction. It can aspire to bring about changes to those norms. Primarily this would be sought through information and education. But its approach must be cautious and self-critical. In discussing whether states have a responsibility under international human rights law to 'change' religious and customary laws, Abdullah Ahmed An-Naim has written that, even if such a duty did exist, this should be approached by 'internal discourse, as supported by cross-cultural dialogue' and that, with regard to *sharia*:

> 'It is up to Muslim women and men to engage in a political struggle to propagate and implement reform of Islamic law in their own communities and countries. ... It is therefore imperative that both the internal actors and their external supporters should avoid acting in a way that might be used as a pretext for undermining the credibility and legitimacy of the process of changing sharia laws'.[54]

---

53   Different considerations arise in commercial matters, where in some circumstances parties might reasonably choose the law of a jurisdiction unconnected with transaction: see C.G. Buys, 'The Arbitrator's Duty to Respect the Parties' Choice of Law in Commercial Arbitration' (2005) 79 *St John's Law Review* 59.
54   A. A. An-Naim, 'State Responsibility under International Human Rights Law to Change Religious and Customary Laws' in R.J. Cook (ed.), *Human Rights of Women: National and International Perspectives*, University of Pennsylvania Press, Philadelphia 1994. I am grateful to Amanda Dale for this reference.

REGULATING THE BAR

Ruth DEECH

Contents

1. INTRODUCTION

Stephen Cretney's professional life ranged across the entire spectrum of the legal profession, save only that of the judiciary (and a fine judge he would have made!). From his wide experience, Cretney's perspective on the role of lawyers in family disputes is of major interest. In his *magnum opus, Family Law in the Twentieth Century: A History*[1] he gives credit to both branches of the profession for transforming the atmosphere in the courts and assisting in making the system more efficient and humane. As he says, no forum whose function it is to resolve the problems of deeply hurt and stressed former spouses can avoid bitterness, distress and humiliation. Nevertheless, the part played by the Bar, of which he is now an honorary member, has come to be seen as vital and helpful.

2. THE CONTRIBUTION OF THE BAR TO FAMILY LAW

Maclean and Eekelaar's study of the Bar at work in family law concludes that: '[t]he barrister is both mentor and guide for the client… we hope we have shown

---

[1] S. CRETNEY, *Family Law in the Twentieth Century: A History*, Oxford University Press, Oxford 2003, p. 77.

that society should value their contribution better.'[2] Noting the long-term failure of mediation as a general substitution for legal proceedings, the authors comment that: 'in some cases counsel effectively plays the role of a mediator with expertise in law and legal process.'[3] Their research showed that where lawyers are involved in family law issues concerning money or children, the majority are resolved without a court process or without a contested hearing, but that where a dispute has to go to court, legal representation supports the parties, assists the court, shortens and focuses the court process and enhances the prospects of resolution. In the same vein, the *Family Justice Review: Interim Report* commented that they were 'impressed by the dedication and capability of those who work in the family justice system. Their work is hugely demanding and often highly stressful. They work to protect children's interests and to promote better outcomes for them.'[4] The final report confirmed this by stating that: 'the supply of properly qualified family lawyers is vital to the protection of children.'[5]

Acknowledging the support given to families by advocates, and considering the planned removal of legal aid from most family law cases from April 2013, it has to be asked whether this support can be replaced by the opening up of lawyers' working structures enabled by the Legal Services Act (LSA) 2007. The relaxation of the rules envisaged in the Act is accompanied by new regulatory systems for the legal profession. However, legal aid is likely to be removed before the supposed beneficial outcomes of the new legal market facilitated by the 2007 Act can take effect, leaving many families in limbo and resorting to self representation, with all the problems that attach to it. There is no evidence that families were unable to *access* legal advice and representation before 2007: the question was whether they could *afford* it. At this stage of the reforms, it seems unlikely that legal advice will be more affordable even if delivered more locally, for example by firms attached to banks and supermarkets. Nor is it likely that internet or telephone advice will assist couples all the way to resolution. Cretney will want to know how families are served by the latest developments and to be reassured that the Bar will remain independent from government. These are the questions to be addressed. As far as the family law bar and its clients are concerned, they face real threats, to some extent from regulation, but more so from reduced legal aid and less access to advocacy. It may be that the way to cope with this is by reforming the substantive law, not the procedure. It could be argued that the *Family Justice Review* of 2011 is starting at the wrong end by tackling procedural issues. In relation to family breakdown, separation and associated money issues, if the law were simpler, fairer and more predictable, if it

---

2   J. Eekelaar and M. Maclean, *Family Law Advocacy: How Barristers Help the Victims of Family Failure*, Hart, Oxford 2009, p.118.

3   Ibid., p. 120.

4   Family Justice Review, *Interim Report*, Ministry of Justice, London 2011, para. 2.27.

5   Family Justice Review, *Final Report*, Ministry of Justice, London 2011, para. 4.179.

were less open to radical shifts in every Supreme Court judgment,[6] the cost of the process and its clarity would be a less pressing issue.

3. THE NEW REGULATORY SYSTEM

The origin of the changes now contemplated lies in the LSA 2007, which facilitates the relaxation of the structures of working that lawyers have known for decades. It also governs the regulation of all branches of the legal profession. New ways for lawyers to work together in the future may be sought not only because they are sensible, but also because they are inevitable under the provisions of the Act and because of the economic pressure on the Bar. Parts of the Bar are hard hit not only by the recession, but because the Ministry of Justice controls the purse strings of legal aid for many of the most socially valuable members of the profession. Arguably, the tail of legal aid cuts is wagging the dog of British justice, at least as far as traditional chambers and self-employment are concerned.

The LSA may yet prove to be a rather unsatisfactory piece of legislation. It is grounded in the 2004 report by Sir David Clementi, a former deputy Governor of the Bank of England.[7] He was concerned with the then over-complex existing regulatory framework (a mixture of oversight by professional bodies and government departments, largely self-regulatory and without sufficient regard to the consumer), as well as the complaints system and the restrictive nature of business practices, though it would be more fair and accurate to say that these two issues were more pertinent to the solicitors' branch of the profession than the Bar. His recommendations differed somewhat from the eventual legislation, the LSA, but the Act did address the problems that he had identified.

In summary, the profession was no longer to be self-regulating, but overseen by a new Legal Services Board (hereinafter the LSB), with a lay majority. Its powers were to some extent to be devolved to the current front line regulators, in the main the Bar Council and the Law Society, but they were both obliged to separate out their regulatory and representative functions (emulating the way the General Medical Council and the British Medical Association fulfil different functions for doctors.) The Bar Council represents the barristers and the Bar Standards Board (hereinafter the BSB) now regulates them; the Law Society represents the solicitors and the Solicitors Regulation Authority (hereinafter the SRA) regulates them. The other regulators are the Council of Legal Conveyancers, the Institute

---

[6]   E.g. *Radmacher v. Granatino* [2010] UKSC 42; and *Jones v. Kernott* [2011] UKSC 53.
[7]   *Report of a Review of the Regulatory Framework for Legal Services in England and Wales*: <http://webarchive.nationalarchives.gov.uk/+http:/www.legal-services-review.org.uk/content/report/index.htm>.

of Legal Executives, with its regulatory arm, the ILEX Professional Standards Board, the Chartered Institute of Patent Attorneys, the Institute of Trade Mark Attorneys, the Intellectual Property Regulation Board, the Association of Costs Lawyers, regulated by the Cost Lawyers Standards Board, and the Master of the Faculties (notaries). For current purposes the focus is on the two biggest regulators, the BSB overseeing 15 000 barristers, and the SRA overseeing about ten times as many solicitors.

The second major change is the introduction of new ownership structures for legal firms and chambers, in particular allowing non-lawyers to own and manage firms. The new firms are called alternative business structures, including legal disciplinary practices or multidisciplinary practices, the latter including non-legal professionals working alongside lawyers, which could amount to a 'one stop shop', sometimes nicknamed 'Tesco law'. A third change was a new system for handling complaints against lawyers.

It does not take much description to see that rather than sorting out the maze of regulation that Clementi identified, the LSA adds to it; it may result in over-regulation, duplication of regulation and competitive regulation, none of it cost-capped. The cost of the LSB and its demands are serious issues, for the practising certificate fee of the Bar has to fund it, at a time of constraint, as well as funding the Board's initiatives, which include quality assessment of advocacy, an overarching education review, changing the traditional prescriptive Bar Code of Conduct to outcomes focused regulatory rules, and the collection of detailed diversity data. In considering the genesis of the legislation, it is clear that the Bar was caught up in the slipstream of the criticisms that had been levelled at the handling of complaints by solicitors in the decades before the new statute, and that the heavy structure of the 2007 Act is not suited to as small a profession as the Bar.

4. THE WAY THE BAR WORKS

Whether the Bar will avail itself of the possibility of new working structures remains to be seen; as yet there is no evidence that they will enable improved services to clients. Cuts in legal aid have exacerbated the non-affordability of legal advice. Not much has been heard from the public about what they want from legal services, despite the proliferation of consumer panels and surveys. The issues may be just too complex and variable, depending on the economic climate, and it may be the latter that thwarts the availability of direct affordable legal advice more than the actions of the lawyers themselves. There may well be risks, especially to families, in the alternative business structures – the influence of outside ownership, profit placed ahead of professional standards, commodification of legal issues, fewer firms in rural areas and in the high street, and rejection of the new firms by legal practices abroad, where other nations have more careful professional rules. Barristers in an entity (as distinct from self-employed barristers) will be conflicted out once one party to potential litigation has engaged a barrister in the entity, whereas at the moment there is no conflict when one barrister in a set of chambers is engaged. It could be that in a small town, where there are not many barristers specialising in family law, and most of those that do have joined in one entity, justice and choice may be restricted. If one of the spouses contemplating divorce engages a barrister in the entity, no other barrister in it will be available for the other spouse to instruct.

If one's first consideration is the client, in the broadest sense, not simply the man and woman who come off the street seeking legal advice, but all those who engage the support of English law, then the preservation of a distinct profession of barrister is actually in the interests of the public. This is because the barrister can and will defend those clients whom commercial legal outfits might ignore, the barrister's duty being to the court, to assist in the development of the law and to protect the needy (witness the significant *pro bono* work undertaken). Sometimes that duty involves telling the court about matters that the client would rather not have revealed. Barristers are bound by the cab rank rule, which means that they take the next client that comes along, regardless of acceptability. It is accordingly recognised that the barrister is not to be personally identified with an unpopular client. Future protection requires that clients should be informed that in-house advocacy within alternative business structures is not the only option. In their interests, the access of regional solicitors' firms to the Bar needs to be kept open, and clients should be protected from the corralling of barristers in big firms that have in-house advocates, reducing their availability at large.

5. A SHORT HISTORY OF REGULATION

How has regulation arrived at this stage? It has come to be widely believed that the governance of the Bar should be taken out of the cloisters of the Inns and the Bar Council, and led blinking into the daylight of Westminster and Whitehall. First because, as has been indicated, legal advice is too expensive. It has moved out of the reach of the middle classes. The advice of a top barrister is affordable by government, by corporate bodies and by wealthy individuals, notably men and the women they divorce. There are many, perhaps the majority of the population, who could never contemplate accessing the advice of a barrister or a city solicitor. It is reported, often with a note of pride (certainly by the journals of the solicitors) that partners in city firms make £1m a year, and that some barristers make similar sums from criminal legal aid.[8] Nevertheless, there are barristers, many of them women and/or from black and ethnic minorities, who undertake largely publicly-funded work in criminal and family issues and make only the most modest of livings. In a survey of the Family Bar conducted by King's College London in 2008/9 it was revealed that 30 per cent of women and black and ethnic minority barristers depend on legal aid for 60–80 per cent of their turnover and that one-third of the family bar relies on public funds for more than 60 per cent of their turnover.[9] Median taxable profits for the family bar are in the region of £66,000 a year, before deducting overheads and expenses. Their pleas are undermined by the excesses at the top end of the Bar earnings scale. In addition, the entire profession was tainted by the tardiness of complaints handling by the Law Society, and the mishandling of claims by miners suffering from lung diseases caused by their work in the mines, where solicitors' firms took more for themselves than for their clients.[10]

Quite rightly, the call has gone up for affordability, access and competence in the legal profession. It has been asked why the changes that have affected business globally should not transform the business of the lawyer. IT, flexiworking, outsourcing should make advice more readily obtainable and cheaper. Other businesses have been affected, or improved, by deregulation, free market competition, the dominance of client choice and consumer sovereignty. So too should the provision of legal services change. This is, of course, to ignore the financial crises of this century, the reasons for and the results of which are still working themselves out, and where the part played by liberalisation of the market has yet to be analysed. It also sits uneasily with the demand, voiced on behalf of the consumer, for accountability and regulation, often where trust was once sufficient (cf. the medical profession and hospitals, banks and journalists). On the one hand, there are calls for ever greater integrity and competence, with accountability; on the other for deregulation, liberalisation and entry into the professions of competitors with different training. This is all hard to square: we have yet to work out the reconciliation of consumerism and ethics.

Second, the old tradition of self-regulation has fallen into disrepute. Self-regulation used to be totally appropriate because of the relatively small size of the Bar, its concentration in London and a few other centres, and the constant surveillance by peers, judges and solicitors. This obviated the need for outside regulation. Now self-regulation has a bad name. Left unchecked it can become self interest. That is the risk that must be guarded against. Appropriate checks

---

8   The amount is disputed and sometimes refers to fees earned over a period of years or shared between several legal professionals.

9   <www.flba.co.uk/public_notices/public_notices/the_work_of_the_family_bar>.

10 <www.timesonline.co.uk/tol/news/politics/article1657755.ece>.

and balances need to be put in place to ensure that self-regulation does what is necessary to reinforce independence, that is, organise the profession to ensure that its members genuinely support the rule of law and the proper administration of justice. It was thought in England and Wales that self-regulation had indeed got too close to being self interest in practice. Arguably, the LSA reforms go too far to control self interest in that they may restrict independence. The pendulum may swing too far in the opposite direction. Proper self-regulation ought to be possible and effective if the profession follows the Nolan principles of integrity in public service and above all controls misconduct swiftly and decently. At the behest of the LSB, itself lay dominated, barristers are now in a minority on the BSB. The Bar has firmly separated the representative and regulatory arms of its governance, and did so even in advance of the 2007 Act. The Bar still controls who becomes a barrister, through the Inns and by the BSB's authorisation of providers of the Bar Professional Training Course, subject of course to the law of the land in relation to discrimination and equality.

The Bar is subject to further *de facto* external controls: there is a new Judicial Appointments Commission, the Bar Code of Conduct is growing in bulk and its work is shaped by the requirements of legal aid. Advancement to the position of QC is also through a commission, and another external body will administer the new scheme of advocacy assessment. Complaints about poor service are handled by the new Office for Legal Complaints, leaving only misconduct complaints under the jurisdiction of the BSB. Third party payers, insurance premiums and the media all play a part in holding the Bar to account to the outside world.

6. THE INDEPENDENCE OF THE BAR

Fusion with the solicitors or any other sector of the legal profession is not on the agenda. It may be difficult for non-lawyers to appreciate why there is virtue in the separateness of the Bar, especially when other common law countries have fused professions and make equally valid claims to independence. In the eyes of this non-practitioner, student and teacher of the law, there is great merit in the division. It fosters independence, not just of practice but of spirit, the shouldering of responsibility for the decision, regardless of anything except the client and the court; it allows for the most advanced development of the skill of advocacy; it ensures that even the most unpopular of clients has representation; it provides a system whereby a barrister may stand up to the government on behalf of, say, a terrorist, without being identified with the client; it fosters the highest standards because each barrister is the object of their fellow barristers' inspection and competitive spirit; it provides the collegiality and protection of the Inns; its very existence is a guarantee of the rule of law because the loyalty is to the client and the court, not to the earning capacity of the entity. Those qualities militate against fusion, even though solicitors are also practising advocacy.

When one takes into account the historical role played by lawyers and the independent judiciary, drawn from them, in the enduring constitutional stability of the UK, there emerge important values needing to be retained no matter how much reform is implemented and necessary. The independence of the legal profession plays a part in the rule of law. This is a concept that common lawyers take for granted, but there have been interesting recent attempts to spell it out, motivated by recognition that this is a time of crisis for the law. It is widely agreed that it means *inter alia* that no one shall be denied the benefit of the law or its consequences.[11] The late Lord Bingham devoted some of his last writings to the rule of law, and amongst the seven defining principles he identified was the independence of judges and lawyers. A Canadian QC put it like this: 'the judgment of lawyers should not be influenced by any consideration other than the need for them to discharge the loyalty they owe each of their clients, subject to the higher duty to themselves, the court, the state and fellow lawyers.'[12] There are several potential conflicts here which could bear analysis, but the general meaning is that lawyers need to be independent in their handling of their clients' cases and independent also of the government.

Lord Bingham was by no means uncritical of the profession. He said that there should be unimpeded access to the courts in order to secure human rights and the rule of law and that there can be no judicial development of these concepts unless the cases are brought to court by the lawyers, often acting under the cab rank rule. He also acknowledged the detrimental effect of excess earnings and the shrinking of legal aid. He concluded that lawyers are necessary to the rule of law but that they are also guilty of impeding it if they price themselves out of reach.

It is widely argued that independence entails that the legal profession should be independent of outside regulation, and be able to regulate its own affairs, conduct its own disciplinary issues and determine its own entrance standards (the implied evil otherwise being government decisions about who may or may not practice – witness the persecution of lawyers in Nazi Germany, which was the first act of Hitler, in Iran today and in certain African countries.) Indeed, the first act of a dictator who wishes to subdue protest is likely to be the control of the lawyers.[13]

---

11 Lord Bingham, 'The Rule of Law' [2007] 66 *Cambridge Law Journal* 67.
12 G. Turriff, 'The Consumption of Lawyer Independence' (2010) 17 *Journal of the Legal Profession* 283.
13 C. Joerges and N.S. Ghaleigh, *Darker Legacies of Law in Europe*, Hart, Oxford 2003; 'The first thing we do, let's kill all the lawyers', *Henry VI, Part 2*; R.W. Gordon, 'The independence of lawyers' (1988) 68 *Boston University Law Review* 1.

Lest this view be thought to be professional self-serving, it is echoed in international conventions. The UN,[14] the European Union,[15] and the International Bar Association[16] have all laid down principles of self-regulation and unimpeded access to clients.

Why does independence matter? It is to enable clients and organisations to challenge the government of the day; it is to secure interpretation and application of the legislation by persons without conflicting loyalties.[17] It is inseparable from the enforcement of human rights. No less a person than Sydney Kentridge has said that in apartheid South Africa there were frequent threats from the government to place the Bar under the control of a central council with government-nominated members. He said that his fears were reawakened by the proposals in the UK that were the forerunners of the LSA 2007, because 'they would obviously increase the power of the government to control the legal profession and ... in the hands of another Lord Chancellor less committed to the independence of the Bar, destroy it.'[18] It also follows from this assertion that the Bar should control the education of its recruits. The nature of the job that they do clearly requires knowledge of the law and procedure, and skill in advocacy, abilities that will not be found in every candidate and need to be tested.

Even Richard Abel, a writer who casts a critical eye over this high-minded approach,[19] accepts the need for a profession that mediates between citizen and state, redresses civil wrongs, manages family disputes and articulates human rights. He points out that while the Bar claims to need a distance between the advocate and his or her client in order to meet conflicting obligations to adversaries and the legal system, this is inconsistent with the demand of the Bar in recent years for more direct access (in order to compete with solicitors). He also comments that there is no evidence that employed barristers' independence is compromised, even though they work for a master.

What does the client want from regulation? They may know nothing about the law and may never before, or ever after, have had recourse to the Bar, but they want their case put to the best of the barrister's ability; they want advice of the highest order, skill and integrity, comparable to the expectations of the patient

---

14   *Basic Principles on the Role of Lawyers, 1990*: 'All persons [should] have effective access to legal services provided by an independent legal profession... lawyers should be entitled to form and join self-governing professional associations to represent their interests, promote their continuing education and training and protect their professional integrity.'

15   *Code of Conduct for Lawyers in the European Union* 1988.

16   *Standards for Independence of the Legal Profession* 1990.

17   The Law Society of Upper Canada, *Task Force on the rule of law and the independence of the Bar* 2006, para.1.

18   J. GAUNTLETT, 'The Bar at the Brink', *Advocate*, April 2011, 6.

19   R. ABEL, *English Lawyers between Market and State*, Oxford University Press, Oxford 2004.

who is referred to a consultant or surgeon. And the barrister needs recognition of the nature of his or her duty. That is, recognition of the overriding duty to the court: otherwise the very system that the client is relying on will not support him or her. Law needs a measure of predictability, and the notion of duty to the court is vital because it ensures impartiality, that all proper disclosures are made, that the law applies to everyone, the opponent, the criminal and the victim, or those he or she does business with, win or lose. In other words, the barrister's behaviour is at the essence of the rule of law. And that is why fusion with the solicitors may not be for the best of all possible worlds.

When it comes to the introduction of the new partnerships in the legal profession, boringly known as 'entities', the BSB will be looking to regulate those who want to specialise in advocacy and sign up to their standards. It will not compete with the regulation offered by the SRA. The BSB entities will not handle client cash and will have restrictive rules about outside investment. It would be contrary to the spirit of the LSA if it did not give free rein to various models of entities. Let a thousand legal flowers bloom. The Bar and the solicitors should agree on differentiating their professions. The solicitors will have in their remit a mixed bag – the magic circle of City firms, and the mixed disciplinary Alternative Business Structures. The Bar will regulate entities that offer, as entities, what the Bar offers as individuals – specialist advice (including that given by the employed bar) and advocacy.

The arguments rehearsed here in favour of independence of the Bar from other sectors of the legal profession, and from the government, are not new. The tussle between independence on the one side, and the alleged desirability of cost control, anti-competitiveness, consumerism and government regulation on the other, goes back some decades. Alternatively this tension may be termed 'professionalism' *versus* 'the market'. The Royal Commission on Legal Services[20] considered all these issues. Its report ruled out partnerships, came down in favour of a two-branch profession, and stressed independence and self-regulation. But the perception of lawyers by the public and in the media remained adverse, little though they may matter. Reform has been formulated expressly to curb the independence of the legal profession, which seemed to some to be a cloak for a self-serving gentlemen's club.

7.   COMPETITION & CONSUMERISM

The genesis of change, as with so much of English law today, was partly European. The European Commission Competition Directorate wanted to make the

---

[20]   (1979) Cmnd 7648.

professions more competitive.[21] The Office of Fair Trading wanted the same, both organisations aiming at removing existing restrictions on forms of business organisation and conduct.[22] The legal profession was changing in any case. It had grown, and more barristers were working in employment, competing with solicitors for the business of price-conscious clients. Many barristers depend on a few large firms for much of their work, or on legal aid. The curbs on the Bar are, in reality, shrinking legal aid, lower remuneration, too many people seeking to come to (and arguably at) the Bar and the possible reduction of reserved services, i.e. those that only lawyers can undertake. Insurers, too, have great power because the rise in premiums might prevent lawyers doing cheaper or more adventurous work.

Despite the responses of the Bar to the needs of clients, the government has played the consumer card (if one takes a cynical approach). Some argue that the claim to regulate in the interests of 'consumers' is a ploy to enable the government to curb the freedom of the Bar, ostensibly in the interests of society, and this is evidenced by disagreement over who the consumer is. On the governmental side, he or she is depicted as the (wo)man in the street needing advice about a divorce or a tenancy. On the legal professional side, the consumer is seen as a broader group of those with an interest in, or affected by the law – the judges, the government departments, business, solicitors, the rule of law itself. There is a genuine need to make legal services more widely available in terms of price, method and competence. This may militate against lawyer independence. The LSA 2007, however, concluded by putting the consumer first (in practice, although there are eight listed objectives for regulators to follow in the Act.[23]) Lord Neuberger has drawn attention to the uneasy compromises, saying that: 'the ethos of consumer society is not necessarily ethical.'[24]

The mechanisms of government control are now in place in the UK. The LSB and its Consumer Panel are appointed with the approval of the Lord Chancellor, who is now firmly a politician himself after his removal from the woolsack.[25] The Consumer Panel and the Office of Fair Trading are to advise the LSB on the

---

[21]   <http://eur-lex.europa.eu/LexUriServ/LexUriServ.do?uri=CELEX:52004DC0083:EN:NOT>.
[22]   OFFICE OF FAIR TRADING, *Competition in the Professions: A Report by the Director General of Fair Trading*, London 2001.
[23]   LSA 2007, s. 1 – the public interest, the rule of law, access to justice, consumers, competition, an independent, strong, diverse and effective legal profession, public understanding of the law, adherence to the professional principles.
[24]   'The Ethics of Professionalism in the 21st Century', Inner Temple, 22.02.2010, www.judiciary.gov.uk/publications_media.
[25]   This change was made to effect the separation of powers: Constitutional Reform Act 2005. The Lord Chancellor is no longer the Speaker of the House of Lords, but functions as the head of the Ministry of Justice.

appointment of approved regulators of the new legal entities.[26] The LSB can cancel the designation of an approved regulator, such as the Bar Council,[27] and the Lord Chancellor could appoint the LSB as an approved regulator,[28] so the LSB could take control of part of the profession with government approval. The Board can recommend cancellation of designation as an approved regulator if the regulator has not observed the regulatory objectives listed in the Act, which include the interests of consumers.[29] It is not clear from the Act whose view is to prevail if the Board and the front line regulators disagree over the meaning of those objectives. This is important, given that the Board has the power to fine,[30] and to levy fees for its support from the profession, which has no way of challenging the budget, save through the Ministry of Justice. There is therefore a real threat, with only the thin possibility of judicial review as a shield.

In this complex economic and regulatory environment, the expressed aim of the BSB in regulating the Bar is to protect its independence, and preserve what is distinctive and best about it in the interests of the rule of law and of society, while allowing it to modernise, indeed to survive. It is, after all, one of the stated objectives of the LSA 2007 to encourage a strong diverse, effective and independent legal profession. If the Bar ever becomes downhearted, it has but to remember what Erskine said on representing Tom Paine in 1792: 'From the moment that any advocate can be permitted to say that he will or will not stand between the Crown and the subject in the court where he daily sits to practise, from that moment the liberties of England are at an end.'[31] There is very good reason in the current climate to be grateful to the Bar for its ability to defend the citizen from his or her government in many countries of the world. And one hopes that the spirit of independence is infectious. It is a spirit that Stephen Cretney exhibited in his professional life.

---

[26]   LSA 2007, Sched. 4, Part 2, paras. 5–9, 11.

[27]   Ibid., s. 45.

[28]   Ibid., s. 62.

[29]   Ibid., s. 45.

[30]   Ibid., s. 38.

[31]   (1792) 22 How. St. Tr. 358, 412.

A FAILED REVOLUTION

Judicial Case Management
of Care Proceedings

Judith MASSON

Contents

1. INTRODUCTION

Whilst others commenting on the Children Act 1989 focused on the creation of a single code unifying public and private law and the relationship between families and the state, Stephen Cretney highlighted the changes the Act brought for the family courts and those who used them. Henceforth, courts hearing children cases would 'have to take an active part in the proceedings rather than simply acting as umpires between the contending parties.'[1] They, not the parties, would be responsible for the progress of cases and, with the assistance of children's guardians, for ensuring that options were fully explored. He reflected:

> '[T]here must be concern that the courts have been given a task which will prove extremely difficult for them to carry out. But perhaps the most striking, and in some ways disturbing feature of the legislation is the revolution which it envisages in judicial practice... Clearly a great deal of thought will have to be given to formulating procedures which will enable these well-intentioned measures to be effective.'[2]

---

[1] DEPARTMENT OF HEALTH, *An Introduction to the Children Act 1989*, HMSO, London 1990.
[2] S. CRETNEY, 'Defining the limits of State Intervention: The Child and the Courts' in D. FREESTONE (ed.), *Children and the Law*, Hull University Press, Hull 1990, 58, 71–2.

These were perceptive comments. Despite legislation and guidance the courts have not been able to take control of proceedings so as to ensure the timely completion of cases. Delay has been a constant concern since the Act was implemented: the duration of care proceedings has risen continually, in the county courts from an average of 28 weeks in March 1993 to 57 weeks in 2010.[3] Delays damage children, who wait in temporary placements,[4] and increase costs for local authorities and the Legal Services Commission.[5] The introduction of judicial case management has not resulted in a revolution in family justice, but rather in resistance, both from the judiciary and the legal profession. Nevertheless, the Family Justice Review sees judicial case management as the way to ensure that care cases are completed more speedily in the future.[6]

Focusing on care proceedings, this chapter examines the twenty-year history of attempts to change the operation of the family courts, outlining the mechanisms for judicial case management and the ways these have been supported and encouraged. Drawing on parallel experiences in civil justice, it reviews the effects of judicial case management and explores the cultural and practical barriers which have made it largely ineffective in care cases. Finally, it considers the changes necessary to ensure the completion of the majority of these cases within six months (26 weeks) as recently proposed.[7]

2. A BRIEF HISTORY OF CASE MANAGEMENT IN ENGLAND AND WALES

In 1990, the idea of judicial control of litigation was relatively new in England and Wales; Children Act proceedings were the first area in which it was introduced. Although wardship was regarded as an inquisitorial jurisdiction, the massive growth in the numbers of applications from the 1970s had overtaken all but the myth of the individual high court judge determining his ward's future.[8]

---

3   Children Act Advisory Committee, *Annual Report 1993–4*, LCD, London 1994, table 5; *Family Justice Review: Interim Report* MoJ, London 2011, para. 2.31.

4   H. Ward, E.R. Munro and C. Dearden, *Babies and Young Children in Care: Life Pathways, Decision Making and Practice*, Jessica Kingsley, London 2006; H. Ward et al., *Infants Suffering, or Likely to Suffer, Significant Harm: A prospective Longitudinal Study*, DFE RB 053, 2010.

5   J. Masson, 'Controlling costs and maintaining services – the reform of legal aid fees for care proceedings' [2008] 20 *Child and Family Law Quarterly* 425.

6   Family Justice Review, *Final Report* MoJ, London 2011, para. 2.148.

7   Ibid., paras. 3.64–3.77.

8   N. Lowe and R. White, *Wards of Court*, Barry Rose, Chichester 1986; J. Masson and S. Morton, 'The use of wardship by local authorities' (1989) 5 *Modern Law Review* 562; cf. Lord Chancellor's Department, *Scoping Study on Delay* LCD, London 1992, para. 156. See further Lowe, this volume.

In 1983, the Matrimonial Causes Procedure Committee consulted on proposals that the courts, rather than the parties, should control the progress of litigation so that there was 'no unnecessary expenditure or delay'.[9] It received a mixed response and accepted that the parties and their advisers should decide what evidence was necessary.[10] These ideas were put aside only be to taken up when a pilot scheme for ancillary relief was introduced in the 1990s.[11]

Case management was not a consideration of those who were responsible for costing the reforms which resulted in the Children Act 1989. They expected disputes about matters such as disclosure 'to be settled between the parties in the majority of cases' and savings to be made by the replacement of wardship by statutory proceedings.[12] Following proposals from the Cleveland Inquiry that there should be an Office of Child Protection to control care proceedings, the Lord Chancellor's Department consulted on a scheme whereby this Office would manage children's guardians and 'eliminate unnecessary disputes or hearings through clarification or resolution of issues.'[13] The response was almost entirely negative; respondents rejected the idea that directions about hearings could be given administratively or that an additional organisation would improve matters. The scheme was dropped; if the management of proceedings was not to be left to the parties it would have to be undertaken by the courts. There was no further consultation and no attempt to build a consensus between practitioners and the judiciary.

The Children Act 1989 required courts hearing care proceedings 'to draw up a timetable with a view to disposing of the application without delay.' Further details were provided in court rules, which also gave courts the power to give directions on the conduct of the proceedings, including on the submission of evidence and experts' reports, and the time allowed for this. Directions could be made on the request of the parties or the court's own motion, and required a hearing where they were not agreed.[14] In the magistrates' courts, directions could be issued by a single magistrate or a magistrates' legal adviser. Although this had a profound effect on the length of final hearings, this process necessitated

---

9   *Report of the Matrimonial Causes Procedure Committee*, LCD, London 1985, para. 3–14–16.
10   Ibid., para. 3–14–16; I. Scott, 'The reform of matrimonial causes procedure' (1986) 5 *Civil Justice Quarterly* 8.
11   KPMG, *Ancillary Relief Pilot Scheme Report*, Lord Chancellor's Department Research Report 98/8 LCD, London 1998.
12   Department of Health and Social Security, *Report of the Working Party on Costing the Review of Child Care Law* DHSS, London 1986, para. 4.59.
13   Lord Chancellor's Department, *Improvement of Care Proceedings Consultation Paper* LCD, London 1988, para. 22f.
14   Section 32 and Family Proceedings Rules 1991 SI 1991/1247, rr. 4.11(4); 4.14(2),(3) and 4.16(1).

additional hearings and increased costs because attendance of the parties, their lawyers and the guardian was required.[15]

Implementation of case management for care proceedings avoided the difficult issues Cretney raised, and focused on two apparently non-contentious aspects – case allocation and timetabling. The system of triple jurisdiction did not create a family court; magistrates' courts and county courts were funded, administered and located separately and used completely different systems for recording or tracking cases.[16] The allocation rules required almost all care proceedings to be commenced in magistrates' courts[17] so a system was required to ensure that difficult cases could be transferred to the appropriate level. Transfer down to the magistrates' court was also possible to ensure the best use of judicial resources.[18] The Lord Chancellor expected that the majority of public law cases would be decided by magistrates;[19] this was reflected in the arrangements made to select and train circuit judges, who had not had an equivalent jurisdiction before the Act[20] and district judges who would manage cases in the county courts.

Lord Woolf's proposals for civil procedure brought case management into mainstream judicial practice. Lord Woolf was concerned that litigation costs denied many people access to the courts. Allowing litigants to remain in control of litigation allowed one party to delay proceedings to the disadvantage of the other. Case management could improve access to justice, increase fairness and cut costs and delay.[21] Strong judicial leadership, a lengthy process of discussion and the involvement of the profession provided a very different context for this reform. The aims were broader: to improve case preparation; reduce delays; and cut the cost of litigation. The mechanics were more developed: pre-action protocols; the allocation of cases to tracks according to their complexity, with consequences for directions particularly on the use of experts; and the introduction of an 'overriding objective' in the Rules to guide courts, lawyers and litigants.[22]

---

[15] CHILDREN ACT ADVISORY COMMITTEE, *Annual Report 1992–3* LCD, London 1993, 50. Legal aid payments are related to the number and length of hearings.

[16] Co-location and shared administration started to be introduced in the mid 2000s.

[17] Children (Allocation of Proceedings) Order 1991 SI 1991/ 1677 r. 3(1)(b).

[18] CHILDREN ACT ADVISORY COMMITTEE, *Annual Report 1991–2*, LCD, London 1992, p. 18.

[19] LORD MACKAY, 'Speech on the inauguration of the Children Act Advisory Committee' London, 10.07.1991.

[20] County courts could commit children to the care of local authorities in matrimonial and various other proceedings but these were effectively extensions of their welfare jurisdiction. Wardships could also be transferred to the county court but only after the primary issue had been determined, see LOWE and WHITE, above n. 8.

[21] LORD WOOLF, *Final Report to the Lord Chancellor on the civil justice system in England and Wales,* HMSO, London 1996; A. ZUCKERMAN and R. CRANSTON (eds.), *Reform of Civil Procedure: Essays on 'Access to Justice'* Clarendon Press, Oxford 1995.

[22] Civil Procedure Rules 1998, 1998/3132, r. 1(1).

Although the civil procedure reforms were welcomed by the profession and applied to practice[23] they have not had the desired effects. Research evidence is limited but Zander has argued convincingly that there has been little impact on the length of proceedings and costs have risen overall. Pre-action protocols front-load case preparation and lead to additional expense in cases that settle, as most do.[24] And time expended in pre-application case preparation can mean that the process is as lengthy for those who litigate. Judicial concerns have focused on litigation costs. Sir Rupert Jackson's Review of civil litigation costs[25] identified failures in case management that contributed to high costs. These included: variable and individualistic approaches from the judiciary;[26] ineffective case management conferences;[27] and non-compliance with pre-action protocols.[28] Jackson LJ admitted that there was only anecdotal evidence but he was convinced that both costs and time were saved by case management by a judge with relevant experience, who 'identified the issues and gave directions focused upon the early resolution of those issues.'[29]

3. JUDICIAL CASE MANAGEMENT IN CHILDREN ACT CASES

Initial training for judges on the Children Act 1989 emphasised the interdisciplinary nature of decisions about children and included a one-day seminar on the criteria for allocation and timetabling rather than focusing on using judicial powers to take control of the litigation.[30] Judicial training did not provide a foundation for a shared understanding of the extent to which the court should control the litigation. Subsequently, Judicial Studies Board lectures on judicial case management reinforced judicial passivity by accepting that judges could generally expect to rely on directions drafted by the parties' lawyers.

The Children Act Advisory Committee had an important role in identifying and resolving issues of practice or resources and dissemination,[31] but its capacity to

---

23   T. PARKES, 'The Civil Procedure Rules ten years on; the practitioners' perspective' in D. DWYER (ed.), *The Civil Procedure Rules Ten Years On*, Oxford University Press, Oxford 2009.

24   M. ZANDER, 'The Woolf reforms: What's the verdict?' in DWYER, above n. 23.

25   R. JACKSON LJ, *Review of Litigation Costs, Final Report*, TSO, London 2010.

26   Ibid., para. 5.1(i).

27   Ibid., para. 5.1(ii).

28   Ibid., para. 6.1.

29   Ibid., para. 5.5.

30   LORD CHANCELLOR'S DEPARTMENT, Information sheet B91, July 1991; CHILDREN ACT ADVISORY COMMITTEE, above n. 15, 80–81.

31   Particularly through a good practice guide published when the Committee was subsumed into the Advisory Board on Family Law in 1997: *Children Act Advisory Committee, Handbook of Best Practice in Children Act cases*, LCD, London 1997.

monitor the operation of the Act required 'accurate diagnostic information on caseload, case progression and case management' not provided by the available statistics. The Committee viewed improving the statistics as a priority task.[32] Twenty years later, there was still 'almost unbelievable lack of management information' available to the Family Justice Review.[33]

Reported decisions highlighted the breadth of judges' powers:

> 'There is a spectrum of procedure for family cases from the ex parte application on minimal evidence to the full and detailed investigations on oral evidence which may be prolonged. Where on that spectrum a judge decides a particular application should be placed is a matter for his discretion.'[34]

Without mechanisms for developing common judicial views, this decision (and many others) resulted in inconsistency rather than greater judicial control. The Court of Appeal noted that sometimes 'corners were cut and procedural rules broken' and stated that judicial discretion and the 'relaxed procedures' of family justice had to be exercised with 'particular care.'[35] Rather than supporting case management, wide judicial discretion encouraged challenge, particularly by those representing parents.

It was only in 1995 that the President of the Family Division attempted to increase consistency by issuing a Practice Direction on Case Management for cases in the High Court or county courts. This applied to family proceedings generally and focused particularly on matters which would help to limit the length of hearings. The Direction stated that reductions of cost and delay 'made it necessary for the court to assert greater control... than has hitherto been customary' and listed a number of issues including '(c) the time allowed for examination and cross-examination of witnesses' and '(d) the issues on which it wishes to be addressed' as matters for the court. The parties and their advisers were enjoined to use 'their best endeavours to reduce or eliminate issues for expert evidence'. The court's greater control was backed by threats of costs orders against practitioners who failed to conduct cases 'economically' and by the introduction of pre-trial reviews for all cases estimated to last five days or more.[36]

---

[32] CHILDREN ACT ADVISORY COMMITTEE, above n. 18, paras. 3.9 and 4.4.
[33] FAMILY JUSTICE REVIEW, *Interim Report* MoJ, London 2011, para. 13.
[34] *Re B (Minors)(Contact)* [1994] 1 FLR 1, 5G *per* Butler-Sloss LJ.
[35] *Re G (A minor)(Care: evidence)* [1994] 2 FLR 785, 797 *per* Waite LJ.
[36] Practice Direction *Case Management* [1995] 1 FLR 456. The President had no power to issue Practice Directions for the family proceedings court.

The problem of increasing delay was not solved. In 2000, the Lord Chancellor's Department established a 'scoping study' to examine once more the reasons for the increased duration of family proceedings, especially those under the Children Act 1989. It noted that a 'set of basic operating principles' had 'evolved through practice and experience' which formed 'the core of what is now referred to as case management.' It also reported that it received very different responses to its questions about case management and concluded that some variations in the time taken to determine cases resulted from 'the lack of a shared or consistent picture with regard to the principles underpinning case management.'[37]

Following this report, in an attempt to change in the whole approach to case management, the President of the Family Division encouraged the Lord Chancellor to establish an Advisory Committee. The Committee largely consisted of judges and lawyers but included representatives from local authorities, CAFCASS and the relevant government departments. The task of the Committee was to approve a draft protocol for care proceedings developed from current best practice.[38] Although the Committee focused on the court's role in reducing delay its Report listed major obstacles to success such as staff shortages in local authorities and CAFCASS;[39] the level of legal aid remuneration; and a shortage of court sitting days. This gave the clear indication that resources had to expand to meet case demands, rather than courts having to manage cases within the available resources.[40] The Protocol was drafted by Ernest Ryder QC with the assistance of two High Court and one County Court judge.[41]

The Protocol divided care proceedings into six stages (5 hearings) through which care proceedings could be completed in 40 weeks. It provided standard directions to assist judges and a code of guidance for experts. The process was supported by a series of checklists for lawyers, CAFCASS and the local authority, a timeline stating when each aspect should be completed and a new Practice Direction. This stated, 'The overriding objective is to enable the Court to deal with every care case a) justly, expeditiously, fairly and with the minimum delay' and also emphasized fairness and proportionate process.[42] The Protocol took up over 80 pages. It mapped out a detailed and complex system, drafted by judges who were

---

37   LORD CHANCELLOR'S DEPARTMENT, above n. 8, paras. 161–2.
38   LORD CHANCELLOR'S ADVISORY COMMITTEE ON JUDICIAL CASE MANAGEMENT IN PUBLIC LAW CHILDREN CASES, *Final Report* LCD, London 2003, published in the PRESIDENT OF THE FAMILY DIVISION AND LORD CHANCELLOR, *Protocol on Judicial Case Management in Public Law Children Act Cases* LCD, London 2003 (hereafter the Protocol).
39   The organization tasked with providing children's guardians and welfare reports.
40   For the opposite view of case management see: A. ZUCKERMAN, 'A reform of civil procedure – Rationing procedure rather than access to justice' (1995) 22 *Journal of Law and Society* 155.
41   Munby J, Coleridge J and HHJ Cryan.
42   Practice Direction (Care Cases, Judicial Continuity and Case Management) [2003] 2 FLR 719, para. 3.1.

experienced in the litigation of care proceedings in the High Court, rather than in the lower courts where the vast majority of cases are decided.

The Protocol failed to ensure case completion within 40 weeks; a review, conducted by those who had devised it, unsurprisingly received positive responses. However, concerns were expressed about the volume of paperwork generated and the inadequacy of judicial resources.[43] The Review suggested refinements, including flexibility in the timetable to fit with the best interests of the child, the extension of district judges' jurisdiction to contested final hearings and a review of the documents required.[44]

These refinements were introduced when the Protocol was replaced by the Public Law Outline (PLO) in 2008.[45] The PLO reduced the number of stages for care proceedings to four and added a pre-proceedings process, which local authorities are required to complete before making an application unless the case is urgent.[46] The Family Procedure Rules 2010 provided a legislative basis for the overriding objective and imposed on courts a legal duty to manage cases 'actively'.[47]

Case management for care proceedings is now clearly modelled on the principles applied in civil proceedings. However, the PLO is no more effective than the Protocol had been. Judges are not able to corral cases into four set hearings; courts continue to be clogged with numerous directions hearings; and timetables are derailed by non compliance by the parties, the failure of experts to submit reports promptly and a lack of court time.[48]

4. CULTURAL BARRIERS TO CASE MANAGEMENT

Entrenched beliefs about care proceedings and the role of the judiciary have made judges unwilling to exercise their case management role and encouraged lawyers to challenge their decisions. First, there is a widely held belief that lay magistrates should not have the power to remove children from their families.

---

[43] JUDICIAL REVIEW TEAM, *Thematic Review of the Protocol for Judicial Case Management in Public Law Children Act Cases* MoJ, London 2005.

[44] Ibid., paras. 26, 33 and 55.

[45] JUDICIARY OF ENGLAND AND WALES AND MINISTRY OF JUSTICE, *Public Law Outline*, MoJ, London 2008.

[46] *Children Act 1989 Guidance and Regulations, Vol 1 Court Orders*, TSO, London 2008, paras. 3.3–4, 3.27–33.

[47] Family Procedure Rules 2010 SI 2010/ 2955, r. 1.1, 1.4(1).

[48] J. PEARCE, J. MASSON and K. BADER, *Just Following Instructions?* School of Law, University of Bristol, Bristol 2011 36–46 and Annex 2 available from <www.bristol.ac.uk/law/research/researchpublications/>; P. JESSIMAN, P. KEOGH and J. BROPHY, *An Early Process Evaluation of the PLO*, Ministry of Justice Research Series 10/09 MoJ, London 2009.

Hard-pressed magistrates' clerks have tended to accede to requests for transfer; as transfer rates increased, confidence in the magistrates' courts declined and county courts became overburdened. Transfer policies and rates vary markedly but the majority of care cases are now heard in county courts.[49]

Secondly, although a strong culture of judicial independence may ensure that judges apply the law even where this conflicts with the will of government, it does not promote consistency or compliance with guidance. Judicial views that 'cases take as long as they need to take' have survived both the Protocol and the PLO, and are reflected in lengthy proceedings where being right is valued far higher than a decision in the child's timescale.[50] Inconsistency also leads to challenges; lawyers are unwilling to advise parents to accept proposals from the other parties if the court might make a more advantageous order.[51]

Thirdly, Pearce and colleagues found that judges and lawyers share understandings about care proceedings which encourage a liberal attitude to matters such as assessments, and discourage robust attitudes to timetabling, narrowing the issues or limiting hearings.[52] The 'draconian' nature of the court's powers, the belief that local authorities provide poor care, the assumption that children's rights generally coincide with parents' rights and the desire to achieve agreed resolution of the proceedings all combine to allow considerable latitude to parents and relatives who seek repeat assessments or adjournments.[53] Moreover, 'independent' assessments were acknowledged to be more influential with parents, who in the face of a negative report might concede, avoiding an unpleasant and time-consuming contest. The alternative, that hopeless contests should be prevented by judicial case management decisions, was not observed, although hearings were shortened in such cases with the agreement of counsel.[54]

5. PRACTICAL BARRIERS TO CASE MANAGEMENT

In order to manage litigation the judge must be knowledgeable about the law, familiar with the case and understand the implications of the directions for the parties. In most courts, the organisation of care proceedings and court

---

[49] Contrary to the Lord Chancellor's expectations, see above n. 19 and Magistrates' Courts Service Inspectorate, *Case administration in the family proceedings courts*, MCSI, London 2001, para. 2.2; J. Masson et al., *Care Profiling Study*, MoJ, London 2008, p. 10.

[50] Pearce, Masson and Bader, above n. 48, p. 52.

[51] R. Mnookin and M. Kornauser, 'Bargaining in the shadow of the law: The case of divorce' [1979] *Current Legal Problems* 65.

[52] Ibid., 49–52.

[53] Ibid., 125–6.

[54] Ibid., 127, 129 and 145.

administration generally contrive to make this impossible. This is not simply the unfortunate consequence of the need to balance competing demands but inherent in the structure established in 1991. Case management in the county courts was largely the work of district judges, who had no jurisdiction to hear contested final hearings.[55] This restriction combined with their lowly status in the judicial hierarchy, their isolation from circuit judges[56] and their lack of experience in contested cases has meant that they had lacked confidence in giving directions.

Judges can only become familiar with the issues in their cases if they read all the case documents. Where judicial continuity ensures that one judge conducts all the hearings then only that judge needs to commit time to reading the file. However, court administration and listing are arranged without much regard to the importance of either judicial continuity or reading time. Booth J, in her report on delay, advised that judges should make greater use of their powers to reserve cases,[57] reflecting the understanding that continuity was exceptional. Moreover, before the jurisdiction of district judges was extended in 2009 to include contested final hearings, continuity could only be achieved if the circuit judge took over the district judge's case management role.[58]

Lacking case familiarity, judges defer to the parties' legal representatives, accepting the proposed directions that the latter have agreed amongst themselves. Shortage of time as a result of busy court lists encourages judges to save time by accepting draft directions without question.[59] This approach to case management is both ineffective and self-defeating. Court time is taken up rubber-stamping directions agreed by the parties because so many directions hearings are crowded into the lists. Moreover, short directions appointments allow no time for contested matters, resulting in adjournments, further hearings and additional litigation costs.[60]

Fear of appeals also inhibits robust decision-making in directions hearings.[61] In care proceedings, the refusal of assessments, adjournments or party status is far more likely to be appealed than their grant.[62] Judges who applied the Public Law

---

55   Family Proceedings (Allocation to the Judiciary) Direction 1991.

56   P. DARBYSHIRE, *Sitting in Judgment*, Hart, Oxford 2011, ch. 12 and pp. 407–410.

57   M. BOOTH, *Avoiding delay in Children Act cases*, LCD, London 1996, para. 2.2.14.

58   Family Proceedings (Allocation to the Judiciary) Direction 2009, replacing [1999] 2 FLR 799.

59   PEARCE, MASSON and BADER, above n. 48; DARBYSHIRE, above n. 56, pp. 283–4.

60   Legal Aid payments for advocacy, including directions hearings are determined by the number and length of such events.

61   Judicial response in focus group conducted as research for the *Care Profiling Study*, below n. 62.

62   J. MASSON et al., *Care Profiling Study*, Ministry of Justice Research Series 4/08 MoJ, London 2008, pp. 50–51.

Outline strictly found that they were overturned by the Court of Appeal.[63] The Family Justice Review noted that 'Court of Appeal judgments have left judges unsupported and unclear whether they can refuse requests for assessments.'[64] In 2010, the President of the Family Division wrote to the family judges advising them of their responsibilities in case management stating that 'no judge should ever deal with a case on the basis that one discretionary outcome rather than another may find greater favour with an appellate tribunal'.[65] Lord Justice Jackson did not accept criticisms of the Court of Appeal's inconsistency in providing guidance on the Civil Procedure Rules but he did state that he considered it 'vital' for that court to support the 'robust but fair' case management decisions.[66]

6. CAN THE FAMILY JUSTICE REVIEW'S LIMIT OF 26 WEEKS[67] BE MADE TO WORK?

A change in culture will be required to make the Family Justice Review's proposed time limit for care proceedings effective.[68] Both the cultural and practical barriers to case management have to be overcome. Six months is a challenging limit – less than half the current average for care proceedings. Implementing it will challenge ingrained beliefs held by many people working in family justice, require judges to exercise their case management powers and lawyers to accept judicial control despite adverse consequences for their clients. In effect, this is the same 'extremely difficult' task that Cretney identified before the Children Act was implemented. Moreover, the history of failure of the earlier initiatives makes it more, not less, difficult; both judges and lawyers have come to accept that lawyers are in control, that cases can be decided by (lengthy) passage of time or by repeated expert assessments.[69] Judges and lawyers will have

---

63   *Re M (A Child)* [2009] EWCA Civ 315; *Re F (A Child)* [2010] EWCA Civ 375; *Re L-S* [2011] EWCA Civ 1022.

64   Family Justice Review, *Final Report*, MoJ, London 2011, para. 3.128.

65   N. Wall, *President's Guidance, Bulletin No 2 Case management decisions and appeals there from* (2010).

66   Rupert Jackson LJ, *Review of litigation costs, Final Report* TSO, London 2010, paras 7.1–2.

67   Family Justice Review, above n. 64, paras. 3.71–3.77.

68   N. Wall, 'Changing the culture: the role of the Bar and the Bench in management of cases involving children' Speech by the President of the Family Division to the Law Reform Committee of the Bar Council, 29.11.2011.

69   J. Masson, 'The use of experts in child care proceedings in England and Wales: benefits costs and controls' Paper presented to the 2nd Annual Conference of the Legal Research Network, Groningen, October 2010, available at <www.bristol.ac.uk/law/research/researchpublications/2011/alrnc2010masson.pdf>.

to change their ways of working and their ideas about what amounts to a fair trial;[70] initially more contested hearings can be expected.[71]

A statutory basis for the limit makes little difference – judges failed to comply with the PLO not because it was *only* a Practice Direction but because they considered it fairer, simpler and more convenient not to do so. Initially at least, the limit will not be readily accepted by practitioners who see it working against their client's interests. The limit or its application in specific cases is likely to be challenged on the basis that the complexity of the case makes such an approach incompatible with the European Convention on Human Rights, Art. 6.

There will certainly be cases, particularly that small minority with unexplained or contested injuries or illnesses, where it will not be possible to have an adequate trial within such a period. These are readily identified at application and should be allocated to a different track, leaving the limit and extension to apply to the majority of cases based on neglect or obvious ill-treatment. Indeed, it will be crucial that the category of cases outside the scheme remains tightly constrained to avoid the system becoming irrelevant.

Restricting cases to six months necessarily means reducing the volume of information considered and the depth of court scrutiny. As a consequence, there will be a reduction in the level of accuracy of decisions, leaving children unprotected or in care, inappropriately.[72] Indeed unless there is some consensus about the evidence required to show that a care order is necessary, local authorities may find themselves accused of failing to provide sufficient information and forced to do as much as now in a shorter time. More positively, a time limit will allow the resources used in court proceedings to be rationed in a more coherent way than through a system of queuing and waiting,[73] which necessarily has adverse consequences for children.

Control by senior judges will not be sufficient to secure consistency and compliance, or for monitoring the effects on other agencies and costs. The case for family justice management information remains at least as strong as when

---

[70] *R v A Local Authority & Others* [2011] EWCA Civ 1451 limiting the right to a further assessment will need to be applied to a wide range of cases where it might be argued that further expert evidence could identify whether a parent could provide adequate care.
[71] FAMILY JUSTICE REVIEW, above n. 64, para. 3.83.
[72] A. ZUCKERMAN, 'Quality and economy in civil procedure – The case for commuting correct judgments for timely judgments' (1994) 14 *Oxford Journal of Legal Studies* 353. The risk may be limited because local authorities currently operate high thresholds for intervention.
[73] B. SCHWARTZ, *Queuing and waiting: studies in the social organization of access and delay* University of Chicago Press, Chicago 1975; A. ZUCKERMAN, 'A reform of civil procedure – Rationing procedure rather than access to justice (1995) 22 *Journal of Law and Society* 155.

the Children Act was introduced. Judges need to be accountable for the resources they use (and those they demand from other agencies, litigants, including local authorities and the Legal Services Commission). The 'overriding objective' – which acknowledges the need for fair allocation of resources between cases – has to be applied on the basis that the resources for delivering justice are finite. Incorporating this into judicial case management and the management of the judiciary will be revolutionary.

OPENNESS AND TRANSPARENCY IN THE FAMILY COURTS

A Policy Journey 2005–2011

Mavis MACLEAN

Contents

1. INTRODUCTION

Stephen Cretney gave us a predominantly optimistic account of the development of family law in his definitive account *Family Law in the Twentieth Century: A History*,[1] which is as deep in its analysis as it is broad in its coverage. He describes how the state extended its control over marriage through defining the rules for eligibility, and the legal consequences of marriage and its termination. He then turns to the establishment of a family justice system constructed on rational principles with professionals committed to a conciliatory approach to adult disputes, and to prioritising the welfare of children at risk.

A good story with the prospect of a happy ending. But the first decade of the twenty-first century has seen increasing dissatisfaction with the world of family law. To some extent this has involved concerns about the law itself, but in recent years the criticism has more often been directed at the working of the family justice system, in particular concerns about delay in dealing with child protection

---

[1] S. CRETNEY, *Family Law in the Twentieth Century: A History*, Oxford University Press, Oxford 2003.

matters, and an overall antipathy to the adversarial and secretive work of the courts and lawyers dealing with family matters.

Public dissatisfaction is perhaps inevitable given the deep personal unhappiness of those who have recourse to family law. It has been fanned by media attention and fuelled by government antipathy to lawyers who are portrayed as profiting from distress and in particular from the public funds being spent on private quarrels through the legal aid scheme. This view survives despite research evidence to the contrary: Philip Lewis's review shows that the policy statements from government about the aggressive behaviour of lawyers are contradicted by a series of empirical studies which found a culture of conciliation.[2] Moreover, the English system remains admired: when experts from a number of other jurisdictions were invited by the Ministry of Justice (MoJ) as part of preparations for the work of the *Family Justice Review*,[3] they expressed widespread appreciation of the child focus of our family law, and admiration for the skilled judges and practitioners.[4]

This is not to say that there is no room for improvement. Any system can be better. There are plenty of ideas under discussion, from better software for listing court hearings, to taking most matters out of the courts and directing people to various other forms of dispute resolution. However, given the demands for reform, a more important question is why doesn't it happen? What happens along the way from ideas and plans for improving the system to achieving change?

This chapter focuses on one example of what appeared to be a widely accepted and sensible proposal for reform, the attempt to open up the family courts to public scrutiny. The story is a long one. The Constitutional Affairs Select Committee (CASC) raised the transparency issue in 2005. Government responded with lengthy consultations and proposals. Rule changes were made in 2009 to permit some increase in media access though not reporting, and legislation to take this further was enacted in the last days of the Labour administration in the Children Schools and Families Act, 2010. But by late 2011 implementation of Part 2 had been put on hold, and the matter had returned to the drawing board. We look here at what stood between a reform proposal and change: the people, the events and the policy landscape.

---

[2] P.S.C. Lewis, 'Assumptions about Lawyers in Policy Statements', Lord Chancellor's Department Research Series 1/00, February 2000.

[3] Set up in 2009: the *Family Justice Review: Final Report* was published by the MoJ in November 2011.

[4] M. Maclean, R. Hunter, F. Wasoff, L. Ferguson, B. Bastard and E. Ryrstedt, 'Family Law in Hard Times: can we learn from other jurisdictions?' (2011) 33 *Journal of Social Welfare and Family Law* 319.

2. THE TRANSPARENCY DEBATE

In 2005 the Constitutional Affairs Select Committee, (CASC) responsible for parliamentary scrutiny of the Department of Constitutional Affairs (now the Ministry of Justice) reported a lack of confidence in the Family Justice System and requested action. This lack of confidence had been extensively reported by the media, fuelled by the complaints from two sources: firstly, fathers groups concerned about the secrecy and perceived bias of the family courts dealing with applications from non-resident fathers for contact and residence, and, secondly, parents involved in care proceedings, who were not able to discuss their cases with advisers or even other experts when seeking to appeal.

In England and Wales family proceedings have traditionally been held in private, unlike criminal matters, on the grounds that the family courts deal with matters which are private to the parties concerned and where the children's welfare requires that their privacy should be protected. But the position was complex and confusing, with different rules for different courts. In the Court of Appeal, which is not a trial court hearing parties or witnesses, hearings are public. But in the trial courts – Family Proceedings Courts, the County Court and the High Court – cases concerning children were mainly held in private though judicial discretion permitted hearings in financial applications relating to children to be open to press and public, and the FPCs (formerly the Magistrates Courts) have always been open though seldom attended. There is, however, an important distinction between access to a court, and what may be reported about what takes place there. In 2005 CASC sought to protect the courts from allegations of secrecy and bias by proposing greater access for press and the public. But at the same time they were concerned to restrict what might be reported. They asked that anonymised judgements should in the normal course of events be delivered in court, but that the press should be restricted to publishing only matters made public by the court.

The transparency debate began with concerns about documents being used outside court after a hearing.[5] But the debate moved swiftly on to incorporate concerns about who should be allowed into court, and what they should be allowed to report. Some argued that allowing the press into court even with reporting restrictions would enable them to act as a proxy for the public and thereby allay public anxiety about secrecy. Others argued that the press would not be interested in attending court if they were not allowed to publish the stories of identifiable individuals.

---

[5]   DCA, *Disclosure of Information in family proceedings Cases involving Children* Cm 6623, HMSO, London 2004.

In September 2005 I chaired a roundtable discussion of the broader issues in Oxford, with judges, lawyers, academics, representatives of children's associations, psychiatrists and psychologists, and officials coming together to discuss whether family courts should continue to be held in private or not, how judgments could be used to improve openness, and how vulnerable adults and children could be protected. These stakeholders were unanimously opposed to the idea of making courts open, and to any increase in reporting. There was however, a growing interest in having more written anonymised judgments to be a source of information to a child involved in a case later in life. The argument was that if a child were to grow up without seeing one or both parents, that child should have access to the decision made by the court and the reasons for that decision as of right. At this meeting participants were also informed about the position in Australia and recent changes in New Zealand. In Australia courts had traditionally been open, then closed in response to sensationalist reporting in the 1970s. The government had reversed the position again in 1983 to a more open system but publishing restrictions were tightly managed and respected by the press, perhaps because the sanctions for breach included a custodial sentence for a serious offence.

Despite this critical stakeholder response the DCA went ahead with a consultation exercise in 2006.[6] The proposals put forward at this stage were that the press should be allowed to attend court hearings on behalf of and for the benefit of the public, though a court could exclude them; there were to be direct reporting restrictions; and new rules should be consistent across all family courts and proceedings. The consultation process continued in October 2006 with a small stakeholder meeting, a 'Day of Perspectives', introduced by the Minister for Family Justice Harriet Harman and chaired again by myself. This meeting to discuss openness was held, to the amusement of the participants, in the Bunker, the secret underground cabinet war rooms below St James Park used in World War II, historically the most secret location in London. Representatives of the family bar and a fathers groups supported greater openness, though for rather different reasons, and the media representative went furthest in demanding total openness, comparing the current position in this jurisdiction to that in the Republic of North Korea. But the judges and medical experts present urged caution, the former to avoid the potential for recognition of a family after hearings in a local court, and the latter describing how such a requirement would contravene ethical medical practice of respect for patient confidentiality. The debate had become clearly divided into, on the one hand, a widespread desire for better accountability and consistency, and, on the other, a concern to protect the privacy and even the safety of vulnerable parties.

---

6   DCA, *Confidence and Confidentiality: Improving transparency and privacy in family courts* Cm 6886, TSO, London 2006.

The following year the responses to the 2006 consultation were published.[7] By this time the government focus had moved a long way from the early emphasis on disclosure of specific documents in specific cases to a focus on broader concerns about confidence in the justice system. This was expressed as more interest in explaining to the wider public how the justice system works, and on the need to give information for children in proceedings to access in later life. In the meantime, however, the CAFCASS Children Panel had met with groups of children and found strong opposition to any public access to information about their private lives.[8] Finally a small expert seminar at the Nuffield Foundation revealed an increasingly critical response to the policy proposals, with concerns now being raised by senior members of the judiciary, some of whom had supported the proposals at an earlier stage, about the need to protect children.

These consultation findings were not welcomed by government, which then decided to hold yet another consultation in June 2007.[9] The approach was new in that it no longer talked about who should have the right to enter the courts, but instead about what information should come out of the courts in order to improve public understanding of court process and confidence in the system. This paper went further than the previous position towards protecting the anonymity of children in proceedings.

As the matter progressed and officials began to work on detailed proposals, the policy appeared to become more complex and the response even more vigorously conflicted. Opposition to the plans grew as the implications became clearer. Organisations for children, lawyers, and medical experts became more critical, and senior members of the judiciary who had originally welcomed the opportunity to show the world how they were doing their difficult job began to worry about the impact of easier access to proceedings on families especially in care proceedings. The response polarised, with those working in the justice system becoming more critical of the plans, while the press became more and more strident in their demand for openness. Even within government there were divided views. The then Lord Chancellor, Lord Falconer, was knowledgeable about the practice of family law including child protection work. His junior minister responsible for family justice was Harriet Harman, whose sister Sarah Harman while practising as a family solicitor had herself been involved in and criticised for her breach of the rules preventing the sharing of information given by expert witnesses in a children case taken to appeal. Harriet Harman was a

---

7   DCA, *Confidence and Confidentiality: Improving transparency and privacy in the family courts – Government Response* Cm 7036, TSO London 2007.

8   The Government published an illustrated 'Young People's Guide to the Confidence and Confidentiality Response Paper' assuring children that their voices were being listened to.

9   MINISTRY OF JUSTICE, *Confidence and Confidentiality: openness in the family courts – A new approach* Cm 7131, TSO, London 2007.

highly visible junior minister with a strong personal commitment to the cause of transparency, and her involvement strengthened the move to legislate.

In December 2008 the MoJ published a reassessment of their views in response to the latest consultation paper together with a new set of proposals from the recently appointed Secretary of State for Justice, Jack Straw. These new proposals moved back towards the original pursuit of openness at all costs and away from the earlier 'new approach' which had placed a greater emphasis on the needs of children both for privacy during proceedings and for access to information about decisions taken and the reasons for them in later life. The 2008 proposals were based on 3 newly-defined principles: to improve confidence in the family courts, to protect the interests of children and vulnerable adults, and to enable more lay support for adults in court, the latter point implying that the openness agenda had become linked with the ministry-wide agenda of trying to keep parties out of the hands of lawyers and courts.

Public information about court procedures was to be improved, and some anonymised judgments were to be placed on a website so that members of the public could see what decisions were being made and the reasons for them. It was also planned that parties were to be given a copy of any judgment made. There would be provision for protecting a child's identity after a case closed, but it would become possible for parties to disclose case information for the purpose of seeking advice, and for onward disclosure to be made to others with the permission of the party making the original disclosure. However, the proposal to allow media presence in all the family courts unless the court decided against it could not be accomplished without primary legislation. New guidelines for media access to the court came into effect in April 2009, with legislation remaining in the wings.

3. OFFICIAL INPUT

In the four years since the Select Committee's original criticism, there had been four consultation exercises, with published responses. The procedures set out for such exercises are precise and demanding. In order to present cogent proposals background statements are required and these must be grounded in precise work on the discrepancies between practice in the different courts, what happens in other jurisdictions, what exactly might be formulated in each set of proposals, and what the implications might be. As this work progresses, the level of detailed consideration given to defining the circumstances in which the media might attend becomes more precise, for example whether accreditation for the press would be needed, what might be recorded and published, whether the media should have access to documents as well as listening to what is said in court (as this forms only a small part of a case, particularly in care cases), should such documents be redacted, what would happen in a small court without a photo copier, could documents be taken out of court to be copied, and so on. The broader published questions posed are then developed in consultation with ministers and informed by stakeholder meetings. The subsequent departmental responses are then prepared based on careful and detailed analysis by officials of the information submitted, for example when the same response was received from large numbers of members of an organisation the report included analysis treating these responses as individual replies but also as a single organisational reply. Finally the broader interpretation placed on the responses is then agreed with ministers.

The amount of official time invested was considerable, especially at a time of pressure on Whitehall to scale down the workforce. Not only policy work but also detailed legal analysis was needed. Concerns about the compatibility of the proposal with Human Rights legislation had to be checked, particularly after government began to indicate that adoption proceedings could be held in public. Harriet Harman argued that if people must marry in public under English law then surely they should also adopt in public. The professionals were horrified at the lack of regard for the privacy of adopters and children, and lawyers were concerned by the apparent blurring of the distinction between the process as part of care proceedings of freeing a child for adoption, which would be subject to the new media access rules, and the actual legal adoption process which is quite separate. Article 8 of the European Convention on Human Rights provides a right to respect for private family life, a right which can on only be interfered with in some circumstances e.g. to protect the child and must be proportionate and temporary. Similarly Article 6 which provides for a fair and public hearing within a reasonable time and for public pronouncement of judgments is qualified to allow the exclusion of the press from a trial where the interests of juveniles or the protection of the private life of parties requires.

In addition to the developmental policy work on moving from a ministerial interest in opening up the family courts to specific workable proposals for change in practice, the new interest in publishing court decisions and the reasons for them led to the need for a pilot project to be known as the Family Court Information Pilot (FCIP). This pilot work would, it was hoped, make a positive contribution to dealing with the problems raised by CASC, without threatening the privacy of families, by increasing public knowledge and understanding of the work of the courts. In cases where a child was to be removed from the care of a parent or prevented from having contact with a parent for a considerable period, a sample of courts were to be asked to prepare an anonymised version of the judgment leading to this separation, to be posted on the BAILII[10] website. This website already published recent judgments of interest to practitioners, and the organisers were willing to support this initiative.

The work involved in setting up this programme of work was extensive. The definition of cases to be included was agreed with the President of the Family Division. Asking courts to participate was not easy, at a time of acute pressures on the system for both courts staff and judiciary. Finally, the Cardiff and Wolverhampton County and Magistrates Courts and Leeds Magistrates Court agreed to help. The MoJ made a contribution towards the cost of court administrative duties, which arose directly from participation, and paid for transcription services for pilot cases. Setting up the pilot required a series of meetings with judiciary, court staff and also the setting up of an advisory group of experts and practitioners, of which I was a member. This group had lively meetings about the aim and scope of the project, which needed to then be brought into line with what the courts were able to do. But from an early stage there was a firm commitment to evaluating the project rigorously, as will be described below.

As the aim of the pilot was to record anonymised decisions and reasons for this group of cases, there was surprise among some members for the Advisory Group on discovering that although the FPCs have always provided decisions and reasons for the decision to parties at the conclusion of a case, that County Court practice differed. Where a case had been contested in a County Court a judgment, either oral and recorded, for which a transcript could be requested and paid for, or written and handed down later would be given setting out the reasons for the order made. But in cases where the matter was not contested it was not unusual for an order to be made without a judgement. Some concern was expressed about these differences, and it was decided in consultation with the President that a short judgment would be requested in cases where there was no other form of explanation of the decision made. The pilot was also asked to look at how copies of judgements could be given to parties at the end of the case, and how they might be stored and made accessible to the children involved in the case in later life. The present position is that the MoJ is only able to store Children Act files for 18 years in county courts and 25 years in the FPCs. Local authority files are kept for 75 years, but do not at present always include a judgement.

As preparation for the FCIP continued during the early part of 2009, there appeared to be a quieter period in the debate, and the prospect of legislation seemed more remote. However, over the summer months of 2009, at a time when the Labour Government was attracting harsh criticism from the press after

---

10   The British and Irish Legal Intelligence Institute: an independent not-for-profit website.

12 years in power, a number of visits were paid to the Justice Secretary Jack Straw in the MoJ by the *Times* journalist Camilla Cavendish who was running a campaign for more openness in the family courts.[11] Her work was welcomed by the media with a journalistic award, and by Jack Straw, just as it had been initially welcomed by all those supporting openness and transparency in the justice system before they became immersed in the detailed implications. It might also be asked whether the re-emergence of an issue which might enable the government to improve its poor treatment by the media might have had some attractions.

Whatever the combination of principled argument and political need, Jack Straw in the height of summer 2009[12] demanded action in the form of a draft bill to enable the press to attend more cases, and to report the substance of a case as long as the parties were not identified. Some sensitive personal information could be excluded, but expert witnesses including medical witnesses were to be named.

Officials at MoJ began work with colleagues at Department for Children Schools and Families (DCSF), which by this time had responsibility for all services for children, including CAFCASS. At this stage a further division arose. In this conflicted debate we had seen already seen the growing divide between the arguments for openness and privacy, and between government and the press versus the professionals working with families in the justice system including the judiciary. Now, as primary legislation was to be drafted, a rift emerged between the two government departments working on the draft bill.

Not surprisingly, the DCSF were not receptive to the apparent failure to give priority to the welfare of children, and were also unhappy at the speed with which the matter was being pursued. A first draft bill taking on board the views of the then Secretary of State at DCSF, Ed Balls, was not acceptable to the Secretary of State for Justice, Jack Straw. He required a second draft to reflect his views more clearly. This second draft was duly prepared by officials for parliamentary draftsmen but remained unacceptable to DCSF.

Neither ministers nor their special advisers were able to bring about a compromise, and the matter was handed back to officials who produced the next draft which divided the proposals into two stages, moving from moderate changes to increase openness to more fundamental changes giving more access to press and better opportunities for reporting after implementation and review of stage 1. The first stage would continue the present position under the 2009

---

[11] See e.g. *The Times*, 09.07.2009.
[12] Public statement 09.07.2009.

rule change on media attendance at court hearings at an expanded group of cases, but would not change access to documents. Children and their families would have life-long anonymity unless the court said otherwise. The media would be able to report the substance of cases they observed if a number of conditions were to be met, but some sensitive information would remain on a banned list. Experts paid by the court could be named, but others giving evidence in the course of their normal employment would have their identity protected. Anyone could publish an anonymised version of the text or summary of a court order except in adoption cases, but court judgments could not be reported unless the court specifically allowed this. The sanction for breach would remain contempt of court. The second stage would remove some of these qualifications, including the banned information list, the restriction on naming any experts and access to documents.

These proposals went far beyond the level of openness established by the recent changes in Australia and New Zealand.[13] The strong concerns of the Interdisciplinary Alliance for Children were not fully reported by the media, but were made known to government. There was a growing expectation that as the Labour government moved towards a general election in May 2010 that these controversial proposals would be quietly lost. But this was not what happened. To the surprise of officials and experts the bill was selected by the Whips for the process known as 'wash up', by which a number of bills are chosen for expedited passage through a parliament reaching the end of its term. The Children Schools and Families Act, of which the transparency clauses are a small part, became law in April 2010.[14]

But a key amendment had been accepted. Commencement of the Second Stage of the Act was not to take place until 18 months after Stage 1, and was also to be dependent on a review of the Transparency and Court Information (Anonymised Judgements) Pilot (better known as the Family Courts Information Pilot, FCIP) being put before parliament by the Secretary of State for Justice.

4. THE FCIP EVALUATION: THE LAST CHAPTER

The Family Court Information Pilot ran in five courts from November 2009 to December 2010. Evaluation had been carefully planned by the Advisory Board to

---

13   J. BROPHY and C. ROBERTS, 'Openness and transparency in Family Courts: what the experience of other countries tell us about reform in England and Wales', Oxford Family Policy Briefing Paper 5, University of Oxford 2009; R.H. GEORGE and C. ROBERTS, 'The Media and the Family Courts – key information and questions about the Children, Schools and Families Bill', Oxford Family Policy Briefing Paper 6, University of Oxford 2009.

14   See also M. MACLEAN and J. KURCZEWSKI, *Making Family Law*, Hart, Oxford 2011, ch. 5 for an account of the early development of the transparency debate.

review the impact of the process on those working in the five courts, the benefits to the parties and the wider public of the availability of a wider range of judgments and the potential cost of rolling out the programme nationally. The department's statisticians had devised a pro forma on which the courts would record the time taken by individual court staff and judiciary on the various tasks, from which the economists could estimate the running costs. The analysts, with myself as an academic adviser, had carried out interviews with judiciary and court staff at each court shortly after the pilot began, and again shortly before the end of the pilot period to seek their views and those of local practitioners on the feasibility and value of the exercise. In addition, a user survey had been run by BAILII to report the views of those who had accessed the website.[15] And finally local press comments on the pilot courts were checked for any comment, but little was found.

Evaluation is always a difficult task. If it is done too soon after a change in practice there is a risk of failing to capture impact which has yet to appear. If it is done too late, events will have moved on, and a particular political context and potential for change may have passed. In this instance the timing was set down in statute, and the process was completed over the summer and the report made available to ministers by the beginning of September 2011. The results were clear, and helpful, making clear how the essential dilemmas of privacy versus transparency play out in practice.

The press, who had pressed long and loudly for change were not satisfied with the process, as while it gave detail on 165 cases it did not provide the names and addresses they wanted. The judiciary, court staff and local professionals were supportive of the aims of increasing understanding of the work of the courts, as were the majority of the 77 users from the wider public who responded to the BAILII user survey. But there remained strong concerns about protecting the privacy of children and families. Court staff saw the additional work as not inherently difficult, but were anxious about a long term additional burden at a time when they were losing staff and resources. The judges too were under pressure, but were able to cope with the process of anonymisation and also spoke of the challenge of being asked to develop the skill to write judgments with a view to being understood by the wider public. But overall, the problem with the website material is that it is large, complex, and difficult to navigate. The most enthusiastic users were academic researchers and policy analysts, for whom it is an invaluable detailed record of a wide range of cases, rather than the material available at present which focuses on cases of legal interest.

---

[15]   56,887 hits were recorded between January 2010 and March 2011.

The FCIP Review was published in September 2011.[16] The Government's Response accepted the recommendation that the measures set out in Part 1 of the Children Schools and Families Act 2010 on how to achieve greater transparency should not be implemented and stated that work should begin afresh.[17] The *Family Justice Review: Final Report* published in November 2011 agreed.

5. CONCLUSION

My final observations are brief. In 2005 the government made a positive response (transparency) to a perceived problem (secrecy and bias). It had a clear aim, senior judiciary were initially sympathetic and the media was strongly supportive. On further reflection (2005–9) problematic implications for practice (harm to children and families through invasion of privacy) were identified. Radical legislation with an inbuilt delaying device was passed in 2010. In 2009–10 a pilot exercise was carried out and evaluated in 2011, and gave rise to suggestions for improving later life access for children to information about orders affecting their family life. A great deal of work was carried out by officials, who worked hard and creatively on these suggestions for reform, but were simply unable to make progress on the matter partly because the precise proposals were limited by poor understanding of the day-to-day working of the court, but mainly because there was genuine non-negotiable conflict between the aims of increasing openness and protecting the privacy of the vulnerable.

A rushed and radical reform was sidestepped, but useful small steps may yet be taken. The road from good idea to good practice is long and hard.

---

16   <www.justice.gov.uk/downloads/publications/policy/moj/family-courts-information-pilot.pdf>.

17   Response (published 13.10.2010) to JUSTICE COMMITTEE, *Operation of the Family Courts: Sixth Report of Session 2010–12*, TSO, London 2011.

FIFTY YEARS IN THE TRANSFORMATION OF AMERICAN FAMILY LAW: 1960–2011

Sanford N. Katz

Contents

1. INTRODUCTION

In his masterwork *Family Law in the Twentieth Century*[1] Stephen Cretney examined the role of Parliament and Royal Commissions in the development of family law during the last century. That focus would not work in the United States, where family law is, for the most part, state law. The federal Congress and the federal Department of Health and Human Services play a limited role mostly dealing with the establishment, administration and funding of federal social and child welfare programs and less with substantive family law issues.[2] Until the 1970s, the United States Supreme Court rarely heard family law cases other than those relating to jurisdictional and procedural issues with the striking exception

---

[1]   S. Cretney, *Family Law In The Twentieth Century: A History*, Oxford University Press, Oxford 2003.

[2]   The federal Congress' enactment of the In Defense of Marriage Act in 1996 is an exception. The Act stated that one state did not have to honor the same-sex marriage laws of another state. In another section, it stated that for federal purposes, marriage was defined as a union of a man and a woman. The effects of the two sections were (1) to limit the Full Faith and Credit Clause of the United States Constitution and (2) to restrict federal benefits to heterosexual marriages: 28 U.S.C. §1738C (2003); 1 U.S.C. §7 (2003). The Act was found unconstitutional by the Federal District Court in Massachusetts in the case of *Gill v. Office of Personnel Management* 699 F.Supp.2d 374 (D. Mass. 2010). There is a proposal in the current session of Congress to repeal the law.

of *Loving v. Virginia*,[3] in which the United States Supreme Court struck down a Virginia miscegenation statute that banned interracial marriages and decided that there was a fundamental right to marry.

During the last half of the twentieth century, state courts and state legislatures both played a major role in family law, a development that reflects a change from the early part of the century when judges, not legislators, were the significant law makers. Indeed, the last half of the twentieth century saw a tension, even a struggle, between the two branches of government in defining the law. Where, for example, family law doctrines, like the best interests of the child or equitable distribution of property were once left to judicial discretion for definition, state legislatures increasingly enacted statutes removing that discretion and mandating judges to apply statutory standards. Child support was another area in which state legislatures set down mandatory guidelines for determining the amount of support to be provided instead of leaving the decision to judicial discretion. By defining terms and determining actual amounts for support, the legislature succeeded in its goal of establishing uniformity in approach to decision-making and outcomes in the case of child support.

In examining family law in the United States during the twentieth century, one is struck by the enormous changes that have occurred from the 1960s until the beginning of the twenty-first century. Looking back, they reflect new developments in society which in most instances law has followed; although in at least two it may have prompted them

2.   THE 1960s AND 1970s

The 1960s were better known for reforms concerning the termination of marriage than for issues regarding formation. In an earlier decade, progress had been made in humanizing the divorce process by introducing mediation and counseling services. What we now refer to as the family court was first established in Ohio. It has provided the prototype for other family courts in the United States. The aim of those courts was and is to provide an informal setting and, in some instances, to minimize the adversarial nature of the divorce procedure. At the same time, divorce law itself was being reformed by the introduction of

---

[3]   388 U.S. 1 (1967). During the 1960s, however, the United States Supreme Court decided *Application of Gault*, 387 U.S. 1 (1967), which held that a juvenile was entitled to the five basic constitutional rights accorded to adults at the adjudicatory phase of a hearing: notice, counsel, confrontation, self-incrimination, and appeal. That case gave rise to a new and defined area of the law. *See generally* S.J. Fox, *Juvenile Courts in a Nutshell,* West, St. Paul 1977. It was during the 1970s and 1980s that the United States Supreme Court began to decide a significant number of family law cases.

'no-fault', with the result that the emphasis in such cases shifted from proving a fault ground, which in some instances was manufactured by the litigants, to the assignment of property and child custody. In a sense, the introduction of no-fault divorce in state statutes was recognition of what was already taking place in divorce practice. Originally, the number of American jurisdictions that offered no-fault divorce was limited, but 50 years later, all American jurisdictions have some sort of no-fault built into their divorce laws.[4]

The assignment of property upon divorce also changed radically. Traditionally, it was determined by title. The new method took into consideration the contribution of the spouses to the acquisition of property and sought to divide the property fairly. Equitable distribution, the term used to describe the new method of assigning property, took into account the contemporary view of marriage, which was based on equality. No longer could it be said that 'marriage is one and that one is the husband.'[5] The demise of the title theory of property division was possible because more and more women were entering the labor force and were able to earn an income. That was in contrast to an earlier period when a woman's wealth was determined by her family relationships, mostly by inheritance, and when she stayed at home caring for the family's house and the children.

In the area of child custody, equality also became a dominant issue. While in the past mothers were more likely to be awarded custody than fathers, the new approach gave fathers an equal chance actively to seek custody. The maternal preference rule, long adhered to both in fact and in law, was basically abandoned and new forms of custodial arrangements took its place, such as the primary caretaker presumption and joint custody.[6] The primary caretaker presumption developed from the influence of psychologists who wrote that the person who tends to the child on a day-to-day basis and has formed a positive emotional attachment to the child should be given preference in a custodial conflict. That was the position expressed in the influential book *Beyond the Best Interests of the Child*, written by Professor Joseph Goldstein, Dr. Albert Solnit and Anna Freud and published in 1973.[7] Joint custody, a disposition that would give mothers and fathers an opportunity to raise their child on a shared basis, recognized the equal

---

4   *See* S.N. KATZ, *Family Law in America*, Oxford, New York 2011, pp. 82–86.

5   Ibid., p. 37.

6   *See* S.N. KATZ, '"That They May Thrive" Goal of Child Custody: Reflections on the Apparent Erosion of the Tender Years Presumption and the Emergence of the Primary Caretaker Presumption' (1992) 8 *Journal of Contemporary Health Law & Policy* 123. See also S. N. KATZ, above n. 4, pp. 104–108.

7   J. GOLDSTEIN, A. SOLNIT and A. FREUD, *Beyond the Best Interests of the Child*, The Free Press, New York 1973.

role played by mothers and fathers in child rearing and began to be awarded in divorce cases.

At the same time, fathers who believed that their legal rights in areas other than divorce cases had been minimized began to assert themselves. Indeed, during this decade and the beginning of the next, laws relating to fatherhood were challenged in courts. Perhaps the best known was *Stanley v. Illinois*,[8] in which the United States Supreme Court decided that an unwed father had rights that should be protected when the custody of his children was involved. That the United States Supreme Court had taken the case may reflect its concern for fathers and perhaps a desire to clarify their rights.

In *Stanley*, Peter Stanley had lived for 18 years with the mother of his three children, whom he had not married, when the mother died. The children were removed from their home and became the subject of a dependency action resulting in their becoming wards of the court. Illinois law at that time declared unwed fathers unfit to have custody of their children without any judicial proceeding. Represented by a legal aid lawyer, Mr. Stanley argued that to treat him differently from a married father resulted in his being denied equal protection of the law guaranteed by the Fourteenth Amendment to the United States Constitution. The Illinois Supreme Court affirmed the removal of the children from his custody, asserting that it was Mr. Stanley's status as an unwed father that was the critical factor, not his fitness for fatherhood. That decision was appealed to the United States Supreme Court.

The United States Supreme Court viewed Mr. Stanley's plight differently, stating that unwed fathers are parents and as such are constitutionally entitled to a hearing on their fitness before their children can be removed from their custody. The Court held that Mr. Stanley was indeed denied his constitutional rights and ordered a hearing at which Mr. Stanley could be present and argue his case, which he did, and won.

The case, however, is best known for footnote 9 in the opinion, which reads:

> 'We note in passing that the incremental cost of offering unwed fathers an opportunity for individualized hearing on fitness, appears to be minimal. If unwed fathers, in the main, do not care about the *disposition* of their children, they will not appear to demand hearings. If they do care, under the scheme here held invalid, Illinois would admittedly at some later time have to afford them a properly focused hearing in a custody or adoption proceeding.

---

8   405 U.S. 645 (1972).

Extending opportunity for hearing to unwed fathers who desire and claim competence to care for their children creates no constitutional or procedural obstacle to foreclosing those unwed fathers who are not so included.'[9]

That statement, buried in a footnote, put in question the constitutionality of state adoption statutes in the United States. Ordinarily, those statutes did not provide for notice or an opportunity to be heard for unwed fathers. Unless they were present and available to assist the birth mother during her pregnancy, unwed fathers were, more or less, invisible figures. Now the highest court in the United States empowered them in the adoption proceeding.

A major question, however, was how to implement the requirement that unwed fathers be notified in an adoption proceeding. Again, if an unwed father's identity and address are known, notice presents little difficulty. It is the absence of those facts that create difficulties. One approach to address this problem was the establishment of Putative Father Registries. These Registries or statutes that act like a Registry are available in 25 states. Their purpose is to give a putative father the opportunity to be notified if a child he fathered is put up for adoption. For example, the Arizona Statute reads:

'A person who is seeking paternity, who wants to receive notice of adoption proceedings, and who is the father or claims to be the father of a child shall file notice of a claim of paternity and of his willingness and intent to support the child to the best of his ability with the State Registrar of Vital Statistics in the Department of Health Services. The Department of Health Services shall provide forms for the purpose of filing the notice of a claim of paternity...'[10]

That the Putative Father Registry in New York did not violate the Due Process and Equal Protection Clauses of the United States Constitution was decided in *Lehr v. Robertson*,[11] the case in which Justice John Paul Stevens wrote his now-famous lines about fatherhood:

'The significance of the biological connection is that it offers the natural father an opportunity that no other male possesses to develop a relationship with his offspring. If he grasps that opportunity and accepts some measure of responsibility for the child's future, he may enjoy the blessings of the parent-child relationship and make uniquely valuable contributions to the child's development. If he fails to do so, the Federal Constitution will not automatically compel a State to listen to his opinion of where the child's best interests lie.'[12]

---

9 Ibid., 657.
10 Ariz. Rev. Stat. §8–106.01(A)-(B) (2007).
11 463 U.S. 248 (1983).
12 Ibid., 262.

The rights of unwed fathers were clarified to some extent by the United States Supreme Court late in the 1970s and in the 1980s, the time period for *Stanley v. Illinois* and *Lehr v. Robertson*. The United States Supreme Court had decided *Quilloin v. Walcott*[13] five years before *Lehr*. In *Quilloin*, the Court held that an unwed father's due process and equal protection rights were not violated by a Georgia statute that only required the consent of the birth mother and not the consent of the putative father in an adoption case if the putative father had not complied with the legitimation procedures, had not supported the child and was generally not involved with the child's upbringing One year later in *Caban v. Mohammed*,[14] the Court was faced with a putative father who had supported his children for a time and had developed a relationship with them. The New York statute had grouped all putative fathers together. The Court held that by so doing, New York's statute was 'over-broad'.

In addition to the 1960s and 1970s being decades in which the United States Supreme Court defined the rights of fathers, it was also the period in which the United States government took the lead in developing model child welfare legislation, which a half century later would prove to be invaluable in terms of protecting children.[15] It was during the 1960s when federal government adoption and foster care specialists recognized that there were a large number of children in foster care for periods longer than a few years, and that the longer the children were in foster care, the more likely it was that they would neither be reunited with their natural parents nor be adopted.

The challenge for the government specialists was to determine the reasons for this state of affairs, and they found them. They were twofold: (1) the inadequacies of state child welfare systems to move children out of the foster care system and into permanent homes and (2) the inability of some suitable adoptive parents, such as foster parents, for example, to adopt the children because of their lack of financial resources. Normally, the federal government does not get involved in child welfare laws. Family law generally and child welfare laws specifically are matters for state legislatures. The role of the federal government is to provide guidance in the form of model legislation and, where appropriate, to provide financial assistance for federal programs. The states can then look to the model legislation for purposes of enacting their own version.

---

[13]   434 U.S. 246 (1978).
[14]   441 U.S. 380 (1979).
[15]   I refer here to the child sexual abuse scandals involving Roman Catholic priests that were uncovered during the 1990s and the beginning of the new century and are still being revealed. See further S.N. KATZ, 'Protecting Children Through State and Federal Laws' in B. ATKIN (ed.), *The International Survey of Family Law 2007*, Jordan, Bristol 2007, pp. 310–11.

A Model Act to Free Children for Permanent Placement[16] was thus developed to provide a new approach to proceedings designed to terminate parental rights. The title given to the Act was meant to illustrate the fact that permanent placement – not termination – was the goal. So the focus was on removing the barriers to placement, but not at the expense of denying natural parents the opportunity to rehabilitate themselves or be rehabilitated.

The two most creative model Acts proposed during this time were the Model State Subsidized Adoption Act[17] and the Model Mandatory Child Abuse and Neglect Reporting Laws.[18] The former was designed to provide a financial subsidy to children who were declared 'hard to place' by reason of their age, their physical or mental health, or their being a member of a sibling group. The most common factor was their age or their need for some kind of long term medical, psychiatric or educational services. Ordinarily these children were in foster care and the likely candidates to be their adoptive parents were their foster parents who were unable to adopt the children due to financial issues. Since adoption terminated foster care payments, subsidized adoption was intended to fulfill those financial needs. Today, 30-plus years after Gallagher and Katz proposed the idea, all American jurisdictions have some sort of subsidized adoption program.

The Model Mandatory Child Abuse and Neglect Reporting Act was controversial because it had the potential for interfering with the privacy of the parent-child relationship and also the doctor-patient relationship. The idea behind the Act was to mandate the reporting of suspected child abuse or neglect by those people, often professionals such as doctors, nurses and teachers, who would be in a position to discover evidence of either abuse or neglect. The recipient of the report would be an appropriate state agency with investigatory powers. If the abuse or neglect was verified, the perpetrator would be subject to criminal prosecution and the child, if in immediate danger, would be removed from the home and placed in a safe and secure environment either on a temporary or more permanent basis pending a hearing. Less severe cases might subject the parents to supervision until they were considered fit to resume parenting on their own. Little did the drafters of this Act realize that 30 years later, child sexual abuse would be revealed as a not-uncommon phenomenon among clergy[19] who had been exempted as a reporter because of the confidentiality of the priest-penitent relationship.

---

16   The Act is reproduced in S.N. Katz, 'Freeing Children for Permanent Placement through a Model Act' (1978) 12 *FLQ (Family Law Quarterly)* 203.

17   The Act is reproduced in S.N. Katz and U.M. Gallagher, 'Subsidized Adoption in America' (1979) 10 *FLQ* 1.

18   Children's Bureau, U.S. Department of Health, Education, & Welfare, *The Abused Child – Principles and Suggested Language for the Reporting of the Physically Abused Child* (1963).

19   See discussion above n. 15 and accompanying text.

During the 1970s, two family law cases were decided in the western and eastern parts of the United States that would have a profound effect on marriage formation and reflect the current reality. When the Florida Supreme Court decided *Posner v. Posner*[20] in 1970, it was called upon to determine whether an antenuptial agreement that settles the rights of parties upon divorce should be enforced. For years, courts held to the view that agreements in contemplation of divorce were unenforceable because it was thought that they would encourage the termination of a marriage. Referring to both the past and the present, Justice Roberts wrote:

'There can be no doubt that the institution of marriage is the foundation of the familial and social structure of our Nation and, as such, continues to be of vital interest to the State; but we cannot blind ourselves to the fact that the concept of the 'sanctity' of marriage – as being practically indissoluble once entered into – held by our ancestors only a few generations ago, has been greatly eroded in the last several decades. This court can take judicial notice of the fact that the ratio of marriages to divorces has reached a disturbing rate in many states; and that a new concept of divorce – in which there is no "guilty" party – is being advocated by many groups and has been adopted by the State of California in a recent revision of its divorce laws providing for dissolution of marriage upon pleading and proof of 'irreconcilable differences" between the parties, without assessing the fault for the failure of the marriage against either party.'[21]

The significance of *Posner* is that, by establishing the principle that an antenuptial agreement that allocates the property of the divorcing couple is enforceable, it acknowledged that the change in public policy toward divorce necessitated a change in the law. Since *Posner* was decided in 1970, antenuptial agreements have been enforced throughout the country, but not without problems. A major issue in enforcing antenuptial agreements is whether they should be treated like ordinary commercial contracts or whether they should be considered as special contracts. An underlying principle in commercial contracts is freedom of contract, meaning that parties are allowed to contract about almost everything without many limitations, except for fraud, coercion and misrepresentation. As special contracts they may be limited in scope and regulated so as to insure both a fair process and fair terms. For example, as a special contract, there may be a requirement that it be in writing, that both sides have a duty to disclose their financial worth to each other, that they both be represented by legal counsel, that alimony may not be waived and that the contract may not be entered into within

---

[20]   233 So.2d 381 (Fla. 1970). Oklahoma is one state that recognized antenuptial agreements before Posner, but it is the exception. *See, e.g., Pence v. Cole*, 205 P. 172 (Okla. 1922); *Talley v. Harris*, 182 P.2d 765 (Okla. 1947); *Clark v. Clark*, 202 P.2d 990 (Okla. 1949); and *Hudson v. Hudson*, 350 P.2d 596 (Okla. 1960).

[21]   233 So.2d 381, 384.

so many days of the wedding. As an ordinary commercial contract, there would be very limited requirements regarding the fairness of the process or the terms.

When *Marvin v. Marvin*[22] was decided by the California Supreme Court in 1976, California did not recognize informal, non-ceremonial marriages, called common law marriages, as they had been abolished by statute in 1895. Thus, it was unusual for that court to recognize a cohabitation arrangement, which originated when the defendant, Lee Marvin, was legally married to another woman. He eventually divorced his wife and continued to live with his companion, Michelle, for six years before he terminated that relationship. Ordinarily, given the facts,, there would be no legal or equitable remedy for Michelle. But the California Supreme Court changed that and decided that Michelle did have a cause of action to recover support payments at the end of her relationship if she could prove that there was an implied or expressed contract or evidence for an equitable remedy. In deciding the case, the California Supreme Court recognized that '[t]he mores of the society have indeed changed' with 'the prevalence of nonmarital relationships in modern society and the social acceptance of them.'[23] Since *Marvin*, at least 26 state appellate state courts and the District of Columbia have approved some form of remedy for a cohabiting person, and only five jurisdictions have denied the enforcement of a cohabitation contract.[24] Without the results in *Marvin,* it is difficult to see how domestic partnerships or civil unions, both marriage-like relationships, would have developed in the United States.

3. THE 1980s AND 1990s

Perhaps the area of family law that had the most dramatic transformation was the definition of parenthood in light of the scientific advancements in human reproduction technology. In 1988 the New Jersey Supreme Court decided *In re Baby M*,[25] the first nationally publicized surrogacy case. The case presented a challenge to both the litigants and to the courts because the facts in the case did not fit neatly into any legal category. The conflict arose between a biological father and a woman who agreed in a written contract to be inseminated by him,

---

[22]   557 P.2d 106 (Cal. 1976).
[23]   Ibid. at 121–22.
[24]   For a full discussion of the *Marvin* case and the reception it received in American courts, see M. GARRISON, 'Nonmarital Cohabitation: Social Revolution and Legal Regulation' (2008) 42 *FLQ* 309. In that article, which is documented with footnotes showing extensive empirical research, Professor Garrison compares the range of social and psychological benefits of formal marriage with contract cohabitation and concludes that marriage provides more of those benefits to the couple and their children than contract cohabitation.
[25]   537 A.2d 1227 (N.J. 1988).

to carry the fetus to term, and deliver the child to him and his wife. Upon the birth of the child, the surrogate mother refused to relinquish her biological child. Was the surrogacy contract legal and enforceable or not, and if it was not enforceable, what legal paradigm would be appropriate for presenting the case in court: contract, adoption, paternity or termination of parental rights? The New Jersey trial court held that the surrogacy contract was valid, terminated the surrogate's parental rights and allowed the wife of the biological father to adopt the child. The New Jersey Supreme Court reversed that decision and held that the contract was not enforceable because it conflicted with state statutes and public policy. Using the best interests of the child test, the court granted custody to the biological father and voided the termination of the birth mother's parental rights and the adoption of the child by the father's wife. The case was remanded to a lower court to decide the custodial arrangement. In essence, the ultimate result of the case – custody to the father and visitation rights to the biological mother – seems like a disposition that would be ordered in a divorce case.

There is no uniformity with regard to the enforcement of surrogacy agreements in the United States. The majority of American jurisdictions will presumably enforce a surrogacy contract under certain conditions and where there are no financial payments made to the surrogate mother beyond reasonable living and medical expenses. A minority of states, however, takes the position that such contracts are against public policy.

Especially difficult is determining the legal mother in cases where the surrogate mother is unrelated to the fetus she is carrying because the fertilized egg that was implanted in her came from another woman. In the now-famous case of *Johnson v. Calvert*,[26] the California Supreme Court held that the surrogate mother (the gestational carrier) who was unrelated to the child she was carrying was not the child's legal mother. Rather, the child's genetic mother was. That result may be the one that prevails in American courts.[27]

4. THE NEW CENTURY

In 2003, the Supreme Judicial Court of Massachusetts published its decision in *Goodridge v. Dept' of Pub. Health*,[28] which held that denying a same-sex couple a license to marry in the Commonwealth of Massachusetts violated that state's equal protection and due process of law clauses in its constitution. That decision,

---

[26]   851 P.2d 776 (Cal. 1993).
[27]   See e.g. *Hodas v. Morin*, 814 N.E.2d 320 (Mass. 2004). See also C. P. KINDREGAN, JR. and M. MCBRIEN, *Assisted Reproductive Technology: A Lawyer's Guide to Emerging Law and Science*, American Bar Association Press, Chicago 2006, pp. 140–91.
[28]   798 N.E.2d 941 (Mass. 2003).

coming at the beginning of the twenty-first century, stands as a high water mark in the history of family law in the United States. Almost 30 years earlier, attempts had been made in Kentucky, Minnesota and the State of Washington to legalize same-sex marriage, but the plaintiffs were all unsuccessful.[29] A similar effort made in Pennsylvania ten years later was equally unsuccessful.[30] What happened in the United States during the latter quarter of the twentieth century to cause the oldest supreme court in the United States to issue such a revolutionary opinion? The answer lies in both the family law decisions in the Commonwealth of Massachusetts and in two other states, and in certain constitutional law decisions in the United States Supreme Court.

The groundwork for the *Goodridge* decision was laid ten years earlier in Hawaii and later in Vermont. In 1993, the highest court in the State of Hawaii decided that to deny a same-sex couple a marriage license in that state infringed on their rights to equal protection of the laws in Hawaii, rights guaranteed under its constitution.[31] However, in 1999 the Hawaii citizens voted to amend its state constitution to limit marriage to heterosexual couples.[32] In 1999, the legislature in the state of Vermont, following the case of *Baker v. State of Vermont*,[33] which stated that it was the function of the legislature to provide a remedy for same-sex couples who want to marry, enacted the Vermont Civil Union Statute, which provides same-sex couples with the benefits of marriage. Two United States Supreme Court cases were also critical to the *Goodridge* holding. In 1967, the highest court in the United States decided *Loving v. Virginia*,[34] which held that the right to marry was a protected constitutional right and struck down the Virginia miscegenation statute. In *Lawrence v. Texas*[35], the Court struck down a Texas statute banning same-sex sodomy as unconstitutional. It has been said that the decision in *Lawrence* represents recognition by certain justices on the United States Supreme Court of changing mores and a new family model.

Another explanation for the decision in *Goodridge* might be that the Supreme Judicial Court of Massachusetts -- in addition to its reputation for expanding individual rights, especially in criminal procedure, beyond what is demanded by

---

29 Kentucky: *Jones v. Callahan*, 501 S.W.2d 588 (Ky. Ct. App. 1973); Minnesota: *Baker v. Nelson*, 191 N.W.2d 185 (Minn. 1971), appeal dismissed, 509 U.S. 810 (1972); Washington: *Singer v. Hara*, 522 P.2d 1187, rev. denied, 84 Wash. 2d 1008 (1974).

30 See *DeSanto v. Barnsley*, 476 A.2d 952 (Pa. Super. 1984).

31 *Behr v. Lewin*, 852 P.2d 44 (Haw. 1993). See also *Baehr v. Miike*, 950 P.2d 1234 (Haw. 1997).

32 Haw. Const. art. I, §23. In 1998, the legislature of Hawaii passed the Hawaii Reciprocal Beneficiary Law, which provided same-sex couples with certain economic benefits that attach to the status of marriage. See Haw. Rev. Stat. ch. 572C-1 to -7 (Michie Supp. 1998). See KATZ, above n. 4, pp. 20–22.

33 744 A.2d 864 (Vt. 1999).

34 388 U.S.1 (1967).

35 539 U.S. 558 (2003).

the United States Supreme Court -- has decided family law cases in a way that has reflected the changes in society, especially with regard to new forms of family arrangements. For example, in *Wilcox v. Trautz*,[36] the court upheld an express contract between two unmarried adults living together. Justice Greany, writing for the court, stated, 'Social mores regarding cohabitation between unmarried parties have changed dramatically in recent years and living arrangements that were once criticized are now relatively common and accepted.'[37] A further example is *E.N.O. v. L.M.M.*,[38] in which the court recognized *de facto* parents in a same-sex custody case. In that case Justice Abrams wrote:

> '[a] child may be a member of a nontraditional family in which he is parented by a legal parent and a de facto parent. A de facto parent is one who has no biological relation to the child, but has participated in the child's life as a member of the child's family. The de facto parent resides with the child, and, with the consent and encouragement of the legal parent, performs a share of caretaking functions at least as great as the legal parent.'[39]

One of the major issues involved in the same-sex marriage cases is whether reshaping the laws regulating marriage is a function of the courts or the legislature. One would have thought that issue was settled in 1888 with the United States Supreme Court case of *Maynard v. Hill*[40] in which Mr. Justice Field wrote:

> 'Marriage, as creating the most important relation in life, as having more to do with the morals and civilization of a people than any other institution, has always been subject to the control of the legislature. The body prescribes the age at which parties may contract to marry, the procedure or form essential to constitute marriage, the duties and obligations it creates, its effects upon the property rights of both, present and prospective and the acts which may constitute grounds for its dissolution.'[41]

However, those words were written long before a series of United States Supreme Court cases interpreted the Equal Protection Clause and the Due Process Clause of the United States Constitution, resulting in the civil rights of an individual trumping separation of powers. The decision in *Goodridge* would have been unthinkable 50 years ago. It reflects the changes in society especially with regard to equality and privacy in marriage and minimizing gender roles.

---

[36] 693 N.E.2d 141 (Mass. 1998).
[37] Ibid., 144.
[38] 711 N.E.2d 866 (Mass. 1999).
[39] Ibid., 891.
[40] 125 U.S. 190 (1988).
[41] Ibid., 205.

The *Goodridge* decision did not herald a widespread legal acceptance of same-sex marriage, but it did become an issue in political elections. Since 2003, Connecticut, Vermont, New Hampshire, Iowa and the District of Columbia have legalized same-sex marriage either by court decision or legislative action. In June 2011, the New York State legislature enacted a law that allows same-sex marriages to be performed in that state.[42] Prior to that, New York courts, like those in New Jersey and Rhode Island currently, had recognized same-sex marriages legally performed in jurisdictions where it was legal.

5. CONCLUSION

From 1960 to the present almost all aspects of family law in America have kept abreast with changes in society. It is rare to find an instance in which it prompted those changes, although in the area of same-sex marriage and child protection, especially with regard to the mandatory reporting of child abuse and neglect that is exactly what has happened. That half-century may be the period that represents the greatest transformation of American family law in American legal history. If the past is any indication, it is hard to predict what the future holds.

---

[42]   Marriage Equality Act (L. 2011, c. 95).

A ROYAL AND CONSTITUTIONAL AFFAIR

The Second Marriage of H.M. King Leopold III of the Belgians

Walter Pintens

Contents

1. ROYALS AND MARRIAGE

A marriage is a private and family affair. It is also a family law matter. But when royals marry, some constitutional problems may arise. This happened not only in the United Kingdom, as we know from Stephen Cretney's work,[1] but also in the Kingdom of Belgium. The second marriage of H.M. King Leopold III not only provoked controversy amongst Belgian politicians and in the population. It was also a major issue in the tragedy of King Leopold III, who had to abdicate in 1951.[2]

---

[1]   See S. Cretney, 'Royal Weddings, Legality and the Rule of Law' [2007] *Family Law* 2007 159; S. Cretney, 'Royal Marriages, Some Legal and Constitutional Issues' (2008) 124 *Law Quarterly Review* 218. See also R. Probert, *The Rights and Wrongs of Royal Marriage: How the law has led to heartbreak, farce and confusion, and why it must be changed*, Kenilworth, Takeaway 2011.

[2]   See on this tragedy R. Cappelle, *Au service du Roi*, 2 vol., Brussels, Dessart 1949; R. Cappelle, *Dix-huit ans auprès du roi Léopold*, Paris, Fayard 1970; G.-H. Dumont, *Léopold III Roi des Belges*, Brussels, Dessart 1944; R. Keyes, *Outrageous Fortune. The Tragedy of Leopold III of the Belgians 1901–1941*, London, Secker & Warburg 1984; R. Keyes, *Leopold III.*

2. KING LEOPOLD III

King Leopold III was born as the son of Crown Prince Albert and Crown Princess Elisabeth, Duchess in Bavaria.[3] Albert became a very popular king.[4] At the beginning of the Great War, Germany posed an ultimatum to Belgium and claimed free passage through Belgium to invade France. Belgium refused in respect of its neutrality imposed by the Conference of London in 1831. On 4 August 1914 Germany declared war. Immediately King Albert took personal command of his troops.[5] However, they were not able to resist the much more forceful German invader, and the King decided to withdraw his troops behind the river Yser in West Flanders. The King stayed four years with his troops and resisted the Germans until the victory of the Allies. A legend was born.[6] King Albert became a hero and entered into history as *le Roi Chevalier*. The history of his father and especially his personal command of the army would have a significant influence on the future King Leopold III.

During the war Leopold was sent to Eton College in the United Kingdom. After the war he continued his education in the United States. On 10 November 1926 Crown Prince Leopold married Princess Astrid of Sweden.[7] Due to her unconventional style she became immensely popular. The couple had three children: Josephine-Charlotte, born in 1927, who became Grand Duchess of Luxemburg, Baudouin, born in 1930, who would become the fifth King of the Belgians and Albert, born in 1934, who is today the reigning King of the Belgians.

On 17 February 1934 King Albert died in a climbing accident. On 23 February 1934 King Leopold III was sworn in as the fourth King of the Belgians. The circumstances could not have been worse.[8] In Germany Hitler had taken power. A new war was foreseeable. King Leopold followed the politics of his father and strove for absolute neutrality of the Kingdom. This influenced his position after Belgium's defeat in 1940 and caused tensions with his ministers. The King's relations with his ministers were anyway not the best. The King did not have a very high opinion of the politicians. The interbellum was a period of instability. As during the French Fourth Republic and the German Republic of Weimar,

---

    Complot tegen de koning 1940–1951, Tielt, Lannoo 1988; J. Velaers and H. Van Goethem, *Leopold III, De koning, het land, de oorlog*, 3th ed., Tielt, Lannoo 2001.

3   A minor branch of the House of Bavaria.

4   See L. Dumont-Wilden, *Albert Ier, Roi des Belges*, Paris, Grasset 1934; J. Willequet, *Albert Ier, roi des Belges*, Paris, Delarge 1979.

5   A. Massart, Le roi Albert et les opérations militaires en 1914–1918, in C. Wyffels (ed.), *Actes du Colloque Roi Albert*, Brussels, Archives de l'Etat en Belgique, 1976, p. 121 ff.

6   See L. Van Yperseele, *Le roi Albert. Histoire d'un mythe*, Ottignies, Quorum, 1995.

7   See G. Rency, *Astrid, Reine des Belges*, Brussels, Bertels, 1936.

8   Velaers and Van Goethem, above n. 2, p. 11 et seq.

political crises were prevalent. In the six years from his accession to the throne, Belgium had nine governments. The King had his doubts as to whether the parliamentary system, with the strong influence of political parties, would be able to cope with the challenges.[9]

Shortly after his accession to the throne, King Leopold III suffered a second terrible loss. On 29 August 1935, while on vacation in Switzerland the King drove the car himself, the Queen sitting at his side. His chauffeur sat in the back. In Küssnacht am Rigi on the shores of Lake Lucerne they had an accident. King Leopold lost control of his car. At the age of twenty-nine the Queen and her unborn child died. Only thirty-four years old, the King was now a widower with three young children.

3. BELGIUM AT WAR

On 10 May 1940 Belgium was at war. German troops invaded the country, although the King had invested all his energy in defending Belgium's neutrality. The Treaty of Versailles had abolished Belgium's neutrality but from mid-1930, the King favoured again a politics of neutrality in order to keep Belgium out of the foreseeable international conflict. France and the United Kingdom were not seen as allies but as guarantors of Belgium's neutrality.

The King rejected the government's proposals to preside immediately over the Council of Ministers and to hold an address from the throne before the United Chambers of Parliament, as his father did when in 1914 the German army invaded Belgium. As commander in chief he immediately took command of the troops. In his father's tradition he took personal command without countersignature of his ministers. Like his father, the King was of the view that, although every other act by the monarch needed the countersignature of his ministers as prescribed by art. 64 of the Constitution,[10] that article was not applicable to art. 68, para. 1 Const.[11] which installed him as commander in chief of the army. Not every constitutionalist agreed with this standpoint.[12] The King's comportment provoked tensions with his ministers.

On the first day of the German offensive, several fortifications were taken. But nevertheless the Belgian army resisted and made the evacuation of the British

---

9 Ibid.
10 Now Art. 106 Const.
11 Now abolished.
12 See W.J. GANSHOF VAN DER MEERSCH, 'Le commandement de l'armée et la responsabilité ministérielle en droit constitutionnel belge' (1948–49) *Revue de l'Université de Bruxelles* 256.

troops from Dunkirk possible. However, further battles would have been disastrous for the army and for the whole population.

On 24 May 1940, a dramatic confrontation took place in the castle of Wijnendale between King Leopold and his ministers.[13] Although some ministers had their doubts, they were eventually convinced that the Allies would win the war and urged the King to follow them to France and to continue the war with the Allies. The King refused.[14] He was confident that the war on the continent would soon be over and that for Belgium the war was almost finished. Further combat was not a matter for Belgium. In his opinion Belgium should not join the Allies to continue the war from abroad. The King thought that strict neutrality would be beneficial to the country. The King believed that a compromise peace between Germany and the United Kingdom would lead to a newly rebuilt European order and that Belgium would still play a role under the house of Saxe-Coburg. The King was sure that he had to stay with his soldiers and that he had to share their experience as a prisoner of war. He was convinced that he would be able to serve his country and that he could have some influence on the occupier in order to improve the living conditions of the population and of the prisoners of war.

Prime Minister Hubert Pierlot drew the attention of the King to the fact that he could not take the decision to capitulate, that being a matter for the government. The ministers could not reach an agreement with the King and left for France. The King tried to build a new government, for which he needed the countersignature of at least one minister of the previous government. The ministers refused.[15] They stayed on as government in France and later in London. After eighteen days of war, the King decided that the war was lost and that the only possibility to save the population was to capitulate and to surrender to the Germans. On 28 May 1940 he declared the end of the war.

The attitude of the King and especially the capitulation were taken badly by the ministers. On the evening of 28 May 1940, Prime Minister Pierlot issued a governmental declaration on the French radio and heavily criticized the King.[16] The Prime Minister announced that against the advice of his government the King had started negotiations with the enemy concerning the capitulation and a peace treaty. History has shown that the King did not negotiate. But Prime Minister Pierlot honestly thought so. Since the King was not covered by his ministers, the King violated the Constitution. The Prime Minister added that the King had broken the bond with his people and that the government was

---

[13]   VELAERS and VAN GOETHEM, above n. 2, p. 226 et seq.
[14]   See J. STENGERS, *Aux origines de la question royale. Léopold III et le gouvernement. Les deux politiques belges de 1940*, Paris, Duculot 1980.
[15]   VELAERS and VAN GOETHEM, above n. 2, p. 252.
[16]   Ibid., p. 269 et seq.

determined to continue the war alongside Britain and France. The same day the ministers decided under application of Art. 82 of the Constitution that the King was unable to reign. Since it was not possible to convoke the Parliament, there was no means of appointing a regent. In the meantime the ministers would exercise the royal power.[17]

The reactions of France and the United Kingdom were also very forthright. French Prime Minister Paul Reynaud called King Leopold a traitor. Prime Minister Churchill criticized King Leopold in the House of Commons on 4 June 1940. Suddenly, without prior consultation, with the least possible notice, without the advice of his ministers and upon his own personal act, Churchill said, the King had sent a plenipotentiary[18] to the German Command, surrendered his Army and exposed 'our' whole flank as means of retreat.[19]

The reactions of the Prime Minister and the allies were not well received by diplomats, judges and lawyers. The population was shocked by the way the King was treated. Many believed that the King had done his best, that he had no other solution than to capitulate and that he simply surrendered without any negotiations with the Germans.[20] The Archbishop of Mechelen, Jozef-Ernest Cardinal Van Roey, who was seen as the highest moral authority in the country, was asked to see the King and to give him the opportunity to defend his honour. After a meeting with the King, the Cardinal wrote a pastoral letter reporting the King's defence, which was read in all the catholic churches.[21] At a later stage the ministers attempted reconciliation with the King but their efforts failed. All this formed the basis for *la question royale* and would lead to the abdication of the King.[22]

The Germans were highly appreciative of the King's decision not to leave the country to join the Allies. They treated him in accordance with his royal dignity.

---

[17]   Governmental decree of 28 May 1940, Moniteur belge 31 May 1940.

[18]   This term is not correct. Originally, the idea of a plenipotentiary was taken into consideration. But since his task was not to negotiate but to receive information about the conditions of the capitulation, the term was modified in 'parlementaire'. See Velaers and Van Goethem, above n. 2, p. 257.

[19]   <www.winstonchurchill.org/learn/speeches/speeches-of-winston-churchill/128-we-shall-fight-on-the-beaches>.

[20]   See F. Balace, 'Fors l'honneur. Ombres et clartés de la capitulation belge' in *Jours de guerre – Jours de défaite*, II, Brussels, Crédit communal 1991, p. 7 et seq.

[21]   See E. Verhoeyen, 'De herderlijke brief van kardinaal Van Roey over de kapitulatie van 28 mei 1940: het aandeel van advokatuur en magistratuur', *Bijdragen tot de geschiedenis van de Tweede Wereldoorlog* 1978, 227 ff.

[22]   See L. De Lichtervelde, 'La question royale' (1947) *Revue générale belge* 321; E. Ramon Arango, *Leopold III and the Belgian royal question*, Baltimore, Hopkins Press 1961; J. Vanwelkenhuyzen, *Quand les chemins se séparent: aux sources de la question royale*, Paris, Duculot 1988.

The royal palace in Laeken was assigned as his residence. The King could keep his staff, even his military advisor General Van Overstraeten.[23] He had a certain freedom of movement. He could travel to the palace in Ciergnon and the royal villa in Knokke, vacation residences of the royal family. He travelled to Austria to undergo dental surgery in Vienna.

That the King stayed in Belgium and was a prisoner of war as were so many other officers and soldiers made him popular within the population. But very soon it would be clear that the King was powerless and that he was not able to improve the living conditions of his population. Even a much-debated visit to Hitler in Berchtesgaden would not offer any guarantees.[24] The popularity of the King decreased.

4. THE MARRIAGE WITH LILIAN BAELS

King Leopold's losses, the death of his father and his wife, his position as a King in an occupied country and the tensions between him and his ministers, of whom some had left France and joined the Allies in London, asked a lot from him. Although he had a certain freedom to move around, he felt isolated. His life as a young widower became a heavy burden.[25]

Here Lilian Baels came to the fore.[26] She was born on 28 November 1916 in London, where her parents lived as refugees during the Great War. Her father was Hendrik Baels, who had been a minister and governor of the province of West Flanders. Her mother was Anne Devischer, daughter of a notary and mayor. Lilian Baels was a beautiful and well-educated lady, very intelligent and with a strong character. The King's mother, Queen Elisabeth, wanted to distract the King and invited Lilian Baels to the royal palace in Laeken. Probably the King had already met her on his visits to West Flanders. Soon there were rumours that the King was having an affair.

On 7 December 1941 not only the population but also the political world was taken by surprise when Cardinal Van Roey, Archbishop of Mechelen, once again came to the fore and announced in a pastoral letter that on 11 September 1941

---

23   See R. Van Overstraeten, *Dans l'étau. Au service de la Belgique*, Paris, Plon 1960; R. Van Overstraeten, *Sous le joug: Léopold III prisonier*, Brussels, Hatier 1986.
24   See A. De Jonghe, Berchtesgaden (19 november 1940): voorgeschiedenis, inhoud en resultaat, Res Publica 1978, 41 et seq.
25   Velaers and Van Goethem, above n. 2, p. 672.
26   See E. Raskin, *Prinses Lilian. De vrouw die Leopold III ten val bracht*, Antwerpen, Houtekiet 1998.

the King had entered into a religious marriage with Lilian Baels.[27] The message was read in every church in the country. It explained that the marriage was celebrated by the Cardinal in the Chapel of the Royal Palace in Laeken. Without further details and omitting the date, the message stated that the civil formalities had also been complied with. The Cardinal continued that he was empowered to add that the marriage only concerned the private and family life of the King and had no public law consequences. The Cardinal made reference to a royal deed stating that the royal consort renounced the title of queen and that she would take the title of princess of Rethy.[28] In the same royal deed the King declared that the offspring of this marriage would be excluded from the throne. Finally, the Cardinal asked for prayers for the King.

Soon it became known that the civil marriage was celebrated on 6 December 1941, the day before the Van Roey announcement, in the royal palace in Laeken by the deputy mayor of the city of Brussels, Jules Coelst. Witnesses were the Grand Marshal of the Court, Louis Count Cornet de Ways-Ruart, and Lucien Van Beirs, procureur du roi[29] at the Court of First Instance in Brussels.

The population was shocked. The time was not ripe for a morganatic marriage. That the King had entered into a new marriage did not correspond to his status as a prisoner of war. The population was angry that the King had paid too much attention to his personal happiness, while so many prisoners of war could not see their wives. In some shops the portrait of the King was replaced by a portrait of the late Queen Astrid, who was still immensely popular. That Lilian Baels would bear the title of Princess of Rethy was taken very badly since the late Queen Astrid used the name Madame de Rethy when she travelled incognito. Since the religious marriage took place two months before the civil marriage, rumours arose that Princess Lilian must be pregnant. This was confirmed by the birth of Prince Alexander on 18 July 1942.

The Royal Family was also dismayed. Queen Elisabeth was against a civil marriage because it would not be possible to keep it secret. For her a religious marriage was enough for the time being. The civil marriage should have waited until the war was over. The brother of the King, Prince Charles, was angry because in 1938 he had wanted to enter into a morganatic marriage with a middle-class lady who was pregnant but had, under pressure from the King, given up the idea.

---

[27]   See VELAERS and VAN GOETHEM, above n. 2, p. 674.
[28]   Rhety is a small village in the province of Antwerp where the royal family has a vacation home.
[29]   Public prosecutor.

5. CONSTITUTIONAL PROBLEMS

The marriage provoked some serious constitutional problems. The religious wedding preceded the civil marriage and therefore violated the Constitution. Art. 16 para. 2 Const. prescribed that the civil wedding should precede the religious wedding.[30] The marriage was valid, but the Cardinal who celebrated the marriage committed a criminal offence and could have been fined under Art. 267 para. 1 Penal Code.

But a more important problem was whether the King had violated Art. 60 of the Constitution.[31] This article prescribed that no act of the King could take effect without the countersignature of a minister, who, in doing so, assumed responsibility for it. The constitution did not, however, explicitly state that Art. 60 was applicable to the marriage of the King. The King was clearly of the opinion that this was not the case. He considered his marriage to be his own private affair. To exclude public law consequences he signed the royal deed that the Cardinal mentioned in his message. But there were also some problems with this document.[32] The Cardinal had lied when he mentioned the existence of the document on 7 December 1941. It was drawn up in the first months of 1943 and antedated to 6 December 1941.

From the Cardinal's pastoral letter we already know that the document contained two elements. First of all Lilian Baels renounced the title of queen. Since this was a matter not regulated by the Constitution, the King was of the view that no constitutional problem arose. The royal deed mentioned that, besides the title of Princess of Rethy, Princess Lilian would, as consort of the King, be entitled to the qualification of Royal Highness and that she could bear the titles of Princess of Belgium, Duchess of Saxony and Princess of Saxe-Coburg-Gotha.

Much more difficult was the second point in the royal deed. Concerning the rights to the throne of the offspring of the new marriage, the authentic deed differs from the pastoral letter of the Cardinal. Where the Cardinal's letter stated that the children would have no rights to the throne, the royal deed reads that it was the King's wish that those children would not accede to the throne, implying a possibility that they might. The King's secretary, Count Capelle, could indeed convince the King that he could not interfere with the Constitution and that its revision by the parliament would be necessary to realize the King's wish.[33] The

---

[30] Now Art. 21 para. 2 Const.
[31] Now Art. 106 Const.
[32] VELAERS and VAN GOETHEM, above n. 2, p. 682 with reference to the papers of the King's secretary Count Capelle.
[33] Ibid., p. 682.

royal deed further specified that the children of the marriage would bear the titles of Royal Highness, Prince and Princess of Belgium, Duke and Duchess of Saxony and Prince and Princess of Saxe-Coburg-Gotha.

King Leopold did not see that the marriage of a king was not only a private but also a public affair since the offspring of the marriage had rights to the throne. From the discussions on the constitution in the National Congress in 1830 we learn that the Congress rejected a proposal to require the consent of the parliament for the marriage of the king, but that the countersignature of a minister was necessary.[34] This does not mean that a minister has to sign the marriage certificate. The consent can also implicitly follow from the presence of a minister. In 1941 the ministers were abroad. But the King had still had the opportunity to approach them and to ask them for their consent.

After the war the constitution was not revised. A commission appointed by the King came to the conclusion that the marriage could not have public law consequences since there had been no ministerial consent.[35] When in 1990 the constitution was revised, Prime Minister Wilfried Martens declared that a minister always had to take responsibility for the marriage of the king. The Prime Minister emphasised that, therefore, the second marriage of King Leopold could have no public law effect and that the children of this marriage were excluded from the throne. The Commission for the revision of the constitution of the Senate unanimously agreed.[36] Also a large majority of constitutional doctrine favours this opinion.[37] In fact, there would have been no chance for Prince Alexander to succeed to the throne, since he himself later entered into a marriage without the consent of King Baudouin.[38]

6. EPILOGUE

On 7 June 1944, the day after the landing of the allies in Normandy, the King was deported to Germany and was held as a prisoner in Castel Hirschstein in Saxony. When the Russian Army was approaching, the King was moved to Strobl in Austria on 7 March 1945. On 7 May 1945 the royal family was freed by the

---

[34]   E. HUYTTENS, *Discussions du Congrès national de Belgique*, II, Brussels, Société typographique de Belgique 1844, p. 482 et seq.

[35]   See VELAERS and VAN GOETHEM, above n. 2, p. 680.

[36]   Ibid., p. 682.

[37]   See e.g. P. WIGNY, *Droit constitutional. Principes et droit positif*, I, Brussels, Bruylant 1952, p. 601 et seq.

[38]   Art. 85, para. 2 of the Constitution prescribes that the descendant who marries without the consent of the King, loses his right to the crown.

United States 106th Cavalry Group. In the meantime the Belgian Parliament had elected the brother of the King, Prince Charles, as Prince Regent of Belgium.

The American and British governments had some worries about the return of the King. They feared that his return could divide the country. The American Army was instructed to keep the King in Germany until contact between him and the Belgian government was established.[39] At first the government strived for reconciliation. But the atmosphere changed when King Leopold took a very stiff standpoint on the conditions of his return. Soon the communist party asked for his abdication, followed after a while by the socialist party. The King went in exile to Pregny-Chambésy near Geneva. Finally, on 12 March 1950 a referendum was held. 57.6 per cent of the voters favoured the King's return. But the result showed an enormous divide between Flanders and Wallonia. In Flanders, where the catholic party was very strong, 72 per cent voted in favour of the King. By contrast, in Wallonia, where the socialist party was the first party, only 42 per cent of the voters were in favour of the King's return, and in Brussels only 48 per cent. After the general election of 4 June 1950, the catholic majority voted on 20 July that there was no longer any difficulty in the King resuming his reign.

On 22 July 1950 King Leopold returned. Strikes, demonstrations and bomb attacks were the result. A few days later three protesters were killed in Grâce-Berleur. The King came under pressure. Now all the political parties understood that the King had no future and feared a revolt. On 1 August 1950 the King resigned in favour of his son Crown Prince Baudouin, the elder son of his first marriage to Queen Astrid. Since he was only 20 years old, he was sworn in as Royal Prince. One year later, on 16 July 1951, the King abdicated and the Royal Prince became King Baudouin and reigned for more than forty years.

King Leopold could keep his title of King. Together with his wife he lived in the royal palace in Laeken and had still a lot of influence on his son. The couple had two more children, Princess Marie-Christine, born in 1951, and Princess Maria-Esmeralda, born in 1956. When in 1960 King Baudouin married Dona Fabiola de Mora y Aragon, King Leopold and Princess Lilian had to leave the palace and take up residence in the castle of Argenteuil. Some pressure by Prime Minister Gaston Eyskens was necessary to get them to leave Laeken.

King Leopold started a new life as a passionate anthropologist and travelled around the world, especially in Brazil, Indonesia and New Guinea. He died on 25 September 1983. Princess Lilian died on 7 June 2002.

---

[39] E. WITTE, J. CRAEYBECKX and A. MEYNEN, *Political history of Belgium from 1830 onwards*, Brussels, ASP 2009, p. 239 et seq.

The abdication of the King was the result of many factors such as the dispute with his ministers in 1940, his visit to Hitler in Berchtesgaden and his stiff attitude in 1945, but the second marriage of the King played a prominent role. It caused the King the loss of his popularity. The later Prime Minister Achille Van Acker considered the marriage the deepest cause of *la question royale*.[40]

---

[40]   Velaers and Van Goethem, above n. 2, p. 677.

INDEX